"NO RELIGION HIGHER THAN TRUTH"

"NO RELIGION
HIGHER THAN TRUTH"

A HISTORY OF THE THEOSOPHICAL

MOVEMENT IN RUSSIA, 1875–1922

Maria Carlson

PRINCETON UNIVERSITY PRESS   PRINCETON, NEW JERSEY

Library of Congress Cataloging-in-Publication Data

Carlson, Maria
No religion higher than truth : a history of the Theosophical
movement in Russia, 1875–1922 / Maria Carlson
p.   cm.
Includes bibliographical references and index.
ISBN 0-691-05682-X (alk. paper)
1. Theosophy—Soviet Union—History—19th century.
2. Theosophy—Soviet Union—History—20th century.
I. Title.
BP550.S6C37   1993
299′.934′094709034—dc20   92-19451   CIP

This book has been composed in Adobe Galliard

Princeton University Press books are printed on acid-free paper,
and meet the guidelines for permanence and durability
of the Committee on Production Guidelines for Book Longevity of
the Council on Library Resources

Printed in the United States of America

10   9   8   7   6   5   4   3   2   1

Contents _____

Illustrations —————————————————————————————

Following p. 104:

Acknowledgments ⎯⎯⎯⎯⎯⎯⎯⎯⎯⎯⎯⎯⎯⎯⎯⎯⎯⎯

I WOULD LIKE to thank the National Endowment for the Humanities for a fellowship, which supported the writing of this book. I would also like to thank the helpful librarians at the Lenin Library in Moscow, the Helsinki Slavonic Library, the Slavic Library at the University of Illinois at Champaign-Urbana, and the Bibliothéque Publique et Universitaire de Genève. My thanks also to Edward Kasinec, Chief of the Slavic and Baltic Division at the New York Public Library. I am grateful to my colleagues at the University of Kansas, William C. Fletcher and Stephen J. Parker, who wrestled manfully with what must have seemed at times a very strange manuscript indeed.

"NO RELIGION HIGHER THAN TRUTH"

Introduction

The Esoteric Tradition and the Russian Silver Age

THIS STUDY of the Russian Theosophical Movement seeks to restore an important missing piece of mosaic tile to the intricate design of fin de siècle Russian culture. The Russian Silver Age (1890–1914) is widely acknowledged as a critical transitional period in Russia's cultural history; as such, its literature, history, art, and philosophy have received widespread and eminently deserved attention from both Russian and Western scholars. As they have learned more about this complex period of great intellectual ferment and social upheaval, scholars have inevitably become aware of certain lacunae in the scholarly mosaic. One such lacuna is the Silver Age's passion for occultism and mysticism in both its refined and vulgar forms. The illegitimate offspring of the Russian religious renaissance, occultism flourished in Russia in the decadent days that preceded world war and revolution.

Like their European contemporaries, the Russians were intrigued by spiritualism, table turning, fortune-telling, magic, and mysticism of every stamp. In terms of intellectual impact, however, the most important form of occultism was modern Theosophy, a contemporary Gnostic gospel invented and disseminated by Helena Blavatsky (1831–1891), an expatriate Russian woman with an enthusiasm for Buddhist thought and a genius for self-promotion. Although her "secret doctrine" succeeded in seducing many leading cultural figures of the Russian Silver Age, it has not received its due as a contributing factor to the aesthetic and philosophical consciousness of the times. Scholars are aware of Theosophy and the other occult and mystical passions of the Silver Age, but erroneously disdain them as trivial; yet, occultism in general and Theosophy in particular are everywhere present, and are, in fact, a major determinant in the artistic and cultural course of the Silver Age. This book outlines the history of the Theosophical Movement in Russia, identifies its leading figures, and begins the documentation of Theosophy's role as a social and intellectual force in Russian society during the fascinating period of the Russian fin de siècle.

Occultism and esotericism have always had their place in intellectual history. The ancient mysteries of the East, the secret rites of the Chaldeans, Egyptians, and Persians, the mystery religions of ancient Greece and the Near East were inherited by medieval Kabbalists, alchemists, Hermeticists, and religious mystics; they were passed on by a superstitious seventeenth century ("century of witchcraft") to the Age of Reason. The eighteenth century, characterized not only by the rationalism of Kant, Hume, and Voltaire, but also by the mysticism of Emanuel Swedenborg, the pseudoscience of Franz Anton Mesmer, and the black arts of the Comtes de Saint-Germain and Cagliostro, helped generate the great popular occult movements of the nineteenth century. Nor has interest in the occult disappeared in the twentieth century. One need only mention the popular interests in extrasensory perception (ESP), Gurdjieff, Satanism, oriental religions, and New Age thought that engages Western society today.

The occult tradition flows parallel to but unseen below the strong surface currents of prevailing wisdom; mysterious and esoteric, it has been hidden by its initiates from the profane eye, but has never disappeared. According to cultural and intellectual fashions, it may run closer to the surface in some ages than in others. This occult current crested in the last third of the nineteenth century, spilling over into the cultural, intellectual, and artistic life of Americans and Europeans.

By the end of the nineteenth century, the European passion for various forms of occultism had been carried eastward to Russia, where it quickly grew in the fertile Russian soil. For some Russians, occultism was entertainment; for others, it was serious science, or philosophy, or even a new faith; for many, it was the merest nonsense, something to ridicule; for almost all, it was a popular topic of discussion. The various forms of occultism were sensationalized in the penny press, dissected in serious journals, debated at public and private lectures, and demonstrated on the stage and at open seances. It was the topic of conversation in fashionable salons and around the family dinner table. "In the journals and newspapers, everywhere, there are publications about books on hypnotism and similar mystical questions," wrote an overwhelmed Russian contemporary. "In bookstore display windows, at the train stations, all these books about spiritualism, chiromancy, occultism, and mysticism in general leap out at you. Even the most innocent books are sold in covers decorated with some kind of mystical emblems and symbols which assault the eye."[1]

Occultism, in a bewildering variety of forms, became the intellectual craze of the time. The Russian Spiritualist journal *Rebus* reported in 1906 that

> according to our correspondent, all of Petersburg is caught up in an unusually powerful mystical movement and at the moment a veritable maelstrom of little religions, cults, and sects has taken shape there. This movement embraces

both the upper and lower levels of society. Among the upper levels we find the Theosophic-Buddhist trend. Admirers of Theosophy are uniting and are even beginning to discuss the question of building a Buddhist lamasery (a dormitory) and a Theosophic-Buddhist temple. On the other hand, we observe a great rise of interest in Freemasonry, as well as a resurgence in long-silent forms of religious movements from the last century.[2]

And not only Petersburg was caught up in the trend. Moscow and the provinces buzzed with new secret societies, demonstrations of hypnotism, public Spiritualist seances, gypsy fortune-tellers, and secret sectarian ecstasies (*radeniia*). Every educated reader who was not a recluse had at least a nodding acquaintance with Theosophy and Spiritualism, but there was also Rosicrucianism, Freemasonry, Martinism, and, of course, those more sensational manifestations of popular, or "boulevard," mysticism: the Tarot, somnambulism, chiromancy, phrenology, mesmerism, astrology, geomancy, and hypnotism. People knew about these things, even if their knowledge was based only on café gossip and sensational newspaper articles in *Novoe Vremia*.

By the eve of the First World War St. Petersburg alone had more than thirty-five officially registered and chartered occult circles; there were also hundreds of unofficial and informal circles. And they were not confined to Moscow and St. Petersburg; occult circles were registered in Viaz'ma in northwestern Russia, Blagoveshchensk in the Russian Far East, Tiflis and Ust'-Kamenogorsk in the south, and every place in between. More than thirty occult journals and newspapers, published in Russia between 1881 and 1918, attest to the extensive popularity of the occult. Given the high level of illiteracy and the rigors of Russian secular and church censorship, this represents a formidable interest in the topic. The oldest of these journals, *Rebus*, was published weekly for thirty-seven years; by 1905 it boasted more than sixteen thousand subscribers. Occult fervor was ubiquitous.

The two most important occult movements in fin de siècle Russia were Theosophy and Spiritualism. They had the largest number of adherents and dominated the journals and publications. Of the two, Theosophy was the more philosophically important and culturally influential, although Spiritualism had the larger membership and a higher public profile.

Theosophy did not appear at the end of the last century by accident; it was called into being by the frustration and dissatisfaction of a growing number of thinking people who felt intellectually and spiritually cut adrift, unwilling or unable to choose between the sterility of scientific positivism and the impotence of a diminished church. They sought the eternal verities and the dignity of man, and they found dirty factories, alienated workers, crime, Philistinism, and decadence. Theosophy offered these bereft modern seekers a resolution to their quandary, together with a highly structured Weltanschauung and a strong moral ethic.

Theosophists defined their doctrine as a syncretic, mystico-religious philosophical system, "the synthesis of Science, Religion, and Philosophy," supposedly based on an ancient esoteric tradition called the "Secret Doctrine." Theosophy claimed to resolve the "crisis of culture and consciousness" then being experienced by European and Russian thought. If faith was no longer alive, Theosophy offered secret knowledge to fill the aching void.

The major impact Theosophy made on Russian fin de siècle culture was certainly not underestimated by its contemporaries. In 1915 Ivanov-Razumnik (Razumnik Vasil'evich Ivanov, 1878–1946), a leading intellectual historian and literary critic, wrote:

> The future historian of literature will undoubtedly have to undertake excavations in the multi-volume "Theosophy" of our time; without this neither Andrei Belyi, nor Viacheslav Ivanov, nor the numerous "Zheorzhii Nulkovs" of Symbolism and pseudo-Symbolism would be comprehensible. The psychologist and the historian will find more than a little to interest them in the study of this distinctive sect of our times; the literary historian cannot afford to pass it by.[3]

Ivanov-Razumnik's suggestion, made so many years ago, deserves to be pursued. A great many pages have already been written in the United States and Western Europe about Theosophy and the Theosophical Society, but practically nothing has been said about the history of the Theosophical Society and its activities in Russia. Yet, Theosophy (and its "Christianized" offshoot, Anthroposophy) went far beyond cheering the lives of civil servants, doctors, lawyers, and society matrons in their personal crises of faith; it also transformed the thought, art, and destinies of many members of the "creative intelligentsia," the leading writers, musicians, philosophers, and artists of the Russian Silver Age. It is no exaggeration to suggest that certain aspects of the period could not be understood without the dimension of Theosophy and its sister theories, arcane though they may seem to us today.

The opulent epoch in Russian cultural history known as the Silver Age spans the period from the last decade of the nineteenth century to the eve of the First World War. A period of cultural schizophrenia, the Silver Age simultaneously experienced two antithetical worlds. One was the bright, rational, scientific world of Karl Marx and historical materialism, Max Planck and quantum mechanics, and Albert Einstein and the theory of relativity (1905); modern science reigned here. The opposite world was the dark, mysterious realm of Friedrich Nietzsche and eternal return, Richard Wagner and the modern mystery drama, the French *poètes maudits*, the haunting canvases of Jean Delville, Odilon Redon, and Gustave Moreau; this was the other world of Mme Blavatsky and the occult.

Like their French predecessors, the Russian Symbolist writers, artists, and God-seekers who dominated Silver Age culture preferred the second world to the first. The physical landscape of the first world consisted of expanding industry, strikes, social unrest, and the vulgarity and mediocrity of a growing middle class. The Russian educated elite feared that it heralded the imminent collapse of culture and civilization. They chose instead to escape from the noisomeness of physical reality into an alternative reality of mind and art where absolute aesthetic and spiritual values still held.

This educated Russian elite, brought up on French decadent literature, influenced by the French occult revival, and trained in German idealist philosophy (infused by Schopenhauer with an undercurrent of Buddhist thought), presided over an aesthetically rich period in which all intellectual endeavors (literature, philosophy, history, theology, music, painting, dance, and theater) interacted with one another and blossomed into the magnificent *Gesamtkunstwerk* that was the Russian Silver Age. In the face of a fragmenting world marching inexorably toward world war and revolution, the Russian creative intelligentsia sought to structure an ultimate synthesis of culture in which art was identified with religion, and aesthetic theory was transformed into a metaphysical worldview. Their search for a meaningful ontological foundation led them past a weakened church toward metaphysical idealism and Theosophical thought. The result was not only a veritable blossoming of the arts, but also a renaissance in religious and idealist philosophy.

Tragically, this magnificent but delicate flower of Russia's Silver Age bloomed over an abyss. Its appearance marked not only the acme of artistic achievement, but also the last moments of a corrupt society: the society of the cafés, of the Mad Monk Rasputin, of champagne for breakfast and illicit trysts at Italian resort hotels, of black ostrich plumes on mauve chapeaux, of salon Satanism and fashionable drug addiction. The Silver Age was not only the idyll of refined Symbolist verse and the haunting and nostalgic paintings of "The World of Art"; it was also a period of pornography, vulgarity, ambiguous sexuality, crime, anti-Semitism, and political terrorism. In this upside-down and inside-out world hovering on the brink of catastrophe, the creative intelligentsia sought eternal verities wherever it could find them; and Theosophy promised to satisfy their spiritual hunger.

Theosophy found its proper niche in Russian Silver Age culture without much effort for a simple reason: despite its exotic coloring, Theosophy in its Russian variant shared the major concerns and vocabulary of the creative and God-seeking intelligentsia. Theosophy rejected physical reality and its deadening positivism, and turned instead to the world of the spirit; Theosophy was obsessed by the history of religious thought, especially by mystery cults and ancient rituals; Theosophy believed in and worked for Russia's cultural mission to the world and subscribed to the "Russian Idea"; Theosophy turned eagerly to Russian sectarian and mystical theology, with its strong neo-Platonic and Gnostic subtext. Theosophy's was a compelling (though now silent and forgotten) voice in the passionate religious dialogues of the Russian Silver Age.

The Silver Age figures whose lives Theosophy touched (for better or worse) are among the most illustrious representatives of the creative and God-seeking intelligentsia. They include the religious philosopher Vladimir Solov'ev; his brother, the novelist Vsevolod Solov'ev; the philanthropist Anna Filosofova; the poets Konstantin Bal'mont and Nikolai Minskii-Vilenkin; the critic and philosopher Dmitrii Merezhkovskii and his wife, the poet Zinaida Hippius; the Symbolist writer and thinker Andrei Belyi; the writer and translator Lev Kobylinskii-Ellis; Aleksei Petrovskii, Pavel Batiushkov, Mikhail Sizov, Nikolai Kiselev (from the Argonaut and Musaget circles); Anna Mintslova, a Mme Blavatsky double who "Theosophized" the eminent scholar, writer, and critic Viacheslav Ivanov; the journalist and philosopher P. D. Uspenskii, who later joined forces with another Russian mystic, Georgii Gurdjieff, before finding his own mystical path; the writer Ol'ga Forsh; the respected religious philosopher Nikolai Berdiaev; the poet Max Voloshin and his wife, the painter Margarita Sabashnikova; the actor and director Mikhail Chekhov; the composer Aleksandr Skriabin; and the painters Nikolai Roerich and Wasily Kandinsky, to name only the most visible figures among the creative intelligentsia who embraced Theosophy. Even Maksim Gor'kii and Anatolii Lunacharskii, both dedicated socialists and colleagues of Vladimir Lenin, were interested at certain points in their lives in Theosophy and occult thought.

The interest of these important Russian cultural figures in Theosophical doctrine affected their work, their philosophy, and, in some extreme cases, even molded their entire worldview. As leading cultural and literary figures with an educated and devoted audience, they were in a position to disseminate certain aspects of Theosophical thought. To understand what motivated them to turn to Theosophy, what they expected to find there, what they did find there, and how it affected their art and their lives, it is imperative to reach some understanding of what Theosophy is and how it fits into the rich mosaic of Silver Age culture.

The importance of Theosophy's role in Silver Age Russian culture is crystallized in the work of Andrei Belyi, whom the idealist philosopher Nikolai Berdiaev called "the most characteristic figure of that epoch."

Berdiaev elaborated: "Belyi is characteristic of the various trends of the beginning of the century because he was unable to remain within the framework of pure literature and aesthetic consciousness; his Symbolism had a mystical and occult character, he reflected all of the spiritual moods and searches of the period."[4] Gifted, admired, influential, profoundly sensitive to the fears, neuroses, and hopes that tortured his generation, Andrei Belyi acted out in his personal life and in his art the symbolic spiritual dramas of his time.

Belyi divided Symbolism into two branches: Symbolism as an aesthetic school, and Symbolism as a worldview. He went so far as to define the Symbolist worldview in Theosophical terms as "a new religious-philosophical doctrine," synthetic in nature, and based on idealist, religious, and occult philosophies. It is fairly easy to spot the Solov'evian and neo-Kantian elements in Belyi's thought, but that third line, occult philosophy, is more problematic for the contemporary scholar. Pursuing this occult line in Belyi's philosophy leads in various directions, but primarily in the direction of Theosophy and its "Westernized" modification, Anthroposophy (or "Christianized Theosophy"), and to its impact on Silver Age thought. Belyi led an entire generation of young, well-educated Russians in this direction; their influence on Russian culture did not cease in 1917, but continued well into the 1930s and is subtly visible even in Russia today.

Those scholars who venture into the elegant and frequently arcane world of the Russian Symbolists are aware that their subjects were, to a greater or lesser extent, involved in these occult movements. Few, however, have explored their history, let alone the importance and implications of this interesting pseudoreligious, philosophical doctrine for the works and thought of the Russian Silver Age. Arcane though it may seem to many, research into Theosophy and Anthroposophy does promise to illuminate certain dark corners of this complex period.

What seems arcane today was not always so. At the turn of the century, Russian readers and critics had little difficulty in recognizing, however superficially, the presence of occult contents and vocabulary in the art, literature, and culture of the Silver Age. Belyi, for instance, was ashamed of his first novel, *Silver Dove*, because it was so "obviously Theosophical," yet one would scarcely use the word *obviously* today. Today many scholars are unaware of the degree to which Theosophical vocabulary and imagery left their subtle mark on the art and literature of the Silver Age: the frequent use—indeed, overuse—of adjectives such as "light," "silent," "bright," "spiritual" (*svetlyi, tikhii, iasnyi, dukhovnyi*); the concept of harmony; the notion of theurgy; the images of Eternity and the Call; the idea of correspondences; the central figure of the Triangle; the images of the spider and web (Maya, the world illusion); the circle, the wheel, and the spiral (of reincarnation); the Initiate and initiation; the idea of the Path; the Abyss; the struggle of Light and Darkness; the notion of the Master and the Brotherhood; the secret society; the color white and the metal silver; exotic Eastern vocabulary; and the like—these are the commonplaces of Theosophy that entered artistic discourse almost unnoticed. An awareness of this occult subtext on the figurative and semantic level opens fresh perspectives that can lead to new interpretive possibilities.

In the second decade of the twentieth century, rapid historical, political, and intellectual change in Russia replaced occult interests with other, more immediate concerns. As a result, the occult dimension of Silver Age culture was overshadowed by other events and philosophies and deprived of the attention it merits. Soviet critics, for many years prisoners of the Russian variant of historical materialism, have not been allowed to study it; Western critics, products of a postwar scientific positivism, have disdained it. This lack of critical attention to occult philosophy, however, does not diminish its importance. For many leading figures of the Russian Silver Age, occult philosophy was not an amusing entertainment, but a lifelong concern that affected all aspects of their personal, spiritual, and creative lives; thus it is eminently worthy of scholarly investigation.

Theosophy, one of the most influential forms of Silver Age speculative mysticism, is an "occult" doctrine, and any discussion of it must necessarily include the words *occult, mystical,* and *esoteric*. These words are not synonymous. Mme Blavatsky, the founder of modern Theosophy, suggests the following working definition for *occultism:* "Occultism embraces the whole range of psychological, physiological, cosmical, physical, and spiritual phenomena. From the word *occult*, hidden or secret; applying therefore to the study of the Kabbala, astrology, alchemy, and all arcane sciences."[5] Her broad definition reveals the basic problem in writing about occultism: determining what it really is. To complicate matters still further, the word *occultism* has been hopelessly distorted in modern popular usage—it means much more than black magic, crystal balls, pentagrams, and seances.

Occultism is a system, a body of knowledge with both a practical and theoretical dimension. Practical occultism focuses on the techniques and procedures used to manipulate and control the supernatural and the unknown, whether by magic, incantation, study, or disciplined will. Theoretical occultism is a broad, synthetic (and frequently syncretic) philosophical system, a worldview that seeks to understand the supernatural and the unknown by penetrating to a hidden mystery wisdom that purports to explain man and the universe. Like every other worldview, occultism is a manner of perceiving reality. It is concerned with the broadening of human consciousness beyond the limitations set by the self-conscious ego and the physical organs of perception. External reality plays a secondary role; occultism addresses the relationship between the inner and outer man, between spiritual and physical reality, and stresses the primacy of the noumenal over the phenomenal.

Such a definition of occultism as a doctrine, a worldview concerned with the broadening of consciousness, leads naturally to the question of how occultism differs from mysticism. Both are exclusive; but while occultism is essentially concealed wisdom, mysticism is secret experience.[6] Church polemics actually clarify the situation. The Christian church denounces occultism since it is a competitive belief system that from the Christian point of view is wrong and thus evil. Mysticism, on the other hand, can exist within the structure and symbology of the church and is therefore good, since "the mystic's experience tends to confirm the religious authority under which he lives; its theology and symbols are projected into his mystical experience."[7]

The British scholar and mystic A. E. Waite (who was also captivated by Theosophy at one time) maintains that the work of the mystic is concerned with "the soul's union with God," and that "this and this only is the end of Mysticism."[8] Another definition of mysticism comes from the eminent scholar Andrew Seth: "It appears in connexion with the endeavor of the human mind to grasp the Divine essence or the ultimate reality of things, and to enjoy the blessedness of actual communion with the highest. . . . The thought that is most intensely present in the mystic is that of a supreme, all-pervading, and in-dwelling Power, in whom all things are one."[9] The theoretical occultist would agree with the mystic that his goal also is "the soul's union with God." The occultist seeks to comprehend the divine essence and achieve unity with it as sincerely as a mystic. The difference between occultism and mysticism is not in *what* is sought, but in *how* it is sought.

A survey of those arcane systems traditionally labeled "occult" (alchemy, astrology, hermetic philosophy, ceremonial magic, and so forth), reveals that they all have some lore or doctrine that must be *learned*. An individual cannot simply *be* an alchemist; one does not come to alchemy through a revelatory experience, but through the study of a body of secret knowledge. One must serve a period of apprenticeship, and, if found worthy, be initiated into an elite and closed society by those who are already alchemists. Hence occultism is *esoteric*, i.e., intended for a small group and concealed from the uninitiated.

Here, then, lies the fundamental distinction between the occultist and the mystic. The ultimate goal—the realization, "in thought and feeling, [of] the immanence of the temporal in the eternal, and of the eternal in the temporal"—may be the same for both;[10] however, the means and expressions differ. The mystic finds his vision nonrationally and intuitively, through the mystical experience, the sudden epiphany, the revelation. For the mystic, "God ceases to be an object, and becomes an experience."[11] This experience of God most often takes place within the traditional structure of a living religious tradition. The occultist, on the other hand, does not seek sudden epiphany or salvation through grace; rather, the occultist seeks to free the divine element within himself through knowledge and study, not through grace or revelation. In this, the occultist is like the scientist; occultism is, in fact, called the "secret science" (*Geheimwissenschaft*). The occultist's conception of knowledge, however, is not quite that of the modern scientist's (although the historical roots of modern science are not coincidentally embedded in medieval occultism); occultism claims a "higher" knowledge—a spiritual, not merely physical, cognition. As the "perennial philosophy," occultism serves as an unstable bridge between the empiricism of modern science and the faith of religion.

The appeal of such a bridge, in the guise of Theosophy, to a fin de siècle European culture cut off from God by excessive rationalism and the rise of modern science and industry, was enormous. The modern European mind had lost its faith; the traditional Church could no longer provide it a direct line to God. The scientific positivism then prevalent in European culture did not offer spiritual revelation; people looked beyond traditional religion and science to meet their spiritual needs:

> Our century will not pass without new discoveries giving us the possibility of more profoundly comprehending the essence of human nature, and, possibly, the day is not far distant when a more profound understanding of it will lead to the reconciliation of feeling and knowledge, will bring peace to the soul and will destroy once and for all the feeling of fear and terror before the unknowable and the infinite that constantly threaten it. One thing we can promise: that if it is fated that this merging occur, then it will not occur in the area of narrow materialism or fruitless metaphysics and traditional theology.[12]

Theosophy, as an occult doctrine, offered the possibility of reaching God "scientifically," with the rationalistic tools at hand, bypassing both "narrow materialism" and "traditional theology." It offered access to the divine not through faith, but through the study of a higher knowledge, through the "secret science." To the modern European mind, whose loss of faith threatened it with fragmentation and alienation, this was a seductive offer indeed.

Theosophy, then, appealed to modern Europeans in three important ways. First, it offered to resolve the contradiction between science and religion, knowledge and faith, thereby curing the post-Enlightenment psychic schizophrenia that had led directly to the crisis of culture and

consciousness. Second, it dispensed with alienating materialism by simply terming it "illusory," and offered modern man an eternal, spiritual
life instead. Third, it replaced a waning Christianity's threat of unendur-
able and eternal torment in hell (or its modern alternative, pessimistic
existentialism) with the more soothing concepts of karma and reincarnation, thus extending the existence of the soul and providing a world that
is cosmically fair and just.

Theosophy appealed to Russians educated in the European manner
for the same reasons it appealed to Europeans. Russians, too, were experiencing a crisis of culture and consciousness. Russians, too, sought to
bridge the gulf between science and religion. The Russians, of course,
refracted Theosophy through the prism of their own particular national
vision, with the result that Russian Theosophy developed a messianic,
distinctly Slavic flavor.

As a cultural and intellectual phenomenon of the Silver Age, Russian
Theosophy is too important to be ignored. Research in this area, however, can be challenging. Material is frequently hard to find; many libraries did not consider the journals and ephemera of the occult movements
worth preserving; and the material available is often unreliable. Many
leading figures of the various occult movements deliberately misrepre-
sented their own history and activities; their faithful adherents, biographers, and hagiographers, although enthusiastic, were rarely objective.
The need to circumvent an unfriendly censorship in Russia took an additional toll on truth in the popular press. Much information must necessarily be based on memoirs, which are subject to the caprices of human
memory. Much of the material reported in contemporary journals is
based on hearsay, rumor, and unsubstantiated comments made with ul-
terior motives, primarily in the unreliable sensational press.

In spite of the particular problems inherent in such research, a study
of Theosophy in Russia can only enhance our understanding and appreciation of the subtleties of Russian Silver Age culture. This book, the
first such study to be written by a scholar not ideologically committed to
Theosophy or Anthroposophy, is designed for a rather specific purpose:
to provide in a single volume a coherent and contextualized documentary history of the Russian Theosophical Movement. The book is intended for cultural and intellectual historians, literary scholars, philosophers, and others who are interested in the cultural life of the Russian
Silver Age.

As a contextual study, this work begins with a survey of the occult
interests of Russian educated society from the seventeenth century into
the modern period. Because Theosophy is a universal, cosmopolitan
phenomenon, this study provides a general history of the parent Theosophical Society and introduces the major figures of the worldwide

Theosophical Movement before focusing on the founding of the Russian Section, its principal members, and the nature of its Theosophical work. It places Mme Blavatsky, Theosophy's founder, in a more Russian context than will be found in Western biographies. The study also covers the independent Russian Theosophical circles (i.e., those not connected administratively with the Parent Society), and traces the impact of the Theosophical-Anthroposophical schism in Europe and Russia. It includes an outline of the basic tenets of Theosophical doctrine and surveys the polemics between the Theosophists and their critics from the areas of Russian Orthodoxy, idealist philosophy, the arts, and the sciences. It indicates Theosophy's role in the philosophical dialogues of the Russian creative intelligentsia. Finally, this study chronicles the demise of the Russian Theosophical and Anthroposophical societies in the postrevolutionary period.

The focus of this book is specifically on Russian Theosophy. Anthroposophy, as a closely related movement, also plays an important role in Russian culture of this period but is not the primary subject of this study. Since the founder of Anthroposophy, Dr. Rudolf Steiner (1861–1925), was himself at one time an influential Theosophist, since he helped to shape modern Theosophy and was inevitably shaped by it, and since his departure from the Theosophical Society did not terminate his dialogue with it, Anthroposophy is included in this study insofar as it relates to and illuminates the Russian Theosophical Movement.[13]

The book contains a glossary of commonly used Theosophical terms, including those that occasionally crop up in Silver Age texts, a bibliography of Theosophical materials, original and secondary, published in Russia between 1881 and 1918, and a general bibliography. The first, more complete bibliography makes it possible to determine when and in what form specific Theosophical texts became readily available to readers of Russian. English, French, and German texts were also accessible, as were Russian translations in manuscript.

This volume does not presume to be exhaustive. Its function is to introduce an important and complex subject, the history of the Russian Theosophical Movement and the general position of Theosophical thought in Russian Silver Age culture, to readers unfamiliar with its general contours. It aims only to provide context; analysis of literary texts or other works of art are beyond its purview. It does, however, lay the groundwork for further research by providing a general framework for future study of Theosophical and occult elements in Silver Age works. Such studies will show concretely the ways in which an understanding of occult philosophies can expand the meaning of Symbolist texts and reveal new interpretive layers.

One

A Historical Survey of Russian Occult Interests

THE RUSSIAN SILVER AGE shared in the unprecedented renascence of interest in occultism and speculative mysticism that swept Europe in the second half of the nineteenth century. That Russians were part of this renascence was in no way exceptional, for mystical interests have often found fertile soil among the Slavs. This late-nineteenth-century fascination of Russian educated society with the occult did not need to be imported from the West; as with other ideas and philosophies, Russian culture simply borrowed from Europe the external structures that gave form and expression to powerful indigenous inclinations. Nineteenth-century occultism in Russia was, in fact, part of a larger cultural tradition and was philosophically reinforced from within. Its roots go back to pre-Christian times.

In Russia certain pagan and occult elements persisted in folk beliefs and coexisted peacefully with Christianity (*dvoeverie*), leaving the Russian mind predisposed to syncretism and tolerant toward independent mystical experience. Long before the nineteenth century, Russia had an extensive and flourishing tradition of witchcraft and sorcery (*znakhari, kolduny, kudesniki, gadalki, ved'my*), as well as mystical sectarianism (*Khlysty, Belye golubi, Skoptsy,* and so on). In addition, the Russian Orthodox church (long noted for its eccentric mystics) did not discourage personal mystical expression, even if such expression did not fit exactly within the prescribed, narrow framework of dogma. Traditional Orthodoxy, rigidly structured on one level, was intellectually adventurous on another; it always left some room for independent, mystical experience. The Gnostic speculations and Sophiology of Orthodox lay and clerical theologians during the Russian religious renaissance of the Silver Age would have resulted in excommunication for heresy in the Western church, but they were cautiously tolerated in the Eastern Christian tradition.

The Earliest Traditions

Occult traditions (as opposed to folk beliefs and superstitions) have always been associated with "secret writings" and "magic books." The earliest extant Russian magic books (*volshebnye knigi*) are from the seventeenth century. Used primarily for fortune-telling (*gadanie*), these "forbidden" manuscripts go back much earlier. Many are compilations of far older geomantic and astrological texts translated from European, Byzantine, Arab, and Persian sources. The titles of these Russian magic books are suggestive: *Rafli, Voronograi, Zodii, Mestokryl, Zvezdechet'i, Ostrolog, Charovnik, Volkhovnik, Aristotelevy Vrata, Tainaia tainykh,* and *Kniga imenuemaia Briusovskoi Kalendar'*. Some of these books continued to interest both scholars and general readers and were reissued by the historians A. N. Pypin and M. N. Speranskii at various times during the nineteenth century. The well-known *Briusovskoi Kalendar'* circulated in numerous exemplars; parts of it were published in the occult journal *Izida* as late as 1911–1912. These magic books never disappeared, but were copied and recopied by generations of Russian readers over the centuries, with new texts added from time to time. They never had the approval of the church, and were forbidden by ecclesiastical authority long before they were officially banned by the Council of the Hundred Chapters (*Stoglav*) in 1551; this, needless to say, enhanced rather than diminished their popularity.[1]

The "rational" eighteenth century was not without its own occult side. In Western Europe the excessive rationalism of the Age of Enlightenment was counterbalanced by a tendency toward the supernatural and occult that expressed itself not only in the refined speculative mysticism of Emanuel Swedenborg (1666–1772), but also in a veritable plague of spirit visitations and widespread werewolf and vampire scares inspired by the folk traditions of the Slavic and Central European lands. The eighteenth century was not just the Age of Voltaire, it was also the Age of Cagliostro, the psychic, occultist, and sorcerer. It was an age of mesmeric passes, seances, prophecies, magic cures, "miracles," astrology, alchemy, anagogy, and occult charlatanism on an international scale.

This dualism was manifested in Russian culture as well. There the eighteenth century began with Peter the Great's ambitious attempt to reform and secularize Russian culture and society. Instituted quickly and brutally, his reforms produced only the veneer of rationalism. Beneath that veneer still lay the analogical, nonlinear, intuitive frame of mind that characterizes Russian thought even today. Over the course of the eighteenth century, this analogical mode of thought, coupled with the feeling of spiritual emptiness induced by "modern" rationalism's separation of man from the "medieval" traditional church and its values, served to turn educated Russians toward other esoteric systems, notably Freemasonry, by the last quarter of the eighteenth century.[2] While Catherine II looked with disdain on the occult, it was during her reign, in 1779, that the notorious Count Cagliostro visited her capital, bringing with him magic cures and new Masonic rites.[3]

Most studies assume (although conclusive documentation has never been presented) that Freemasonry first came to Russia in 1731, early in the reign of Empress Anne, when either Captain John Phillips or General James Keith was named Provincial Grand Master for Moscow by Lord Lovell, then head of the Grand Lodge of England. The popular story of Peter the Great having undergone a Masonic initiation in England is probably apocryphal. By the mid-eighteenth century, numerous Masonic lodges had formed in Moscow, St. Petersburg, and the provinces, and had quickly established connections with their French, Swedish, and German counterparts. Freemasonry flourished in Russia among the upper classes. Leading Russian Freemasons of the period included the writer and journalist Nikolai Novikov (1744–1818), Professor I. G. Shvarts, I. V. Lopukhin, and Count I. P. Elagin.

As a result of this occult, particularly Masonic, activity, a new type of esoteric literature appeared in Russia at the end of the eighteenth century. It reflected occult interests that were Western rather than indigenously Russian: Martinism (a blend of theosophy, Rosicrucianism, and mystical Freemasonry attributed to Louis Claude de Saint-Martin [1743–1803]), the Rose Cross, Illuminism, ancient mystery cults, philosophical alchemy, and other subjects associated with European Freemasonry. The occult texts that began appearing in the last quarter of the eighteenth century were almost exclusively translations of European works and were published in Russia either by Nikolai Novikov, who operated the university press, or by Ivan Lopukhin, who had a secret printing plant in addition to his regular press. Numbering more than a hundred titles, these texts include translations of Masonic classics, Rosicrucian texts, the *Bhagavad Gita*, the works of Karl von Eckartshausen, Louis Claude de Saint-Martin, Paracelsus, as well as anthologies of mystical thought, supernatural events, and prophetic dreams, much of it anecdotal.[4] Many of the incidents recorded would be told and retold in journals and anthologies throughout the nineteenth and early twentieth centuries. All of these texts were popular in their time and were sought after again at the beginning of the twentieth century, when they were advertised not only in occult publications, but in popular journals and even in national bibliographies, such as *Knizhnaia letopis'*.

If the prominent contemporary writer and historian Nikolai Karamzin called mysticism "preposterology" (*vzdorologiia*), and if Catherine the Great viewed spectral visitations with contempt and Masonic lodges with apprehension, her mystically inclined grandson, Tsar Alexander I, surrounded himself with intimates who were involved with the Swedenborgians, Freemasons, Russian mystical sectarians, and the Bible Society (these included Prince Aleksandr Golitsyn, Rodion Koshelev, the

Baroness von Krüdener, and Ekaterina Tatarinova).[5] It was rumored that Alexander I himself became a Freemason in 1803. Under Prince Golitsyn's patronage (he was Chief Procurator of the Holy Synod and later Minister of Religious Affairs and Education) occult texts and journals (e.g., *Sionskii Vestnik*) circulated with relative freedom, despite official ecclesiastical disapproval.

By the summer of 1822 the Orthodox church, taking advantage of Archimandrite Photius's considerable influence on the Tsar, convinced Alexander to confiscate occult books and to ban all mystical and secret societies on the grounds that they were engaged in revolutionary activity, an accusation with considerable foundation, as Nicholas I had opportunity to discover in the Decembrist Uprising of 1825. The royal decree, however, did not eradicate Russian Freemasonry; the Masonic lodges exercised greater secrecy but did not discontinue their meetings and rituals. Over the course of the century many Russian Freemasons also became members of French, German, English, and Belgian lodges.

Although Nicholas's court, which was most unlike Alexander's, remained untouched by occult tendencies, educated society's interest in the subject did not lessen; only the means of its expression was transformed. The wave of German romanticism that spilled into Russia during the first quarter of the nineteenth century had carried with it a passion for things occult, fantastic, and supernatural, both on a popular and esoteric level. One result was the appearance of a large body of supernatural fiction, again imitating Western trends and models. The period from 1825 to mid-century was characterized by the flowering of the Russian supernatural short story, which involved both minor and major writers (Antonii Pogorel'skii, M. N. Zagoskin, A. K. Tolstoi, V. F. Odoevskii, Nikolai Gogol', Aleksandr Pushkin, and others).

If fewer occult materials were being published in Russia by the mid-nineteenth century, it was more the result of the increasingly restrictive system of censorship created by Nicholas I than the counteracting effect of modern science and philosophical positivism. Books on occult topics had to be passed by both government and church censors, and anything that looked suspiciously like a threat to the teachings or hierarchy of the Orthodox church was not published. While certain eccentricities of personal behavior (such as attending private seances) might be overlooked, occultism in print was tantamount to spiritual sedition. The result was that in the second half of the nineteenth century Russian presses were set up in outposts of the Russian Empire and in European cities, notably in Warsaw and Leipzig, and the books printed there were then either quietly smuggled or occasionally "imported" into central Russia as "foreign" publications (which came under a different set of censorship restrictions). Materials also circulated in manuscript copies.

The French Occult Revival

The second half of the nineteenth century witnessed a tremendous boom in occultism. It started in France and inevitably spilled over into Russia where, after the death of the unimaginative Nicholas I in 1855, the last three Russian Tsars embraced it enthusiastically. The doyen of nineteenth-century philosophical occultism, the author of the French occult revival, the man who is revered as "one of the key figures in the history of modern occultism," was Eliphas Lévi (pseudonym of Alphonse Louis Constant [1810–1875]).[6] Lévi was a defrocked French priest who had a long-standing interest in occultism and mystical philosophy. Starting almost alone, he soon gathered around him a group of disciples and made France the vanguard of the occult movement. His studies, although vague, romantic, and often contradictory, became increasingly popular and are even today considered classics of philosophical occultism. His major works, circulating in Russia in translated manuscript, were *Dogme et rituel de la haute magie* (Paris, 1856), *Histoire de la magie* (Paris, 1860), and *La Clef des grands mystères* (Paris, 1861).

Eliphas Lévi was an extremely influential figure. Not only did he initiate the occult revival of the second half of the nineteenth century, he also influenced the work of many others: the French Symbolist writers (Charles Baudelaire, Arthur Rimbaud, Paul Verlaine, Philippe Villiers de l'Isle-Adam, Joris Karl Huysmans, Sâr [Joséphin] Péladan), the painters of the Salon de la Rose-Croix, the Nabis (especially Paul Serusier and Paul Ranson), Odilon Redon, Puvis de Chavannes, Gustave Moreau, Jean Delville, as well as the Dutch artist Jan Toorop, the English pre-Raphaelite painters, and the scandalous poets Charles Algernon Swinburne and Oscar Wilde.[7] The British writer Edward Bulwer-Lytton, himself a Rosicrucian, put Lévi and his philosophy into his popular novels.[8] The Hermetic Order of the Golden Dawn, whose members included Irish poet William Butler Yeats and the scholar A. E. Waite, attempted to synthesize the vast and bewildering body of occult material into a system, using Lévi as its foundation. Many other occultists based their studies on Lévi's; even the eccentric Mme Blavatsky leaned heavily on Lévi's work for her own Theosophical classics. Writing about the period in general, the popular author Anatole France observed: "A certain knowledge of the occult sciences became necessary for the understanding of a great number of literary works of this period. Magic occupied a large place in the imagination of our poets and novelists. The vertigo of the invisible seized them, the idea of the unknown haunted them."[9]

In France, Eliphas Lévi's principal disciple was Stanislas de Guaita (1860–1897). De Guaita, a morphine addict and decadent poet, earned his place in the occult movement with the publication of two works. The first (and more important) was *Le Serpent de la Genèse* (Paris, 1891), which consisted of two parts, *Le Temple de Satan* and *La Clef de la magie noire*. The other work was *Essais de sciences maudites* (Paris, 1894). De Guaita, together with the Kabbalist Oswald Wirth, Papus, and others, dreamed of uniting occultists everywhere into a single, universal Rosicrucian brotherhood, for occultism has traditionally been a cosmopolitan and not a nationalist phenomenon. There was to be a place for Russian occultists in this brotherhood as well. Leading Russian and Polish occultists had studied abroad with their European mentors, and European occultists regularly visited Russia; all necessary lines of communication were already in place.

Another contributor to the French occult revival was the Polish mathematician and occultist Joseph Hoene-Wroński (1778–1853), who strove for the synthesis of rationalism, religion, and belief in human progress. He was the author of *Messianisme, ou Réforme absolue du savoir humaine* (Paris, 1847), which advocated the union of religion and philosophy. The works of Eliphas Lévi and Hoene-Wroński subsequently influenced Joseph Saint-Yves d'Alveydre (1842–1910), a student of Eastern and Western occult traditions, and his disciple, Gerard Encausse (1865–1916), who wrote prolifically on Kabbalism, alchemy, spiritualism, Rosicrucianism, Freemasonry, Theosophy, and the Tarot, under the name, famous all over Europe, of Papus. He was translated into all the European languages, and eleven of his major works appeared in Russian. He headed the Faculté des Sciences Hermétiques of the Université Libre des Hautes Etudes in Paris, which attracted Russian students and whose program formed the basis of numerous private occult study courses in Russia. Papus was also the head of *L'Ordre du Martinisme* and its affiliate, *L'Ordre Kabbalistique de la Rose-Croix*.

Two French occultists became particularly influential in the Russian court of Nicholas II. The first was Dr. Philippe (Nizier-Anthèlme Vachod, 1849–1905), who preceded Grigorii Rasputin as spiritual mentor of the royal family. The second was the celebrated Papus, who was a popular and welcome visitor at the Russian court. By 1899 Dr. Philippe and Papus had established a Martinist Order in the court circle of St. Petersburg. Tsar Nicholas II was an initiate of this Order, but left the Lodge when he became more seriously committed to Russian Orthodoxy. His uncles, the Grand Princes Nikolai Nikolaevich and Petr Nikolaevich, as well as other members of the royal family and numerous members of the government, continued as members of Martinist and other Masonic orders. Nina Berberova, in her book on Russian Freemasonry and the Russian Revolution, pointed out that by 1914 "there was no profession, no institution, no official or private society, organization or group in Russia without Freemasons."[10]

The French occult revival, once started, generated interest in many occult and mystical systems. Gnosticism, ancient Hermeticism, medieval philosophical alchemy, Kabbalism, and Rosicrucianism were rediscovered and popularized. Serious scholars of these disciplines could choose from many reprints and translations of original texts, as well as new studies of the material, among them Marcellin Berthelot's three-volume *Collection des anciens alchimistes Grecs* (Paris, 1887–1888), A. E. Waite's *Hermetic Museum* (London, 1893), C. W. King's *Gnostics and Their Remains* (2d ed., London, 1887), and G. R. S. Mead's three-volume *Thrice-Greatest Hermes* (London, 1906).[11] Interest in Kabbalism produced its own body of literature, including Adolphe Franck's now classic *La Kabbale* (2d ed., Paris, 1889), Papus's *La Qabalah* (Paris, 1892), and Lévi's own Kabbalistic studies, *La Clef des grands mystères* (Paris, 1861) and *Le Livre des splendeurs* (Paris, 1894). Paul Christian's *Histoire de la magie, du monde surnaturel et de la fatalité à travers les temps et les peuples* (Paris, 1870) became a basic textbook for aspiring occultists and journeyman astrologers. Classics of medieval mysticism, religion, and occultism were reprinted, making the works of Paracelsus, Agrippa von Nettesheim, Heinrich Khunrath, Raimon Lully, and Jacob Boehme, as well as the later works of Emanuel Swedenborg and Karl von Eckartshausen, easily available to an interested reading public, along with new studies of these mystics and others. This huge body of occult material, much of it in French and thus easily accessible to educated Russians, soon found its way into Russia.

The Russian middle class and the creative intelligentsia, cosmopolitan and fairly well read, were acquainted with these French occult classics. Works by Papus, Lévi, St. Yves d'Alveydre, Karl DuPrel, Camille Flammarion, Allan Kardec, and Paul Sédir were translated into Russian after 1905. Many Russian readers also read the works of European authors influenced by Lévi and his disciples. Russian literary journals carried articles by and about them. Their literature was accessible to those who did not read French and English through the competent translations of Bal'mont, Briusov, and other Russian Symbolist writers.

The authors of the occult revival are represented in numerous popular texts, such Sofia Ivanovna Tukholka's *Okkul'tizm i magiia*, which predigested the major nineteenth-century occult trends for the middle-class reader, or Vladimir Zapriagaev's series of paraphrases, in which he retold Western occult texts for a specifically Russian audience unable to read them in the original.[12] On a more plebeian level were works like the *Domashniaia volshebnaia knizhka*, a reference book of fortune-telling and black and white magic, which had been published in its thirteenth edition by 1909. Books on dream interpretation, horoscope casting, and collections of supernatural anecdotes and "true stories" were also immensely popular.

The Golden Age of Russian occultism came only at the beginning of the twentieth century, when secret societies and esoteric publications proliferated at an astonishing rate. This was due to the easing of censorship restrictions by the Manifesto of October 17, 1905, which guaranteed fundamental civil liberties, including freedom of opinion, of the press, of assembly, and of association. Even the more restrictive "provisional rules" of November 24, 1905, which negated some of the advances made in October, did not change the fact that things were much freer than they had been on October 16. Most important, church censorship was considerably curtailed, thus at last allowing the widespread publication of occult material in Russia. Spreading doctrines contrary or inimical to the Orthodox church was no longer punishable by exile to Siberia.

Russian occult interests ran the entire gamut: Spiritualism and Theosophy attracted the most attention and generated the largest number of publications, but there was also Rosicrucianism, alchemy, psychographology, phrenology, Kabbalism, Yoga, sectarianism, Hermeticism, hypnotism, Egyptian religion, astrology, chiromancy, animal magnetism, fakirism, telepathy, the Tarot, and magic (both black and white). Freemasonry experienced a particular popularity, since several members of the royal family were active members and protected the movement with their patronage. Hundreds of occult societies and circles, registered and unregistered, were formed in every major city and in the provinces. More than eight hundred occult titles (excluding belles lettres) were published in Russia between 1881, when the passion for the occult that had America and Europe firmly in its grip finally penetrated the Russian Empire, and 1918, when scores of occult societies found themselves banned, their books confiscated, their members arrested, and their presses closed down by lack of paper and by Bolshevik order. If works of fiction, original and translated, are added to this count, the number of occult publications climbs much higher. Between 1881 and 1918 some thirty occult journals were published, their titles reflecting the wide range of occult interests: *Rebus, Vestnik Teosofii, Izida, Mentalizm, Ottuda, Russkii Frank-mason, Spiritualist, Voprosy khiromantii i gipnotizma, Zhurnal psikho-grafologii*, and others.

Spiritualism

By far the most popular and widespread nineteenth-century occult movement in Russia was Spiritualism. Spiritualism is a belief in the continued existence of the dead and in the ability of the living to communicate with them through a sensitive, or medium. Manifestations of spirit presence include rapping, table turning, automatic writing, spirit voices, and ectoplasmic materialization. Nineteenth-century Spiritualism took one of two forms. The first was *scientific spiritualism* (Anglo-American "modern Spiritualism"), which, regardless of its "occult" trappings, was essentially positivistic in its insistence that the various Spiritualist phenomena were indeed consistent with modern science and would eventually be explained according to the laws of nature; "scientific" spiritualism attracted the attention of numerous scientists, who carried out laboratory research in an attempt to discover these natural laws. The second was *mystical spiritualism* (the French *"Spiritisme"* of Allan Kardec [Hippolyte Leon Denizard Rivail, 1804–1869]), an alternative "religion" with a doctrine of compulsory reincarnation (a "soul" achieves spiritual perfection through a sequence of reincarnations). Both forms of spiritualism gained popularity in Russia.

Modern Spiritualism traditionally dates from March 31, 1848, when two sisters, Kate and Margaret Fox, spoke with the spirit of a murdered peddler in a farmhouse in Hydesville, New York. In the early 1850s it became the rage in Europe, attracting the attention of the educated public, and converting such divers persons as the artist Alphonse Mucha, the actress Sarah Bernhardt, the writers Victor Hugo and Elizabeth Barrett Browning, and Queen Victoria. Russians who traveled abroad had brought Spiritualism back to the capitals with them by the winter of 1852. Initially viewed as a salon entertainment, early Russian Spiritualism consisted primarily of table turning and automatic writing; two decades would pass before it would be taken seriously in Russia.

French Spiritism had come to Russia by 1854, introduced by General Apollon Boltin.[13] The general accessibility of the French language to educated Russians ensured that mystical French Spiritism, rather than Anglo-American Spiritualism, was the first to become popular in Russia. By the end of the century, however, most educated Russians had come to prefer "scientific" Spiritualism to its mystical French variant.

At first Russian Spiritualism was limited to a small circle of aristocratic enthusiasts, heirs of the occult interests of the Schopenhauer-oriented Odoevskii circle and intimates of the court. Their most prominent representative was the writer A. K. Tolstoi (1817–1875), who had always expressed strong interest in the occult and supernatural and who incorporated such elements into his novels, poems, and short stories. The Russian philosopher Vladimir Solov'ev (1853–1900) later became part of this circle; Solov'ev at one time indulged his interest in Spiritualism and even engaged in automatic writing. Other prominent early Spiritualists included Count Grigorii Kushelev-Bezborodko; Vladimir Dal', the compiler of the famous *Tolkovyi slovar'*; Professor P. D. Iurkevich, a religious philosopher and Vladimir Solov'ev's teacher at Moscow University; and Academician M. V. Ostrogradskii.

When the internationally famous medium Daniel Dunglas Home (1833–1886) visited Russia, he was a frequent guest at the estate of A. K. Tolstoi. Home was but one of the many Spiritualists and mediums invited to Russia to give seances for the court of Alexander II. Home further strengthened his ties to Russia by marrying Count Kushelev-Bezborodko's sister-in-law, Alexandrina de Kroll, and spending a large part of every year in Russia.[14] Spiritualism continued to be a "hobby" pursued by the Russian courts of Alexander III and Nicholas II. They sponsored Spiritualists, occultists, and mystics of various stamps, and in the face of ecclesiastical disapproval gave them the limited protection afforded by royal patronage.[15]

In the 1870s the figure of Aleksandr Nikolaevich Aksakov (1823–1903), nephew of the writer Sergei Timofeevich Aksakov and younger cousin of the Slavophile thinkers Ivan and Konstantin Aksakov, came to dominate the field of Russian Spiritualism. A. N. Aksakov's early passion for Swedenborg soon awakened a more general interest in spiritualism and mysticism. Pursuing this interest in Russia, however, was decidedly difficult. The church censorship prevented him from printing Spiritualist texts in Russia and his requests to publish a Russian Spiritualist journal were repeatedly rejected. Aksakov published many translations of well-known European Spiritualist works, frequently at his own expense, at a press in Leipzig.

A. N. Aksakov was also an author of original works on Spiritualism. His *Animism and Spiritism* (first Russian edition, 1893), in which he strove to be as scientific and objective as possible, remains an important work in the history of Spiritualism even today; Karl DuPrel, the German mystical philosopher, called it "the phenomenology of Spiritualism." Founder, editor, and publisher of the prestigious journal *Psychische Studien* (Leipzig, 1874–1934), Aksakov was well known and respected in Spiritualist circles in Petersburg, London, and on the continent. In 1900 he was invited to chair the Paris Spiritualist Congress.

A. N. Aksakov was aided in his work in Russia by two professors from the Imperial University in St. Petersburg, the chemist Aleksandr Mikhailovich Butlerov (1828–1886; Butlerov was married to A. N. Aksakov's cousin) and the zoologist Nikolai Petrovich Vagner (1829–1907). The two professors, by their cautious support of the validity of mediumistic phenomena, took Spiritualism out of the realm of a mere diversion for a bored, sensation-seeking society or a serious pursuit for only a small elite group of scientists and philosophers, and turned it into an earnest controversy in the Russian press. Professor Vagner wrote a letter to the editor of *Vestnik Evropy*, "Po povodu spiritualizma"; it was published in the April 1875 issue. This letter was followed by a storm of articles in the press, especially in *Peterburgskie Vedomosti, Novoe Vremia,* and *Birzhevye Vedomosti*. More serious polemics continued in the monthly journals. It was tremendous free advertising for Spiritualism.

In the winter of 1875–1876 a Scientific Commission for the Study of Mediumistic Phenomena, headed by Dmitrii Mendeleev (1834–1907), the internationally known chemist and father of the Periodic Table of Elements, was formed at the St. Petersburg Imperial University. Scandal tore the Commission apart when Mendeleev was accused of attempting to sabotage the investigation by publishing his negative conclusions (*Materialy dlia suzhdeniia o spiritizme* [1876]) before the investigation had properly begun.[16] Opposing prejudices battled it out in the press. Public opinion came down on the side of the Spiritualists, and Russian Spiritualism became solidly entrenched in the culture of its time.

The Spiritualists were determined to extract a full recantation from Mendeleev; the best they would do, however, was a contemptuous, grudging admission of the existence of mediumistic phenomena some twenty years later. In January 1894, the Spiritualist V. I. Pribytkov gleefully reported that Mendeleev had finally admitted the existence of such phenomena. "Do you now admit, Dmitrii Ivanovich, the possibility of the phenomena themselves?" asked Pribytkov. "They exist. I've seen them, but they happen very rarely. They are not worth paying attention to, and no serious, busy person is going to get involved with them," answered Mendeleev.[17]

The popularity of Spiritualism continued to increase in Russia. On October 11, 1881, the Spiritualists cautiously launched their first Russian journal, *Rebus*. *Rebus* was the brainchild of Viktor Ivanovich Pribytkov (d. 1910). He and his wife, the medium Elizaveta Dmitrievna Pribytkova (d. 1896), were prominent St. Petersburg Spiritualists. *Rebus* ("Man is the most immediate and most complex of rebuses") began publication camouflaged as a weekly games and popular entertainment magazine. It gradually became apparent, however, that one of the "games" involved was Spiritualism. Articles on automatic writing, Theosophy, animal magnetism, and other related topics soon appeared among the puzzles and rebuses. Thomas Berry, in his survey of Russian Spiritualism, suggests that *Rebus* was allowed to exist specifically "because of the interest in Spiritualism by the royal family and high society."[18] Even with royal tolerance, certain censorship problems could not be avoided in 1881 and the new journal had its share of editorial headaches; not until the end of 1905 do the words "Independent Organ of the Russian Spiritualists" appear on *Rebus*'s title page.

Pribytkov remained editor of *Rebus* until December 1903, when illness forced him to surrender editorship of the journal to Pavel Aleksandrovich Chistiakov. *Rebus*'s offices moved from St. Petersburg to the Arbat in Moscow. As an editor, Chistiakov was more biting, more sarcastic than Pribytkov; he was less saccharine, more penetrating and witty. *Rebus* took on a different format and a decidedly different flavor. Chistiakov's own column, "On the Path," has some of the journal's more interesting comments.

On October 31, 1905, almost immediately after the October Manifesto, Chistiakov applied to the Russian authorities for official registration of his unofficial Moscow Spiritualist Circle, which had been meeting openly since 1897. The resulting "Russian Spiritualist Society for Study in the Areas of Experimental Psychology, Psychic Phenomena, and Spiritualism" was chartered in early 1906 and had its first official meeting on May 26 of that year. It began with thirty-eight charter members but membership soon grew into the hundreds.

One of the first official acts of the Russian Spiritualist Society was to organize a Russian Congress. On October 20–27, 1906, the long-planned Congress of Spiritualists was finally held in Moscow.[19] Although it was a closed Congress for subscribers and collaborators of *Rebus* and their invited guests, more than four hundred people attended; more than three hundred had to be turned away because they lacked invitations (and the hall could not hold them anyway). V. I. Pribytkov was named honorary chairman while P. A. Chistiakov chaired the sessions. The week-long Spiritualist Congress allowed representation by other occult groups, including the Theosophists, who used the Congress as a forum to acquaint interested Russians with their founder and their doctrine. In addition to all aspects of Spiritualism and Spiritism, other occult sciences included in the program of the Congress were numerology, astrology, alchemy, and Kabbalistic studies. This was not surprising, as many people had an interest in more than one area of occultism.

After 1906, *Rebus* and the Russian Spiritualist Society were no longer the exclusive arbiters of Russian Spiritualism, although they continued to dominate it. Vladimir Pavlovich Bykov, leader of the Moscow Circle of Dogmatic Spiritualists, immediately initiated a number of new Spiritualist journals and newspapers (*Spiritualist, Golos Vseobshchei Liubvi*, and *Ottuda*) in competition with *Rebus*.[20] If *Rebus* represented the point of view of "scientific Spiritualism," then Bykov's *Spiritualist* focused on the "religious" dimension of Spiritualism; it frequently represented French mystical Spiritism, but with a Christian twist. Each issue of *Spiritualist* had some articles on Christian morality and ethics, theoretical Spiritualism, and practical Spiritualism (records of seances, descriptions of phenomena). Bykov and Chistiakov polemicized with each other, at times rancorously, in *Spiritualist* and *Rebus*. Bykov finally gave up Spiritualism and returned to the Orthodox church.[21]

Spiritualism exuded a strong influence on Russian middle- and upper-class society. Vladimir Bykov estimated that 1,672 Spiritualist circles, official and unofficial, existed in Moscow and St. Petersburg at the beginning of the century. Bykov also offered figures that provide a general profile of the Spiritualists among the Russian population. He claimed that his three publications had more than fifty thousand subscribers. "Categorizing my subscribers on the basis of employment and social position, it is possible to determine quite accurately that persons living in the countryside constituted 27% of my readers; civil servants and military personnel, 53%; professionals and the independently wealthy, 12%; clerics, who doubtlessly subscribed to my publications and journals with the goal of preparing themselves for the struggle against this evil, 8%."[22] Bykov is one of the few Spiritualists (or ex-Spiritualists) actually to offer something approaching statistics, but all commentators, both pro- and anti-Spiritualist, stress that Spiritualism involved an enormous number of people.

Spiritualism's primary impact was on the middle and upper classes. Its considerable influence among members of the court and the government has yet to be specifically documented, but it cannot be denied. Among the creative intelligentsia, Spiritualism appealed primarily to those who modeled themselves and their lives on the French Decadents, many of whom openly indulged their occult and spiritualist interests. Thus the Symbolist poet Aleksandr Blok attended seances, presided over by the famous Polish medium Jan Guzik, at Professor Anichkov's home, while Valerii Briusov, an occasional contributor to *Rebus* and a frequenter of seances, contemplated writing a novel called *The Medium*. The young Symbolist Andrei Belyi, who had a falling out with Briusov, quite seriously accused the older poet of being "a powerful hypnotist" who was attacking him with "mediumistic manifestations."[23] Belyi also caricatured the mystical anarchist Georgii Chulkov, himself passionately interested in extrasensory and spiritualist phenomena, as Chukholka, an unconscious medium transmitting demonic forces, in his novel *The Silver Dove*. Spiritualism also inspired a large body of popular reading, especially the many novels of Vera Kryzhanovskaia ("Rochester"), a socially prominent St. Petersburg Spiritualist, A. A. fon-Nol'de, Andrei Zarin, and Mme Blavatsky's sister, Vera Zhelikhovskaia.

Spiritualism's popularity did not sit well with the Orthodox church, despite many Spiritualists claiming to be "Christian Spiritualists" (as opposed to "pagan Spiritualists" and "atheist" or "heretical" [Buddhist] Theosophists"). Bykov described a typical meeting of "Christian Spiritualists" in his own Circle: "After the singing of the usual prayers of the Christian church, a lecture about the Christian-Spiritualist movement is read; this is followed by a general discussion and an experimental mediumistic seance."[24] While Spiritualism easily made room for Christianity, and Spiritualists prepared themselves by prayer and fasting to withstand the "dark forces" that sometimes manifested themselves at seances, the converse was not true: Christianity could not make room for Spiritualism. The clergy invoked the Biblical prohibition against Spiritualism and all forms of magic: "There shall not be found among you any one that maketh his son or his daughter to pass through the fire, or that useth divination, or an observer of times, or an enchanter, or a witch, or a charmer, or a consulter with familiar spirits, or a wizard, or a necromancer, For all that do these things are an abomination unto the Lord" (Deut. 18:10–12). They clinched their arguments with references to Saul's fateful visit to the Witch of Endor (1 Sam. 28). But their arguments did not stop serious Spiritualists.

Spiritualism appealed to its practitioners for various reasons. For many, it was just fun. Ladies and gentlemen were given an opportunity to sit together in darkened rooms, holding hands without censure; critics frequently leveled the accusation that Spiritualism openly encouraged sexual depravity. Spiritualism also titillated and amused with immediate "miracles": levitating furniture, strange knocks, automatic writing, spirit voices, disembodied hands, apparitions, unseen violins, flowers dropping from the ceiling, a spooky encounter with the land "beyond." For some it brought consolation, contact with their dear departed, and "proof" that death would not really be the end of themselves either, at a time when the church's promises of an afterlife were no longer so convincing. For others it was an entirely new direction in "scientific research," one that stood on the threshold of a breakthrough to a new set of natural laws "proving" the existence of life beyond death. Spiritualism spoke to the plethora of neuroses generated by a disintegrating, morbid, and decadent age.

Theosophy

Although not as strong in terms of numbers of adherents as Spiritualism, Theosophy was the most important occult trend of the late nineteenth century in terms of cultural and philosophical content. Allegedly coined by the neo-Platonist Ammonius Saccas (c. 160–242), the word *theosophy* comes from the Late Greek and means "Divine Wisdom" (*theos*, "god," and *sophia*, "wisdom"). The term *theosophy* may be used to refer to any system of speculative mysticism, from neo-Platonism to the philosophy of Vladimir Solov'ev. Over the years it has come to be specifically associated with the esoteric philosophies of the medieval mystics (Jacob

Boehme, Meister Eckhart, Paracelsus, and others). Theosophy (with a small "t") as speculative mysticism should be distinguished from Theosophy (with a capital "T") as an organized movement of the late nineteenth century.

Theosophy (with a capital "T") was the creation of Helena Petrovna Blavatsky (1831–1891), an expatriate Russian then living in New York City.[25] In 1875, this enigmatic woman, assisted by the American Colonel Henry Steel Olcott (1832–1907), organized the Theosophical Society. The Society became popular and soon claimed tens of thousands of members worldwide, spreading eventually to Russia and attracting numerous adherents from the educated middle classes. Modern Theosophy, regardless of its subsequent contempt for Spiritualism (its greatest competitor for the hearts and minds of the mystically inclined), evolved out of Spiritualism. The two founders of Theosophy, Colonel Henry Olcott and Mme Blavatsky, both began their occult careers in Spiritualism, the former as a journalist, the latter as a medium. Although Mme Blavatsky would continue to believe in mediumistic phenomena as psychic manifestation, she and the Theosophical program rejected the idea of "spirits." Theosophy's and Spiritualism's "theological" divergences did not inhibit people from adhering simultaneously to both movements.

The Charter of the Theosophical Society (1875) states that the principal aim and object of the Society is to form the nucleus of a Universal Brotherhood of Humanity, without distinction by race, color, creed, sex, or caste. The Universal Brotherhood is based on the idea of the One Life, prevalent in Buddhism and Hinduism, which lies at the core of Theosophy. The One Life is the Soul of the World, the ultimate reality in which each living thing shares. Although Theosophists deny it, their doctrine is essentially a form of pantheism. Thus all human beings have a single spiritual nature and strive toward a single spiritual goal. The Society's subsidiary goals are to sponsor the study of ancient and modern religions, philosophies, and sciences, and to demonstrate the importance of such study, since only in this way can the single Mystery Wisdom be distilled out of them, and finally to investigate the unexplained laws of nature and the psychical powers latent in human beings. On this last point scientific Spiritualism and Theosophy have some things in common, and the movements might have drawn closer together had it not been for Mme Blavatsky's personal animosity toward the London Society for Psychical Research and toward leading Spiritualists, who colluded to expose her celebrated psychic manifestations as sophisticated trickery and by whom she consequently felt betrayed.

Theosophy provides its adherents with a structured Weltanschauung, yet at the same time it is amorphous enough to accommodate interests in other forms of mysticism, occultism, and religion. Mrs. Annie Besant (1874–1933), one of the Movement's leaders, pointed out that Theosophy,

> As the origin and basis of all religions, . . . cannot be the antagonist of any; it is indeed their purifier, revealing the valuable inner meaning of much that has become mischievous in its external presentation by the perverseness of ignorance and the accretions of superstition; but it recognizes and defends itself in each, and seeks in each to unveil its hidden wisdom. No man in becoming a Theosophist need cease to be a Christian, a Buddhist, a Hindu; he will but acquire a deeper insight into his own faith, a firmer hold on its spiritual truths, a broader understanding of its sacred teachings.[26]

From the Theosophical point of view, an enlightened individual could lay out the Tarot on Tuesday night, participate in sectarian ecstasy on Wednesday, speak to his Theosophical circle on Thursday, and receive the Eucharist on Sunday with no violence done to his inner convictions. Theosophy as a system catered to the eclectic spirit of the age.

Leading Theosophists defined their doctrine as a syncretic, mystico-religious philosophical system, "at once an adequate philosophy and an all-embracing religion and ethic," which is founded on an ancient esoteric tradition.[27] Mme Blavatsky called this tradition, which she considered the one supreme source of all the religions in the world, the Mystery Wisdom, or the Secret Doctrine. This "esoteric philosophy reconciles all religions, strips every one of its outward, human garments, and shows the root of each to be identical with that of every other great religion."[28] Thus Theosophy affirms "the antiquity, continuity, and essential unity of esoteric teaching." The Theosophists claimed that "sages and prophets belonging to the most diverse ages have reached conclusions identical in substance though differing in form, regarding the first and last of truths, and always along the same path of interior initiation and meditation."[29] Studying the world's great religions through a method of "comparative esotericism," Theosophy attempted to distill out this universal mother doctrine.

This Secret Doctrine, Mme Blavatsky alleged, had been jealously guarded for thousands of years by a Brotherhood of ageless adepts (she called them Masters, or "Mahatmas") who had long concealed it from profane eyes. "Proofs of its diffusion, authentic records of its history, a complete chain of documents, showing its character and presence in every land, together with the teaching of all its great adepts," she insisted, "exist to this day in the secret crypts of libraries belonging to the Occult Fraternity."[30] Mrs. Besant elaborated further:

> The common property of the religions of the world asserts the existence of an original teaching in the custody of a Brotherhood of great spiritual Teachers,

who—Themselves the outcome of past cycles of evolution—acted as the in-
structors and guides of the child humanity of our planet, imparting to its races
and nations in turn the fundamental truths of religion in the form most
adapted to the idiosyncrasies of the recipients.[31]

In the second half of the nineteenth century, the "Brotherhood of the
White Lodge, the Hierarchy of Adepts who watch over and guide the
evolution of humanity, and who have preserved these truths unim-
paired," decided that the time had come for these truths to be revealed
to the world.[32] Using Mme Blavatsky as a channel, the Masters "or-
dered" her to found the Theosophical Society as a means of disseminating this universal occult doctrine to those prepared to benefit from it.
Taking control of her thoughts, the Masters communicated through her
the two major texts of the Movement, *Isis Unveiled* and *The Secret Doctrine*, which she then wrote down.

Mme Blavatsky's personal fascination with Eastern religions, Buddhism in particular, led to the inclusion of a vast quantity of Buddhist
material in Theosophy. Buddhism's greatest contribution to Theosophy
was an exotic vocabulary and an involved cosmology that lent Theosophy a certain piquancy. Adherents also borrowed the unfamiliar but ex-
citing activities of meditation, chanting, and incense burning; some
made a habit of wearing oriental garments. Theosophical practices
added excitement to the mundaneness of everyday life.

Although Theosophy is sometimes called "neo-Buddhism," "Western Buddhism," and even "esoteric Buddhism," it would be facile to
dismiss Theosophy as nothing more than a form of Buddhism, since it
did not adopt Eastern ideas (maya, karma, reincarnation, nirvana) consistently and without some Western refinements. And Theosophy borrowed not only from Buddhism; it borrowed selectively from any and all
times and thought systems in its attempt to show the fundamental unity
of the esoteric tradition; it then laid the resulting, highly syncretic material over a quasi-Buddhist cosmology. The result is a mystical *mélange
d'idées* that draws from all world religions, major and minor, past and
present, from occult systems such as Kabbalism, Hermeticism, Gnosticism, and alchemy, from ancient mystery cults (of Osiris, Adonis,
Dionysos, Mithra, the Mysteries of Eleusis, Orphism), and from
any philosophical-religious system that may come to mind (Platonism
and neo-Platonism, Pythagoreanism, medieval speculative mysticism,
French occultism).

As an international movement, Theosophy was by no means monolithic. Many individuals embraced Theosophy, but were unable to
embrace the Theosophical Society, preferring to work alone or in small
circles of like-minded, independent Theosophists, or even to combine
their Theosophy with the teachings of rival occult schools. Others, al-

though working within the framework of the Society, followed their own radically different visions. The Society was also heir to all the ills that plague any large organization, such as financial problems, bureaucracy, personal rivalries, and struggles for power. It experienced several schisms and considerable fragmentation after the death of its founder in 1891.

After Mme Blavatsky's demise, Colonel Olcott presided over the Society until his own death in 1907, at which time Mrs. Annie Besant, a social reformer and Fabian socialist who came to Theosophy only in 1889, took over the Society and found in it a new outlet for her activism. Mrs. Besant's strong emphasis on Brahmanism, her personal involvement in Indian colonial politics, her excessive deference to morally questionable elements within the Theosophical administration in the face of strong opposition from the membership, and the direction of her leadership (the proclamation of a young Brahmin boy as the new Messiah) lost the Theosophical Society many members. The first years of her presidency saw the resignation of the highly respected scholar, G. R. S. Mead, who had been Mme Blavatsky's private secretary and then editor of *The Theosophical Review*, and seven hundred British members to form a separate Quest Society. Mrs. Besant's tenure also saw the secession of the enormous American Section from the parent Society because of irreconcilable administrative and personal disagreements. While Mrs. Besant, who headed the Theosophical Society until her death at an advanced age in 1933, was able to inspire passionate devotion and admiration, she was also capable of inspiring their opposites.

The most durable intellectual challenge to Theosophy came from Anthroposophy, a movement founded by the German Theosophist Rudolf Steiner (1861–1925). The Austrian-born Dr. Steiner, scholar, philosopher, and occultist, first became affiliated with the Theosophical Society in 1902. In October of that year, Mrs. Besant traveled to Germany to officially charter the German Section and to accept Rudolf Steiner into the Esoteric School, an elite inner circle of advanced occultists. He was a man destined to succeed: his knowledge was universal, his gifts considerable, his personal honor unimpeachable, and his energy boundless.

Steiner joined the Theosophical Society because at the time he shared a large part of its vision; he most certainly found it advantageous to have the power and support of an international organization behind him. Within a few years it became clear to Mrs. Besant and to other Theosophists that, while Dr. Steiner's occult science had much in common with Theosophy, there were also critical differences. Nor could it have escaped Mrs. Besant's notice that Dr. Steiner was potentially charismatic and by 1905 had developed his own cult following, all quite legitimately within the perimeters of the Theosophical Society. His following grew every year.

Steiner's relations with Mrs. Besant became increasingly complex, for he was not a follower and could not approve of either her leadership style or its direction. His connection with the Theosophical Society finally ended on January 14, 1913, when Mrs. Besant withdrew the Charter of the German Section. Almost three thousand Theosophists, more than half the entire German Section, seceded with Steiner to form the Anthroposophical Society on February 2, 1913. Mrs. Besant realized the rift was inevitable, but sincerely hoped that Anthroposophy would continue to contribute to the general Work.

Although he gave his movement a different name, Rudolf Steiner's Anthroposophy is a refinement and redirection of Theosophy, not a mutually exclusive movement. Strongly influenced by Mme Blavatsky's neo-Buddhistic works, Steiner was able to structure and systematize her rather amorphous esoteric universe, but he warned against either an exclusively oriental or an exclusively occidental process of thinking. The general worldview and the basic cosmology of her Theosophy and his Anthroposophy, however, even given some difference in emphasis and terminology, remained similar. Both movements sought to achieve clairvoyance through the use of intellect and reason; both sought to overcome materialism and return the spiritual dimension to human life; both desired to heal the rift between religion and science; both represented a modern gnosis.

While Theosophy emphasized the oriental, intuitive, passive principle as the means toward occult ends, Anthroposophy focused on the occidental, rational, active principle. Steiner avoided the Theosophists' excessive dependence on oriental vocabulary and sought to present religious and occult concepts using Western terms. "The essential difference between Indian Theosophy and Anthroposophy," explained Edouard Schuré, a Theosophist much taken with the Steinerian variant, "lies in the supreme role attributed by Anthroposophy to the Christ in human evolution and also in its connection with the Rosicrucian tradition," a specifically Western, not Eastern, esoteric tradition.[33] Steiner's Anthroposophy, in fact, offered a "Christian Theosophy," a "Western gnosis," as an alternative to the "Hindu gnosis" of Mme Blavatsky's Theosophy.[34] The disagreement between Theosophy and Anthroposophy was more a matter of means and method, not of ultimate goal.

Steiner's major appeal was therefore to those who felt drawn to the basic concept of Theosophy, but who felt uncomfortable with its alien Buddhism. For them Steiner had a Western vocabulary, based on Western European occult, religious, and philosophical traditions to which they could relate. For those who were unwilling or unable to substitute Mme Blavatsky's Himalayan Mahatmas for the Christ, Steiner formulated the "Christ Impulse," showing Christ to be the axis of human evolution, and not just one of the Theosophists' Mahatmas.

And Steiner had a different style; a certain Theosophical faction found his more disciplined, masculine, "Germanic" scientific-philosophical approach to *Geheimwissenschaft* more convincing than the relatively chaotic, feminine, intuitive Theosophy of Mme Blavatsky and Mrs. Besant. Theosophy was undoubtedly a movement dominated by strong women. It was founded by a woman, its most notable leader was a woman, most Theosophical circles were run by women, the membership was preponderantly female, and Theosophy was closely connected with the Women's Movement. Such an environment must certainly have been threatening to many European males of the period; to them Dr. Steiner appeared more "serious" and "intellectual," as well as less "sentimental." His style and "rational" approach to occult thought certainly appealed to many young decadents looking for a strong masculine role model.

The popularity of Theosophy and similar movements is consistent with several related developments in nineteenth-century intellectual history. These include the beginnings of analytical psychology, expanded new research in comparative religion and myth, the growth of oriental studies, and a new, more sophisticated appreciation of Eastern arts. Growing out of romanticism's interest in mythology and religion (J. G. Herder, Antoine Pernety, the Schlegels, Schelling, Schopenhauer, Friedrich Creuzer, and others), this interest exploded in the second half of the nineteenth century in the works of the Orientologists Friedrich Max Müller and Paul Deussen, the ethnologist Sir James Frazer and the Cambridge School, and in the work of Wilhelm Wundt, Gustav Fechner, Edouard von Hartmann, Harald Höffding, and Emile Boutroux on the philosophy and psychology of religion. New translations of important Hindu works (particularly the Upanishads and the *Bhagavad Gita*), advances in Egyptology and the archaeology of the Holy Land, and new discoveries of Gnostic texts made available to European readers the previously unknown spiritual records of other cultures at precisely the time when their own religious culture was collapsing. Theosophy picked up these various interests, packaged them, and made them available to a large popular audience.

Essentially, the immense popularity of Spiritualism, Theosophy, and other occult movements was an expression of society's discontent with the materialism that dominated the second half of the nineteenth century. Materialism, with its scientific positivism, its analytical, fragmenting nature, its denial of supersensory phenomena and spiritual experience, and its emphasis on scientific method, threatened to unseat man from his central position in the universe and his spiritual kinship with God. The occult movements hoped to balance the materialism of the age by reminding man of his spiritual, intuitive side. Spiritualism sought to resolve the metaphysical dilemma by using science against itself to "prove" the existence of the spiritual world. Theosophy recognized both a physical and spiritual reality, and sought to show that "Nature is not 'a fortuitous concurrence of atoms,' and to assign to man his rightful place in the scheme of the Universe." "The occult side of Nature," exclaimed the Theosophists, "has never been approached by the Science of modern civilization."[35]

Theosophy offered something important to its adherents: a seemingly stable belief system with claims to a venerable past. When both nineteenth-century scientists and metaphysicians began to expose traditional Christianity as incapable of meeting the needs of modern man, people turned to other belief systems to fill the void. Theosophy appeared at a time of crisis, when it seemed to many that science and religion had become mutually exclusive, that Christian morality was petit-bourgeois, and that cultural traditions had become generally discredited. Theosophy promised the union of science and religion; Mme Blavatsky even used the subtitle "The Synthesis of Science, Religion, and Philosophy" for her major work, *The Secret Doctrine*. A. P. Sinnett claimed the esoteric doctrine was "the missing link between materialism and spirituality," and insisted that "the esoteric doctrine finds itself under no obligation to keep its science and religion in separate compartments. Its theory of physics and its theory of spirituality are not only reconcilable with each other, they are intimately blended together and interdependent."[36] Theosophy also promised a millenia-old esoteric tradition that would dispel "the restless discontent which arises chiefly from the impatient and hopeless feeling that life is unintelligible, unjust, and unmanageable," and that was a great deal.[37] It accounted, to a large extent, for Theosophy's immense popularity. Thus the Theosophists were seekers, making their own contribution to the waning century's search for timeless truths, new values, and a sense of order to replace what had been lost.

In spite of its laudable humanitarian goals and extravagant claims to be the synthesis of science, religion, and philosophy, Theosophy was unable to provide the panacea that would cure the twentieth century's crisis of culture and consciousness. It did not really have the power to change anything. Although the Theosophists termed their cosmology "scientific," it was no more scientifically demonstrable than that of the Spiritualists; in fact, both Spiritualism and Theosophy were destined to be the victims of scientific positivism. With the rise of contemporary science and especially the tremendous advances in nuclear physics, the exotic Buddhist cosmology, reified by the Theosophists, looked like a fairytale, while Spiritualism's "scientific" seances were repeatedly exposed as the manipulation of gullible dupes by ingenious mediums.

In its popular, exoteric form, Theosophy became a pseudoscientific and pseudoreligious means of perpetuating, in spite of its Buddhistic coloring, an essentially Christian morality, but as a doctrine it lacked the power to fill the spiritual vacuum left by lost religious faith. Theosophy advocated "right thinking," giving Theosophical explanations in place of Christian ones. On closer examination, Mrs. Besant's Theosophical "right thinking," in spite of her personal conversion to Brahmanism, revealed her original roots in Fabian socialism and bore an uncanny resemblance to Judeo-Christian ethics. Theosophy offered consolation to a suffering humanity in a seemingly cruel and irrational world, but its doctrine turned out to be spiritually impotent. Theosophy offered a "modern" religion with exotic terminology and different ritual, but ultimately it was no more than a modern sect, philosophically undisciplined and offering a questionable gnosis.

Even if Theosophy was old wine in new bottles, we must not lose sight of its immense popularity and the international enthusiasm with which it was received at the beginning of the twentieth century. Nor should we forget that in Russia it was not merely a nostrum for the educated middle class's spiritual indisposition, but also one possible solution to the literary and artistic elite's crisis of culture and consciousness. Even if it is an aberrant twig on the tree of Russian Silver Age religious and philosophical thought, Theosophy must necessarily be included in any discussion of this period, especially since so many of its major representatives engaged in serious dialogue with it (Vladimir Solov'ev, Nikolai Berdiaev, Andrei Belyi, Dmitrii Merezhkovskii). Theosophy shared the visionary goals of the Russian religious renaissance: it stressed the birth of the "New Man," sought to recover God, and emphasized the primacy of the noumenal over the phenomenal. Like the Nietzsche-influenced, God-seeking intelligentsia, Theosophists looked to the "revaluation of all values" and the birth of a new culture. They subscribed to the "Russian Idea" and saw in Theosophy that spiritual union of East and West that would bring Russia out of its long sleep and send it forth to save decaying Western civilization from the deadening hand of positivism and scientific materialism.

The fundamental features of the Theosophical worldview brought it into close philosophical affinity with the Russian Symbolist movement and even contributed to the positing of Symbolism as worldview. Like Theosophy, Symbolism (as conceived by Andrei Belyi and Viacheslav Ivanov, for example) was a broadly philosophical-religious movement; like Theosophy, its nature was essentially synthetic and eclectic; like Theosophy it hoped to herald a new, more spiritual age. Writing about Theosophy in 1901, the optimistic young Andrei Belyi, just on the threshold of his career, saw Theosophy as "preparing mankind for the acceptance of the Approaching Truth."[38]

It is not surprising that Russians participated so wholeheartedly in the late-nineteenth-century occult revival, or that they embraced what Theosophy claimed to offer. The British scholar E. M. Butler observes that "the kind of mysticism that accompanies the more ambiguous types of magic pullulates in that enigmatic country [Russia], so much more closely akin to the East than to the West. It has harboured in the past and doubtless will continue to harbour hundreds of thousands of mystics, mages, sages, magicians, and holy men of every conceivable description."[39] The Russians certainly took a leading role in producing mages at the turn of the century. If, in the second half of the last century, the Russian empire contributed Turgenev, Dostoevsky, Tolstoi, and Chekhov to world literature, if it gave Tchaikovsky to world music, Lobachevskii to mathematics, Mendeleev to science, and Lenin to politics, then it also gave the world, within a few years of each other, Grigorii Rasputin (1873?–1916), a sectarian monk who rose from Siberian obscurity to direct the fate of Russia by controlling the royal family; Georgii Gurdjieff (1872–1949), who, together with P. D. Ouspensky (1878–1947), developed a form of Yoga for the Western mind; and Mme Blavatsky, who invented a new "religion of reason" that survives to this day.

Two

The Early Days of Theosophy in Russia (1875–1901)

The Magnificent Madame

The world came to know the founder of Theosophy variously as Helena Blavatsky, Mme Blavatsky, or H. P. B. At the beginning she was Elena Petrovna Gan, the daughter of Captain Peter Alekseevich Gan (1798–1873; of the Hahn von Rottenstein-Hahn family, princes of Mecklenburg) and Elena Andreevna Gan (née Fadeeva, 1814–1842). Elena Petrovna was born in Ekaterinoslav on July 31 (O.S.), 1831. From childhood she created for herself a private world of imaginative fantasy; her younger sister, Vera Zhelikhovskaia (1835–1896), would later claim that Elena Petrovna had revealed a tendency toward somnambulism and mediumism at an early age. She was only eleven years old when her mother died, at which time she went to live with her maternal grandmother, the scholarly Elena Pavlovna Fadeeva (née Princess Dolgorukaia, 1787–1860), in Saratov and then in Tiflis. Her life with the Fadeevs was privileged. She was brought up by governesses, tutored to speak several languages, given the run of an excellent library, and allowed to travel with her aristocratic cousins.[1]

The Fadeevs were known for their intelligence and creativity. From their midst came several writers: Elena Andreevna Gan, Elena Petrovna's mother, was a novelist of the 1840s who wrote under the pseudonym "Zinaida R-va"; the critic Belinskii called her "the Russian George Sand." General Rostislav Andreevich Fadeev, Elena Petrovna's uncle, was a charming man known for his war tales. Vera Petrovna Zhelikhovskaia, Elena Petrovna's sister, was a journalist and prolific, if minor, novelist. One of Elena Petrovna's maternal aunts was a Witte by marriage; her famous son, Count Sergei Witte (Minister of Finance under Alexander III and Nicholas II) was Elena Petrovna's cousin, as was the travel writer and journalist Evgenii L'vovich Markov.

Elena Petrovna began her "occult education" while living with the Fadeevs. Her great-grandfather, Prince Pavel Dolgorukii, had been interested in occultism and his extensive library was available to Elena Petrovna as she was growing up in her grandmother's home. One of the frequent visitors to the Fadeev household was Prince Aleksandr Golitsyn, rumored to be a Freemason and occultist (the Golitsyn family had for generations been interested in occultism; this Prince Golitsyn was apparently the grandson of Alexander I's intimate); he took a strong interest in the precocious and eccentric young girl. Shortly after Prince Golitsyn's departure from Tiflis in 1849, Elena Petrovna, almost eighteen, married forty-year-old Nikifor Vasil'evich Blavatskii (1809–?), vice governor of Erevan.[2] Within three months she had left her husband and started an exotic life of traveling, possibly with Prince Golitsyn's assistance.

Relatively little is known about Elena Petrovna's life between 1849 and 1859. She left Russia through Constantinople and later claimed to have been in Egypt, India, Tibet, the Middle East, and other out-of-the-way places. These claims are now a traditional part of the Blavatsky "mythology," but they remain undocumented and unsubstantiated. She probably did travel to Turkey, Greece, Egypt, France, and England. Theosophical biographers, however, provide a detailed itinerary for these years that takes Elena Petrovna around the world and even places her in New Orleans, investigating voodoo cults, visiting Indians, and crossing the United States in a covered wagon.[3] It is an incredible itinerary that would have been extremely difficult (if not impossible) even for a woman of unlimited means in the nineteenth century, and Elena Petrovna, despite her aristocratic lineage, did not have unlimited means. Russian letters and memoirs indicate that Elena Petrovna was indeed traveling, but with an opera singer named Agardii Metrovich and within the Russian Empire and in Europe. Certainly she was in London in the early 1850s, and in 1858 she met the medium D. D. Home in Paris where she became an habituée of Spiritualist circles, learning the techniques and style she later wielded so successfully.

In the winter of 1859–1860 Elena Petrovna returned to Russia and went to stay for a time with her recently widowed sister, Vera Petrovna Zhelikhovskaia (then Iakhontova), in the northern Russian city of Pskov. Zhelikhovskaia later wrote about her sister's return, describing how Elena Petrovna came accompanied by *esprits frappeurs* and soon became the center of attention as curious Pskovians came to observe her mediumistic phenomena.[4] She recounted how Elena Petrovna levitated tables (or made them too heavy to pick up), held seances at which the Russian poet Aleksandr Pushkin appeared, and unmasked a murderer by means of her incredible psychic powers. Elena Petrovna allegedly had the ability to "see" people who had lived in a particular room or house in the past; she was a superb clairvoyante. Thus, by 1859, Elena Petrovna was already assiduously cultivating the occult aura that would surround her for the rest of her life.

After visiting in Pskov with her sister, Elena Petrovna traveled south, to see family in Odessa and Tiflis. She spent considerable time mollifying relatives who were less than anxious to receive the itinerant black sheep of the Fadeev family. Later she claimed that she left Russia again in 1863 to travel in Italy, Greece, Egypt, the Far East, and again in Tibet, where she allegedly became a *chela* (disciple) and received instruction in occultism from the Mahatmas of the Great White Brotherhood. This journey, too, is undocumented, although sensational rumors circulated concerning her various activities, occult and secular, during this period. She actually remained in Russia much of this time, had an affair, became pregnant, and gave birth to an illegitimate child. A cripple, her son died when she went abroad again with Agardii Metrovich in 1864 or 1865. She returned home to bury the child and left Russia again only in 1871. It is highly unlikely that she reached the Tibetan border during this period or became a disciple of the Mahatmas, as some biographers claim.[5] Had she done so, she would have experienced difficulties in communication; although she spoke several European languages, she knew no oriental languages, ancient or modern.

By 1873 Mme Blavatsky, as Elena Petrovna now called herself, had made her way to the United States. Having settled in New York, she supported herself by writing sensationalistic newspaper articles of an anti-Jesuit and anti-Papal tenor; she contributed exotic descriptions of the Caucasus for American readers; and she wrote on Spiritualism, the rage of the day. She had become intimately acquainted with various Eastern occult systems and actively encouraged her American colleagues to see her as a clairvoyant, a medium, and a mystic. In those days she was committed to Spiritualism, but Mme Blavatsky was not born to be a follower in other people's movements. In New York City, on September 8, 1875, she and Colonel Henry Olcott (1832–1907) pioneered a new direction in occultism by founding the Theosophical Society. Olcott later chose to use November 17, the Society's ceremonial inauguration date, as the official founding date.

Meeting with limited success in the United States (even after the publication of her massive occult textbook, *Isis Unveiled*), Mme Blavatsky and Colonel Olcott decided in 1878 to travel to India to set up an Indian headquarters for the Society. In India they found a natural ally for their work in Dayananda Saraswati, who was promulgating a revised modern variant of Hinduism, the *Arya Samaj*. Mme Blavatsky also agitated among the natives against English rule and succeeded in convincing the local authorities that she was a spy for the Russians (Great Britain was much exercised over the "Great Game," and feared a Russian incursion into India during those years). This accusation of spying would occasionally resurface during the remainder of her life, but Mme Blavatsky reveled in the notoriety.[6] These two Theosophists traveled extensively on the subcontinent, setting up numerous branches of their new Society and locating its headquarters in Adyar, Madras, where the parent branch of the Society remains to this day. Mme Blavatsky kept an account of their journey and sent it to the Russian newspaper, *Moskovskie Vedomosti*, to earn extra money.[7]

Early in 1884 Mme Blavatsky was ready to return to Europe, and by March she was in Paris to proselytize for the Theosophical Society. By then, the English Society for Psychical Research (SPR) had become interested in the phenomena attributed to the Theosophical Society's enigmatic leader.[8] Mme Blavatsky's arrival in Europe presented the SPR with an opportunity to investigate her claim that she indeed possessed psychic powers, and to settle once and for all the question of the existence of Madame's Mahatmas. An endorsement from the SPR would have guaranteed the success of the Theosophical Society, but Mme Blavatsky was understandably wary of their investigation.

Aside from her questionable psychic powers, Madame's Mahatmas and the Great White Brotherhood were the single greatest problems in establishing the credibility of the Theosophical Movement. In the beginning, Mme Blavatsky's own Teachers (whom she identified as Master Morya and Koot Hoomi), as well as the other "adepts," had remained more or less aloof and isolated in the Himalayas, communicating with the world only through their *chela*, Mme Blavatsky. Their existence had not been empirically demonstrated and rested exclusively on the claims of Mme Blavatsky herself and the corroboration of her suggestible colleagues, Colonel Olcott, A. P. Sinnett (1840–1921), and the Reverend C. W. Leadbeater (1847–1934). Mystics and visionaries may experience subjective hallucinations that are entirely real to them, and these may have been the origin of Mme Blavatsky's Mahatmas. But her Mahatmas had recently become impatient with psychic communication; they had taken to crafting letters or communicating directly with various leading members of the Theosophical Society. These letters would drop from the ceiling or be mysteriously delivered in other ways. The written communications of the Mahatmas could not be explained by subjective hallucination and were unconvincing as mediumistic phenomena ("precipitation"). When tall, silent, ascetic Hindus, turbaned and dressed in white, actually began to appear to individuals, the SPR suspected a hoax.

By May 1884 a major scandal became inevitable when Mme Blavatsky learned that her old friend and confederate back at Theosophical Headquarters in Adyar, Mrs. Emma Coulomb, had turned on her. Privy to the details of Mme Blavatsky's past, Mrs. Coulomb publicly announced that "Madame Blavatsky was a fraud, . . . Madame had forced her [Mrs. Coulomb's] husband to build a trapdoor to deliver Mahatma letters and trick apparatus in the Occult Room." She added that "Madame had borrowed money from her in Cairo and never repaid it; Madame had once had a husband named Agardi Metrovitch; all of the English were dupes and idiots who had been taken in by H. P. B.'s invented Mahatmas; the *real* purpose of the Theosophical Society was to overthrow British rule in India."[9] Emma Coulomb then proceeded to publish Mme Blavatsky's incriminating letters in a local colonial paper. This did not help Mme Blavatsky's case with the Society for Psychical Research. They sent a member, Richard Hodgson, to India to investigate in situ. When he arrived in Adyar he discovered that the evidence in the Occult Room had been destroyed and its walls newly plastered.

In the end, the SPR did not find for Mme Blavatsky. After three months in Adyar, Hodgson concluded that Mme Blavatsky was guilty of palpable fraud and her followers of excessive credulity. He discovered that the Mahatma letters were written exclusively in English, in Mme Blavatsky's handwriting, and drew his own conclusions. He also learned that the Hindus living at the Theosophical Headquarters were accessories to the plot. There was nothing at all occult about the Occult Room. Given the evidence, Richard Hodgson was generous in his summation for the SPR regarding Mme Blavatsky: "For our own part, we regard her neither as the mouthpiece of hidden seers, nor as a mere vulgar adventuress; we think that she has achieved a title to permanent remembrance as one of the most accomplished, ingenious, and interesting impostors in history."[10]

Mme Blavatsky had little choice but to brazen out the ensuing scandal. The SPR may have blackened her personal reputation, but it was unable to destroy the Theosophical Society. She defended herself with portentous references to mysterious "Forces of Darkness" that were trying to discredit her and the Movement. But in spite of the disgrace, she continued to win new converts to Theosophy. Her success was due as much to her personality as to the appeal of her Secret Doctrine. The magnificent Madame was a master of occult publicity. Circumstances dictated that she continue generating the mediumistic phenomena even when it became clear that exposure was inevitable. She had begun her professional life as a Spiritualist and knew just how convincing such phenomena could be; they were second nature to her, and she was obviously good at producing them without detection. She also felt that her followers *wanted* phenomena, and she was right, because even after her "exposure" the Mahatmas and their "miracles" continued to capture people's imaginations. There were numerous cases of true believers hallucinating their own Masters—photographs, letters, and all.[11]

When Colonel Olcott politely but firmly refused to allow her to return to Adyar after the scandal, Mme Blavatsky took up permanent residence in London in May 1887. Her home at 17 Lansdowne Road became a place of pilgrimage. Writers, painters, scholars, aristocrats, and would-be occultists of every persuasion came to see the large Russian woman with enormous, protruding, hypnotic eyes, long tapered fingers and elegant hands, and an acidic tongue. Mme Blavatsky was inevitably dressed in loose, black, flowing garments of ambiguous construction. She smoked constantly. All of London loved her; she was an original.

In London Mme Blavatsky and her supporters opened a new branch of the Theosophical Society, the Blavatsky Lodge, and began their own journal, *Lucifer*. In Lansdowne Road she wrote her second major occult text, *The Secret Doctrine*.[12] She died there on May 8, 1891, after a long illness and much pain (she suffered from rheumatism, edema, and other ills). The Theosophical Society celebrates the day of her "departure from the physical plane" as the Day of the White Lotus (the mystical flower of the East, it symbolizes both the Buddha-Avatar and the Unity that is concealed by multiplicity). In the end, Helena Petrovna Blavatsky succeeded in living up to her name: *Elena* (Helen) means "the bright, shining one," "the torch." Her patronymic connects her with the founder of another church, St. Peter, *petros*, the rock.

An accurate and completely factual biography of this remarkable woman will never be written.[13] Mme Blavatsky spent a lifetime ensuring that it would be impossible to separate fact from her fantasy. She post-dated and predated, concealed, created, and camouflaged "evidence." Although she lied to others and to herself with equal facility, her charisma evoked passionate devotion from many of her followers. Her entire life, personal and professional, consisted of appearance, illusion, and effect. An untraditional, creative, and stimulating woman, she loved to shock and astound, to be the center of attention at any cost. Existing biographical material, most of it written by starry-eyed adherents (for whom she is a divine guru) or militant anti-Theosophists (who see her as a temperamental, nasty charlatan), excludes material that does not fit the selected mythic paradigm. The fact remains that this imaginative woman consciously mythologized her very existence; day by day she "created" her own life and legend. Her "creatively lived life" was performance art, raised to a new level by her undoubtedly charismatic, hypnotic personality. She infected an entire generation with her myth. She has been called a genius and a charlatan as though the two were mutually exclusive; Mme Blavatsky was clearly both. No one would be more pleased than she to know that the mystification she engendered in her lifetime continues a century after her death.

The Introduction of Theosophy into Russia

For a woman who had chosen to lead an unorthodox life and who existed *pour épater la galerie*, Mme Blavatsky seemed unduly obsessed with her social and professional reputation in her native land. She maintained her professional contacts with influential Russian Spiritualists even after publicly denouncing Spiritualism. She corresponded regularly with Aleksandr Aksakov and Viktor Pribytkov, who occasionally found translation and writing work for her. She wrote hysterical letters to Aksakov, begging him not to reveal her sordid past to fellow Russian Spiritualists, and pressed her sister, Vera Zhelikhovskaia, and her aunt, Nadezhda Fadeeva, to defend her and to propagandize her "phenomena" and her philosophy at home. And yet for all Mme Blavatsky's genuine love for Russia, her concern for her reputation, and her desire for recognition at home, her Theosophical Society trod a thorny path in her native land because of her personality and reputation.

The very earliest Russian conceptions of Theosophy as a doctrine were nebulous at best. Before 1881 Theosophy hardly rated a mention in the Russian press. This is not surprising, since the new Movement did not immediately gather sufficient strength to attract serious international attention. Between 1881 and 1901 the journal *Rebus*, edited by the sympathetic and kindly Pribytkov, served as the major Russian vehicle for Theosophy. Its articles reveal the changing popular perceptions of the Theosophical Movement through the prism of *Rebus*'s own Spiritualist concerns. *Rebus* emphasized Mme Blavatsky's phenomena and commented on the high points of Theosophical doctrine. The obliging Spiritualists published an occasional letter from Mme Blavatsky, advertised her journal, *The Theosophist*, and offered, for only one ruble, a photographic portrait of the Madame herself. Frequently, *Rebus* indulged in light polemics with the Theosophists about the nature of spiritualism.[14] Such polemics often ended with the Spiritualists throwing down the gauntlet to the Theosophists: "You maintain that you possess higher, undoubtable truths. Prove them to us with scientific arguments and factual corroboration, and we will believe you."[15] *Rebus* also published translations from European occult journals, including Mme Blavatsky's own *Theosophist*. Additional information about Theosophy entered Russia through European books and journals in which Mme Blavatsky, the Mahatma scandal, and the Society received considerable attention.

Although brief references to Mme Blavatsky and Theosophy had occasionally been made in some of the more sensational Russian newspapers, the first serious discussions of the doctrinal aspects of Theosophy appeared only in 1883. That fall Vera Zhelikhovskaia, Mme Blavatsky's sister and her most ardent Russian supporter in the early days, provided extensive advertising for the Theosophical Society in her lengthy catalogue of Mme Blavatsky's mediumistic feats for *Rebus*.[16] Zhelikhovskaia took the Russian press to task for constantly attacking their eccentric but talented countrywoman, brought "proof" that her sister possessed incredible mediumistic powers, and outlined Theosophical doctrine in a very general and diffuse way. Her series attracted considerable attention among the growing number of people interested in occultism.

After Zhelikhovskaia's major contribution, short pieces on Theosophy, a number of them inaccurate, began to appear in *Rebus* regularly. A brief article, published April 22, 1884, reported that Mme Blavatsky was currently in Paris with Colonel Olcott as a representative of the Theosophical Society, but it seemed unaware that they were the founders of the Society or that it was a Western, not an Indian, Society. The article announced that the Society

> has as its goals to found an international brotherhood of peoples without differentiation of race or creed; to study the literature of the Eastern peoples and magic; to strive to know the hidden laws of nature and psychic powers hidden in man. "The Society" is tremendously important in the East, where more than a hundred sections have been opened in India and Ceylon. At present its influence is penetrating to the West, having found not a few proselytes in New York and other American cities. The Paris and London sections of the Society count many famous scholars among their members.[17]

More information on the Theosophical Society appeared in *Odesskii Vestnik, Novorossiiskii Telegraf*, and *Rebus* in the summer of 1884, in the form of epistolary essays from the prolific pen of Vera Zhelikhovskaia.[18] Visiting her sister in Paris that summer, Zhelikhovskaia was again upset by the way in which the Russian press was treating Mme Blavatsky and falsifying her mission. "*Novoe Vremia* and many other newspapers have announced that she came to Paris in order to destroy Christianity and to build a temple to Buddha. She and others devoted to the Theosophical Society never even dreamed of such a thing," she wrote in *Rebus* on one such essay.[19] Zhelikhovskaia took advantage of the essay's publication to give a summary of Theosophy's main goals and to speak of the Mahatmas and Mme Blavatsky's "miracles."

Later that same year E. F. Barabash, whose relatively objective articles did much to propagandize Theosophy in Russia in the early days, wrote a lengthy piece for *Rebus* in which he outlined in some detail the tenets and general cosmology of the Theosophical doctrine. Barabash argued with Theosophy from the point of view of Spiritualism, but remained essentially friendly toward the Movement:

> The ideas and goals of this Society are of more than a little interest, for thinking people in general and for those who have had the opportunity to be convinced of the reality of mediumistic phenomena in particular, because these ideas are intimately connected with the new Spiritualist movement, because they represent an entirely *original* point of view on mediumistic phenomena held by the adepts of the Society, and because of the important role which the

founders of the Theosophical Society, H. P. Blavatsky and Colonel Olcott, played in the new Spiritualism.[20]

Although Barabash briefly mentions the Mahatmas, his article focuses primarily on Theosophy as a secular faith, stressing its search for the hidden laws of nature and its humanitarian ideals, its goal of uniting all of mankind into a single Brotherhood, thereby destroying prejudice, intolerance, social inequality, and racism. Barabash was also flattering to Theosophy and Mme Blavatsky in his survey of Spiritualism throughout history.[21]

By 1887 enough had been said about the Theosophical Society in the Russian press for the sedate journal *Russkaia Mysl'* to acquaint its readership with the Society's basic contours. The tone of V. V. Lesevich's article for that journal was skeptical and condescending; he presented the Society as a curiosity, although he did lay out the basic tenets of Theosophy in a relatively straightforward manner. Lesevich was unimpressed by Mme Blavatsky's abilities as a thinker: "She took it into her head to explicate the philosophy of Plato and ended up babbling out a tremendous lot of all kinds of rubbish," he concluded.[22] Through articles like those of Barabash and Lesevich, information about Mme Blavatsky and the Theosophical doctrine, most of it negative, was seeping slowly but surely into Russia in spite of the censorship.

That Mme Blavatsky and Theosophy were being taken seriously was made clear in 1890, when the respected philosopher Vladimir Solov'ev (1853–1900) reviewed her book, *Key to Theosophy*, in the journal *Russkoe Obozrenie*.[23] Solov'ev, a true theosophist (with a small "t") who was acquainted with the various traditions of speculative mysticism, including Gnosticism, Kabbalism, and medieval mysticism, immediately caught the point that Mme Blavatsky's Theosophical secret doctrine "does not refer to the wisdom of God, but to divine wisdom," an important distinction for an understanding of the Godhead.[24] Written in a slightly ironic tone, especially when touching upon the ubiquitous Mahatmas, Vl. Solov'ev's review gave a general summary of the principles of the doctrine, but concluded that "unfortunately, the positive side of this doctrine is a lot less clear and less defined than its negative side," and that Mme Blavatsky's Theosophy remains "shaky and vague."[25]

If Solov'ev's review was problematic, the article about Mme Blavatsky that he published in 1892 in S. A. Vengerov's biographical dictionary was annihilating.[26] Solov'ev began his essay by pointing out that true "theosophy" and "Buddhism" are, in fact, mutually exclusive. "The basic characteristic of Buddhism is its non-recognition of God, i.e. as a single, absolute being."[27] In its fundamental understanding of the Godhead, then, Mme Blavatsky's Theosophy is already inimical to Christian-

ity. Her Theosophy, Solov'ev went on, is "an anti-religious, anti-philo-
sophical, and anti-scientific doctrine" that criticizes European science
for not wanting to accept Asian fables as truth. A doctrine whose starting point is the assumption of the reality of Mahatmas who lead a secret
existence in the Himalayas and from there control human development
can scarcely call itself a serious doctrine, he pointed out. "In the 'Theosophy' of Mme Blavatsky and Company we see the attempt of a charlatan
to adapt actual Asiatic Buddhism to the mystical and metaphysical needs
of a half-educated European society that is dissatisfied, for one reason or
another, with its own religious institutions and doctrines."[28] The best
that this "untenable and false" doctrine can achieve is only a "relative
truth."[29] Solov'ev's philosophically trained mind immediately discerned
and revealed the inconsistencies and contradictions of Theosophy. His
stature among the creative intelligentsia ensured that this article would
become the basis of what the Theosophists would bellicosely call "anti-
Theosophical prejudice."

Solov'ev's position did not prevent the Russian Theosophists from
elevating him to patron saint of their movement after his death. They
saw his "Sophia, Wisdom of God" as a variant of their own "Theo-
Sophia." For the next twenty years they were faced with the problem of
claiming Vladimir Solov'ev as their own while explaining away his attack
on Theosophy and its founder. Years later, Elena Pisareva would insist
that his article was "based on the purest misunderstanding."[30] Anna
Kamenskaia, head of the St. Petersburg Theosophists, would write (in
Rebus) that Theosophy "is still completely unknown among us; moreover, it evokes prejudices against it, prejudices based on rather complex
reasons. One of them consists of the fact that, in his article about Theosophy, Vladimir Solov'ev described this movement as an attempt to disseminate neo-Buddhism." But Theosophy, she goes on to say, "could
not rest on Buddhism alone, it gradually turned to Brahmanism, to the
religion of Zarathustra, and finally to Christianity." To explain away the
criticism of the much-admired Solov'ev, Kamenskaia pointed out that
"Vladimir Solov'ev, who became acquainted with Theosophy through
the first Theosophical books, could have inadvertently erred by confusing the historical moment with the general attitude of the movement."[31]

Vladimir Solov'ev's article was not the only setback to Theosophy in
Russia that year. Early in 1892 Vsevolod Solov'ev (1849–1903), the
philosopher's older brother and a popular romantic and historical novelist, began the publication of *Sovremennaia zhritsa Izidy* (*Moe znakom-
stvo s E. P. Blavatskoi*) in installments in the popular journal, *Russkii
Vestnik*.[32] Although Mme Blavatsky was not as well known in Russia as
in Europe, the book nevertheless upset many Russian Theosophists who
saw it as Vs. Solov'ev's attempt to slander Mme Blavatsky because of

private differences. Solov'ev's book was successful enough to go through several Russian editions and was soon translated into English as *A Modern Priestess of Isis.*[33]

Vsevolod Solov'ev had met Mme Blavatsky in Paris in May 1884, when he was taking a cure for nerves and she was proselytizing for the new Society on the continent. She impressed him tremendously and managed to persuade him of the authenticity of her mediumistic powers and the vast extent of her popularity and influence. He was convinced enough by her mediumistic demonstrations to write an "eyewitness" letter to *Rebus* extolling her abilities.[34] Late in 1885 he returned to St. Petersburg, where he became better acquainted with Vera Zhelikhovskaia and quickly became an intimate of the family. In confidence Zhelikhovskaia, then still ambivalent about her sister's chosen career and the role of Russian "prophet" that Mme Blavatsky had forced on her, told Solov'ev the details of Mme Blavatsky's lurid past (the second "marriage" to Agardii Metrovich, various affairs, the illegitimate child, and so forth). Although Solov'ev himself was not without skeletons in his own closet (some "irregularities" in his relations with his sister-in-law), he felt shocked and betrayed. When he returned to Europe in February 1886, he spread among his confidants the malicious stories he had learned from Zhelikhovskaia.[35] Just as they had earlier been intimate friends, he and Mme Blavatsky were now unforgiving enemies.

Mme Blavatsky's scandals might have been a nine days' wonder in Russia had they not been kept alive by both Vsevolod Solov'ev and Vera Zhelikhovskaia. Solov'ev felt that Mme Blavatsky had tricked him in a weak moment; his vanity was bruised. For him, she was a charlatan, although he paid her the generous compliment of considering her the superior of Count Cagliostro.[36] The extent to which he turned on Mme Blavatsky probably reflected the degree to which he felt he had been duped by her. At least he waited until she was dead before publishing his book. In *Zhritsa* Vs. Solov'ev explained his motives through a reference to a conversation he had had with Zhelikhovskaia:

> In Russia very little is known about the "Theosophical Society" and its founder, and it would be best not to speak of them at all. I promise you [i.e. Zhelikhovskaia] that as long as there are no misrepresentations about the "Theosophical Society" and Helena Petrovna in the Russian press, I will remain silent. But if there is talk of all this, and false talk at that, I will consider it my duty to speak the truth in print, to tell what I know. That is my last word.[37]

Zhelikhovskaia's hagiographic biography of Mme Blavatsky, published as a necrology in the last two issues of *Russkoe Obozrenie* for 1891 (she died May 8 of that year), served as the cue for the appearance of his own version of the Blavatsky myth.

Although Vsevolod Solov'ev was by no means an impartial observer, his book did a great deal of harm, not only to Mme Blavatsky personally but also to the Russian Theosophical Movement. He made many damaging accusations and brought damning evidence. Zhelikhovskaia worked as hard as she could to defuse his attacks since, by then, she and her three daughters had committed themselves completely to propagandizing Theosophy in Russia. Blood was thicker than water, and they saw themselves as Mme Blavatsky's rightful Russian champions (although there were individual Theosophists in Russia in 1893, it would still be another fifteen years before Russia would have an organized Theosophical Society to protect the beloved preceptress's name).[38] Ironically, the panegyrical prose with which Zhelikhovskaia answered Solov'ev's accusations did little to establish her own credibility; on the contrary, it served to make Zhelikhovskaia appear credulous and placed the Society itself in a questionable light.

After Zhelikhovskaia's treacly, inflated memoirs of her sister, Solov'ev's tart answer must have sounded like the voice of reason to many readers. In fairness to him it must be pointed out that, while he illuminated some of the more horrid sides of Mme Blavatsky's character (supported by many of the numerous biographies that have appeared since her death), he shows some understanding and sympathy for her as well. "In her quiet and good moments," he writes, "she was an incredibly sympathetic individual. She had a certain charm. . . . The reason for the 'modern priestess of Isis's' strange sympathy must be sought in her originality, her unique, fiery talent, and in her stormy, wild energy. Such talent and energy are an elemental force which is difficult to withstand." Nevertheless, Solov'ev adds, "this force, united with a perversity of the soul, with some sort of savage inability to understand 'in life' the difference between good and evil, created one of the most interesting and representative phenomena of the end of the nineteenth century—the 'Theosophical Society.' "[39]

Vera Zhelikhovskaia answered Vsevolod Solov'ev's *Zhritsa* in a book of her own, *E. P. Blavatskaia i sovremennyi zhrets istiny* (1893). The battle between them was vituperative. Solov'ev's talented prose, although petty and self-serving, avoided Zhelikhovskaia's less talented but equally self-serving hysteria; as point and counterpoint their polemics were fascinating reading and were avidly followed by Russians looking for sensational entertainment. Russian Theosophists later criticized Solov'ev's book, but their accusations against him sounded naive and ignorant. While Solov'ev himself was scarcely objective, his documentation was superior and convincing, and he knew the principal personally. The Theosophists were forced to admit that his book "played a rather fateful role in Russian society's opinion of H. P. Blavatsky; animated and vividly written, the book was read by many."[40]

In 1893 Solov'ev followed up *Sovremennaia zhritsa Izidy* with an article in the prestigious journal *Voprosy Filosofii i Psikhologii,* outlining
the basic premises of Theosophical belief.[41] Using the French translation
of A. P. Sinnett's *Esoteric Buddhism* (London, 1883; Paris, 1891) and
Louis Dramard's *La Science occulte, étude sur la doctrine ésotérique*
(Paris, 1886) as his source texts, Solov'ev gave a thorough and conscientious presentation that highlighted the internal contradictions and
weaknesses of Theosophical cosmogenesis and anthropogenesis. This,
however, was insufficient for the editor, who felt obliged to add his own
comments to those of the author. Solov'ev "speaks partly in the tone of
a disenchanted adept," said the editor,

> But the character of the presented doctrine is set forth clearly, and several
> directions (particularly at the end of the article) are enough to warn the reader
> against the attractions of this pseudophilosophical and ignorant doctrine.
> There is good reason to present it in our journal as a warning to Russian soci-
> ety against the attraction of the absurd ravings of Western European scien-
> tific-religious sectarians. It is useful to become acquainted with the fantastic
> inventions of the neo-Buddhists.[42]

Neither Solov'ev's straightforward outline of Theosophy's extravagant
cosmology nor the editor's contemptuous comments could have done
much to enhance the reputation of Theosophy in Russia.

The perception of Mme Blavatsky and Theosophy in Russia after this
would never return to what it was during the 1880s. The focus of the
press throughout the 1890s was not on her Society, but on her excesses
and her scandals. Even *Rebus,* which had more or less objectively documented the growth of the Theosophical Society abroad, chose not to
publish an obituary when she died in 1891. The Russian press scrupu-
lously weighed Mme Blavatsky's European career and found it wanting.
"All serious [occult] researchers have recently begun to cleanse the area
of their search of everything that even hints at charlatanism and mystification. Mme Blavatsky and her Theosophical Society have come under
particularly severe attacks from all sides," reported *Rebus.*[43] Even the
Mahatmas returned to haunt the Society again. In 1894 Edmund Garrett published a sensational study of the Mahatma episode, *Isis Very
Much Unveiled; The Story of the Great Mahatma Hoax,* in London.
Within months Mikhail Petrovo-Solovovo's lengthy review of Edmund
Garrett's book for *Rebus* indelicately raked over every horrid detail of
the Mahatma scandal and made certain that the facts were well known in
Russia.[44]

The Theosophical doctrine received as much criticism as Mme Blavatsky herself. Theosophy itself was "shady," pointed out Boris Taits in
1894.[45] "M. G-v," citing the eminent Orientalist Max Müller, wrote

that Theosophy was no more than "misconstrued, misunderstood, caricatured Buddhism" and "Theosophical ravings."[46] Papus wrote about Theosophy in his *Course méthodique de science occulte*, and excerpts of it were immediately translated in *Rebus*. The famous French occultist wrote:

> What will the reader, curious enough to look into the works of Mme Blavatsky, find? Here are our own impressions: 1) Complete absence of any system . . . 2) An overwhelming quantity of various assertions, some of which have been taken out of context, others deprived of all basis. 3) Numerous contradictions in the most basic things . . . 4) Nasty attacks on Christians and on scholars, and simultaneously a defense of those scholars, but not of Christians. In all of these books [Mme Blavatsky] maintains a doctrine which is difficult to define: a mixture of gnosticism, Buddhism, Spiritism, the Kabbala. Part of it is taken from Origen, part from Tibetan encyclopedias . . . All of it is presented under the name "Theosophy." In the beginning of our researches we, too, joined the Society, considering it to be serious, but we soon saw what was going on and withdrew.[47]

Mme Blavatsky's Russian reputation did not rest entirely on her notoriety; she was also recognized for her literary work. Like the rest of her remarkable family, she turned out to be a prolific and imaginative writer. Her articles and stories in American and European newspapers, magazines, and esoteric journals are numerous; less familiar are her articles and books published in Russia. Between 1879 and 1886, she wrote for *Rebus, Moskovskie Vedomosti, Pravda* (Odessa), *Russkii Vestnik, Novoe Vremia,* and *Tiflisskii Vestnik* under various pseudonyms, principally the exotic "Radda-Bai." Over the course of 1878 she wrote eight installments of the series "Golos s togo sveta" (signed "Golos") for *Tiflisskii Vestnik* and another series for the Odessa newspaper *Pravda*. She also wrote a short story that appeared in *Rebus*.[48]

Mme Blavatsky's major work written in Russian is *Iz peshcher i debrei Indostana*, a series of unusual travel notes. It began serialization in Mikhail Katkov's *Moskovskie Vedomosti* on November 30, 1879, and ran until January 1882, when it ceased abruptly and was not completed. It resumed serialization a year later in Katkov's journal, *Russkii Vestnik*, and ran until August 1886. The literary merit of *Iz peshcher i debrei Indostana* is undeniable. Like her personality, Mme Blavatsky's style is lively and untraditional. Her account of her travels around the Indian subcontinent in 1879 is awash with Hindu words and local color. She inserts anecdotes, tales, religious myths, and stories of semi-occult, "fantastic" events into the tapestry of her narrative seemingly to amuse more than to instruct. Readers seeking exotica, entertainment, and sensation loved her work; it was popular. This para-Theosophical work also had woven into it a crash course in the Buddhist and Hindu religions, with a healthy dose of comparative religions and some facile and highly suspicious etymologies (the inevitable result of Mme Blavatsky's superficial acquaintance with exotic and classical languages). The novelist Vsevolod Solov'ev, himself no stranger to stylistic excess, had high praise for her wit and style, but correctly warned the reader against taking her travelogues seriously as fact.[49]

For some time, Mme Blavatsky was viewed in Russia as either the colorful author Radda-Bai, or a Spiritualist gone bad, or a notorious charlatan unmasked by the London Society for Psychical Research, or all three. It was not until the turn of the century that her notoriety, mitigated by time, receded into the background and the Theosophical Movement was able to stand on its own merits. Even so, the Russian Theosophists were never allowed to forget her scandalous background entirely; it was periodically trotted out and used as a bludgeon against them, and her notoriety was a major factor in retarding the Movement's development in Russia. Russian Theosophy never really lived down Elena Petrovna, and she was never honored as a prophet in her own country.

The Theosophical Society abroad learned to emphasize Mme Blavatsky's works but to play down her personality; the Russian Society would be forced to answer for that personality again and again. The Russians dealt with the problem of Mme Blavatsky's scandals by attempting to hold to the dichotomous view, first postulated by Zhelikhovskaia, that Mme Blavatsky's private life did not affect the validity of her revelation; Russian Theosophists tried simply to ignore ad hominem attacks or to dismiss them as petty. Dmitrii Stranden, a pillar of the Russian Theosophical Society, wrote in 1913 that "the truth of the Theosophical doctrine rests not on the perfection of that individual who proclaimed it in our time, but on a considerably more solid foundation—on the agreement of this doctrine with the voices of reason, conscience, and spiritual intuition."[50] Elena Pisareva, for whom Mme Blavatsky was "a prophetess of high idealism," pointed out that "in spite of all indications of her profoundly sincere, wide open and madly bold nature, completely incompatible with any kind of cunning and crookedness, the contemporaries of H. P. [Blavatsky] found it easier to believe every slander against her than to admit that she *really* did possess extraordinary psychic powers."[51] Pisareva's and Stranden's naiveté and sincerity could not convince those who did not see life through Theosophical spectacles, and Mme Blavatsky continued to be a target; her disgrace was used in general to discredit occult tendencies in Russian society. The Theosophists were still dismissing attacks on Mme Blavatsky's character up to the very moment of the Russian Society's dissolution. Old habits die hard; Mme

Blavatsky continued to appear in the role of occult ogre in Soviet anti-occult and anti-Masonic publications well into the modern period.

Only after the turn of the century, when Theosophy managed at last to distance itself somewhat from Mme Blavatsky's extravagant personality and questionable "miracles," did the Movement become a real cultural force in Russia. That it achieved substantial popularity between 1901 and 1922 says much about what it had to offer those who were living through the Silver Age's crisis of culture and consciousness. After Mme Blavatsky's death in 1891, the Theosophical Society came more and more under the influence of Mrs. Annie Besant's paradoxically sober, bourgeois approach to occult knowledge. Less emphasis was placed on Mme Blavatsky's personality and, instead, her major work, *The Secret Doctrine*, became more of the focus, along with Mrs. Besant's more "Christian" texts. This change was noticeable in the Russian press as well. After 1901 the tone of many articles changed and Theosophy, pro and contra, became a serious topic of discussion in middle-class salons. Theosophy was practiced by genteel ladies and sober gentlemen who emphasized the philosophical and philanthropic aspects of the doctrine. Legitimate endeavor, commitment, and study finally edged out the sensational miracle working associated with the name of Mme Blavatsky.

Three

The Theosophical Society in Russia (1901–1917)

The First Circles (1901–1908)

Before 1901, individual Theosophists and a few small, private circles did exist in the Russian provinces and in Moscow and St. Petersburg; however, the Russian public at large still had only a general notion of the Theosophical Movement and its aims. By 1901 this had changed, thanks to the proselytizing efforts of Vera Zhelikhovskaia, the press coverage provided by *Rebus* and a handful of other journals and newspapers, and the increasing number of individuals, Russian and European, who brought Theosophy with them to Russia from the continent and England. And so Theosophy spread across Russia, thanks to individuals such as Mr. Zorn of Odessa, who in the 1880s collected one of the first Theosophical libraries in Russia; Mme Maria Robinovich of Vladikavkaz in the Caucasus, who became interested in Mme Blavatsky's works in the 1890s and was further inspired after meeting Mrs. Annie Besant on a trip to England; and other Russians who had succumbed to the attractions of Theosophy while abroad and shared their discovery and their books with friends and colleagues at home.[1]

Attempts to spread the new doctrine in Russia were not always immediately successful. Mme Robinovich's efforts serve as a cautionary example. She tried to organize a circle in Vladikavkaz when she returned from abroad, but immediately encountered difficulties with the local authorities who viewed her activities not only as an heretical infringement on the Russian Orthodox church's prerogative to spiritual hegemony, but as politically suspicious. Her Theosophy perforce remained within her domestic circle; she converted her children and her mother. Maria Robinovich was among the first to begin translating Theosophical literature into Russian. For many years Theosophical literature circulated in Russia either as smuggled foreign volumes (principally English and French), or as manuscript translations.

After 1901, the Russian Theosophical Movement became inextricably linked with the name of Anna Alekseevna Kamenskaia (1867–1952). Raised and educated in Switzerland, Kamenskaia returned to Russia and became a private teacher. She was associated with Maria Stoiunina's progressive gymnasium in St. Petersburg, from which she retired in 1915 after twenty-five years of teaching. She and another Theosophist,

Tsetsiliia Liudvigovna Gel'mbol'dt (d. 1936), taught together briefly in their own progressive school. A woman with a highly developed social consciousness, Kamenskaia was also active in social work (she taught evening courses for factory workers) and the growing Russian Women's Movement. This energetic, strong-willed, and dedicated woman was the driving force behind the Russian Theosophical Society; she built it and she held it together. Under the pseudonym "Alba," Kamenskaia produced a huge body of original articles and translations of Theosophical classics; she lectured tirelessly (and ceaselessly); she edited the Society's journal, *Vestnik Teosofii*, and she oversaw the numerous publications of the Society.

Kamenskaia was introduced to Theosophy by an acquaintance of Maria Robinovich and a pioneer of the Russian Theosophical Movement, Nina Konstantinovna Gernet (d. 1932). Mme Gernet was a member of the English Theosophical Society and worked with branches in Germany, Switzerland, France, and Italy. She frequently traveled between Europe and Russia, smuggling forbidden Theosophical books into her native land. Interested in Eastern religions and mysticism from an early age, Mme Gernet became an ardent Theosophist when she discovered that Theosophy could provide her with an outlet for her interests and a purpose in life. Many Russians first came to Theosophy through her efforts. She also maintained a high profile within the English Theosophical Society and published in their main organ, the *Theosophical Review*.[2] Nina Gernet's extensive and complete personal collection of Theosophical literature eventually became the central library of the Russian Section.

Anna Kamenskaia and Nina Gernet were childhood friends, having gone to school together in Switzerland. Once, when Kamenskaia was immobilized with a broken leg, her friend brought her a box of Theosophical books. Kamenskaia was initially uninterested, because "amidst the suffering and ignorance which surrounded us, I believed that all our energy ought to be given to the struggle for light and so I was at first antagonistic to Theosophy. I mistook it for an aristocratic teaching, good only for a few, and dangerous because it might turn away some of the force needed to help the helpless."[3] Unable to work because of her broken leg, bored with doing nothing, Kamenskaia at last decided to look at some of the books Gernet had left for her: "Suddenly I remembered the coffer with the 'strange' literature and I took the first book I saw in it, [Mrs. Besant's] *In the Outer Court*. I had not read two pages before I was deeply interested and as I read farther I grew so moved and excited that I could not take a meal, or speak, nor sleep till I had finished it. I read it the whole night through and then thrice again. . . . It changed my whole life and I shall never forget it."[4] Kamenskaia's interest soon communicated itself to her close friend and colleague, Tsetsiliia Gel'mbol'dt, who would become Kamenskaia's closest associate after the formation of the Society.

In the summer of 1902 Kamenskaia accompanied Gernet to England for two weeks; there, on several occasions, she heard Mrs. Annie Besant speak about Theosophy. At the time Mrs. Besant, who would become the Society's president in 1907, was one of the most influential Theosophists in the Society. Born and raised in London, unsuccessfully married to an Anglican clergyman, she had begun her professional life as a social reformer by embracing atheism and Fabian Socialism. Then, in 1889, she read Mme Blavatsky's *Secret Doctrine*, met the creator of Theosophy herself, and soon afterward became her anointed successor. At the time of Mme Blavatsky's death in 1891 Mrs. Besant had achieved considerable prominence within the Society. She traveled to Adyar in 1893 and adopted Brahmanism (she claimed that in many of her previous incarnations she had been a Hindu, as well as Hypatia and Giordano Bruno).

Annie Besant was attractive, sincere, and enthusiastic; she immediately won over Anna Kamenskaia. "After that, every time A[nnie] B[esant] was in Europe, I went to hear her," wrote Kamenskaia. "I attended all the Theosophical Congresses and occasionally accompanied A. B. during her *tournées*. When I was in London, she invited me to come to her, and I would spend a part of the morning working in her room."[5] Throughout the rest of her life Kamenskaia would remain a personal friend and resolute defender of Mrs. Besant, whom she called "my friend and my guru." Kamenskaia's personal devotion to Mrs. Besant played a definitive role in forming the character of the Russian Society and eventually determined Kamenskaia's own fate. Then and there in 1902 she made the decision to carry the torch of Theosophy to Russia.

Anna Kamenskaia, now a registered member of the English Section of the Theosophical Society, returned to Russia from England filled with Theosophical notions and went to work immediately. A good, if not original, speaker, she gave lectures on comparative religion and Theosophy in select private salons of St. Petersburg. She soon discovered willing comrades, among them Maria von Strauch-Spettini (1847–1904), an actress recently retired from the Imperial Theater in St. Petersburg.[6] Von Strauch was a member of the Berlin branch of the Theosophical Society and had already considered starting a branch in St. Petersburg. "I have met together several times with Fräulein Kamenskaia and now we are in constant contact," she wrote from Petersburg on October 31, 1902, to her close friend Marie von Sivers, who was then in Berlin working with Dr. Rudolf Steiner:

> Do you know, I have suggested to her that we start meeting once a month in order to lay the foundation of a small Theosophical organization. On Satur-

day, November 2, we are going to have a tea at my house. I have invited Frau
Sch., Frau W., her mother, and Frau von H. to come, then your sister [Olga
von Sivers], and both of the Fräuleins Helmboldt [Tsetsiliia Gel'mbol'dt and
her sister Liutsiia]. . . . I have no idea as yet how it will all turn out, but hope-
fully the plan is viable and will be of use to all concerned. Fräulein
K[amenskaia] wanted to invite a few more ladies and gentlemen. That means
we already have ten people for a German circle, and she will form just such
another Russian one.[7]

The result of Maria von Strauch's Saturday afternoon tea was the first
branch of what would become, almost exactly six years later, the Russian
Theosophical Society. After her premature death at the end of 1904,
this first Theosophical circle was named for her.

By 1905 the Maria Strauch Circle had grown large enough to form a
second unit, the Hypatia Circle.[8] Soon two more circles were organized
and the Theosophists were able to look organizationally beyond St. Petersburg. A growing number of unofficial Theosophical circles pros-
pered in various cities of the empire, largely because of the contribution
of the itinerant Nina Gernet, who was an early uniting force within the
growing Russian Movement. Through her, Kamenskaia eventually met
Elena Pisareva from Kaluga, Nina Pshenetskaia and Pavel Batiushkov
from Moscow, Elizaveta Radzevich from Kiev, and many other individuals who would later play major roles in the creation of the official Russian Society.

The most prominent founding member of the Russian Theosophical
Society was Anna Pavlovna Filosofova (née Diagileva, 1837–1912). An
influential woman in her own right, she was also the mother of the
writer and philosopher Dmitrii Filosofov and the aunt of Serge Dia-
ghilev, the organizer of the Russian "World of Art" Movement and the
Ballet Russe. Filosofova was born into the wealthy gentry. The eldest of
nine children, she married Vladimir Dmitrievich Filosofov in 1856,
when she was only nineteen. Filosofov, a public figure, a reformer, and
a highly placed bureaucrat, was fifteen years her senior; he did much to
mold his young wife's character and interests. Liberal and charitable,
Filosofova soon became involved with the Women's Movement and
worked with the peasants, establishing schools, missions, and hospitals
for the poor. In the fall of 1879 she was exiled abroad for her progressive ideas and political leanings, unacceptable in the wife of a highly
placed public figure. She went to Wiesbaden, where she discovered Theosophy. Early in 1881 she was permitted to return to Russia and to continue her philanthropic and feminist activities.

Anna Filosofova first met Anna Kamenskaia in 1902, when she attended one of Kamenskaia's private Theosophical lectures. Filosofova
had familiarized herself with Theosophical doctrine during her years

abroad "and found in it not only a complete expression of her own most sacred convictions, but also a clear explanation of that active idealism which imbued her entire life."[9] Russia provided no outlet for this interest, however. Kamenskaia enthusiastically informed Filosofova that a small Theosophical circle was already active in St. Petersburg, and soon Anna Pavlovna became a member of Maria von Strauch-Spettini's circle. The joining of forces by these two dynamic women, Kamenskaia and Filosofova, was to greatly advance the Theosophical Movement in Russia.

A leading figure among Russian Theosophists, Filosofova supported them with her considerable financial means, worked for the cause, and made her prestigious salon, frequented by the cream of St. Petersburg society and intelligentsia, available for disseminating the Secret Doctrine through discussion and lecture. She was frequently one of the Russian representatives at various Theosophical Congresses and meetings abroad. She also worked to popularize Theosophy at home: she was the logical choice, for example, to lead the Theosophical delegation to the Congress of Russian Spiritualists in Moscow in 1906.[10] Filosofova continued to be an active and visible member of the Russian Theosophical Society until her death on March 17, 1912. On the Day of the White Lotus (May 8, the anniversary of Mme Blavatsky's "departure from the physical plane"), Filosofova's portrait joined Mme Blavatsky's and Olcott's in prominent display at the Society's Headquarters as a "pioneer of the movement in Russia." Her contributions to Russian society in general and to the Russian Theosophical Movement in particular were considerable.

The Theosophical circles continued their unobtrusive work through the early years of the new century. There was talk of starting a journal, registering as an official organization, and finally joining the parent Theosophical Society, but for several years it was unfeasible: a Theosophical Society would not be tolerated by the Orthodox church and would certainly be denied a charter. The situation changed radically with the Revolution of 1905–1906, which liberalized Russian censorship regulations. The first priority of the Russian Theosophists in this changed context was the dissemination of Theosophical texts. Their first publications were a journal, *Vestnik Teosofii* (the first issue appeared on January 7, 1908), and a collection of Theosophical articles, *Voprosy Teosofii*, which went on sale in December 1907.

The five sections of the first volume of *Voprosy Teosofii* were dedicated almost exclusively to translations and paraphrases of recent lectures and articles by leading Theosophists, most of them prepared by Anna Kamenskaia, Elena Pisareva, Dmitrii Stranden, Pavel Batiushkov, and Anna Mintslova. These included works by Annie Besant ("The Search for God," "Theosophy and the New Psychology," "Does Theosophy Contradict Christianity?" and "The Necessity of Reincarnation"), Rudolf Steiner ("The Culture of the Fifth Aryan Race," "*Faust*"), Edith Ward ("Theosophy and Science"), Edouard Schuré ("Dionysos and Persephone"), and Mme Blavatsky's *Voice of the Silence*. Excerpts from the *Bhagavad Gita* were also included.

A second volume of *Voprosy Teosofii* appeared in 1910 (and was reissued in 1911); this volume was dedicated to Mme Blavatsky and included a new biography by Elena Pisareva, a discussion of the leader's mission by Anna Kamenskaia, and memoirs by Mme Blavatsky's Theosophical colleagues. The most important material in this second volume was Mme Blavatsky's "Introductory" and "Proem" to *The Secret Doctrine*, seven stanzas from the Book of Dzyan (*The Secret Doctrine* is an extensive commentary on these stanzas), her article, "Practical Occultism," and several minor pieces, including her short story "Zakoldovannaia zhizn'." The publication of *Voprosy Teosofii* signaled the official debut of the Theosophists in Russian society and raised their profile among educated Russians.

This debut did not pass unnoticed. *Rebus* reported that "in early January [1908], a meeting of representatives from the Russian Theosophical circles took place in Moscow; certain measures were outlined to facilitate the unification of the circles, and *Vestnik Teosofii*'s relation to the European Theosophical Movement was clarified."[11] Many Russian Theosophists, however, were in no hurry to affiliate themselves with the Parent Society. "The participants of the meeting arrived at the conclusion that such a step was premature and that it was generally undesirable to subordinate the Theosophical Movement in Russia to directives from England," reported the correspondent for *Russkii Frankmason*.[12]

Continuing their discussions over the course of 1908, the representatives of the various circles finally reached a majority decision to organize (with a significant number of circles choosing to remain independent). They overcame numerous bureaucratic impediments and officially registered the new Russian Theosophical Society ("Rossiiskoe Teosoficheskoe Obshchestvo"; RTO) with the authorities in St. Petersburg on September 30, 1908. Now chartered, the RTO could become a National Section (the Russian Section) of the worldwide Theosophical Society, affiliated with Mrs. Besant and the Theosophical Society Headquarters in Adyar.[13] The Inaugural Meeting of the Russian Theosophical Society was held on November 17, 1908 (the thirty-third anniversary of the founding of the Society by Mme Blavatsky and Colonel Olcott) in St. Petersburg, where the new Section would be headquartered. Anna Kamenskaia was elected General Secretary.

Theosophical Work (1908–1914)

Membership

Determining the number of Theosophists in Russia is difficult, since various factors affected membership count both abroad and at home. After Mme Blavatsky's death in 1891, the Theosophical Society soon splintered into fragments that for political, administrative, moral, or doctrinal reasons cut their connections to Colonel Olcott, Mrs. Besant, and the parent Society. Mme Blavatsky's Mahatmas, the scandalous accusations of pedophilia against the Reverend C. W. Leadbeater (as well as his generally eccentric behavior), and Mrs. Besant's showy Hinduism, culminating in the Krishnamurti affair, contributed in no small way to this.[14]

The first major schism in 1895 broke off most of the enormous American Section (more than six thousand members) from the Society. In 1909 another group separated to form the United Lodge of Theosophists, while that same year Mme Blavatsky's personal secretary, G. R. S. Mead, left the Theosophical Society to form the Quest Society. In 1913 Dr. Rudolf Steiner, an uneasy colleague of Mrs. Besant's from the start, took almost the entire German Society with him when he seceded to form the Anthroposophical Society. The members of these various organizations remained in the Theosophical mainstream, but could not be counted members of the Theosophical Society.

Theosophical ideas and texts were also reworked and incorporated into other esoteric movements, such as the British Order of the Golden Dawn and the Stella Matutina, Alice Bailey's Arcane School, and the Rosicrucian Fellowship (AMORC). Many individuals were attracted to certain aspects of Theosophy, but never joined any society at all; they preferred to read and study alone or in small, independent circles. Other individuals with an interest in Theosophy had primary affiliations with other occult groups, such as the Spiritualists or Freemasons. Thus, the actual dissemination and impact of Theosophical ideas was considerably greater than membership statistics alone would indicate.

The Russian Theosophical Society (RTO) was an officially recognized national Section of the original Theosophical Society and loyal to Mrs. Besant. Russian Theosophists, however, were affected by the same political and doctrinal arguments that beset Theosophy as a whole, and so the membership statistics of the RTO are but the tip of the Russian Theosophical iceberg. Shortly before the formation of the RTO, an editorial in *Rebus* pointed out:

> There are several factions within the Theosophical movement, the most rational of which, and closest to patterns of Western European thought, is the

German faction under the leadership of Rudolf Steiner. It must also be noted that the Anglo-Indian faction has at the present time put forward a clearly delineated, dogmatic position, which gives it a rather sectarian character. This situation has resulted in the appearance of many [Russian] Theosophical organizations not affiliated with the centers of the Theosophical Movement, but proclaiming themselves independent followers of the Theosophical doctrine. Such, for instance, are a Theosophical circle in Moscow, another in Odessa.[15]

On the eve of the First World War probably several thousand Russians were sympathetic to Theosophy, although only three hundred were registered officially with the RTO in St. Petersburg in 1913.[16] This figure represents more than three times the official membership of the Society when it was chartered in late 1908, and the Society continued to grow steadily.[17] As a point of comparison, Finland had 518 registered members, America 4,145 (with thousands more in the separate American Society), and England 2,280 in 1913. Germany's membership had dropped to 218 (compared to 2,447 the previous year), reflecting the defection of German members to Rudolf Steiner's Anthroposophical Society. Worldwide membership for 1913 is given as 25,000 for the Adyar-based Society, but the number of interested parties was much higher. In 1911 there were more than fifty Theosophical journals, reflecting the entire range of allegiances, being published in Europe, America, and India. Four were published in Russia, only one of which spoke for the RTO. In all, some thirty occult journals appeared in Russia between 1881 and 1918, and most of them, although not devoted exclusively to Theosophy, also included Theosophical material.

In the case of the Russian Section, official membership figures do not accurately reflect actual interest. Some Russian Theosophists had registered as members of European branches (notably in Belgium, England, and Germany) before 1907 and never changed official membership to the Russian Section, although they attended meetings and participated in RTO functions. Other interested persons chose not to register officially because the Russian Orthodox church, of which many Theosophists were active members, did not approve of the Society. Conservative government agencies (and many Theosophists were in civil and military service) also disapproved of employees who belonged to an organization frowned on by the Orthodox church. The Society did experience occasional harassment and its middle-class adherents often found it expedient not to be officially listed.

Most of those who were registered members lived in the major cities where there were active branches; nevertheless, Theosophists in the provinces sometimes never bothered to register. Other interested individuals were attracted to Theosophy but expressed their disapproval of

Mrs. Besant and C. W. Leadbeater by not joining. These individuals joined independent Theosophical circles which, for a variety of valid reasons, chose not to affiliate with the Russian Section and so did not enter into its statistics. There was as much internal politicking among the Russian Theosophists as among the European and American branches. Thousands of Russians all over the country, however, managed to attend Theosophical lectures and other functions regularly. The RTO's public functions were remarkably well attended.

The vast majority of the Russian Theosophical Society's members came from the petty gentry, the middle grades of civil service, the military, the professions, the creative intelligentsia, and from other elements within the small but growing Russian educated middle class. Theosophy also attracted members from the aristocracy.[18] The Russian Theosophical Society was dominated by women; available information indicates that less than a third of its members were men. Women held most of the top administrative positions in the Russian Section. Within the Russian educated class, which was still very small on the eve of the First World War, the Theosophists formed a respectable contingent, numerically and financially.

Of the seven branches that made up the Russian Section of the Theosophical Society, the largest was the St. Petersburg branch.[19] It had ten circles, probably representing more than half the total RTO membership. Reflecting the particular interests of the St. Petersburg Theosophists, these included the Maria Strauch Circle, Hypatia Circle, the Eastern Circle, the Pedagogical Circle, the Artistic Circle, the Dr. Steiner Study Circle, the *Secret Doctrine* Study Circle, the Christian Circle, and the Union of Races Circle. The active Kiev branch had more than forty registered members; Moscow had about thirty, plus two study circles (the Annie Besant and the Vladimir Solov'ev Study Circles).[20] The Kaluga branch, established on April 21, 1909, had fewer than twenty formally registered members, although it had the highest profile after the St. Petersburg branch. The newest branch in Yalta, which opened on April 7, 1914, was the smallest; Kamenskaia mentioned that fewer than a dozen members belonged in February 1914, but there were more than thirty "interested parties," which perhaps gives some rough indication of the ratio of registered to unregistered Theosophists.[21] Tiflis, Rostov-na-Donu (opened on May 10, 1910), and the provinces shared the rest. There were regional affiliates, but no branches, in Khar'kov, Poltava, Riga, and Iaroslavl'. The various branches had different interests: Kaluga's, for instance, was music and handicrafts, Kiev's was philosophy (many members were also active in the Kiev Religious-Philosophical Society); the Tiflis circle was interested in all forms of occult philosophy and spiritualism.

The Kaluga branch of the RTO, despite its small size, was the most important after St. Petersburg because of its president, Elena Fedorovna Pisareva, and her family. Pisareva first began holding Theosophical meetings for interested friends in Kaluga in 1906, although she had already been a Theosophist for some years. She was acquainted with Maria von Strauch and was a close friend of Anna Filosofova. Her husband, Nikolai Pisarev (secretary of the Kaluga branch), owned the Lotos Publishing House, the first Theosophical press in Russia. Lotos published twenty-one titles between 1905 and October 1917, when its press and stock were destroyed by the Bolsheviks. The Pisarev's daughter, Natalia, was also involved in the Movement as a translator of Theosophical texts; she eventually married the Italian Theosophist Pietro Bocca and moved abroad.

The Pisarev family offered their country estate outside Kaluga, Podborki, as a Theosophical center. Podborki was only 18 versts (about 12 miles) from the monastery of Optina Pustyn', where the Theosophists were frequent visitors.[22] Many Theosophists stayed at Podborki. Anna Kamenskaia began spending her summers there in 1903, and wrote about it several years later: "Over the years [Podborki] became a spiritual center in which active Theosophical work went on and toward which seeking and hungering hearts were drawn."[23] Podborki became the Russian version of the Headquarters House in Adyar, Madras.

Elena Pisareva was well known among European Theosophists. She was personally acquainted with Mrs. Annie Besant, Dr. Rudolf Steiner, Marie von Sivers, G. R. S. Mead, Mrs. Cooper-Oakley, and Bertram Keightley. Although she lived in Kaluga, she frequented Theosophical circles in St. Petersburg and Moscow, and her contacts included the major unofficial Theosophical circles as well as affiliates of the Russian Section. After Filosofova's death, Kamenskaia and Pisareva became, without a doubt, the two most internationally visible Russian Theosophists. During the years when no Russian Section existed, they had learned to participate in European Theosophical events and to maintain a high European profile. Kamenskaia, Pisareva, and their Russian colleagues unfailingly attended Theosophical Congresses, conferences, summer courses, lecture series, and other activities in England and on the continent, bringing back lectures, lessons, and other materials to share with colleagues at home. Little time elapsed between European events and publications, and Russian knowledge of them.

Elena Pisareva's original affiliation was with the German Section of the Theosophical Society; she became a member of the Berlin branch in 1905 and from 1908 headed the Rudolf Steiner branch in Kaluga. Pisareva arranged for Steiner to give a special lecture cycle designed for the Russians in May and June of 1906, in conjunction with the World Theosophical Congress then taking place in Paris (June 3–6). Attending Steiner's Paris cycle were the writers Konstantin Bal'mont, Nikolai Minskii [Vilenkin], Dmitrii Merezhkovskii and his wife Zinaida Hippius, the critic Dmitrii Filosofov (Anna Filosofova's son), Maksimilian Voloshin and his wife and Margarita Sabashnikova, and other members of the Russian community in Paris, as well as the delegation of Theosophists from Russia (more than a dozen individuals, including Pisareva herself, Anna Kamenskaia, Nina Gernet, Anna Filosofova, and Anna Mintslova).

The Paris Cycle was not the first lecture series that Steiner had prepared for the Russians, nor would it be the last. In both 1904 and 1905 Steiner had read cycles specifically designed for Russian audiences; he would also read special lectures for the Russians in 1912 and 1913. Russian Theosophists, remarkably peripatetic, would often stop in Berlin or Cologne on their way home from European meetings to hear Dr. Steiner's lectures.[24] The Paris Cycle, however, was historically important, both for Steiner and for the further development of Russian Theosophy. The topic of these important lectures (the evolution of the cosmos, the earth, and man) already contained the core of much of Steiner's subsequent thought and made a lasting impression on his audiences. Many of the Theosophists who attended took notes, which they later read in their circles at home, accounting in part for Steiner's high profile among Russian occultists.

The meeting with Steiner and the 1906 Paris Congress also served to introduce the Russian Theosophists to each other. Here the leading role was taken by the generous and hospitable Anna Filosofova. Her close friend, the Theosophist A. V. Tyrkova, wrote, "There were many Russian Theosophists at the Congress. They had not yet organized; in fact, many of them were not even acquainted, but they soon became friends in [Filosofova's] drawing room."[25]

Pisareva's overall contribution to the Russian Theosophical Society was great. In addition to actively promoting Steiner's variant of Theosophy, she translated numerous Theosophical texts, wrote a Russian biography of Mme Blavatsky, published pamphlets, served as liaison between RTO and non-RTO circles and between the Russian and German Sections, contributed her editorial efforts to *Vestnik Teosofii*, and lectured extensively. Like Kamenskaia and Filosofova, Elena Pisareva devoted her life to the Theosophical cause. Even after the Bolshevik Revolution, when she was obliged to emigrate in 1922, she went to Italy and continued to work, with Kamenskaia in Geneva, for the Russian Theosophical Society Outside Russia.

A third member of the small but vigorous Kaluga branch was Aleksandra Vasil'evna Unkovskaia (1857–1929). A graduate of the St. Petersburg Conservatory of Music, a professional violinist, and the widow of the famous operatic baritone N. V. Unkovskii, the popular Aleksandra Vasil'evna worked on sound-color synesthesia, which she interpreted in a mystical way. She lectured and wrote on the Theosophical dimensions of sounds, colors, and music. She was a close friend of Kamenskaia and contributed extensively to *Vestnik Teosofii*. Unkovskaia traveled frequently and, like Pisareva and Kamenskaia, had numerous contacts with European Theosophists. She also was acquainted with many leading figures in the world of music and art.[26]

The Kiev and Moscow branches followed St. Petersburg and Kaluga in visibility. The Kiev branch was founded by Ariadna Vel'ts and Elizaveta Vil'gel'movna Rodzevich. Leading members included E. G. Berdiaeva, who was also a member of the Kiev Religious-Philosophical Society and leader of the short-lived Sophia Circle for the study of Theosophy and Christianity (founded February 15, 1915), Vasilii Alekseevich Sobolev, Evgenii Kuz'min, and Evgeniia Vasil'evna Pal'shau.

The Moscow branch was officially established on March 14, 1910, but never attracted many members. This is not an indication, however, that Muscovites were uninterested in Theosophy; on the contrary, Moscow actually had the largest number of independent Theosophical circles in Russia. The administration of the Moscow branch was in the capable hands of Anna Iakovlevna Rabinovich, a dentist with offices on the Arbat. Its first president was Iu. N. Kirpichnikova. Other visible Moscow Theosophists included Nikolai Karlovich Boianus, A. V. Bornio, Sofia Vladimirovna Ger'e (who would, as its president, see the Moscow branch through the Bolshevik Revolution, and die soon after), E. E. Lineva, E. Nedovich, and Princess Sofia Urusova, who also served as president of the branch.

Theosophical Life

The Russian Theosophists had their own particular life-style. Their "season" opened on September 18 (October 1 [N.S.]), which was Mrs. Besant's birthday. It closed on April 25 (May 8 [N.S.]), on the Day of the White Lotus. The major event of the fall season was the anniversary celebration of the founding of the Theosophical Society on November 17. By tradition, the provincial members of the RTO would come to St. Petersburg for this "Golden Week" (*zolotaia nedelia*), where they would enjoy a series of special lectures, teas, musical performances, exhibits of Indian art, and other Theosophical entertainments.

Each week during the season, the St. Petersburg branch would hold two or three open meetings, which the general public was welcome to attend. These were so successful that by the fall of 1913 the RTO began using the main hall of the Tenishev Academy (seating 413) for their public lectures. Many of the leading members also traveled extensively to lecture in the provinces. The Theosophists were enthusiastic lecturers and frequently packed auditoriums with talks on "Theosophy and Life," "The Structure of the Cosmos and the Structure of Man," "Reincarnation," "The Doctrine of Karma and Dharma," "The Development of Psychic Powers and the Education of the New Man," and "The Path of Discipleship and the Mission of Mankind."[27]

The public lectures would be reviewed in the local press and occasionally in *Rebus*, which continued to monitor the Russian Theosophical Movement. From the first day of the Society's formation Pavel Chistiakov, *Rebus*'s editor, reported on its activities and aims, feeling it his duty to inform the public and keep the Theosophists honest. While having few objections to Mrs. Besant herself, Chistiakov was not well disposed toward her retinue. Thus when Iu. M. Kirpichnikova, the president of the Moscow branch, read the persistently problematic C. W. Leadbeater's "Outline of Theosophy" at a lecture, Chistiakov wrote:

> We have already had cause more than once on the pages of *Rebus* to take note of the fantastic fabrications of Mr. Leadbeater . . . , for instance, [his discussion of] which kind of harp the *Logos* plays or of what color, in which countries nymphs can be found. . . . Any serious movement should steer clear of such unrestrainable adepts, and we think that the Theosophical Society in Petersburg would do well to take over the Moscow branch for a certain period of time, in order to prevent its appearing in public with such risk-laden and compromising names and ideas.[28]

On the whole, however, Russian Theosophists managed to avoid most of the eccentric excesses toward which a certain faction within Theosophy seemed inclined.

Each week there would also be an equal number of closed meetings, open only to members and their specially invited guests. Small, intimate meetings of the various circles, for members exclusively, were held regularly. At these meetings the chairman would frequently read the latest article by the Parent Society's leading lights or conduct a symposium on Theosophical classics or some aspect of doctrine. The public lectures and the lecture cycles for members were still a part of "exoteric Theosophy," accessible to anyone who cared to join and do the readings; the Society also had an inner, secret "Esoteric Section" for the select few whose spiritual development was more advanced and who were capable of absorbing and understanding the most sophisticated occult philosophy.[29] All meetings frequently included musical interludes, recitation of inspirational verse and Hindu scriptures, and burning of incense. Fridays were for tea and open conversation at the elegant, gilded RTO Headquarters, which had to be expanded to hold at least a hundred members for closed meetings.

Theosophists attended not only their own lectures, but also those of their detractors. When Mentin lectured against Theosophy in Kaluga early in 1912 (Theosophy is "a dangerous epidemic"), Elena Pisareva, her husband N. V. Pisarev, and G. Gagarin were present to defend the Society. In Poltava, when the unfriendly rector of the local seminary, Archimandrite Varlaam, lectured on the "harmful influence of fashionable Theosophical doctrine, which is beginning strongly to attract our youth," Theosophists were there to defend their position at the lecture and in the local newspaper.[30]

The Theosophists preferred their own company and spent their free time with Theosophical comrades. They had their own vegetarian restaurants and even a vegetarian *dacha-pension*, the "Vasanta," in the village of Samopomoshch', forty-five minutes from St. Petersburg, where they could recoup their strength in the fresh air and the Theosophical atmosphere. The gift of a member, Ivan Anuchkin, it burned down in December 1915. By that time the Theosophists were already collecting money to build a modern Theosophical sanatorium, to be called the "Bela," on the Black Sea coast. The Pisarevs' "Podborki" also offered a refuge when needed. Finally, the Society was enthusiastically involved in plans to build a Buddhist temple in St. Petersburg.[31]

Although Theosophists as a group were perceived by many as being elitist and exclusive, even haughty, they were not isolated from other social movements.[32] The growth of the Theosophical Society actually went hand in hand with the Women's Movement. One reason for this might be the high visibility and assertiveness of the Theosophical women. Mme Blavatsky was a unique woman for her time; charlatan or no, she can be credited for accomplishing what few men could have achieved in that age. Her grandmother was a dominant personality, her mother was an early feminist writer. Anna Kamenskaia was professionally involved in pedagogy and child rearing. Nina Gernet was a remarkably independent and peripatetic woman for the end of the nineteenth century. Many women within the Theosophical Movement owned their own businesses or were themselves doctors, dentists, teachers, or other professionals. Anna Filosofova was instrumental in involving the Theosophical Movement in philanthropic and social projects. Filosofova was a major figure in the Russian Women's Movement; with Dr. A. N. Shabanova, she helped organize the first All-Russian Women's Congress (1908), in which many Theosophists, both men and women, participated. She was also involved in numerous philanthropic projects, including the building of the first dormitory for working women in St. Petersburg.

The Women's Movement saw a natural ally in the Theosophical Society because it was a minority group with a large female constituency and scope for social activism. The Theosophists saw an ally in the Women's Movement because the women involved had "vision": "The voices from the Higher Planes [i.e., the voices of the Great Teachers] find the greatest response in the heart of woman. For this reason the Women's Movement is strong, and for this reason it must be successful. In its dream of human brotherhood, regardless of sex and class, it approaches and unites with Theosophy," explained Nadezhda Trofimenko-Dmitrieva.[33] In this view Russian Theosophists echoed the views of the League of Free Women in London and other international women's organizations. They were pro-family, as well as advocates for higher educational opportunities for women and complete equality with men.

The Theosophical Movement was involved in a variety of philanthropic organizations. Theosophists opened vegetarian cafeterias and food kitchens for the poor, worked in hospitals, ran kindergartens, provided day care, put up Christmas trees for the children of the poor, distributed candy, books, and toys, and held entertainments for the penurious elderly. The Theosophists were among the first to express interest in Maria Montessori's new teaching method and to apply it to their own educational efforts; they were active in pedagogy. The RTO had a Pedagogical Circle that met regularly, worked with kindergartens, and produced a small body of literature on upbringing and primary education.[34]

Finally, the Theosophists also participated in various arts and crafts movements, on the theory that people would be healthier and happier if they worked with their hands. The Russian Theosophical Society was associated with the International Union of Handiwork. Particularly active in this aspect of Theosophical life was Aleksandr Loginovna Pogosskaia, who wrote and translated for *Vestnik Teosofii* under the pseudonym "Dana." Pogosskaia had lived in Florida and England and frequently returned to Russia to visit and lecture for the Kaluga branch. For twenty-two years she was involved in the export of Russian peasant handicrafts abroad. An enthusiastic liaison between Russian and English Theosophists, she traveled frequently between the two countries.

Contemporaries were not unaware of this dimension of the Theosophical Society. In his book on Theosophy, Father Dmitrevskii wrote:

> In order to give a real notion of the social power of this movement, it is sufficient to list those leagues and unions, which currently enter into the charter of the Theosophical Society. Here they are: "The League for the Dissemina-

tion of Theosophical Literature"; "The League of the Power of Thought with the Aim of Providing Work for Self-Improvement"; "The League of the Aesthetic," the goal of which is to spread the ideal of Beauty in society; "The League of Moral Education of Youth"; "The 'Isis' Union," whose goal is to bring beauty and the understanding of art into the life of the poor; "The Brotherhood of Workers," who advance the idea of the holiness of labor and the solidarity of workers; "The International Union of Handiwork"; "The Union for the Protection of Animals"; "The League for Action against Vivisection and Grafts."[35]

The Theosophists were indefatigable philanthropists. In fact, the majority of RTO members were well-meaning, generous, idealistic men and women who saw in Theosophy not only a quasi-religion or an esoteric doctrine, but a social and philanthropic outlet as well. They believed fervently in Theosophy's concept of "active idealism" and subscribed to its tenet that "in the social sphere Theosophy teaches the necessity of building a new life on the basis of brotherhood and moral responsibility of each individual for other people, and of all other people for each individual."[36] Theosophy satisfied their need to "belong" and to do "good deeds" for "mankind" in the name of a higher idea. That is why Dmitrii Merezhkovskii patronizingly called them "mercilessly kind."

The Herald of Theosophy: Vestnik Teosofii

The central organ of the Russian Theosophical Society was *Vestnik Teosofii* (*Theosophical Herald*).[37] On the front page was the credo of the Society: "Net Religii vyshe Istiny" ("There Is No Religion Higher Than Truth"), which Mme Blavatsky had claimed in *Iz peshcher i debrei Indostana* was the *devise* of the Maharajah of Benares. The journal's program was to: (1) include original articles and articles in translation on Theosophy, comparative religions, occultism, studies of the psychic forces hidden in nature and in man, and psychology and other related fields of knowledge; (2) provide news of the Theosophical Movement in Russia and abroad and of other related spiritual and social movements; (3) include biographies of leading representatives of the Theosophical worldview; 4) have an artistic and literary section, showing the reflection of the spiritual in art; (5) review books on questions of Theosophy, psychology, spiritualism, and so forth; and (6) provide a reference section and answers to subscribers' questions.

The *Vestnik Teosofii* had several regular features. These included the "Scientific Section" (for health, diet, and science); the "Survey of Theosophical Literature," a selective review of all the major foreign Theo-

sophical journals, compiled by Varvara Nikolaevna Pushkina; "Chronicle of the Theosophical Movement," written by Alba-Kamenskaia;
"Chronicle of Life," which dealt primarily with the minutiae of Russian
intellectual life; "From the Newspapers and Journals," which ran excerpts from the Russian press on items of interest to Theosophists; a
book review section that reviewed books on the oddest subjects, most of
them unrelated to Theosophy but probably reflecting the interests and
hobbies of the reviewers; a "Question and Answer" column patterned
on the dialogue structure of Mme Blavatsky's *Key to Theosophy*; and
"From a Theosophist's Diary," personal and professional excerpts from
Alba-Kamenskaia's journal. Sprinkled throughout each issue were gems
of wisdom mined from various sources: Goethe, oriental scriptures,
L. N. Tolstoi, Theosophical classics, the Bible, the Gnostics, and so
forth. Over the years the *Vestnik* discussed the various topics of particular peripheral interest to Russian Theosophists: morality, vegetarianism,
education, Atlantis, philanthropy, problems of European culture, crime,
labor, the Women's Movement, sectarianism, and quality of life.

The format of *Vestnik Teosofii* was based primarily on the London
journal, *The Theosophical Review*.[38] Its early years were haunted by financial problems, and the journal probably never showed a profit. Much of
the publication costs after 1912 were covered by the editors and pub-
lishers (Kamenskaia and Gel'mbol'dt) themselves. Only readers' support
and contributions kept it going. The *Vestnik Teosofii* was aimed at a specific audience; while it met the needs of that audience, it could not have
had a broad appeal. It was written primarily (but not exclusively) in
"Theosophical language," a marked form of discourse studded with
platitudes, Hinduisms, and the excessive use of "gentle" vocabulary
(*svetlyi, tikhii, liubimyi, dorogoi*). Its tone ranged from sermonizing to
being self-righteous and even ecstatic.

Over its eleven years of publication, *Vestnik* made available to its readers numerous Theosophical classics in Russian translation. Some items,
especially those that did not get by the censorship, circulated in manuscript only to members and interested parties. The quality of the translations was uneven; some were competent, others only approximate paraphrases. Alba-Kamenskaia and the editorial board of *Vestnik* were not
above excising sensitive passages, or rephrasing wording so as not to irri-
tate the censorship, the authorities, or the readership.

In spite of Kamenskaia's efforts to avoid official attention, she was
invited to visit the offices of the Third Section on several occasions. One
time she was briefly detained for material published in *Vestnik*. On
March 12, 1912 Kamenskaia had her day in court. She was sued for allowing a disparaging comment about St. Constantine the Great to appear in the March 1912 issue of *Vestnik Teosofii*, but she was acquitted

on May 18, 1912. It was her most serious, but not her only, brush with the Tsarist secret police, who constantly kept the Theosophists under surveillance.

The serialization of three important and influential texts—Mrs. Besant's *Ancient Wisdom* (1897), Edouard Schuré's *Les Grand Initiés* (1889), and Rudolf Steiner's *Wie erlangt man Erkenntnisse der höheren Welten* (1904)—in *Vestnik Teosofii* were completed by the end of 1909 and made immediately available, in attractive editions, to the general reading public. While texts by various Theosophists and occultists appeared on the pages of *Vestnik*, the Russian Theosophical Movement was hampered by the unavailability in Russian of two of its most important texts, Mme Blavatsky's *Isis Unveiled* and *The Secret Doctrine*. Not until 1913 did the journal began to serialize excerpts from *The Secret Doctrine* under the title *Evoliutsiia simvolizma*. Mme Blavatsky's at times virulently anti-Christian position consistently ran into problems with the censorship and prevented publication of this classic Theosophical text. Subscription to the Russian translation of *The Secret Doctrine* had originally been announced in *Vestnik* in 1911, but was subsequently disallowed by the censorship. The January 1912 issue of *Vestnik* announced that "publication of *The Secret Doctrine* is deferred due to circumstances beyond the control of the editorial board," and offered a refund. Only after the February 1917 revolution could the work appear in a more complete form. It was typeset and ready for printing when the Bolsheviks confiscated the plates in 1918 and closed the press.

Vestnik Teosofii published many works by leading American and European Theosophists, notably Mrs. Besant and Dr. Steiner, but also Dr. Théophile Pascal, Mabel Collins, A. P. Sinnett, G. R. S. Mead, C. W. Leadbeater, Dr. Franz Hartmann, and Michael Wood.[39] Beginning in January 1910, *Vestnik* published large segments of a translation (by Kamenskaia and Irma Mantsiarli) of the *Bhagavad Gita* into Russian, as well as Rudolf Steiner's biographical series on medieval mystics from Meister Eckhart to Giordano Bruno, *Die Mystik im Aufgange des neuzeitlichen Geisteslebens* (1895). The translation of Louis Ménard's *Hermes Trismegistus* in 1911 made available for the first time certain ancient hermetic texts in Russian. Almost all of these major Theosophical works subsequently appeared in separate editions, many being reprinted several times, and sold not only at RTO lectures but also in many exclusive speciality bookshops.[40]

The journal also published Indian myths, the stories of Rabindranath Tagore, fragments from Indian and Chinese religious classics, and inspirational poetry by the philosopher Vladimir Solov'ev, the poet Max Voloshin, and the poet-sectarian Aleksandr Dobroliubov, whom Kamenskaia considered a "profound mystic" and a "popular theosophist."

There were also articles on Russian Orthodox saints and elders popular with the Theosophists, especially St. Serafim of Sarov (also revered by the Russian royal family and the Sophiologists). Although the preponderance of material was Theosophical, every facet of ancient and contemporary occultism, religion, and speculative philosophy, with the exception of black magic, found a place in the pages of *Vestnik Teosofii*.

Although the vast bulk of *Vestnik*'s contents was material translated from European sources, also included was original Russian material, only some of it of interest. The largest single Russian contributor was Anna Kamenskaia. Not only did she write many of the regular features, but as the president of the RTO she had her own column, "From a Theosophist's Diary" (and after the start of the war in 1914, also "On Watch"). Kamenskaia's articles, while well intentioned, were not very stimulating. She trained as a teacher, not as a thinker or a prophet; her profession was apparent in her articles. As early as 1903 Maria von Strauch-Spettini observed of her: "I have a great yearning for deeper insights, and Fräulein Kamenskaia, as dear and as good as she is, is not substantial enough to give them to me. Both ladies (Frl. Gernet) can only repeat what I can and already have read for myself. But I yearn for glimmerings that would unlock deeper insights, that would awaken that which cannot awaken by itself."[41] What Kamenskaia lacked in flair, however, she certainly made up for with commitment and hard work. *Vestnik Teosofii* was a success first and foremost because of her efforts.

Another important contributor to *Vestnik Teosofii* was Pavel Nikolaevich Batiushkov (1864–c. 1930), the grandson of the poet Konstantin Batiushkov. Batiushkov was interested in both spiritualism and Theosophy. His Theosophical interests antedate the formation of the RTO and can probably be traced to his cousin, Anna Sergeevna Goncharova (a relative of Pushkin's wife, Nataliia Goncharova), who returned to Moscow from Paris in 1901 a confirmed Theosophist. Goncharova shared her new passion with her cousin and his friends, the Symbolist writer Andrei Belyi and the other members of the Moscow Argonaut Circle. A quiet, studious individual, Batiushkov worked at the Rumiantsev Museum in Moscow.

Batiushkov wrote more than a dozen original Theosophical articles (on spiritual alchemy, karma, and mysticism and poetry, among other subjects) and was a regular contributor to *Vestnik Teosofii*. He also translated excerpts from several Theosophical texts, including Mabel Collins's *Light on the Path*; this latter he published in the first book of the Symbolist anthology *Svobodnaia Sovest'* in 1906. While Batiushkov's contribution was not profound, he lent the Society his scholarly respectability and was a reliable and much-liked colleague. He also disseminated Theosophical ideas in Symbolist literary circles. Viewing Theosophy as a living philosophical system, he strove to take certain basic Theosophical concepts beyond their rote presentation in Theosophical brochures and to place them in a more general philosophical context, frequently relating them to the theory of "Symbolism as a worldview" advocated by his friends and colleagues among the Argonauts.

As *Vestnik Teosofii* continued to grow in size and circulation, other Russian contributors emerged to balance the heavily European content of the first two years of publication. Aleksandra Unkovskaia wrote articles on color, sound, and number ("Tsvet-zvuk-chislo"), on Richard Wagner, and on other musical topics. She contributed irregular "Letters on Music," in which she discussed her "color-sound" (*tsvetozvuk*) synesthetic theories, and began her "spiritual" memoirs in *Vestnik*. Anna Kamenskaia's sister, Margarita Alekseevna, wrote letters from India in 1912, where she was a guest at the Adyar Headquarters, as well as an article on the history of Buddhism. Konstantin Kudriavtsev wrote on pseudoscientific topics associated with hypnotism and spiritualism. Evgenii Kuz'min, an active member of the Kiev branch, wrote several summary articles for *Vestnik Teosofii*, which were later published as popular brochures. Elena Pisareva contributed both general articles and biographical material on Mme Blavatsky. Dmitrii Vladimirovich Stranden helped spread the Theosophical word not only in occasional articles for *Vestnik*, but in his books as well. His interests were sectarianism, esoteric Christianity, and philosophy. Other contributors included P. I. Timofeevskii; M. F. Gardenina, who reviewed books; Aleksandra Pogosskaia, who wrote on the virtues of labor and wrote an occasional column, "Letters from England"; Varvara Pushkina, who supported Mrs. Besant's Order of the Star in the East; Vera Rudich and Anna Veselovskaia, who both translated and wrote original occult verse for the journal; and, of course, Nina Gernet, to name but a few. Many more Theosophists worked on translations of European Theosophical texts for the journal. At its peak, *Vestnik Teosofii* distributed some thousand copies a month. Under Russian conditions, and considering the esoteric nature of the Theosophical doctrine, this was an extraordinary circulation.

A Theosophical Thinker: P. D. Uspenskii (1878–1947)

The Russian Theosophical Society did not produce from within its ranks anyone of the stature of Mme Blavatsky, Mrs. Annie Besant, or Dr. Rudolf Steiner. The most important and visible Theosophical thinker in Russia was Petr Demianovich Uspenskii (Ouspensky; 1878–1947). He came to Theosophy in 1907, although for him it was only a way station on his own esoteric path. He wrote:

> In 1907 I found Theosophical literature, which was prohibited in Russia—Blavatsky, Olcott, Annie Besant, Sinnett, etc. It produced a very strong impression on me although I at once saw its weak side. The weak side was that, such as it was, it had no continuation. But it opened doors for me into a new and bigger world. I discovered the idea of esotericism, found a possible approach for the study of religion and mysticism, and received a new impulse for the study of "higher dimensions."[42]

Although he left Theosophy after seven years of apprenticeship, Uspenskii never underestimated its importance in his life and thought. Much of his subsequent occult system was clearly rooted in Theosophy: in its moral dimension, its emphasis on comparative religion, and its attempt to unite science, philosophy, and religion. And he made his own contribution to the Movement, as well; Berdiaev called him "the most independent and talented Theosophical writer we have" in Russia.[43]

A mathematician by training and a journalist by profession, Uspenskii was the RTO's most prominent philosopher, author, and lecturer until he left the Society in 1914. His major contribution to Russian Theosophical thought is contained in three books, *Chetvertoe izmerenie, Tertium Organum,* and *Vnutrennii krug. Chetvertoe izmerenie* and another text, *Simvoly Taro,* were published in *Vestnik Teosofii.* Uspenskii maintained that the three spatial dimensions and the one linear temporal dimension characteristic of the perceived phenomenal world are actually the product of Maya, the World Illusion. In maya, time appears unidimensional: a straight line, a series of points with past, present, and future being three consecutive points on that line. The order of those points cannot be changed, and, once passed, those points cannot be repeated. New points become new past, new present, new future. But, claimed Uspenskii, this is all illusion. Time is not really a straight line. It is a curve, or perhaps (as Andrei Belyi would also subsequently suggest), a spiral. Other dimensions, such as eternity, actually exist, but these higher dimensions are accessible only to the "new man," the superman, who has developed "supersensible" (occult) sight. In his eclectic theories, Uspenskii united the "higher man" of the Theosophists, Vladimir Solov'ev's *Bogochelovek,* and Nietzsche's *Übermensch,* placing them in the context of mystical Darwinism. "The major content of the Theosophical system," he wrote, "must be considered *synthetic philosophy, evolutionary morality, and the doctrine of the superman.*[44]

Uspenskii's syncretic approach was characteristic of the peculiar mental fermentation that took place during the Russian Silver Age; it strove to synthesize all the major intellectual trends of the time. Uspenskii sought to unite Western philosophy and Eastern mysticism in a more balanced fashion and to correct the Theosophical list toward Buddhism.

He brought in Nietzsche's concepts of the superman and eternal recurrence, integrated them with Buddhist notions of the higher self, reincarnation, and the One Life, and grafted them onto Solov'ev's concepts of the All-Unity and the Godman.

Nor did Uspenskii's thought lack the necessary scientific dimension. Reincarnation became "evolution of the spirit," Darwinism of the soul rather than of the organism. Uspenskii "proved" his theory of dimensions with mystical mathematics, an example of "scientific occultism"; his mystical mathematics of space later influenced Russian abstract art (Matiushin, Malevich, and others). The importance and influence of Uspenskii as a synthesizer and popularizer of fashionable philosophies in early twentieth century Russia has been underestimated.

In November 1914 Uspenskii returned to Russia from a lengthy trip, curtailed by the outbreak of the First World War, which had taken him to Egypt, Ceylon, and India. He spent two months of his "search for the miraculous" in India, where he visited Mrs. Besant at the Theosophical Headquarters in Adyar. He returned disappointed. Uspenskii had already decided to leave the Theosophical Society when he gave, early in 1915, three lectures sponsored by the Theosophists about his foreign adventures. *Vestnik* reported:

P. D. Uspenskii's three lectures attracted a huge audience, but they evoked perplexity. The lecturer promised in the program to talk about India. In fact he talked only about disillusionment in seeking the miraculous and about his understanding of occultism at variance with its understanding by Theosophists and the Theosophical Society. With indignation he said that the Theosophists selected ethics and philosophy, not occultism, as their field of effort, and that ethics and philosophy are unnecessary to the Society and unrelated to occultism. . . . He also accused the Theosophical Society of arrogance and sectarianism.[45]

Uspenskii's presence and popular speeches were sorely missed by the RTO after his departure.

Uspenskii broke away from Theosophy because he was looking for a more refined esoteric tradition, as well as a more Christian-oriented alternative to the Theosophists' Buddhism. Early in 1915 he told his friend Anna Butkovskaia, then also a member of the RTO, that he "intended to leave the Society whose members were just sheep, showing no evidence of independent thought; and although he had been invited to join their 'inner circle' with the promise of enlightenment not accessible to the rank and file, he felt that there he would only encounter bigger sheep."[46] Uspenskii's decision to leave was reinforced by a meeting with Gurdjieff in the spring of 1915, a meeting that changed his life, although his and Gurdjieff's philosophy would develop in different directions and the two men would subsequently part ways. In August 1921 Uspenskii lectured in London for the Quest Society, formed by G. R. S. Mead (another Theosophical "expatriate"), and eventually developed his own following. He never returned to Russia, but his ideas did not emigrate with him. Uspenskii's Russian disciples to this day continue to read and study his books.[47]

Russian Theosophy during the First World War (1914–1918)

In 1915, a year after the start of the First World War, the Russian Theosophical Society celebrated the seventh anniversary of its Theosophical work. This was a major milestone, for the principle of "seven," important in almost all occult systems, here designates one complete cycle, or phase, in the process of spiritual development. This first seven-year cycle had been devoted to building a Society and propagandizing Theosophy to Russian society at large; on the eve of the war the RTO had enough members and interested parties to state without reservation that the Theosophists had indeed established a visible cultural and social presence within Russian society.

By 1916, at the start of the second seven-year cycle, the Theosophists were a social force to be reckoned with. People regularly had to be turned away from their lectures for lack of space, and, at each such gathering, sales of books and pamphlets, costing only kopeks, would often exceed 100 rubles. Theosophical publications were regularly included for serious review by major journals, such as *Russkaia Mysl'*. In 1916 Kamenskaia, who was wary of overstatement and rarely exaggerated the dimensions of Russian Theosophy, proudly pointed out that "over the course of the first phase of our existence (the first seven years), we were a new phenomenon, incomprehensible to and unacknowledged by Russian society; we were not taken into consideration, we were what science calls a '*quantité négligeable*.' But things have now changed: . . . people now view us with consideration, they have begun to acknowledge us, and to come to us for assistance and advice."[48] During the First World War the Russian Theosophical Society was at the pinnacle of its success and influence.

Success in numbers, however, was not the Theosophical Society's mission in Russia. Taking stock of the Society's considerable achievements, Kamenskaia concluded that in the next seven-year cycle the Theosophists would have an even more important role to play in Russian (and world) culture:

We are undoubtedly moving on to a higher level of world life. Not without purpose have all the veils been torn away and previous illusions are burning in the fire of difficult, and, at the same time, profoundly meaningful experiences; not without purpose are we passing through so many shocks; not without purpose are all minds and hearts opening to new ideas and inspirations. But what kind of world view will be capable of expressing this higher level of consciousness? Only that world view which can unify all the complex needs of human life and provide the strength to build life on earth on the basis of brotherhood, love, and mutual assistance. Theosophy provides such a world view.[49]

The Theosophists were people of vision. Theosophy, and specifically Russian Theosophy, was to facilitate the cultural and spiritual renewal of the world; it was the hope of the future for a world at war.

While some Russian occultists allowed the beginning of the First World War to pass them by as an illusory tempest in a phenomenal teacup (it went unremarked in several occult publications, including *Rebus*), the war did not go unnoticed by the Theosophists. In September 1914, Kamenskaia began writing "On Watch" ("Na storozhevom postu"), a new opening section in *Vestnik Teosofii* that continued to appear until the demise of the journal itself. Kamenskaia urged Theosophists to see the war as a cosmic event of occult significance, a cleansing fire in whose heat would be forged a new, spiritual union of the religious East and the scientific West, mediated by Russian spirituality. Russia, with such an important historical mission, was sure to be victorious. Kamenskaia's point of view, not to mention her imagery and terminology, was shared by many representatives of the creative and God-seeking intelligentsia.

In Adyar, Mrs. Besant had issued a statement about the war almost immediately, although her remarks did not appear in *Vestnik Teosofii* until October 1915.[50] She pointed out that Universal Brotherhood was a fact, war was a fact (a repeating fact of evolution), God was a fact, and the Brotherhood of Adepts was a fact. Therefore, war was an evil out of which good would come. Theosophists should trust the Brotherhood of Adepts to see the world through this period of carnage and suffering; they knew what they were doing, even if ordinary mortals did not. War, she felt, was worthwhile, since the extraordinary opportunities it evoked for exhibition of bravery, mercy, and self-sacrifice allowed the soul to achieve in days, weeks, months what would ordinarily take many lifetimes to achieve. War was the great leveler. It highlighted injustice and the crimes of society. And, of course, war was inevitable if it was karma. Mrs. Besant urged Theosophists to accept what was happening and to adopt a neutral position.

Writing about the war at its outbreak, Kamenskaia also recognized it as "a frightening phantom of world karma not overcome." But Kamenskaia could not quite advocate the neutrality that Mrs. Besant urged. Good Theosophists do not run from war, she pointed out. They recognize it as an indicator of the low level of humanity, and they differentiate between a righteous war (the defense of the unfortunate) and a sinful war (an offensive, grasping war). They feel themselves part of their own nation and must be prepared to carry their share of national karma.[51] Kamenskaia perceived Russia's karma to be connected with its Slavic mission, and hoped that Russia would understand that she was destined, through Theosophy, "to become the link between the West and the East, of which Vladimir Solov'ev dreamed."[52] Her earliest comments were about the growing unity of the Russian people, about the war as an opportunity to realize the best aspects of the rich Slavic soul, about the mission of the Slavs to heal and renew the world through Theosophy. "Saint Sophia, Theosophy, opens to us the path toward the fulfillment" of this task, she wrote. "This task is close to the Russian soul, and all of Slavic culture, now arising, is consciously and unconsciously directed toward its realization. . . . The soul of the Russian people feels this very strongly, and because it feels this so strongly, it will undoubtedly approach the realization of its mission, it will illuminate the life of this world with the light of St. Sophia."[53]

Not surprisingly, the Russian Theosophists shared in the messianic vision of the God-seeking intelligentsia; many Theosophists were members of that intelligentsia. Like many educated Russians, they, too, had invested a great deal of emotional and intellectual energy in the German culture of Schopenhauer, Goethe, Schiller, Schelling, and Nietzsche, not to mention German scholarship and science. Immediately after the outbreak of the war, Nikolai Roerich, Dmitrii Filosofov, Dmitrii Merezhkovskii, Sergei Bulgakov, E. N. Trubetskoi, and many other leading intellectuals wrote in the newspapers and journals about how shocked they were by "cultured" Germans, so long admired and imitated, breaking out in their "animal guise"; the generally high regard they had for German culture made it difficult, if not impossible, for them to understand this fiercely warlike aspect of the German nation. The God-seeking intelligentsia felt that they alone were left in the world to carry on the banner of culture.

The Theosophists shared their position: "The old, embittered, egoistic, isolated world is dying. The utilitarian, materialist culture is falling apart; contemporary Germany is a vivid example. The days of educated barbarianism, which replaced the idea of humanity and justice with the idea of brute force, supported by utilitarian science, are ending. Should we grieve for the fall of such a civilization?" asked Kamenskaia. "Isn't it time to replace the idol of external culture and utilitarian science with a religious ideal? Does not the mission of the Slavs, the mission of Russia consist of this task?"[54]

The outbreak of the First World War clearly revealed the extent to which the Russian Theosophists' vision of the "Path of St. Sophia" and the "Russian Idea" of the God-seekers coincided. The rhetoric might be dressed in universal Theosophical garments, but behind "On Watch" and the other indignant articles that proliferated in *Vestnik Teosofii* lay the same manifestations of Great Russian chauvinism and patriotic optimism mingled with feelings of guilt and condescension toward the Russian common people (*narod*), the same faith in Russian spirituality, the same advocacy of a religious solution to the problem at hand, the same apocalyptic vision, as expressed by the God-seekers. The Theosophists sang the same song as the God-seeking intelligentsia: it was the mission of uncultured but spiritualized Russia to show the cultured but soul-dead West just what *real* culture should be. Both expressed their vision by urging self-sacrifice; both used the Christian imagery of passion, crucifixion, and resurrection. Kamenskaia wrote about the need to "bravely drink the cup of suffering to its dregs, never ceasing to serve Russia."[55] This all fit the Theosophical paradigm of the initiatory path: to be born one must die; to advance spiritually, one must suffer.

That was what the war meant. The resurrection of Russia would come, the spiritual regeneration of the Russian people would happen, but only after suffering and death. The war was the passion of the Russian nation, the distorted manifestation of a noumenal reality in phenomenal time and space. The attack of the "dark forces of evil" provided the opportunity to prove spiritual mettle. The brave words of the Theosophists, frequently repeated in the pages of *Vestnik* and sounding in the lecture halls, were an echo of Berdiaev's earlier statement that Russia "can pass on to new awareness only through repentance and self-indictment," or Sergei Bulgakov's warning against the "dark forces" that are torturing the body of Russia and his call to "a free, spiritual act, invisible but entirely real," to dispel the forces of darkness.[56] The Theosophists and the God-seeking intelligentsia even used the same vocabulary: crisis of consciousness, dark forces, carrying the cross, Russia's mission, God-bearing people (*narod-bogonosets*), sacrifice, crucifixion, spiritual renewal, resurrection, new path, and bright future.

The war showed no signs of ending quickly. The Theosophists reined in the rhetoric and went back to their lecturing activity, devotional and occult literature, and usual concerns. The war remained with them, however, as Theosophists were called up and went to fight. The Theosophists also worked for the war effort. The RTO had a "Kruzhok sluzheniia," led by V. N. Pushkina and Ts. L. Gel'mbol'dt, which engaged in volunteer work and war service. The Service Circle worked closely with existing relief organizations, such as the International Red Cross. The Theosophists organized vegetarian soup kitchens for soldiers and for their families, left behind without support; made and collected underwear and clothing for soldiers and refugees; donated reading matter and read aloud to invalids in the military hospitals; helped with bookkeeping and records; did pedagogical work; taught first aid; subsidized hospital beds, and volunteered in the wards. Many went to the front as Sisters of Mercy.

In 1916 the Theosophists felt the pinch of war economy, as did all Russians. All publications, including *Vestnik Teosofii*, were unable to find competent typesetters, suffered from the paper shortage, and were hamstrung by rising printing costs. The cost of *Vestnik Teosofii* had gone up to seven rubles in 1916 (it would rise to twenty-one rubles by 1918). Kamenskaia begged her readership for support: "At this critical moment in Russian life the voice of *Vestnik* should not be silenced, the hearthfire should not go out. The Editorial Board hopes that those who warmed themselves at this hearthfire will not leave it in this difficult moment and will help to carry forward the light of Eternity into the world."[57] Each succeeding volume was, nevertheless, shorter than the one before. The regular features disappeared. *Vestnik Teosofii* itself faded away without fanfare in 1918. It seemed, for all intents and purposes, to mark the end of Theosophy in Russia.

Four

Other Russian Theosophical Movements

The Smolensk Theosophists

Not all Russian Theosophists were affiliated with the Russian Theosophical Society, nor could that organization even claim the right of primogeniture. The very first attempt to establish a Theosophical Society in Russia took place not in the capital of St. Petersburg, but in the provincial city of Smolensk, more than a full year before the RTO was officially chartered.

Inaugurated on July 30, 1907, the Smolensk Theosophical Society had a strong patriotic and Russian Orthodox coloring from its inception.[1] The Smolensk Theosophists considered themselves under the protection of the icon of St. Michael of Chernigov; Archimandrite Ignatii, a senior Russian Orthodox monk and a member of the Society's board, served a liturgy in its honor, with prayers for the Romanovs; the service was attended by clergy from a nearby monastery. The Society sent a telegram to Tsar Nicholas II, asking for his support, and sent messages to local Orthodox prelates: "The Smolensk Theosophical Society, having as its goal the unification of all in brotherhood and love, believing in and knowing the power that prayer to the Lord God gives all people, begs your holy and warm prayers and blessings for our new Society."[2] *Rebus* welcomed it, calling its charter "an interesting case of the refraction of the principles of Theosophy through the prism of Russian Christian mysticism."[3]

The most interesting feature of the Smolensk Theosophical Society was its ecumenical Christian dimension. Its credo was published on the back cover of every issue of its journal, *Teosofskaia Zhizn'*:

> What is the Theosophical Society? The Theosophical Society forms the nucleus of a Christian brotherhood, which studies religious systems, philosophy, and sciences; which investigates the forces of nature latent in man; which struggles against the material side of human nature; which disseminates the principles of the knowledge of the spirit of truth; which develops its spiritual powers; and which establishes the power of spirit over matter.
>
> The main credo of the Society's members is "Love thy neighbor as thyself." Their main task is to truly live the life of a Christian; to be unsatisfied with only being called a Christian; to exhort others to do the same; and to serve as a true example and model of Christian life, both in word and in deed.

The Theosophical Society is not a secret society, nor a sect, nor a specific faith. It seeks to collect all Christians beneath its banner—in fact, not just in stated intention.

The members of the Theosophical Society treat all people, according to the example of their Divine Teacher, with honor, love, tolerance, deference, and gentleness; they strictly observe Christian-Theosophical principles and do not digress from the charter of the Society.

Consequently: not in words, but in deeds: Love God, love thy neighbor, know thyself, develop strength of spirit, suppress the power of the passions, serve as a good example to thy neighbor, teach him, be honest, just, tolerant, deferential, gentle, and true to the Charter.

Clearly the Smolensk Theosophists spoke of Theosophy, but affirmed ethical Christianity and Christian charity. Their credo led *Rebus* to observe: "We are not dealing here with Theosophy as much as with something we should really call 'Christianized Theosophy.'" *Rebus* praised the new Society for its recognition that, given the peculiarities of the Russian national consciousness, the "exotic flowers of Hindu thought" would not grow well in Russian soil without some serious grafting on of Orthodox thought.[4]

Vladimir Ivanovich Shtal'berg, the editor of *Teosofskaia Zhizn'* and prominent member of the Smolensk Society, claimed that Russia was a fundamentally Christian country; even its sectarians, he opined, were truly Christian. "And really," he asked, "what is the sense of transplanting pure Theosophy into Russian soil? Its principles would not merge with the Russian spiritual outlook, but would remain only an excrescence on the spiritual and moral organism of the Russian people, having nothing in common with them."[5] The Smolensk Theosophists wanted to give Russian Theosophy its own, inherently Slavic face, and that meant injecting a strong Orthodox element.

In this the Smolensk Society had the assistance of a certain faction within the local clergy. Archimandrite Aleksandr, like founding member Archimandrite Ignatii, viewed the rising interest in Theosophy as one more expression of the growth of spirituality in Russia. The participation of the clergy in the Smolensk Society, however, was short-lived. Even if a few archimandrites were intoxicated by this heretical doctrine, the rest of the Smolensk clergy remained spiritually sober. Arguments were of no avail; the archimandrites received orders from their spiritual superiors to leave the Society a few short months after they had helped to found it. In vain Shtal'berg petitioned the Synod to allow clerical members to continue their participation, arguing that the Society had received a legal charter. The Holy Synod, by decree on April 25, 1908, did not find the activity of the Theosophical Society immoral, anti-Christian, or sinful; the Synod did, however, consider it specifically alien to Orthodox Christian doctrine and could not allow Orthodox clergy to participate in or support such a society.[6]

The Synod was not pleased with the publicity that the archimandrites' membership in the Smolensk Theosophical Society generated. Criticism of clerical participation began to appear in the Russian press. Writing in *Kolokol*, a newspaper associated with the reactionary but powerful Black Hundreds, N. Mariupol'skii expressed a typical reactionary attitude toward Theosophy. "Last year a 'Theosophical Society' was organized in Smolensk. Similar 'societies' are now springing up like mushrooms," he complained. "Nevertheless, their stance is unquestionably anti-Christian." He was appalled that "now, at a time when the Orthodox Church is being ruined by various sects and a lack of faith, we find among the monastic brethren, and even among the monastery leaders, those who establish societies inimical to Christianity, who organize lectures on spiritualism, occultism, telepathy, clairvoyance, somnambulism, and other -isms, and even arrange seances!"[7] Obviously this must all be part of a Masonic conspiracy; how, Mariupol'skii wondered, did the governor ever permit the registration of such a society?

The activities and publications of the Smolensk Theosophical Society could most generously be described as eclectic. Several members, notably A. S. Kellet, L. F. fon-der-Raab Tilen, Fedor Potekhin, N. K. Boianus, and A. V. Bornio, wrote summary articles about different forms of occultism and their history for *Teosofskaia Zhizn'*. As editor, V. I. Shtal'berg contributed a regular column, "The Struggle of the Spirit with Matter," that addressed ethics and morality. The journal mixed Theosophical materials (translations of Rudolf Steiner's *Wie erlangt man Erkenntnisse höherer Welten*, paraphrases of Mrs. Besant's articles, and some hagiographic musings about Mme Blavatsky) with works by traditional mystics (Emanuel Swedenborg, Eckartshausen) and Spiritualists, seasoning the whole with local members' poems and descriptions of strange and inexplicable things that had happened to them or their friends. The result was an amateur mystical mélange of no identifiable occult persuasion.

The journal soon revealed that the Smolensk Society's interests lay not only in Theosophy, but also in spiritualism and hypnotism. "An occult-mentalist group has been organized within the Smolensk Theosophical Society for the study and practical application of spiritual forces in man," announced the January 1908 issue. The members had an "occult-mental prayer" that they all recited at exactly 10:33 P.M. Smolensk time, no matter where they were; they found it remarkably efficacious.[8] Soon the journal was publishing condensed stenographic reports of local spiritualist seances. Letters to *Teosofskaia Zhizn'* indicate its close ties to Sergei Dmitrievich Volkov (d. 1909), an occultist, Freemason, Spiritualist, and leader of a large unaffiliated Theosophical circle in Moscow.

The Smolensk Theosophists were not content to remain quietly in Smolensk. In February 1908, a month after the meeting of all Russian Theosophical circles in Moscow had reached some basic agreement about the establishment of a Russian Section, an interesting commentary about the new Smolensk Society appeared in *Rebus*:

> We have been informed by our English correspondents that the administration of the [Parent] Theosophical Society was somewhat shocked and surprised by the announcement it received from the Smolensk Theosophical Society about the latter's joining it. We find this surprise entirely understandable, and we sincerely advise the Smolensk Theosophists to forget the whole idea and to go about their business independently. We are familiar with several Theosophical circles in Odessa and Moscow which, quite to the contrary, not only are not seeking to join, but have actually declined joining even when invited to do so by the English Theosophists. After all, the situation threatens to be full of practical difficulties: the position of a legalized Russian Society which is simultaneously a section of the foreign Society will be inconvenient at the very least. It's worth thinking about.[9]

(The request of the Smolensk Theosophical Society for affiliation was declined by the English Theosophists.)

In September 1908 the Smolensk Society took stock of their year's work; Shtal'berg was forced to conclude that its members had certainly "trod a thorny path." On the debit side were the "apathy, mockery, spite, and curses" to which they had been subjected. They had been accused of Freemasonry. They had only thirty-three regular members and *Teosofskaia Zhizn'* was 58 rubles, 50 kopeks, in the red. They had sought to provide spiritual food for a nation hungering for spiritual sustenance, and yet were attacked on all sides for their pains. On the credit side, the thirty-three members represented double the original membership of sixteen; their journal had 130 annual subscribers and 10 six-month subscribers; in addition, they had sold 105 separate issues.[10]

As the first such organization in Russia, the Smolensk Theosophical Society (even after changing its name to the Smolensk *Christian* Theosophical Society at the end of 1908) bore the brunt of the criticism that the more conservative elements in Russia obviously had in store for Theosophy:

> First of all the false assertion was made, thanks to a certain faction among the press, that the Theosophical Society is really secret Freemasonry; then a pow-

erful opinion was expressed that Theosophical principles are alien to Christianity and as such are unacceptable to Christianity; and then the persecutions began: there were cases of members of the Theosophical organization being refused Holy Communion, the journal had to be sent out in plain brown paper wrappers so that those receiving it and their nearest and dearest would be spared great unpleasantness [and so on].[11]

In August 1909 Shtal'berg decided it had been a mistake to use the word *Theosophy* in his journal's title and to decorate the cover with Theosophical symbols. In January 1910 he began publication of a new journal, *Zhizn' Dukha*, which he described as a spiritualist, religious, and philosophical journal. *Zhizn' Dukha* appeared over the course of twelve months, when it "temporarily" ceased publication forever. This new journal was clearly a continuation of *Teosofskaia Zhizn'*; the format was identical. *Zhizn' Dukha* no longer made any attempt to identify itself as strictly Theosophical and, as the program on the back cover announced, included articles on "all branches of the sacred sciences." Without using the word *Theosophy*, the new journal still urged its readers to "Love thy neighbor as thyself" and advocated goodness, brotherhood, tolerance, and other Christian and Theosophical virtues.

The pages of *Zhizn' Dukha* were graced with the presence of Vera Ivanovna Kryzhanovskaia, touted as a regular contributor. Kryzhanovskaia was a well-known St. Petersburg writer, the darling of the occult set, and the author of a series of immensely popular romantic and historical novels with extensive spiritualist and esoteric content.[12] The journal continued to carry advertisements for the Smolensk Christian Theosophical Society (which was still extant, although not for long). Several of the regular contributors now sent in articles only with the understanding that they would be printed under pseudonyms. The considerable spiritualist bias of the Society's members became even clearer than before.

It was inevitable that the Smolensk Theosophical Society would soon cease its activity. It collapsed in early 1911, but many of its members continued their occult activities in other organizations. A. V. Bornio joined the Moscow branch of the RTO, Dr. Nikolai Boianus joined K. P. Khristoforova's unaffiliated Theosophical circle in Moscow, Fedor Potekhin attached himself to the independent occultists associated with the hermetic journal *Izida*, contributing to it and to the new *Teosoficheskoe Obozrenie*. The more powerful St. Petersburg RTO and its new journal posed serious competition, however, and Shtal'berg gave up the struggle. The provinces had clearly not been the place from which to launch Russian Theosophy.

Vasilii Bogushevskii and *Teosoficheskoe Obozrenie*

The Smolensk Theosophists began their activity and their journal just one month before the appearance of another Theosophical journal, *Teosoficheskoe Obozrenie*, published in St. Petersburg by Vasilii L'vovich Bogushevskii. This new journal claimed no affiliation with any particular branch or splinter group within the Theosophical Movement, although it took the *devise* of the parent Society, "There Is No Religion Higher than Truth," as its own. It advocated the same principle of the brotherhood of nations and urged the study of comparative religions and the investigation of the psychic powers latent in man. Bogushevskii stated that his journal simply sought to provide interested Russian readers with information about Theosophy in Russia and abroad:

> *Teosoficheskoe Obozrenie* is a free and independent organ of the press and does not have as its goal the formation of a new sect or the dissemination of any sort of specific doctrine; instead, it calls upon every believer, regardless of the religion he espouses, to examine those truths which form the foundations of his own religion. . . . The journal recognizes no authority except reason. The journal does not speak for any Theosophical Society, and none of the extant Societies is responsible for the opinions expressed in its articles.[13]

The stated goal of *Teosoficheskoe Obozrenie* was to acquaint readers with "the all-encompassing world view that is the foundation of all religious systems, philosophies, and sciences." "We are firmly convinced that Russia, too," said Bogushevskii, "will have its own original word to say and will bring to Theosophy its own uniquely Russian element."[14]

Rebus reviewed the new journal: "We are forced to conclude that the acquaintance of the journal's administration with Theosophy is of a rather casual sort." Still, Chistiakov, the editor of *Rebus* and the author of the review, praised it for its "lively selection of articles and the absence of sectarian narrowmindedness in this selection. We are familiar with many Theosophical publications and this [narrowminded] spirit can be seen in them everywhere."[15]

The first few issues certainly contained lively and diverse materials. They included articles by Annie Besant, Dr. Franz Hartmann, Wilhelm Hübbe-Schleiden (then a colleague of Dr. Steiner's in the German Branch), Charles Johnston (Mme Blavatsky's nephew-in-law), Mabel Collins, and Edouard Schuré, all well-known English and European Theosophists, as well as an essay on Spinoza and Theosophy by Bogushevskii, materials on the spiritual education of children, Fedor Potekhin's article on the Dukhobors, and material on Esperanto by Professor Radvan-Rypinskii.[16] The Russian contributions tended toward fiction and devotional essays, on the order of "Two Years in the City of Happiness" by "Strannik" [the Wanderer], and the deservedly anonymous "I Love the Whole World; a Fairytale." A chronicle section gave the details of the Worldwide Theosophical Congress in Munich, held May 18–21, 1907, and was pleased to report that a lecture had been read there on the growing Theosophical Movement in Russia.

In his article on "The Dawn of Theosophy in Russia," Bogushevskii optimistically observed: "Theosophy is gradually beginning to lay a path into Russia, the homeland of its founder, Helena Petrovna Blavatsky. Several circles have been formed in St. Petersburg; they intend to work regularly, read lectures, and disseminate information. Other groups have formed in Moscow, Kiev, Kaluga, and Vladikavkaz. Several articles on Theosophy have been published in the periodical press."[17] He reported on the newly formed Smolensk Society and urged cooperation among all Russian Theosophists. When *Vestnik Teosofii* began publication in January 1908 he reviewed it enthusiastically, but labeled it "very theoretical."[18]

Bogushevskii's *Teosoficheskoe Obozrenie* was an interesting third voice in the Russian Theosophical Movement. If the Smolensk *Teosofskaia Zhizn'* preached Christianity and practiced Spiritualism, and if *Vestnik Teosofii* represented theoretical Theosophy with the odd concession to Russian reality, then the editorial bias of *Teosoficheskoe Obozrenie* was clearly toward practical Theosophy, as practiced by the American Theosophists, then led by Katherine Tingley.[19] Despite Bogushevskii's particular focus, however, the journal continued to accommodate all Theosophical points of view.

Teosoficheskoe Obozrenie was short-lived: it ceased publication in September 1908, after exactly twelve issues. In an effort to recoup his investment, Bogushevskii renamed the journal *Mir*, expanded its program to include popular science, social and political trends, and popular literature, and continued to publish until January 1912. *Rebus*, as usual, had the last word after the almost inevitable demise of Bogushevskii's journal. "Obviously the demand for Theosophy has not yet reached the point where it can provide a sufficiently large contingent of subscribers to support three similar journals," observed the editor.[20]

The failure of *Teosoficheskoe Obozrenie* and the Smolensk *Teosofskaia Zhizn'* was not due entirely to the appearance in 1908 of the superior publication, *Vestnik Teosofii*, or to the growing presence of the RTO. The first two journals simply did not offer primary Theosophical texts in competent translations. Their Russian offerings were weak, derivative, and excessively sentimental. *Teosoficheskoe Obozrenie* did not have the unified vision of an organized Society behind it, while *Teosofskaia Zhizn'* was published by well-intentioned but amateur Theosophists. Distribution was irregular. Neither had a wealthy patron to provide financial support. All three journals had solid competition for the occult readership in the well-established, well-organized, and interesting *Rebus*, whose subscribers numbered in the tens of thousands, and in the other Russian Spiritualist and hermetic journals and newspapers. Being essentially middle-class, educated people, many Theosophists read French, German, or English, and preferred to subscribe to the superior European Theosophical journals.

By 1910 *Vestnik Teosofii* and the Russian Theosophical Society had consolidated their position in the vanguard of the Russian Theosophical Movement. The RTO's beautifully formatted journal, flexible but coherent editorial policy, and easily accessible, inexpensive translations of Theosophical classics easily accommodated the needs not only of the main Society, but those of the independent Theosophical circles as well.

An Independent: Khristoforova's Moscow Circle

There is little information about the independent Theosophical circles in Russia in the first years of the twentieth century. These circles rarely published or even kept notes to become a matter of public record; what records did exist were destroyed or confiscated shortly after the Revolution. The usual sources of such information, memoirs and letters, are not available, since most of the people in these circles were not famous and their personal papers were lost.

Rebus made several references to a large Theosophical circle in Odessa. The Odessa circle may well have been composed primarily of foreigners or Russians of foreign extraction residing in that city; its few communications are signed "Smith" and "Gordon." Another large Theosophical circle in Moscow (with ties to the Smolensk Theosophical Society) was headed by Sergei Dmitrievich Volkov (d. 1909). Volkov, who also claimed to be a Freemason and was considered a charlatan by some, was interested not only in theoretical Theosophy, but in various forms of applied occultism (mentalism, clairvoyance, and hypnotism). Like many independent circles, Volkov's Theosophical circle was interested in many branches of occultism, not only in Theosophy.

The one exception to the general dearth of information is the Moscow circle of Kleopatra Petrovna Khristoforova (d. 1934), a well-to-do woman from Moscow's merchant class. Her circle, while probably not entirely representative of the independent circles as a whole, did reflect the traditional Moscow philosophical bias (as opposed to St. Petersburg's literary emphasis). Some of its participants were members of the Russian Theosophical Society; most were not. The Khristoforova circle is relatively better documented because several leading literary and cultural figures were among its members. It played a subtle but important role in Russian Silver Age culture.

K. P. Khristoforova's circle met at her home near Devich'e Pole in Moscow. Its members included the Symbolist writer Andrei Belyi (Boris Nikolaevich Bugaev, 1880–1934); his mother (and Khristoforova's old friend), Aleksandra Dmitrievna Bugaeva (1858–1922); Belyi's friend, the prominent Theosophist and Argonaut Pavel Batiushkov; the future head of the Russian Anthroposophical Society, Boris Pavlovich Grigorov (1883–1945); Grigorov's soon-to-be wife, Nadezhda Afanas'evna Baryshkina (1885–1964); Ekaterina Mikhailovna Kokhmanskaia (whose own Theosophical circle Belyi began attending in the autumn of 1902); Nina Valentinovna Pshenetskaia (d. 1933), one of Russia's Theosophical pioneers and a translator of Theosophical texts; the historian Mikhail Aleksandrovich Ertel', son of the populist writer, Aleksandr Ertel'; Dr. Nikolai Karlovich Boianus and his wife, Olga; Dmitrii Nedovich, a Hermeticist, occultist, and later Belyi's colleague at the "Musaget" journal, *Trudy i Dni*; Princess Sofiia Urusova, then secretary, later president, of the Moscow branch of the Russian Theosophical Society; an assortment of interested university students; and Elena Pisareva, who frequently visited Moscow from Kaluga and through whom Khristoforova's circle was in touch with the Russian Section of the Theosophical Society. Occasional visitors to this circle included Belyi's literary friends Lev L'vovich Kobylinskii-Ellis (1879–1947) and Aleksei Sergeevich Petrovskii (1881–1958), as well as the famous writer and scholar, Viacheslav Ivanov. Arguably the most influential member of this circle was Anna Mintslova.

After Mme Blavatsky herself, Anna Rudol'fovna Mintslova ((1865–1910?) was certainly the most extraordinary individual in the history of Russian Theosophy. The well-educated daughter of a Moscow barrister, she was aware of her resemblance to the extraordinary Mme Blavatsky and consciously cultivated it.[21] Both women had the same intense blue-grey eyes, the same hypnotic stare, and the same plump hands with tapering fingers. They both wore the same black, baggy garments of ambiguous cut to cover their obesity. Both were driven by a need for attention and desire for power over others. Like Mme Blavatsky, Mintslova claimed to be clairvoyant and frequently experienced hallucinations, trance states, and other paraoccult phenomena; she read palms, and Ekaterina Bal'mont called her "Anna the Prophetess." Mintslova was also hysterical, smothering, demanding, and neurotic. Like Mme Blavatsky, she claimed to have her own Mahatma who guided her spiritual work. She felt herself "chosen" to be the liaison between the Brotherhood of Adepts and the most spiritually advanced Russian Theosophists.

Mintslova began her studies of Theosophy with classic works by Mme Blavatsky, A. P. Sinnett, C. W. Leadbeater, and Mrs. Besant, but soon discovered the teachings of Rudolf Steiner. Peripatetic by inclination (she seemed to have no home of her own, and constantly stayed with friends), she began to frequent Dr. Steiner's European lecture courses and to bring back notes to share with Theosophical friends in Russia. She and her colleague, Elena Pisareva, maintained a direct line to Dr. Steiner through their St. Petersburg friend, Marie von Sivers, who was his secretary. They worked to popularize his variant of Theosophy in the Esoteric Section of the RTO and among intellectual Theosophists, notably in the Moscow circle of Khristoforova.

Various contemporaries have left descriptions of Anna Mintslova. Andrei Belyi probably exaggerated less than usual when he described how

> A heavy and large head would move among us, with yellow disheveled locks rising high above it; and no matter how she tried to comb them, the locks stuck out like serpents, tufting above a browless, enormous forehead; and her small, weak-sighted, and watery blue eyes were narrowed, but open them up, and they became like two wheels, not eyes at all; and when they darkened, they seemed to be bottomless; and they would snap open, and she would sit immobile, horribly reminiscent of those stone sculptures, the female-shaped Scythian statues amid the burnt-out steppes.[22]

Nikolai Berdiaev, whose personal relationship with Mintslova was less intellectually intimate than Belyi's, offered the most sobering description: "She was an ugly, fat woman with bulging eyes. She bore a certain resemblance to Mme Blavatsky. Her appearance was rather repulsive. . . . Mintslova was an intelligent woman, gifted in her own way, and endowed with great ability to approach people; she knew how to speak with whom."[23]

Anna Mintslova was remarkably well connected among the literary elite of the Silver Age, counting among her closest friends the poet Konstantin Bal'mont, his first wife, Ekaterina, the poet Maksimilian Voloshin, and his wife (Ekaterina Bal'mont's niece), Margarita Sabashnikova; Andrei Belyi and Viacheslav Ivanov were her intimates up to the moment of her mysterious disappearance in 1910. She was present at the literary soirées in Ivanov's Tower apartment and acquainted with most major and minor writers of the period. For many she was almost a caricature of the eccentric lady Theosophist, for others she was a spiritual danger (Berdiaev, in particular, found her threatening), and for some she became a guru.

Max Voloshin and Margarita Sabashnikova, recently returned from Europe and enthusiastic about Theosophy, first introduced Mintslova to Viacheslav Ivanov in late 1906. Voloshin had met Mrs. Besant abroad in

1894; he met Mintslova at about the same time. Ivanov's wife, the writer Lidiia Dmitrievna Zinov'eva-Annibal (1872–1907), was fascinated by the exotic Mintslova and began to study the "secret science" under her tutelage. Ivanov himself soon became interested and in a short time was also receiving pages and pages of occult "lessons" dictated by Mintslova's "Voices." For the three years following his wife's death, Mintslova took control of Ivanov's life. His grief, his weakness, and his curiosity made him particularly receptive to her promise that with her spiritual help he would be able to communicate with his beloved wife.

Andrei Belyi had previously met Mintslova both at the home of the Symbolist writer Valerii Briusov in Moscow and at Ivanov's Tower in St. Petersburg, but she became a serious force in his life only in 1908, when he became truly committed to Theosophy. Drawn to Theosophy since 1896, Belyi left the Movement and returned to it several times during the first decade of the twentieth century. By 1908 he had read all the major works of Mrs. Besant, Mme Blavatsky, A. P. Sinnett, C. W. Leadbeater, Dr. Théophile Pascal, and Edouard Schuré, given to him by his mother's friend and Mintslova's intimate, Kleopatra Khristoforova. By 1908 he was well acquainted with the leading Moscow Theosophists and had become an avid reader of *Vestnik Teosofii*, where he was particularly taken by Steiner's *Knowledge of the Higher Worlds and Its Attainment*.[24] That fall he was regularly attending Khristoforova's circle, then directed by Mikhail Ertel', who, like Mintslova, was a follower of Steiner.[25]

Working together, Khristoforova and Mintslova soon convinced Belyi that Mintslova was an agent of "the secret BROTHERHOOD in the Himalayas that observes us all, with the help of radiant forces." She was "inspired by *them*. Kleopatra Petrovna [Khristoforova] strengthened this belief: 'Have courage. . . . You have been chosen as a disciple,'" she told Belyi.[26] The two women, he felt, were clearly preparing him for something important.

In 1909 Mintslova separately proposed to Belyi and Viacheslav Ivanov that they form a secret "Brotherhood of the Knights of Truth" to serve as conduits of Spirit and Truth in order to save the world from Eastern occultists and demonic powers. She showed them pictures of two of Mme Blavatsky's Mahatmas, Koot Hoomi and Master Morya: "This one here is Blavatsky's teacher, and that one is Besant's; you choose—under whose sign do you want to stand?"[27] Her proposal was an eclectic blend of Blavatsky's Theosophy, Steiner's Rosicrucianism, Russian messianism, and her own personal vision. The motifs and images generated by their discussions were echoed later in the literary and philosophical works of both Belyi and Ivanov: the threatening East

(Solov'ev's panmongolism blended with Mintslova's Eastern occultists and Chinese Tatars), secret enemies, demonic illusion, powers of Darkness and Light, knighthood, the chivalric theme, the Rose and the Cross, the spirituality of Russia and Russia's salvation.[28]

Although Mintslova told Ivanov that Belyi was the third leg of their "Mystical Triangle," she did not tell Belyi about Ivanov until the end of January 1910. The two writers, she claimed, were the Rose and the Cross, the representatives of the North and the South, who were to build the new Chivalric Order of Truth.[29] It is not known if Viacheslav Ivanov seriously attempted to recruit anyone at all for Mintslova's Rosicrucian Brotherhood, as she requested. Mintslova approached several individuals, including Nikolai Berdiaev and Aleksandr Blok, apparently unsuccessfully. The enthusiastic Andrei Belyi shared his Theosophical-Rosicrucian expectations with his friends at the Musaget Publishing House: the serious, erudite, and intellectual Emilii Karlovich Metner (1872–1936), critic and head of Musaget; Nikolai Petrovich Kiselev (1884–1965), one of the Argonauts and Musaget's secretary; Mikhail Ivanovich Sizov (1884–1956), a Theosophist devoted to Mintslova and, with Kiselev, an active member of the Russian Spiritualist Society; and Aleksei Petrovskii, Theosophist, librarian, and translator of the German medieval mystic, Jacob Boehme.[30]

Mintslova, aided and supported by her friend Khristoforova, introduced Viacheslav Ivanov into the Moscow circle, the better to continue their Rosicrucian work. Her project failed, however, when Belyi, who had taken Mintslova's plans seriously, was disappointed by the revelation that the mysterious "Other" whom she had been praising was not a learned Rosicrucian sage, but only his old colleague, Viacheslav Ivanov. Belyi complained, "I loved Ivanov, but I saw that he, having accepted many teachings and formulas of the occult world, was playing with these teachings in the manner of a dilettante; and Mintslova was hiding his dilettantism under the cover of responsibility."[31] At the same time Emilii Metner, who resented Mintslova's unilateral exclusion of their friend, Lev Kobylinskii-Ellis, from their group of "knights," warned Belyi about her instability. A sense of tremendous disappointment soon settled over the young Moscow occultists and communicated itself to the high-strung Mintslova. Belyi now saw "Mintslova's fantastic myths, interwoven with everyday life, together with her frequent references to occult brotherhoods," as nothing more than an indication "that we were dealing with an ailing, very nervous, and exhausted woman."[32] He withdrew from the Mystical Triangle.

Mintslova regarded her failure to organize a Russian Rosicrucian Brotherhood among the Symbolist elite as fateful. She convinced herself that she had failed in the mission that "They" had assigned her, and that "They" were subsequently removing her from the physical plane. Suffering from an acute persecution complex, she felt she was being followed by evil forces from the East; strange men in turbans, she claimed, were trying to smother her, kidnap her, sabotage her occult mission.

In 1910 Mintslova left Moscow, then she left Russia. She sent several letters from Germany, and then she disappeared. No one missed her at first because she was constantly traveling; everyone assumed she was staying with someone else. Viacheslav Ivanov and Nikolai Berdiaev later thought she might have gone to Italy and entered a convent with Rosicrucian connections; Andrei Belyi suggested that she had gone to Norway and thrown herself into a fjord (she loved Norway). No one ever saw her again and all attempts to trace her failed.

Mintslova was regarded by some as Steiner's "secret emissary" to Russia. Their relationship before 1909, when Mintslova was satisfied to be Steiner's disciple, appears to have been cordial; their later relationship was complicated by Mintslova's conviction that she had reached a level of initiation as high as Steiner's and was his occult equal; Steiner would have viewed this as hubris and self-delusion. While he certainly felt that the Slavic folk soul had an important role to play in the future of occult science, it is unlikely that the exceedingly sober Steiner would have selected the neurotic and visionary Mintslova to represent him in Russia. Her increasingly subjective interpretation of his teachings would also have precluded his trusting her with such a mission. Still, she did help to popularize Steiner's philosophy in Russia, even if she warned Belyi (ironically, as it became evident) that Steiner was not for him.[33]

Steiner eventually repudiated Mintslova. Belyi reported that other Anthroposophists whom he met later in Dornach claimed she was "an epileptic, a sick and unhappy woman! Her illness took the form of charlatanism; having fallen into the hands of occult societies, she is just such a Charybdis of our movement, as atheism and skepticism of the spirit are its Scylla."[34] "Such individuals as Mintslova," concluded Nikolai Berdiaev, "could wield so much influence only in the culturally elitist atmosphere characteristic of the times, which were permeated by occult tendencies and searches. In this atmosphere there was a great deal of unconscious mendacity and self-deceit, and little love for truth. People wanted to be deceived and seduced."[35] Gurus like Mintslova, until she vanished, catered to those wants.

Kleopatra Khristoforova's Theosophical circle did not long survive Mintslova's disappearance: Khristoforova herself became ill; Mikhail Ertel' had a nervous breakdown; Belyi, Grigorov, Kobylinskii-Ellis, Sizov, and Petrovskii left Khristoforova to form their own Steinerian circle; all of them soon left Russia and traveled to Western Europe to hear in person the lectures of the "Christian Theosophist" Rudolf Steiner, who had displaced Mme Blavatsky from the occult zodiac.

The Russian Anthroposophists: Steiner and Russia

Rudolf Steiner, the son of an Austrian railway official, was born in Kral-jevic (near the Hungarian-Croatian border) on February 27, 1861. A boundlessly energetic philosopher, scholar, and educator, he was a specialist on the scientific works of Goethe and one of the editors of the Goethe Standard Edition. Steiner first became involved with Theosophy in 1900, when the prominent German Theosophists, the Count and Countess von Brockdorff, invited him to speak about Nietzsche to a largely Theosophical audience in Berlin. At the time Steiner was in the process of defining the contours of his own occult system based on the traditions of Western mysticism. Steiner was an excellent and inspiring speaker; he soon became a frequent lecturer at the Brockdorffs' *Theosophische Bibliothek*. There, while lecturing on European mysticism in November 1900, he met the young and attractive Marie von Sivers from St. Petersburg.

Marie von Sivers, who would eventually become Frau Steiner on Christmas Eve 1914, was born on March 14, 1867, in Włotzławek (Warsaw province), Poland, then part of the Russian Empire. She came from a German-Baltic Evangelical family with a tradition of Russian civil and military service. When she was ten years old, her father retired and took the family to St. Petersburg. While studying artistic recitation (she came to be an inspiring speaker), Marie von Sivers had the opportunity to travel and spent considerable time in Western Europe. She translated works by the famous French Theosophist Edouard Schuré; through him she became acquainted with the Theosophy of Mme Blavatsky. Both she and her sister, Olga von Sivers (d. 1917), became fervent Theosophists, finding additional support from their friend and mentor in St. Petersburg, Maria von Strauch-Spettini.

Steiner and Fräulein von Sivers were soon working together at the *Theosophische Bibliothek* in Berlin. They approached Mrs. Besant and Colonel Henry Olcott (then president of the Theosophical Society) at the Theosophical Congress in London in July 1902 to request an official charter for the German branches. Mrs. Besant herself came to Berlin on October 19–21, 1902, to oversee the founding of the German Section. Steiner was elected secretary general of the new section and Marie von Sivers became his assistant.

Over the next few years Steiner took an active and leading role in the

Theosophical Society, using its support, administrative structure, and platform to lay the foundation of his own version of *Geheimwissenschaft*, which he first called "anthroposophy" in late 1902. During this period he lectured ceaselessly to both Theosophical and non-Theosophical audiences in the German-speaking areas of central Europe and Scandinavia; he also wrote three important, programmatic books: *Das Christentum als mystische Tatsache und die Mysterien des Altertums* (1902), *Theosophie* (1904), and *Wie erlangt man Erkenntnisse höherer Welten* (1904).

By 1906 it had become clear that Steiner was diverging from the Theosophical canon as preached by Mrs. Besant, although he was still within most of the boundaries set by Mme Blavatsky's more synthetic Theosophical vision. Steiner's Theosophy gradually minimized the oriental dimension and replaced it with a more Christian vision, although that vision was Gnostic, not traditional, in character. Formally trained in German science and philosophy, Steiner was a more structured thinker than either Mme Blavatsky or Mrs. Besant; his Theosophy was placed over a supporting framework of German idealist thought and scientific method.[36] Steiner opposed dogmatism in occultism and based his own *Geisteswissenschaft*, a systematic approach to "spiritual science," on personal experience and experimentation. While Divine Wisdom was still his goal (as it was also the goal of the Theosophists), his geography of the Path leading to the achievement of that wisdom was different; Steiner's more disciplined Path wound Westward, not Eastward.

Early in his career Steiner came to believe that the Slavic "folk soul" (*die slavische Volksseele*) would play a major role in the future evolution of a spiritual humanity. Himself the author of two significant philosophical works, *Die Philosophie der Freiheit: Grundzüge einer modernen Weltanschauung* (1893) and *Die Rätsel der Philosophie* (1914), he was aware of the various religious and philosophical developments in Russia. He particularly admired the thought of Vladimir Solov'ev, whom he saw as a mediator between East and West.

Steiner's initial source of contact with the Russians was through Marie von Sivers. "Mariia Iakovlevna" maintained the ties that bound her to St. Petersburg and to her particular friends, Maria von Strauch-Spettini and Elena Pisareva, both founding members of the Russian Theosophical Movement. She was also acquainted with Anna Mintslova, Kleopatra Khristoforova, and a handful of other Russian members with close ties to the German Section. When Russians wished to be received by Dr. Steiner, they wrote first to Fräulein von Sivers.[37]

Elena Pisareva was Rudolf Steiner's first major supporter in Russia. Marie von Sivers introduced her to Steiner and to his *Geheimwissenschaft*, first by correspondence and then in person. Pisareva joined the

German Section in 1905. That spring she visited Marie von Sivers in
Berlin, and the two planned to bring Steiner to Russia for a lecture series: "We agreed on a lecture cycle at an estate near Kaluga [Pisareva's
Podborki] for June 1906. It did not come about. It was the year of the
Revolution which followed the war with Japan. The situation was uncertain." Concerned about the disorders in Russia that summer, Rudolf
Steiner prudently chose not to travel there. Nevertheless, "the Russian
friends asked to hold the cycle in Paris, where there has always been a
sizable Russian émigré group. Rudolf Steiner agreed; it was also the year
in which the Theosophists held their general meeting in Paris."[38]

Steiner lectured in Passy and Paris in May and June 1906. The text of
those lectures did not survive, but notes of his cycle of eighteen lectures
on "Esoteric Cosmology," read between May 25 and June 14, were
taken by several of the Russians in attendance, as well as by the French
Theosophist and author, Edouard Schuré, who also attended at
Steiner's and von Sivers' personal invitation.[39] This cycle was especially
important because it represented the final fruits of a critical stage in
Steiner's occult development. It was well attended.

Among those present were Margarita Sabashnikova and Max Voloshin, then on their wedding trip; Konstantin Bal'mont and his wife;
and Nikolai Minskii-Vilenkin. Dmitrii Merezhkovskii and his wife,
Zinaida Hippius, in Paris with Dmitrii Filosofov (Anna Filosofova's
son), asked Margarita Sabashnikova if they might also attend the lectures. The chemistry between the Merezhkovskiis and Steiner was
dreadful. Sabashnikova described their meeting in her memoirs:

> Merezhkovskii came prejudiced against Rudolf Steiner. Zinaida Hippius
> curled up on the couch and observed Steiner in an arrogant manner through
> her lorgnette, as if he were some sort of curious object. Merezhkovskii him-
> self, very excited, interrogated Steiner in the style of an inquisitor. "We are
> naked and poor and thirsty," he cried, "and long for truth." One had the
> feeling, however, that they did not feel at all poor, and were convinced that
> they already had the truth. "Tell us of the ultimate mystery!" bawled Me-
> rezhkovskii, to which Steiner answered, "Only if you tell us of the penulti-
> mate one."[40]

The meeting ended badly, with ill feeling against Merezhkovskii and his
attempt at what the Theosophists felt were "cheap polemics."

After Steiner's Paris lectures for the Russian Theosophists, Elena Pisareva and Anna Mintslova attempted to promote his variant of Theosophy back in Russia. Pisareva organized a small Steiner circle in Kaluga.
Both women brought back and circulated notes from those of Steiner's
European lectures they attended, as well as materials that their friend
from St. Petersburg, Marie von Sivers, sent them.[41] Mintslova translated

Steiner's fundamental text, *Theosophy*, into Russian.[42] She also attempted to persuade Steiner to lecture in Russia in 1908; like the 1906 visit, however, the 1908 visit did not take place.[43] Pisareva's and Mintslova's greatest contribution to Steiner's cause was to share his more coherent variant of Theosophical doctrine with the members of Khristoforova's private circle in Moscow.

Between 1908 and 1912 Steiner worked within the structure and hierarchy of the Theosophical Society and seemed content to do so. He sensed considerable interest among the Theosophists in his brand of esotericism and had no objection to an Anthroposophical workshop under the auspices of the Theosophical Society. He only wanted it understood that the section he led "would never work merely according to set dogmas; it would engage in independent spiritual research, and, in meetings with the whole Society, seek mutual understanding about the cultivation of genuine spiritual life."[44]

His position proved to be divisive. The relationship between Steiner and Mrs. Besant was never particularly cordial or intimate. He viewed her increasingly Hindu inclinations and maternalistic dogmatism as a violation of the Society's spiritual integrity. He was particularly offended by her proclamation of the young Hindu, Jiddu Krishnamurti (1895–1986), an avatar of the Christ; this he saw as a critical misreading of spiritual reality, a "deterioration to a fearsome degree" of the parent Society's integrity. Her establishment in 1911 of the Order of the Star in the East to sponsor Krishnamurti and his mission became the *causa finalis* that heralded the end of Steiner's association with Mrs. Besant. Throughout 1912 he discussed breaking with the Theosophical Society with the various members of the German Section who were fiercely loyal to him; his decision to withdraw was made in early September. In his *Autobiography* he explained:

> Since 1906 things occurred in the [Theosophical] Society—upon whose leadership I had no influence whatever—which had the character of spiritualistic aberrations and made it necessary for me to stress ever more emphatically that the section of the Society led by me had absolutely nothing to do with these things. The climax of all this came when it was asserted that Christ would appear in a new earth-life within a certain Hindu boy. For the propagation of this absurdity a special society, *The Star of the East*, was founded within the Theosophical Society. It was quite impossible for my friends and myself to accept as members of the German Section the members of this *Star of the East*, as they, and more especially Annie Besant the president of the Theosophical Society, wished.[45]

After receiving a telegram from Steiner's section demanding her resignation, Mrs. Besant withdrew the German Section's charter on January 14,

1913. On February 2–3, the originally scheduled Eleventh General Meeting of the German Section of the Theosophical Society in Berlin became the First General Meeting of the newly formed Anthroposophical Society.

The schism was felt not only in Germany, but throughout the national sections. In Russia, where Rudolf Steiner had a small but devoted following, the break did not appear particularly rancorous, although *Vestnik Teosofii* lamented the division:

> We have received sad tidings from the German Section. Over the last year a definitely isolated and somewhat fanatical atmosphere has formed, expressing itself through the refusal of the members of the German Section to recognize the doctrine of Theosophy in any form that does not correspond to the doctrine of the head of the German Section, Dr. Rudolf Steiner. This atmosphere thickened, and it became clear that a schism in the T. S. was imminent. Recently the last act of this sad event was played out: The Council of the German Section expressed its conviction (in a telegram, sent to Adyar), that only the resignation of the President [Mrs. Besant] from her post would allow the continued existence of the T. S.

Reluctantly, *Vestnik Teosofii* concluded, "both for them and for us, it would be better if they organized separately."[46] Anna Kamenskaia, with her strong Eastern interests and her passionate personal devotion to Annie Besant, continued to support the Adyar-based parent Society and the Order of the Eastern Star. Her dominant personality kept the RTO in line. Even Elena Pisareva, despite her close personal ties to Marie von Sivers and her preference for Steiner's Theosophy (she was his primary translator for *Vestnik Teosofii*), sided with Kamenskaia and remained with the parent Society. The loss to the Russian Theosophical Society in terms of membership was minimal; most Russian Theosophists who subsequently became Anthroposophists had never officially registered with the Theosophical Society. The rigorous philosophical basis and the academic elitism of the Steiner variant also made it less broadly appealing than Theosophy in Russia, producing relatively few new converts.

The birthplace of Anthroposophy in Russia was Kleopatra Khristoforova's Theosophical circle. The leading lights of what eventually became the Russian Anthroposophical Society—Andrei Belyi, Mikhail Sizov, Aleksei Petrovskii, Nikolai Kiselev, Lev Kobylinskii-Ellis, Mikhail Ertel', Boris Grigorov (who would head the Moscow branch), and Nadezhda Baryshkina-Grigorova—all came to Rudolf Steiner and Anthroposophy through the primary influence of Elena Pisareva, Anna Mintslova, and Kleopatra Khristoforova, yet the older generation chose not to leave the Theosophical path.[47]

In 1911, when Khristoforova's circle began to dissolve, Boris Grigorov and Lev Kobylinskii-Ellis invited certain of its members to join a separate Steiner study group. This new group added to the growing number of Russian Steinerians the amateur classicist Vladimir Nilender, Egyptologist V. M. Vikent'ev, Mikhail Sizov's wife and sister, Trofim Trapeznikov, the artist Anna Alekseevna (Asya) Turgeneva, her sister Nataliia, the minor critic Dmitrii Nedovich, and several others. By early 1912 the Moscow Steinerians had coalesced around a core group of young Symbolist writers and critics associated with the Musaget Publishing House: Belyi, Kobylinskii-Ellis, Sizov, and Kiselev. Viacheslav Ivanov and Emilii Metner, both deeply involved in Musaget, were interested in, but not totally committed to, Steiner's Anthroposophy. Emilii Metner eventually rejected Steiner's thought and embraced the depth psychology of C. G. Jung; Steiner himself turned down Ivanov's request to join the Anthroposophical group in 1912.[48]

On May 8, 1913, three months after the founding of the Anthroposophical Society in Berlin, the Russian Anthroposophical Society (*Russkoe Antroposoficheskoe Obshchestvo;* RAO) was chartered in Moscow (Registration No. 58). Its charter stated: "The Society has as its goal a fraternal association of people on the grounds of their recognition of the general spiritual foundations of life, on their common investigations into the spiritual nature of man, and on their study of the common nucleus of the world views and faiths of different times and peoples."[49] The original membership was small, but enthusiastic.

The founding meeting of the Russian Anthroposophical Society took place in Moscow on September 7/20 (O.S./N.S.), 1913, the eve of the feast of the Birth of the Blessed Virgin, in a basement room next to the Church of the Dormition of the Virgin Among the Graves, on Mertvyi pereulok, 13 (now Pereulok N. A. Ostrovskogo). All of the women wore white. A police officer was present to observe order. Margarita Sabashnikova had come from Germany, from Steiner himself, for the ceremony. She read Vladimir Solov'ev's "Three Encounters," a narrative poem in which he described his three meetings with Sophia, the Wisdom of God; afterward she spoke of Russia's mission.

The newly organized Russian Anthroposophists assumed that the Russian Society would be named for the mystic philosopher Vladimir Solov'ev. "We asked Rudolf Steiner for a name for the working group in Moscow, and expected it to be named for Vladimir Solov'ev or another great mystic," wrote Margarita Sabashnikova. "We were astonished, even displeased, as we heard the name 'Mikhail Lomonosov.' Whoever would have thought of Mikhail Lomonosov!"[50]

Steiner had suggested "Mikhail Lomonosov" for a good reason. Mikhail Vasil'evich Lomonosov (1711–1765)—Russian scientist, scholar, critic, and poet—was the quintessential man of the Russian Enlightenment. A peasant by birth, he emerged from obscurity to become an internationally known member of the newly formed St. Petersburg Academy of Sciences. Lomonosov was to Russian literature and culture what Peter the Great was to Russian government and society. He rejected the passivity and spiritual conservatism of the Russian Middle Ages and brought the Enlightenment, the "New Age," to Russia. Steiner explained: "There is a different regent of earth life for every epoch, as it were; one regent follows another. Until 1879 the spirit acting out of the spiritual world was the one we call the spirit Gabriel, if a name is to be used. From 1879 onwards it was the spirit we call Michael. It is Michael who directs events in our times."[51] From the Anthroposophical point of view, "Mikhail" Lomonosov was the embodiment of the "Michaelic Spirit," which uses intellect and reason to attain clairvoyance; thus he was the logical choice to inspire the new Anthroposophical Lodge in Moscow.

The question of whether or not the first Russian lodge accepted Steiner's choice has not been completely settled. Sabashnikova, who was present at the founding of the RAO and who continued to work within the Society until she left for Germany in 1922, insisted in her memoirs that they did. M. Zhemchuzhnikova, a Moscow Anthroposophist who was only fourteen when the Russian Society was formed and who attended her first Anthroposophical lecture only after the Revolution, claimed that the Moscow Anthroposophists decided to name the Moscow Lodge for Vladimir Solov'ev against Steiner's advice. According to Zhemchuzhnikova, only after the Revolution, when the Moscow Lodge split into two, did the practical Anthroposophists (under the leadership of M. P. Stoliarov, K. N. Bugaeva, and V. O. Anisimova-Stanevich) take the name "Mikhail Lomonosov," while the esoteric Anthroposophists (under the continuing leadership of Boris Grigorov) retained the name "Vladimir Solov'ev."[52]

In 1912, before the Anthroposophical Society was founded, the Musaget Steinerians had established their own press, called "Dukhovnoe Znanie" (Spiritual Knowledge), as an alternative to the RTO Press and Suvorin's popularizing "Novyi Chelovek" (New Man). After the Russian Anthroposophical Society received its official charter in spring 1913, Dukhovnoe Znanie became publicly affiliated with it, claiming in its advertising that it adhered to the same principles served by the Anthroposophical Society. Dukhovnoe Znanie was a branch of Emilii Metner's modernist Musaget Publishing House; the editorial offices of the Symbolist journal *Trudy i Dni*, the philosophical and culturological journal *Logos*, Dukhovnoe Znanie, and Musaget itself were all located at Prechistenskii Boulevard, 31, apartment 9. Dukhovnoe Znanie published theosophical and esoteric texts, which, according to an advertising insert, touched on "problems of the Spirit, the tasks and foundations of spiritual culture, the manifestation of the spiritual powers of man, classics of the past, which have preserved evidence of spiritual knowledge, and the works of contemporary authors." They included Margarita Sabashnikova's book on St. Serafim of Sarov, her translation of Meister Eckhart, Aleksei Petrovskii's translation of Jacob Boehme's *Aurora*, Andrei Belyi's answer to Emilii Metner's critique of Steiner (published by Musaget), and numerous translations of the major works of Rudolf Steiner (see bibliography).

An event of great importance to the Anthroposophical Society as a whole took place on the same day that the RAO held its founding meeting: on September 20, 1913, Rudolf Steiner laid the foundation stone of the Anthroposophical temple on a hill at the edge of the Swiss town of Dornach, not far from Basel.[53] It was to be called the "Goetheanum." Steiner first contemplated such a building in 1911, when he discovered that ordinary theaters were unsuitable for staging the mystery dramas that had become an integral part of his spiritual work. Symbolic, archetypal, and highly abstract, these mystery plays served as an aesthetic prelude to his more important lecture cycles.[54] Steiner conceived of a special, "new" style of building as the proper physical setting for the Anthroposophical mystery dramas.

That Rudolf Steiner named his Anthroposophical temple in Dornach the Goetheanum was a reminder of the identity he felt between his and Goethe's spiritual-scientific work and of the importance of "Goetheanism" as a concept in Steiner's own thought. The Goetheanum was also sometimes called the "Johannesbau," after an important character in Steiner's mystery dramas. (Another character from the dramas, Benedictus, gave his name to the Petrograd Lodge of the Russian Anthroposophical Society, headed by Boris Lehmann.)

Anthroposophists from seventeen countries lived with Steiner in the Anthroposophical community in Dornach and helped to build the Goetheanum. Among them were several Russians who had joined Steiner in 1911 and 1912, had become members of his new Anthroposophical Society while abroad, and now were building the Goetheanum with their own hands. These included (at various times) Andrei Belyi, his wife, the artist Asya Turgeneva, her sister Natasha Turgeneva, her husband Aleksandr Mikhailovich Pozzo (1882–1941), Trofim Trapeznikov, Margarita Sabashnikova, and Mikhail Sizov; Max Voloshin also visited. The Russian Anthroposophists carved wood, etched glass, hauled materials, painted, and took their turn at night watch. From Dornach they welcomed the formation of a Russian Anthroposophical Society in Moscow.

In 1912 and 1913 Rudolf Steiner gave two series of lectures in Helsingfors; both series included special presentations for Russian members.[55] Russians of both Theosophical and Steinerian persuasion came from St. Petersburg and Moscow to hear him speak; they were joined by other Russians who had been following Steiner as he lectured throughout Europe and Scandinavia. The 1913 series attracted more than forty Russians, among them Nikolai Berdiaev, who was profoundly interested in Anthroposophy and in Steiner at the time. Berdiaev received a more hospitable reception from Steiner than Viacheslav Ivanov had in Basel the previous September.

Steiner's Helsingfors lectures brought several new members to Anthroposophy, including Boris Lehmann, Margarita Sabashnikova's friend from St. Petersburg and the future head of the Benedictus Lodge in Petrograd, and Aleksandr Pozzo, who would become Andrei Belyi's brother-in-law. The 1913 lectures also attracted Kleopatra Khristoforova, Asya and Natasha Turgeneva, Andrei Belyi, Mikhail Sizov, Kobylinskii-Ellis, Trapeznikov, and Vikent'ev. After the lectures, the Russians would gather in Belyi's rooms, and he, as one of Steiner's own students, would go through the materials and explain the more esoteric complexities.

To the Russians Steiner spoke of the importance of the Slavic folk soul as a spiritual bridge between the passive Orient and the active Occident. The religious thought of the Orient belongs to the past; the philosophical-scientific thought of the Occident belongs to the present; the Slavic soul will bridge the two and create a pathway to a spiritual future (in the Sixth Post-Atlantean Age). More than any other national soul, claimed Steiner, the Slavic folk soul strives to realize the world of the spirit. Being still very young, the Slavic soul experiences the pull of material existence and (because of its closeness to the Aryan soul) the sway of oriental thought; therein lies a certain danger. But when it finally manifests itself fully and becomes independent of Western materialism and Eastern passivity, the noble and beautiful Russian soul will have much to say to the world. Steiner pointed out the importance of Tolstoi, Dostoevskii, and Vladimir Solov'ev for the occidental spiritual impulse; he felt that those thinkers had a great deal to say to the West. Steiner's sympathy for and knowledge of Russian culture, his understanding of the "Mission of Russia," endeared him to his Russian followers.

The Russian Anthroposophical Movement continued to grow, but very slowly. Although it never attracted a large group of adherents, those who chose to embrace it tended to be more intellectually rigorous and philosophically inclined than those who chose Theosophy. The Russian Anthroposophists tended to be well educated; a higher percentage of academics, philosophers, and writers were among them than among the Theosophists, who were more likely to be from the professional classes, the civil service, and the gentry. Russian Anthroposophy was a remarkably homogeneous movement, attracting specifically a small core of intellectual seekers who came to the problem of Russia's

crisis of culture and consciousness through the focus of German idealism, cultural philosophy, and European cosmopolitanism. University
trained, saturated with neo-Kantianism, steeped in Troitskii, Hartmann,
Windelband, Wundt, and Höffding, but still responsive to a religious
urge and the creative impulse, they demanded a coherent methodology,
scientific discipline, and aesthetic style in their occultism.[56]

Despite their respect for oriental thought, the Russian Anthroposophists distrusted oriental elements ("panmongolism") in Russian culture; they were no less dissatisfied with its overtly "Westernizing" elements (excessive materialism and rationalism). On the whole they were
pro-Slav and wanted to build on the Slavophile tradition without being
trapped in the cul-de-sac of traditional dichotomies (the masses versus
the intelligentsia, Slavophiles versus Westernizers, and so forth). They
were "synthesizers"; they emphasized "creative will" as the catalyst that
would transform a stagnating Russia into a synthesis of the finest features of both Eastern and Western culture. "Its geographic location
places Russia between two extreme, monolithic cultures—between the
materialist countries of the West and the passive, world-denying countries of the East. It is appropriate that Russia creatively unite these
extremes," wrote Anthroposophist Nikolai Belotsvetov.[57] Because
Steiner's contact with Russians was in fact contact with the God-seeking
intelligentsia, his theory of the Slavic folk soul not surprisingly reflected
many features of this synthetic Slavophilism.

Despite their hopes for Russian culture and their good intentions
(more or less the same hopes and intentions, expressed in different imagery, as those of the rest of Russia's creative intelligentsia), the Anthroposophists were perceived by their society as being effete and recondite.
In the St. Petersburg daily, *Rech'*, Dmitrii Filosofov attacked the Musaget Steinerians for their withdrawal from Russian reality:

> The falseness, the futility, and the non-historicity of the Musagetians consists
> of the fact that, in a country thirsting for the building of culture, where even
> aged graybeards destroy in the name of an unclear future, some refined indi-
> viduals, "burdened by the victories of (not even their own, but Western) civi-
> lization," strive toward contemplative peace, toward Buddhism, and Rudolf
> Steiner, and neo-Platonism. Russia has aged graybeards, while the Mus-
> agetians keep talking about the end of the beginning, or they start building,
> as Ellis and Andrei Belyi, together with Steiner, are building, some sort of
> Indo-European temple near Basel. . . . And our unwashed Russia is left aside
> somewhere. There is no room for Russia in Rudolf Steiner's temple near
> Basel.[58]

Although they lived in a highly rarefied atmosphere, the Russian Anthroposophists exerted an influence disproportionate to their small
numbers. Victor Fedjuschin estimates that the number of Russian An-

throposophists on the eve of the Revolution was actually less than a hundred.[59] Many of them, however, were highly visible and respected *intelligenty*—writers, professors, scholars, and artists. Like the Theosophists, the Socialists, the God-seekers, and the God-builders, they, too, were convinced of Russia's important cultural mission and inspired by an optimistic vision of Russia's radiant future. They left an indelible mark on the intellectual history of their time, and the history of Silver Age culture cannot be written without them.

1. Mme Blavatsky, at the time of writing *Isis Unveiled* (1877)

2. Mme Blavatsky with her sister, Vera Zhelikhovskaia; behind them are Mme Blavatsky's niece, Vera Johnston, and her husband, Charles; on the right is Colonel Olcott

3. Mrs. Annie Besant in 1885

4. Vsevolod Solov'ev, author of *Sovremennaia zhritsa Izidy* (1892)

5. Anna Mintslova, seated with the writer and scholar, Viacheslav Ivanov; seated with them is the writer and composer Mikhail Kuzmin; immediately behind Kuzmin is Margarita Sabashnikova (?), and family members

6. Andrei Belyi, the Symbolist writer and leading
Anthroposophist in the 1920s

7. Aleksandr Aksakov, leading Russian Spiritualist

8. Viktor Pribytkov, Russian Spiritualist and founder of the journal *Rebus*

9. "Alba," Anna Kamenskaia, President of the Russian Theosophical Society

10. Elena Pisareva, Russian Theosophist; she was one of the first to introduce Rudolf Steiner into Russia

11. Founder of the Anthroposophical Society, Rudolf Steiner, with his wife, Marie von Sivers-Steiner

8-й годъ изданія.

ВѢСТНИКЪ ТЕОСОФІИ

РЕЛИГІОЗНО-ФИЛОСОФСКО-
НАУЧНЫЙ ЖУРНАЛЪ.

Satyât Nâsti Paro Dharmah

(Нѣтъ религіи выше истины).

7 іюля—7 августа.

ПЕТРОГРАДЪ.

1915.

№ 7—8.

12. Title page of *Vestnik teosofii*, chief organ of the RTO

Годъ 1-й   Мартъ.   № 6.

Теософическое Обозрѣніе

Путь къ Всемірному Братству

журналъ,

посвященный

Братству человѣчества, теософіи

и изученію

этики, философіи, наукъ и искусствъ.

Содержаніе № 6.

АДРЕСЪ РЕДАКЦІИ

С.-Петербургъ, Васильевскій Островъ, 6 линія, д. 5.

1908.

13. Title page of unaffiliated journal, *Teosoficheskoe obozrenie*

Теософская жизнь.

Ежемѣсячное издание, посвящено Теософскому движенію.

Изученію философіи, наукъ и религій.

СТРЕМИСЬ КЪ ИСТИНѢ

№ 10-11 ІЮНЬ—ІЮЛЬ. 1908.

СОДЕРЖАНІЕ:

14. Title page of *Teosofskaia zhizn'*, chief organ of the Smolensk Theosophists

Five

Theosophical Doctrine: An Outline

THE UNDERLYING PREMISE of Theosophy is that there exists a single, universal occult tradition (the Secret Doctrine), ancient but ageless, on which all religions, past and present, are in part based. This ancient "wisdom-tradition," claim Theosophists, unites religion, science, and philosophy into one grand synthesis that explains everything: God, the Universe, Man, Being, and Creation. This comprehensive worldview, "a mine of entirely trustworthy knowledge from which all religions and philosophies have derived whatever they possess of truth," has always been known to the great religious figures and spiritual adepts of the world, from the ancient Egyptian Magi to Mme Blavatsky herself.[1] Mme Blavatsky always insisted that this "mother doctrine" was not a religion (unless it was a "religion of reason"), but a belief system based on absolute knowledge.

As such a belief system, Theosophy is a form of gnosis. It conceives of itself not as a faith or an ecstatic revelation, but as "esoteric knowledge" and "spiritual science" (Rudolf Steiner's *Geisteswissenschaft*).[2] The profoundly gnostic worldview of Theosophy is especially clear in the cosmogenesis and anthropogenesis that Mme Blavatsky presents in her commentaries to the "Stanzas of Dzyan"; these "Stanzas" form the basis of her massive study, *The Secret Doctrine*.[3] Later major Theosophical texts (Mrs. Besant's *Ancient Wisdom* and *Esoteric Christianity*, A. P. Sinnett's *Esoteric Buddhism*, and Rudolf Steiner's *Theosophy* and *Outline of Occult Science*) all attempt to give system and coherence to Theosophy as originally outlined in *The Secret Doctrine* and in Mme Blavatsky's earlier occult epic, *Isis Unveiled*; the basic principles of Theosophical doctrine, however, are all contained in her two fundamental works.

Theosophical cosmology—its understanding of the origin, structure, and dynamics of the universe—is complex, intricate, and, at times, disconcertingly contradictory.[4] While Theosophical literature boasts numerous books and articles about its finer doctrinal points, and while some general summaries have been attempted by pro-Theosophists and anti-Theosophists, few efforts have been made to provide a general outline of the doctrine by non-Theosophists for non-Theosophists, particularly with any scholarly rigor. Yet, if Theosophy's particular role in the philosophical fermentation of the Russian Silver Age is to be understood, one must understand the idiosyncratic worldview that informs Theosophical thought. An acquaintance with this worldview can illuminate certain dark corners of Russian Symbolism and expand the cultural framework in which we understand the God-seeking of the Russian Silver Age.

What Is Modern Theosophy?

Briefly stated, the Theosophical doctrine, as originally conceived by Mme Blavatsky, is a modern form of metaphysical monism, pantheism, and emanationism. As such, it traces all existence back to emanations of a single reality and identifies God with the Universe. The human soul, likewise an emanation of this single reality, transmigrates through an enormous number of lifetimes, first downward into matter, then upward into spirit, each incarnation shaped by the karma generated by good or evil acts. The present era of earth history marks a turning point at which the downward march of humanity into matter must be reversed; enlightened individuals, aided by the revelations of Theosophical doctrine, are ready to begin the ascent to the realm of the spirit.

All-embracing, Theosophy derives its particular psychology and complex cosmology from sacred Hindu texts, mystery religions, Gnosticism, neo-Platonism, and the vast body of Western occultism, both ancient and modern, with interpolations from the natural and social sciences, comparative religion, archaeology, medicine, and evolutionism. The result is an unusual blend of pantheism, occultism, and facile rationalism. Vastly tolerant itself of other creeds and even of atheism, Theosophy was absolutely unacceptable to the Christian church, especially to the Orthodox Christianity of Russia.

The exotic vocabulary that distinctively colors Theosophical cosmology is taken generally from Buddhism because, as A. P. Sinnett explained, "Buddhism remained in closer union with the esoteric doctrine than any other popular religion."[5] Mme Blavatsky made it clear, however, that her Theosophy did not derive from Buddhism in its traditional, orthodox form; instead, she postulated an *esoteric* Buddhism whose vocabulary and cosmology are similar to, but not identical with, those of traditional Buddhism. This esoteric Buddhism was conveniently hidden from the profane eyes of the uninitiated (as well as from legitimate Sanskrit and Pali scholars who might contradict Theosophical exegesis). The following exposition outlines the basic tenets of modern Theosophy and considers the manner in which its worldview accounts for God, the Universe, and Man.

Theosophy and God

For the Theosophists, the Divine Principle is unknowable, undefinable, and ineffable. It has many names, and may be called the One Absolute Reality, the Infinite and Eternal, the Omnipresent Principle, the Original Creative Impulse, the Primal Source, the Abyss, the One Unity, the Divine Thought. It is unborn and undying, the source and content of all. Everything from the macrocosm to the microcosm is but a differentiated or transformed aspect of this One Unity and contains some element of its Truth and Nature.[6] The Divine is the All in All and cannot be comprehended by human thought.

This One Unity of Absolute Being and Nonbeing simply *is*. This Primal Source, as the First or Great Monad, periodically manifests itself in a finite series of emanations of lesser monads without diminishing Itself in any way.[7] Here Theosophy grafts Gnosticism onto neo-Buddhism, for the initial emanation of the Divine Principle, in most Theosophical paradigms, is the First Logos, or the Primal Word. The Divine Principle *thinks* the paradigm of the universe, then *speaks* the word of creation, and then the word, as sound, becomes the matter of the cosmos. Thus divine thought becomes creative word, and creative word becomes dense matter. This refined form of Gnostic emanationism was retained in the Christian tradition and, in modified form, can be found in the opening verses of the Gospel of St. John.[8]

As Divine Thought reveals Itself in a sevenfold process, it moves from the perfect to the less perfect, first creating spiritual Essences that will control the order of the Cosmos, then the Cosmos itself, then Nature, then Matter.[9] Matter, as the opposite and imperfect end of Spirit, is called Darkness and Evil. Darkness and Evil, however, are relative concepts in Theosophy, being not the opposite of Divinity, but only the most distant and hence most imperfect and distorted forms of Divine emanation.

From the One Life emanate individual lives, from the Universal Over-Soul (Mme Blavatsky's *Anima Supra-mundi*) emanate individual souls; these divine sparks are wrapped in matter and become microcosmic human monads. The human monad is thus "a god in the animal form";[10] it contains "within itself germinally, or in a state of latency, all the divine powers and attributes" of God, albeit trapped within a material, physical shell.[11] As an emanation of the Divine, each microcosmic human monad duplicates perfectly the macrocosmic Great Monad. Each human monad, or soul, is thus more than the mirror of God; it *is* God. The human monad's real self is eternal and one with the Universe. Divinity resides a priori not only in every man, but in every atom of the

Universe, since all is an emanation of the Divine. Pantheistic in its apprehension of Divinity as permeating all of creation (even of being identified with it), Theosophy rejects the idea of a personal God or individual immortality, accepting only an all-embracing One Divine Principle that informs everything.

Theosophy and the Universe

The Universe of the Theosophists, based on a Buddhist paradigm, is characterized by periodicity and pulsation and ruled by the law of cycles. Symbolized by the circle and the spiral, the Universe is the greatest example of the cyclical nature of Being, for "Nature works always in complete curves, and travels always in paths which return into themselves."[12] Being and Nonbeing alternate in a cycle of *manvantaras,* or periods of manifestation and activity, separated from each other by *pralayas,* or periods of dissolution (obscuration) and rest.

A complete cycle of *manvantaras* and *pralayas,* according to Mme Blavatsky, is called a Day and a Night of Brahma, or the Waking and Sleeping of the Universe. She cites 308,448,000 human years as the duration of a single *manvantara*. To this she adds that "14 'Manvantaras' *plus* the period of one *Satya Yuga* make ONE DAY OF BRAHMA, or a complete [major] Manvantara and make . . . 4,320,000,000 years." When 360 Days and Nights of Brahma have passed, a Year of Brahma is completed. One Age of Brahma, or a *Maha-Kalpa*, being 100 Years of Brahma, reaches into the trillions, even quadrillions of human years.[13] Huge blocks of time, incomprehensible to the human mind, are involved in the existence of the universe. Such enormous numbers create a sense of eternity; nevertheless, this near-eternity is ultimately finite, for the trillions of years pass in an alternation of activity and dissolution, and finally the universe itself dissolves and rests. Eventually the universe will become manifest again and another cycle of equally unimaginable duration will begin. The cycles continue without end.

During each *manvantara*, each solar system, or planetary chain, goes through a cycle of seven planetary reincarnations; this is described as One Revolution of the Wheel. On each of the seven planets there are seven waves of seven kingdoms of nature (various degrees of mineral, vegetable, animal, human, and superhuman); the seventh wave is Humanity (the human monads). On each planet Humanity consists of seven root races; each root race has seven sub-races; each sub-race has seven branches. Between planetary rounds there is a minor *pralaya* while the planets rest. Each planetary incarnation is "under the supervision and guidance of special 'Builders' and 'Watchers'—the various *Dhyan-*

Chohans [divine intelligent Essences charged with supervision of the Cosmos]."[14] According to Theosophical cosmology, Humanity is currently in the fourth round, the Earth incarnation, and experiencing the fifth root race, the Aryan. The Slavs are the seventh sub-race (i.e., the youngest branch) of the Aryan root race; their cosmic duty, or mission (dharma), based on the Slavic folk soul's ability to conceptualize and to receive the contents of other cultures, is to assist in the realization of a more spiritualized humanity that will be achieved with the sixth root race.

In the Theosophical paradigm Man is a god who, pulled by desires, has descended from spirit into the coils of matter and is working his way out of material existence back to his spiritual home. Theosophy's understanding of matter, particularly in its relationship to spirit, is profoundly Gnostic: Spirit is a relatively positive value, while matter, associated in this world with "evil," is a relatively negative value that must be overcome. "The body is the tomb of the soul," wrote the ancient Gnostics; "the body is the sepulchre, the prison of the soul," wrote Mme Blavatsky.[15] Like the Gnostics, the Theosophists interpreted the Fall as "the Fall of Spirit into generation [matter], not the Fall of mortal man" into sin.[16]

During the Revolution of the Wheel the human monads, as they move from planet to planet, are Pilgrim-Souls that descend from spirit into matter and ascend back to spirit through a series of reincarnational cycles.[17] The Universe, explained Mme Blavatsky,

> manifests periodically, for purposes of the collective progress of the countless *lives*, the outbreathing of the One *Life*; in order that through the *Ever-Becoming*, every cosmic atom in this infinite Universe, passing from the formless and the intangible, through the mixed natures of the semi-terrestrial, down to matter in full generation, and then back again, reascending at each new period higher and nearer the final goal; that each atom, we say, *may reach through individual merits and efforts* that plane where it re-becomes the one unconditioned ALL. But between the Alpha and the Omega there is the weary "Road" hedged in by thorns, that "goes down first, then
>
> > Winds up hill all the way
> > Yes, to the very end."[18]

Only by completing such a journey can the Pilgrim-Soul become a fully conscious divine agent. Employing the metaphor of the journey, this pilgrimage of the soul expresses a divine archetype in the Jungian sense; in the Theosophical sense, it microcosmically expresses a macrocosmic reality. The world's great myths of the dying and resurrected gods (such as Osiris, Dionysus, Attis, and Christ) thus become Theosophical symbols, expressions in metaphorical human terms of the greater Drama of the Soul: the soul's descent into the illusion and darkness of matter, its comprehension of the illusory nature of the material world, its realization that behind the manifestations in imperfect matter one can "read" a noumenal truth, and, finally, its conscious and freely desired return to the light of the Divine One.[19]

On each planet the Pilgrim-Soul, or human monad, undergoes a complicated evolutionary sequence, involving, according to Mme Blavatsky's estimate, some eight hundred incarnations. The present Earth incarnation is the round in which the human monad penetrates most deeply into matter. "The essential mission of this epoch of civilization is to adapt man to the physical plane to develop reason and practical logic, to immerse intelligence in physical matter so that matter may be understood and finally mastered."[20] Once this mission has been accomplished, "evolution has reached its acme of physical development, crowned its work with the perfect physical man, and, from this point, begins its work spirit-ward."[21] This is, in fact, the reason that Mme Blavatsky's Mahatmas, the adepts of the Great White Brotherhood, chose this historical moment to reveal Theosophy to the masses through their disciple: the human monads have completed their descent into matter, and are now ready to receive knowledge of the Secret Doctrine that will guide them in their journey "spirit-ward" toward their ultimate reunion with the Divine One.

Following the greater cyclical pattern of *manvantara* and *pralaya*, the alternating manifestations of the seven root races on each planet are also separated from each other by periods of obscuration. The approach of such a period is signaled by cataclysms of fire or water, eschatological signs, and a general sense of impending apocalypse. Theosophy predicted that the Aryan root race, the fifth, most material race in the Earth incarnation, had already reached the zenith of "physical intellectuality," the highest point of its civilization, and was coming to the end of its particular cycle. History would now move into a period of "obscuration," accompanied by chaos and cataclysm.

From the Theosophical point of view, this physical intellectuality, uninformed by spirit, was clearly manifested in the materialism and scientific positivism that characterized European culture at the end of the nineteenth century. Having reached this point, humanity's progress toward "absolute evil" (in Theosophical terms, the monad's completed involution, or descent, into matter) would be arrested and the civilization of the fifth root race destroyed. "When physical intellect, unguarded by elevated morality, runs over into the proper region of spiritual advancement, . . . natural law provides for its violent repression," wrote Sinnett.[22] Given the intellectual and political climate of fin de siècle Europe, given the sinister atmosphere of senseless evil, rampant materialism, and the much-heralded death of God, the Theosophical view of human evolution offered a seemingly coherent explanation of why things were bad, as well as hope that things at their worst must cease. This explanation fed the general eschatological expectations of the age. In Russia, given the innate tendency toward philosophical apocalypticism, given the social and political upheavals caused by the Russo-Japanese War, the Revolution of 1905, and the First World War, and given the growing rift between positivism and idealism, all viewed through the focus of the Russian religious renascence, the Theosophical interpretation of events seemed logical enough to many.

Theosophy and Man

On the basis of the occult principle of correspondences ("That which is above is like that which is below, to perpetuate the mystery of the One Thing," we read in the *Tabula Smaragdina* of Hermes Trismegistus), the human microcosm replicates the macrocosm of the greater universe. Man is ternary in his essence, consisting of matter, intellect, and spirit (or body, soul, and spirit), and septenary in his evolutionary composition. The seven principles of man, which constitute an upper, eternal, spiritual triad, and a lower, mortal, physical quaternary, are:

Spiritual Principles:
1. *Atma*. Pure, Universal Spirit. An emanation of the Absolute.
2. *Buddhi*. Spiritual Soul. The vehicle of Universal Spirit.
3. Higher *Manas*. Mind. Intelligence. Human, or Consciousness Soul.

Physical Principles:
4. *Kama Rupa*. (Lower *Manas*), or Animal Soul, the seat of animal desires and passions. Line of demarcation between the mortal and immortal elements. The agent of Will during the lifetime.
5. *Linga Sharira*. Astral Body (vehicle of life). Sentient soul.
6. *Prana*. The Etheric Double. Life essence, vital power. Matter as Force.
7. *Rupa*. The Dense Body. Gross, physical matter.

The three lowest principles—the physical, etheric, and astral bodies—exist in the phenomenal world of space, matter, and time. They constitute the *material* man. The reincarnational cycles are manifested in these three bodies, " 'the three worlds' through which lies the pilgrimage of the soul, again and again repeated. In these three worlds revolves the wheel of human life, and souls are bound to that wheel throughout their evolution, and are carried by it to each of these worlds in turn."[23]

The two intermediary principles of the higher and lower *Manas* are the *mental* principles, the highest *human* aspect of God in man. The further evolution of these two principles belongs to the future of the human race, although some chosen vessels, well advanced in spiritual evolution, may attain them now. In most human beings, however, the higher *Manas* is not yet developed.[24] The sixth and seventh principles are the *spiritual* planes. "What lies beyond on the sixth and seventh planes is hidden in the unimaginable light of God."[25] In time man will develop all seven principles and become perfect; this will happen at the end of the seven times seventh round of reincarnations, at which time the spiritually developed individual will be God.

Theosophical doctrine further distinguishes between a lower and a higher human Ego; the Ego it defines simply as man's sense of "I am." The lower, mortal, personal Ego, incorporated in the three lower bodies, is associated with a particular historical incarnation, and is called "personality." The higher, immortal, impersonal Ego, associated with the higher bodies, remains unchanged through the reincarnational sequence, and is called "individuality."

Since the universe and man are septenary in structure and function, the planes of existence are also seven. These seven planes are:

1. Physical Plane
2. Astral Plane
3. Mental (Manas or Devachanic) Plane
4. Intuitional (Buddhic) Plane
5. Spiritual (Nirvanic) Plane
6. Monadic (Para-nirvanic) Plane
7. Divine (Maha-para-nirvanic) Plane

All seven planes exist simultaneously, although man has not yet become sufficiently "spiritualized" in this Earth incarnation to perceive more than three or (in some highly advanced individuals) four planes.

Man is constantly aware of the physical plane because his gross and etheric bodies (which sustain the life function) and his animal desires dwell in it. The physical senses, however, are no reliable measure of reality, the physical plane being only one of several planes, and the least refined at that. Man becomes aware of other planes only when he alters his consciousness (whether by spiritual exercise, madness, drugs, dreams, or death).

What Theosophy terms the "astral world" or the "astral plane" is "not a place, but a *state*, or condition, of existence. It surrounds us and we are immersed in it while we live on Earth."[26] The individual is able to perceive the astral plane passively through dreams, drugged states, or insanity, and actively through consciously developed spiritual sight. The occultist can train his astral body to leave the gross body under certain circumstances of trance or sleep; it is then free to travel and act on the astral plane (astral projection).

Feelings, ideas, and thoughts experienced in the physical world exist on the astral plane as concrete animal forms: Steiner explained that "a feeling of hatred against another being appears [on the astral plane] as an attacking demon," while "a lie in the physical world becomes an agent of destruction in the astral world. A lie is a murder in the astral world."[27] Thus every *idea* or *thought*, good and harmful, assumes a visible *form* on the astral plane; the act of thought becomes an act of actual creation. The imperishable astral impression of every thought, feeling, and action since the Earth incarnation began is preserved as "living tableaux" on the Akashic Record. For those with "supersensible sight," the Akashic Record is an open book in which world history literally comes to life.

Events on the astral and physical planes are closely, although inversely, related: the one is the mirror image of the other. Thus the number 1,000,000 in the physical world is the number 0000001 on the astral plane, and the harmless thought, "Enfranshish," to take an example from Andrei Belyi's "astral novel," *Peterburg*, becomes the dangerous demon, "Shishnarfne." Life on the astral plane is also lived in reverse order. Thus, "all that we throw out of ourselves into the astral world at one time will reappear in times to come, on the physical plane. What we sow in the astral world we reap on Earth in future times."[28]

Finally, the appearance of objects on the astral plane is quite different from their form on the physical plane; in the astral world one perceives material objects from all sides at once. Moreover, certain forms of matter, invisible to the physical eye, become visible to the supersensible eye on the astral plane. Every material object also has an astral counterpart, being in effect doubled. Some occultists describe the astral plane as the fourth dimension.

Those who are able to penetrate the astral plane learn that "each living creature is surrounded with an atmosphere of its own, usually called its aura." The human body produces (as does every animate and inanimate object) an aura, a radiant energy field that "is seen as an oval mass of luminous mist of highly complex structure," a cloud of color and light.[29] A trained occultist who can project his astral body to the astral plane can "read" a person's aura by its colors, and can interpret the state of that individual's health, feelings, character, and even karma.

The human aura is tripartite, consisting of the lowest sheath (showing the influence of the body on the soul), the middle sheath (reflecting the life of the soul), and the highest sheath (the spiritual state). The precise interpretation of aura colors differs, but it is generally agreed that an obtrusive, dark red is associated with sensual desires and lust, while rose pink connotes motherly love or selfless affection; green is associated with lower natures and a sympathy to the physical world, brown and orange with egotism, pride, and ambition, yellow with intellect, blue with spirituality, piety, and wisdom, violet with religious fervor, white with transcendence and sanctity, black with malice and evil. The duller and muddier the colors, the more related they are to the body; the purer and brighter, the more they pertain to the spiritual in man.[30]

The third plane accessible to the human monad of the Earth incarnation (i.e., the human being) is the Devachanic plane. This is the "abode of the Gods," and corresponds roughly to the Christian concept of heaven. The human monad, in the intermediate stage between incarnations, ascends to Devachan and there integrates its past experiences and prepares for the next life. The higher planes above Devachan will be reached only in the distant future, when the human monad is further along on the spiritual path to the Divine One.

The Meaning of the Path

The human monad's task in this, its most material sequence of incarnations, is to recognize that the bondage of matter is illusory and to begin its journey back to spirit. For the Theosophists, as for the Gnostics, matter (understood as the entire phenomenal world) is an illusion. Theoretically monistic, but practically dualistic, most esoteric philosophies (including Theosophy) postulate the opposition of phenomenal (material) and noumenal (spiritual) reality. *Real* reality is changeless and eternal; that which changes is illusory: "Spirit is the only reality," wrote Edouard Schuré. "Matter is nothing but its lower, changing, ephemeral expression, its dynamism in space and time."[31] To comprehend this and to overcome the illusion of matter is Theosophical wisdom. This point of view is remarkably similar to that of the Valentinian gnosis.

The illusion of matter is perpetrated in Buddhist (and Theosophical) mythology by Maya, the Spider who weaves the material web of the world illusion, or the phenomenal world. "Maya or illusion is an element which enters into all finite things, for everything that exists has only a relative, not an absolute, reality, since the appearance which the hidden noumenon assumes for any observer depends upon his power of cognition," explained Mme Blavatsky. "Nothing is permanent except the one hidden absolute existence which contains in itself the noumena of all realities."[32] Noumena and phenomena are connected by analogy and correspondence. Events in matter are distorted, at times parodic, even grotesque reflections of events occurring on the spiritual plane. The noumenon is enciphered in the phenomenal event, and the occultist who has developed his "spiritual sight" can see behind the distorted pseudoreality of the manifested mechanical Universe to the real meaning of the noumenon that informs it.[33]

If the world of Spirit is the realm of the One, the All-Unity, then the world of Matter, *maya*, is the world of the Two, of dichotomy. In imperfect matter the divine Unity appears as duality so that man's consciousness might comprehend empirically what he perceives: Light is empirically comprehensible only in relation to Darkness, Good in relation to Evil, Life to Death, Male to Female. While man's spiritual self is aware that duality is an illusion of material existence, man's inferior physical self is easily misled by the illusion. Man must read Nature as a mystical text, learn to understand his own dualistic nature (spiritual and material), recognize the illusion of the phenomenal world, and desire to return to the One.

The three deceptions of *maya*, the three primary illusions of the phenomenal world, are Death, Time, and Evil. Death is illusory because only the human monad's material shell, a product of maya, dies. The human monad itself, being an emanation of the Divine, is eternal. Paradoxically, life in the material body becomes a form of death, a "burial" in matter, while earthly death is liberation, a return to the real world of pure spirit, unpolluted by matter. Here, again, Theosophy coincides with Gnosticism.

Time is illusory because it exists only in the material world; the All-Unity, the Divine One, exists in Eternity, which alone is real. Chronological time is perceived as the opposite of eternity in dichotomous material existence. The individual who has developed supersensible sight can sense the presence of Eternity in Time, and learn to "hear the call" of Eternity, awakening him to the realization of his divine nature.

Evil is illusory because it is not absolute, but relative. Neither good nor evil exist per se; each is generated and created out of the other; they are, in fact, the dichotomous expression of a single truth. Evil is no more than divine light condensed into material form. Thus Satan, or Lucifer, is an essentially positive concept for Theosophy, which claims that God and the Devil are but the two sides of a single coin: *Demon est Deus inversus*. As the just and retributive agent of karma, the Devil is the servant of God. Mme Blavatsky went so far as to say that "that which the clergy of every dogmatic religion—preeminently the Christian—points out as Satan, the enemy of God, is in reality, the highest divine Spirit— (occult Wisdom on Earth)—in its naturally antagonistic character to every worldly, evanescent illusion, dogmatic or ecclesiastical religions included."[34] Theosophy considered that Christianity, by polarizing God and Satan, simply misunderstood the homogeneity of the Divine One, unable to look beyond its bifurcated manifestation in matter.

The task of the human monad in his material existence is to realize that matter is illusory and to overcome it, thus returning, step by reincarnational step, to the pure spirit of the Divine One. While subject to the cyclical law of reincarnation, the Pilgrim-Soul is bound by the law of karma. A doctrine fundamental to Brahmanism and Buddhism, karma was easily incorporated into the syncretistic philosophy of the Theosophists. Karma is understood as a cosmic law of cause and effect that determines one's human condition in any incarnation based on one's behavior in previous incarnations: What one sows in this life, whether good or evil, one reaps in a later reincarnation; all that is done, is done for all eternity. Mme Blavatsky defined karma as

> the LAW OF RETRIBUTION; the Law of Cause and Effect or Ethical Causation. . . . It is the power that controls all things, the resultant of moral action, the metaphysical Samskara, or the moral effect of an act committed for the attainment of something which gratifies a personal desire. There is the Karma of merit and the Karma of demerit. Karma neither punishes nor rewards; it is simply *the one* Universal LAW which guides unerringly and, so to say, blindly, all other laws productive of certain effects along the grooves of their respective causations.[35]

The situation is complicated in that an individual is involved not only in his or her own karma, but in the karma of the groups to which the individual belongs. "While a man makes his own individual karma he also connects himself thereby with others, thus becoming a member of various groups—family, national, racial—and as a member he shares in the collective karma of each of these groups."[36]

Karma, according to Theosophy, does not deny the concept of free will. Man's free will lies in his ability to control the karma he creates in the life being lived. "Let man be left free to choose his own actions," wrote Mrs. Besant, "but let every action bring about an inevitable result; let him run loose amid all objects of desire and seize whatever he will, but let him have all the results of his choice, be they delightful or grievous." The remainder of her explanation shows karma to be a form of cosmic shock therapy. If man experiences pain often enough in the wake of "bad" choices, he will presently "freely reject the objects whose possession ultimately causes him pain; he will no longer desire them when he has experienced to the full that their possession ends in sorrow. . . . The lesson will be repeated any number of times found necessary."[37]

Neither does karma limit the individual in any way; on the contrary, it frees the individual for conscious creativity on a large scale. By understanding one's karma and acting accordingly, the individual can consciously design his or her own present and future lives. Seeing one's present existence as part of a larger, unfinished tapestry, one is able to fashion one's own "creatively lived life" (in the words of the Russian Symbolists) and determine the direction of future incarnations.

Through its particular understanding of karma, Theosophy was able to modify subtly one important aspect of pantheism. While at first glance the Theosophical understanding of man seems to dissolve the individual in the enormous collectivity of the cosmos (a specifically oriental feature), in fact it continues the tradition of occidental individualism through its particular revision of karma. Each individual becomes the conscious determiner of his or her own fate, becomes his or her own "lawgiver," who knowingly chooses the direction of this and of future lives.

Reincarnation and karma were the opiate of the Theosophical masses; when the thought of eternal life in the paradise of traditional Christianity could no longer console, Theosophy, with its notion of reincarnation, could. Mrs. Besant wrote that there is a "fundamental necessity for reincarnation if life is to be made intelligible, and if injustice and cruelty are not to mock the helplessness of man. With reincarnation man is a dignified, immortal being, evolving toward a divinely glorious end; without it, he is a tossing straw on the stream of chance circumstances, irresponsible for his character, for his actions, for his destiny."[38]

The law of karma proved that evil and suffering are neither arbitrary nor random. It gave different meaning to the concept of Fate, in that blind chance was no longer the controlling factor of one's existence. A higher, logical law of spiritual causation (in which enlightened individuals themselves participated) determined into what time and place those individuals were born and what they had to overcome or accomplish in this particular life. In the last analysis, all that happened was just. Karma provided a consoling explanation of why things went wrong, why innocent people suffered, why cruelty and viciousness existed, and why life was unfair: it was all the result of karma that had not been worked out in previous reincarnations.

The goal of one's lives was to balance out bad karma with good, and then to act as little as possible, thus reducing the amount of karma created. If the human monad could in this life reduce the "karma of demerit" for future lives and avoid the creation of new karma, it would eventually reach a state of perfect balance and harmony, the final degree of which is the extinction of existence in matter. It would be freed from human passion and animal desires; it would reach the state of absolute existence, nirvana, and escape the wheel of material reincarnation altogether.

To the Western mind, reincarnation, karma, and nirvana are not congenial concepts. First, they are difficult for the Western mind to comprehend in the manner originally intended by Eastern thought, and so they
reach the Western mind in a distorted form, frequently as an attempt,
conscious or unconscious, to revise the Christian explanation of suffering as the result of original sin. Second, they encourage passivity and
withdrawal from society and reality in Western man. One is inclined to
spend one's life inducing dreams, visions, and meditative states (as many
turn-of-the-century Russian intellectuals did), since these are perceived
as the means of contact with the spiritual world. The analytical psychologist C. G. Jung, who spent a lifetime studying alchemy and other occult sciences, considered Theosophy actually dangerous to the Western
mind:

> The usual mistake of Western man when faced with this problem of grasping
> the ideas of the East is like that of the student in *Faust*. Misled by the devil,
> he contemptuously turns his back on science and, carried away by Eastern
> occultism, takes over yoga practices word for word and becomes a pitiable
> imitator. (Theosophy is our best example of this.) Thus he abandons the one
> sure foundation of the Western mind and loses himself in a mist of words and
> ideas that could never have originated in European brains and can never be
> profitably grafted upon them.[39]

Jung's conclusion, reached in 1929, echoes the words of the Russian
philosopher, Nikolai Berdiaev, from 1916. Berdiaev complained that
Theosophy oversimplified complex Eastern doctrines and, in this oversimplified form, presented psychic truths, relevant to Eastern thought,
to unprepared and uncomprehending Western minds. "There is something in the Hindu understanding of God that is incapable of being expressed in our language, that is untranslatable into our Western concepts," he wrote.[40]

Ready as the Russian Theosophists were to embrace the enticingly
exotic oriental trappings of Theosophy, much as they might insist that
Russian Theosophy would facilitate the union of oriental religion and
Western science and philosophy, it was the Gnostic, rather than the
Buddhist, dimension in Theosophical cosmology that in the end made
it particularly appealing to Theosophically inclined members of the Russian creative intelligentsia. Russian Orthodox mystical theology has bent
more than a little in the direction of the Gnostic heresy, and at no time
was this as true as during the Silver Age. The Gnostic influence appears
in Vladimir Solov'ev's Sophiology (in which the concept of the "All-
Unity" and the Valentinian model figure prominently), and in the elaboration of his work by the priests Sergei Bulgakov and Pavel Florenskii.

At one point even Nikolai Berdiaev welcomed the tendency toward Gnosticism and urged that "Gnosticism should be revived and should enter into our life for all time."[41]

This Gnostic dimension also found expression in Russian mystical sectarianism at the turn of the century. The *Khlysty* ("Flagellants") embraced the same idea of identity with divinity and called their elders "Christs." Many contemporary Russian scholars actually claimed that the roots of this heretical sect lay in the Gnostic movements of the sixth century and the Manichaeanism of the medieval Bogomils.[42] This Gnostic model, which underlies Russian neo-Christianity, Sophiology, sectarian beliefs, and Theosophy, fed the worldview of the second-generation Symbolist writers and can be detected in Russian literature as late as the 1930s (in Mikhail Bulgakov's novel *Master i Margarita*, for example).

In the end, Theosophy (as well as Spiritualism and other occult movements) fostered the passivity that stems from rejection of concrete reality. Escape from contemporary reality, whether it be into the past, into exotica, into dreams, or into the world of imagination, is also characteristic of Russian Symbolist art and literature. One need only look at the occult journals still being published during the First World War and the Revolution, particularly *Rebus*. No historian could discover sufficient material there to document the disintegration of the monarchy, the dreadful defeats of the war, or the excesses of revolutionary activity. One wonders if this passive withdrawal, this *Weltflucht*, would play a role in the events of 1918 and afterward, when the Russian middle class and the intelligentsia became the submissive victims of Bolshevik excesses.

Anthroposophical Refinements: Rudolf Steiner's Spiritual Science

For the ten years between 1902 (when he first became a member) and 1912 (when he resigned), Rudolf Steiner was a visible member of the Theosophical Society, contributing more to the systematization of Theosophical doctrine than most leaders of the Society later cared to admit.[43] During that time he developed his own variant of theosophical occultism, which he called Anthroposophy. The term was not original to Steiner. It was first used by the alchemist and Hermeticist Thomas Vaughan, twin brother of the English metaphysical poet Henry Vaughan, in the seventeenth century. Steiner selected it for its Rosicrucian associations; the Rosicrucianism initiation plays a central role in Steiner's Anthroposophy.

During his years as a Theosophist, Steiner did not tamper overmuch with traditional Theosophical doctrine, at least as it was presented by

A. P. Sinnett and Mme Blavatsky. What he did, however, was to purge the system of Mme Blavatsky's confusing (and confused) layers of comparative religion, questionable etymologies, and creative mythology. He minimized the presence of oriental thought and vocabulary, extracted what he believed to be the essence of the doctrine, and arranged the whole in a relatively coherent, systematic form couched in vocabulary taken from the natural sciences, psychology, and Western philosophy. He thereby changed the names, if not the functions, of traditional Theosophical concepts. The *prana* of Theosophy became Steiner's "etheric nature," the *chela* became a "spiritual researcher" who investigates a spiritual (not merely physical) science, and so on. This change in terminology was one of the factors that made Steiner's occult science more accessible and acceptable to the educated European mind; nevertheless, there remained a definite doctrinal continuity between the Theosophy of Mme Blavatsky and Steiner's Anthroposophy, particularly in regard to the central concepts of karma and reincarnation.

Another modification was Steiner's shift in emphasis from purely intuitive cognition to a combination of intuitive, inspirational, and intellectual cognition. Steiner called his more disciplined method "spiritual *science*" (*Geisteswissenschaft*), or "supersensible knowledge." It attempts to make occult science a legitimate discipline, with its own body of facts and its own empirical knowledge, qualitatively different from but no less valid than that of traditional science, and closely related to it. By following Steiner's recommended method of study, exercises, and meditations aimed at developing the spiritual organs of perception, spiritual researchers could train themselves to operate consciously on a level of "supersensible" cognition. Steiner did not scorn the advances of modern science. "There can be no doubt whatever that the method of thought derived from natural science is the greatest power in modern spiritual life," he wrote. "One who is investigating the nature of the spirit can only learn from natural science."[44] This apparent acceptance of modern science was a fundamental feature of the Anthroposophical Way, or Path, and also contributed to its appeal to the modern Western mind.

Steiner was opposed to anything that smacked of superstition or could not be "proved" by individual spiritual experimentation. He himself claimed to have experienced, in addition to the waking and dreaming states, an additional "soul state" of imaginative cognition in which the soul, although in a state similar to sleep, still retains consciousness and is able to immerse itself in "symbolic visualization," taking control of events that occur to the "Self" on other planes. Steiner was convinced that spiritually advanced human beings were capable of developing conscious control not only of their physical body, but also of their etheric and astral bodies. By purifying and refashioning the astral body through meditation, concentration, and other exercises, thus enabling it to acquire higher organs of supersensible perception, trained spiritual researchers could participate actively in the spiritual world.[45] They would achieve complete and unbroken consciousness; they would remember past incarnations and would control subsequent incarnations so as to return as the same physical self (thus creating the illusion among the unenlightened that they had lived for hundreds, even thousands, of years).

Even before his break with the Theosophical Society at the end of 1912, Steiner was open about what he specifically found objectionable in Theosophy. He felt that Mme Blavatsky had been premature in revealing certain esoteric truths to the world. Nothing should have been revealed until the very end of the nineteenth century (at the end of every century, according to Steiner, the Heavenly Hierarchy sends the human race some additional spiritual assistance), and then that revelation had to be of a particular kind, suitable for the soul, mind, and body of Western man. Unfortunately, in Dr. Steiner's view, Mme Blavatsky's own soul was unformed and chaotic; it distorted the wisdom that Western Rosicrucian adepts sent through it. Consequently, Eastern adepts were able to take control of it and insert their own form of specifically oriental spiritual knowledge. Hence the unexpected (and erroneous) Buddhist nature of her revelation to Western humanity. Eventually, the excessive chaos of Mme Blavatsky's soul forced all adepts to withdraw from it, leaving it an open and dangerous channel for negative occult forces.[46]

Steiner's rejection of Theosophy's oriental dimension did not mean he was contemptuous of oriental wisdom; he simply felt that nothing within the oriental tradition would aid Western man in overcoming the power of scientific materialism from which he had to escape to begin his journey spiritward. The illumination of Western man could come only from within the Western tradition itself. Scientific materialism, in Steiner's view, was the Golgotha of the human mind; no passive oriental tradition could possibly give man the strength to sacrifice himself actively on this particular cross.[47]

Steiner identified three kinds of initiation: "the ancient Yoga, the really specific Christian initiation, and that initiation which is entirely appropriate for men of the present day, the Christian-Rosicrucian initiation":[48]

> There are three different kinds of initiation, all of which lead to the same goal.
> There are three paths, the choice of one of which depends upon a man's individuality. One initiation is that of wisdom; it is the fitting goal for Indian and
> Oriental training. This path is fraught with great dangers for European and
> Western bodies and is therefore not the right one. The second initiation is

based upon the life of feeling; it is the fundamentally Christian path. Only few individuals can still take this path because it demands a strong power of devotion and piety. The third path is the Rosicrucian training, the path of the initiation of thinking and of will. It leads to union with the forces of the other paths of initiation. . . .to genuine spiritual sight and knowledge of the spiritual world based on actual experience.[49]

Steiner clearly differentiated the Eastern soul, mind, and body from the Western. He characterized the Eastern initiation as passive, achieved while the initiate was in a trance or sleep state. The Western, or Rosicrucian, initiation he himself proposed taught the initiate to work actively and consciously through mind, reason, and intellect to achieve enlightenment. Unlike the Eastern guru, who merely imparts occult knowledge, the Western teacher provides an intellectual stimulus and waits for the developed mind to reach its own spiritual conclusions. Steiner made no demands of faith or belief in his system; he asked only that his disciples approach it without prejudice.

The Rosicrucian initiation rests on a Christian foundation but has deeper roots in Western medieval Gnostic and Hermetic philosophies, all strongly colored by esoteric Christianity. Steiner named the Brotherhood of St. John, the Knights of the Grail, the Albigenses and Cathars, the Rosicrucian Fraternity, the Knights Templar, and, of course, Anthroposophy, as preservers of this Western initiation and clothed some aspects of his Anthroposophy in their metaphors and vocabulary.

The Christ Impulse

Steiner's Christian-Rosicrucian initiation laid great stress on the role of the Christ Impulse in human spiritual development. His commitment to restoring the Christ concept to a rationalistic and materialistic world is perhaps his greatest point of departure from traditional Theosophy. Both Steiner and the Theosophists agreed that Christianity, as promulgated by the organized Church, was a distorted and materialistic form of the original teaching; both agreed that spiritual truth lay in an esoteric Christianity that was not popularly disseminated; both saw this esoteric Christianity as based solidly on Gnostic thought. Beyond that, Mme Blavatsky had little time for Christianity and, although she referred to it occasionally in order to criticize it, did not make it a major feature of her neo-Buddhist worldview. Annie Besant, the author of a major Theosophical text on *Esoteric Christianity* (1901), divided the Christ into historical, mythical, and mystical figures. Jesus was a human being who had achieved a certain level of spiritual development and, at the moment of his initiation into the "mysteries," became a "son of God." She denied to the Theosophical Christ the role of personal Savior and did not consider his existence to be a unique historical event, since any successful initiate can become a "son of God." Mrs. Besant's Gnosticism leaned toward the oriental variant in its insistence that the goal of esoteric Christian initiation was to escape the cycle of rebirth and the circle of generation.[50]

The primary role of the Christ in Steiner's system is as cultural symbol of man's emerging sense of individuality, of the egoconsciousness (Steiner's "I AM"). "His mission consisted in bringing to mankind the full force of the ego, an inner independence in the soul."[51] For Steiner,

> Christ Jesus is not only a Universal Principle; Christ is a Being who appeared once, and once only, at a definite moment in history. In human form, He revealed by His words and His life, a state of perfection which it is possible for all men ultimately to acquire by their own free will. Christ came to the Earth at a critical moment, when the descending arc of human evolution was about to reach its lowest point of materialization. In order that the Christ-Principle might awaken in man, the life of Christ Himself on Earth was necessary in a human body. . . . The Christ Impulse intervenes in [the] karmic process and becomes its central pivot. Since He came to Earth the Christ has lived in the depths of every human soul."[52]

Steiner's Christ, for all of his presence and uniqueness, is not more traditionally Christian than the Christ of the Theosophists; Steiner's form of Christianity is still the expression of a pantheistic worldview, for his Son of God is the son of an eternal, hidden Father who is concealed in Nature. "God is magically concealed in the world. And you need His own force in order to find Him. This force you must awaken within yourself."[53]

Steiner called this force the Christ Impulse. He provided a further clarification of his peculiar understanding of the Christ in his commentary to the most Gnostic of the Christian gospels, the Gospel of St. John:

> The earth exists in order that full self-consciousness, the "I AM," may be given to mankind. Previously, everything was a preparation for this self-consciousness, for this "I AM"; and the Christ was that Being Who gave the impulse that made it possible for every human being—each as an individual—to experience the "I AM." Only with His advent was the powerful impulse given which carries earth humanity forward with a mighty bound.[54]

Thus Steiner's Christ is the "quickener" of the "I AM," the self-conscious, rational, individual ego (as opposed to the unconscious, intuitive, group ego that characterizes the psyche of primitive man).

The Christ Impulse was necessary if the human monad was to be aided in its spiritual journey. The pilgrimage of the soul necessitated the human monad's descent entirely into matter, because only by descending into matter could he lose his sense of one-ness with the Divine All and be completely alone with his own Self. Once isolated in matter, man would be able to identify and develop his individual ego consciousness through intellect, allowing his own "I AM" to emerge. Only by developing his Self (the "I AM") could man comprehend that he alone was responsible for his own actions and that he had free will. The "I AM" was the only possible vehicle for man's conscious, rational, and freely chosen return to the Divine All. The human monad's ego consciousness emerged, however, at the very point when humanity was completely trapped in matter and had lost every memory of its spiritual heredity. At this point in human history the time had come for the appearance of the Christ, who came to break the illusory bonds of matter and to "give again the impulse for finding the path back to the Universal."[55]

The Christ Impulse, claimed Steiner, is unique to the Western Path. The Eastern (and ancient) Path, with its different tasks and different history, attempted to restore the human monad's original unity with the Divine not by accepting the reality of matter and actively overcoming it, but by completely rejecting matter as an illusion and yielding to reassimilation into Brahman (the All-Spirit); such passive dissolution in the Godhead obliterates the "I AM," destroys individual ego consciousness, and negates free will. Western man, had he followed this path, would never have created his material culture or achieved free will or found spiritual redemption. Mme Blavatsky, with her Eastern Theosophy, advocated a wrong, even a dangerous, Path for Western humanity; Steiner's Anthroposophy returned it to the straight and narrow Path that led to a true understanding of the Mystery of Golgotha.

Ahriman and Lucifer

Steiner's Anthroposophy also further developed the Theosophical understanding of evil. Evil, as an illusion perpetrated in matter, cannot exist sui generis; evil is only an agent of karma. And as there is no personal God in Theosophy, there can be no personal Devil. Mme Blavatsky explained Lucifer's current satanic image in Christian culture as an act of defamation: Lucifer, the "'Luminous Son of the Morning,' or manvantaric Dawn" was actually "transformed by the Church into Lucifer or Satan, because he is higher and older than Jehovah, and had to be sacrificed to the new dogma,"[56] when in fact he is "allegorized as Good, and Sacrifice, a God of Wisdom, under different names."[57] She agreed with the French occultist Eliphas Lévi that Lucifer was actually a vehicle of light (Lucifer literally means "Light bearer") and "a mediating force diffused throughout creation; that it serves for creation and destruction." Furthermore, she held that "the light in question is of the nature of fire, that it is warming and vivifying in its prudent use, but that it burns, dissolves, and destroys in its excess."[58]

For Steiner, this was too effulgent an explanation; he offered a more streamlined one. Steiner maintained, like the Theosophists, that "*there is no essential evil*. Everything evil arises from this: something that is good in one direction is put to use in the world in another direction and thereby turned to evil."[59] In Anthroposophical doctrine evil is intrinsically associated with two impulses: the luciferian and the ahrimanic. In the mythic figures of Lucifer and Ahriman, Steiner created metaphors of the potentially dark forces that are part of the universal order of things.[60]

According to Steiner, Ahriman (the Zoroastrian Prince of Darkness) "is the Lord of Death, far and wide the ruler of all the powers that have to bring about in the physical sense world what this world has to have, the annihilation and death of its entities"; Ahriman is the lawful ruler of the ordering of death. As such, he "should not be regarded as an evil power but as one whose influence in the general world order is fully legitimate."[61] Steiner uses the adjectives *dark, hard, rigid, cold, descending, and lower* to delineate the aspects of the ahrimanic impulse. Ahriman controls human thought. When he brings his rigid, earth-bound impulse to human thought he materializes it. As the arbiter of thought, Ahriman, when allowed to outweigh Lucifer, facilitates the development of the exclusively mechanistic aspect of modern science and the exclusively economic and material concerns of society. Steiner felt that Ahriman was the predominant force in modern times.

Lucifer, the force in opposition to Ahriman, is the power of Will that tears human beings away from the world of the senses and helps them be creative, imaginative, and artistic. Steiner describes Lucifer as *light, heat, motion, flexibility, ascent*. What is great and sublime in humanity's art and culture comes from the luciferian impulse. But too much luciferian influence leads to egotism, willfulness, fanaticism, extravagant idealism, and the loss of a grip on reality. When the luciferian impulse predominates in a human being, the individual becomes a slave to his or her passions, emotions, desires, and impulses.

"The whole art of life," wrote Steiner, "consists in finding the true balance between them," between Lucifer and Ahriman.[62] Life should not be an attempt to escape struggle and conflict and rest eternally in a passive state of nirvana; life should be an active and constant attempt to achieve a balance of opposing forces, a balance between luciferian and ahrimanic impulses. In their rightful places, and held in check by each other, Lucifer and Ahriman work beneficially in the human being. When the balance is upset, the overwhelming element, whether luciferian or ahrimanic, becomes demonic and is experienced by the psyche as the Devil.

Historically, the Christ figure stands midway between Lucifer, incarnated three thousand years ago and associated with the Pagan Gnosis (the emergence of intellect without the moral principle), and Ahriman, whose incarnation is yet to come. "Just as there was an incarnation of Lucifer in the flesh and an incarnation of Christ in the flesh, so, before only a part of the third millennium of the post-Christian era has elapsed, there will be, in the West, an actual incarnation of Ahriman," predicted Steiner.[63] He assimilated the future incarnation of Ahriman to the predicted appearance of the Antichrist, whose birth was to be accompanied by shattering, cataclysmic events on the physical plane. Only by developing spiritual perception and becoming aware of the movement of spiritual forces that inform the concrete events that occur in the physical world can humanity avoid being forever held prisoner in matter by the dark materialistic and intellectual forces of Ahriman.

By creating his own coherent system of "spiritual science," or "rational mysticism" (Anthroposophy), Steiner hoped to avoid the vagaries of mysticism, for he was more aware than most that "again and again you will find that truths which come from the spiritual world lay themselves open to the charge of being contradictory."[64] He claimed that his system of Observation, Thinking, Reason, and Experience was indeed a "scientific" approach to occult phenomena, the penetration of the mysteries through the use of a disciplined, "mystical" cognition. "Spiritual Science," he claimed, "has no desire to lead to *belief*, but to *knowledge*" of the right and logical universal order of things.[65] This knowledge eventually became the subject of more than 150 books and 6,000 lectures that Steiner wrote and delivered during his lifetime. The evolution of Steiner's system of occult knowledge was remarkably consistent, from his first occult writings at the very beginning of the twentieth century, through the Theosophical years, until his death in Dornach on March 30, 1925.

During his association with the Theosophical Society and after his break with it, Steiner's Anthroposophy continued to be intimately related to Theosophy (although some Anthroposophists, being closely attuned to the finest nuances of doctrinal divergence, may disagree). Steiner's differences with Theosophy were personal, administrative, and methodological, but not essentially theological. Both Theosophy and Anthroposophy are a modern gnosis; both are forms of pantheism and metaphysical monism; both are emanationist; both claim to purvey objective knowledge rather than blind faith; both have fantastic cosmologies based, in large part, on Buddhist paradigms; both believe in reincarnation and karma; both advocate an esoteric Christianity based on Gnostic models (although Anthroposophy emphasizes it more). Anthroposophy's scientific vocabulary, its restrained, "pedagogical" tone, its preference for occidental over oriental terminology and tradition, and its logical coherence (the result of Steiner's brilliant gift for systematization and organization) make it appear far more divergent from Theosophy than it, in fact, is. The underlying philosophical assumptions and general worldview (perceptions of reality, time, space, the I and the not-I, and so forth) of both doctrines remain remarkably similar. Both turned out to be "positivistic religions," offering a seemingly logical theology based on pseudoscience. The difference between them is essentially one of style and emphasis, although Steiner's pointedly Christian dimension and Western vocabulary undoubtedly ensured that his Anthroposophy would have the more profound appeal to the educated European mind that hungered for a *Christian* Theosophy.

Six

The Russian Reception of Theosophical Thought

THE THEOSOPHISTS were correct in their often repeated lament that their critics did not understand Theosophy or they would not spread such silly reports about it. Like their European brethren, the Russian Theosophists expended oceans of ink trying to set their critics straight. Rarely have so many repeated themselves so often to so little avail. To them it seemed that non-Theosophists willfully conspired to misunderstand the fundamental premises of Theosophy and to confuse it with vulgar occultism of the basest sort.

And it was true: the vast majority (but by no means all) of Theosophy's critics were abysmally ignorant of the basic tenets of the Movement and terribly prejudiced against it. Their articles clearly reveal that they were not confused by any real knowledge or understanding of Theosophy. Other critics, like the *Rebus* faction, had doctrinal differences with Theosophy; they criticized Theosophy's divergence from their own particular point of view but remained open to occult thought in general. The Theosophical Society also attracted considerable criticism from the church and the intellectual establishment. Still, certain critics had been adherents themselves of Theosophy or had studied it seriously, and their criticism is pertinent indeed, for it clearly reflects the social and cultural currents of the period. The most serious attack on the Russian Theosophical Society was, in fact, made by a defector from their ranks.

That defector, Konstantin Kudriavtsev, was, in many ways, an archetypal Russian Theosophist. He was a middle-ranking St. Petersburg bureaucrat; one of his duties was to edit the *Izvestiia Sankt-Peterburgskoi gorodskoi dumy*. He was also a philanthropist, as far as his means allowed, and he worked with the St. Petersburg Society for the Protection of Children from Cruelty. Finally, Kudriavtsev was a representative, if discontented, "seeker" who had sampled various occult movements before settling, briefly, on Theosophy. He had practiced hypnotism and belonged to various esoteric groups, including the Russian Spiritualist Society (he was keen to take spirit photographs in his spare time); he contributed to various journals, notably the Spiritualist publications *Rebus* and *Iz Mraka k Svetu*. Kudriavtsev continued to have good relations with the Spiritualists, who "personally attested that Mr. Kudriavtsev was a man of the highest honor and sincerity."[1]

Kudriavtsev was entirely devoted to the Theosophical Society during the years he was a member. He was one of the Russian Society's founders; he fought for its charter with the St. Petersburg authorities; he served as the First Secretary of the RTO; he did a great deal of editorial work for *Vestnik Teosofii*; he lectured frequently on behalf of the Society. Suddenly, and apparently unexpectedly, he left the Theosophical Society in the winter of 1911–1912 and attacked it in a sensationalist pamphlet, *Chto takoe teosofiia i Teosoficheskoe Obshchestvo.*[2] Kudriavtsev's tract is of particular interest because it clearly verbalized the objections many Russians felt not to Theosophy per se, but to Theosophy as practiced and disseminated by the official Theosophical Society. It also pointed out several of the inconsistencies in Theosophical doctrine and behavior. Kudriavtsev's arguments carried additional weight because he had been a highly visible and obviously sincere Theosophist. His accusations serve as a paradigm of the Theosophical/anti-Theosophical debate in Russia.

The burden of Kudriavtsev's critique was that as a true Orthodox Christian believer he could not ultimately reconcile Theosophy with Christianity, regardless of the former's claim that the two systems were eminently compatible. Kudriavtsev found he did not, after all, care for the "foreign dogmas, grown in distant and alien soil," that comprise Theosophy. "I have become convinced," he wrote, "that the Theosophical Society is not a society seeking knowledge, but an external organ of the 'Universal Brotherhood.' "[3] He had looked to Theosophy to show him a new spiritual path, a new gnosis that would deepen his own Christian faith. And now he had discovered that Theosophy was misrepresenting itself as a gnosis; it was, in fact, a *religion*, a new, secret church inimical to the Christian church and representing dangerous Eastern elements. He had been promised the union of Science, Religion, and Philosophy and, instead, had been given a cabal of Mahatmas.

Kudriavtsev particularly objected to the strong Buddhist element in Theosophy. He pointed out that Mme Blavatsky had converted to Buddhism; that the first president of the Theosophical Society, Henry Olcott, had converted to Buddhism; that the current president of the Theosophical Society, Mrs. Besant, had embraced Brahmanism. "Why does Buddhism blossom in the heart of the Theosophical Society and why is it necessary to convert from Christianity to Buddhism if all religions are the revelations of one and the same truth?" Kudriavtsev asked.[4] Why, he went on, are Theosophists asked to venerate Master Morya and Koot Hoomi, Mme Blavatsky's Mahatma "teachers," and not Jesus Christ? In what way is Jesus Christ inferior to them or to Buddha? And why denigrate Christianity? Kudriavtsev finally decided that Theosophy was a "betrayal of Christ" and offered the suggestion, only partly in jest, that the existence of "the Theosophical Society might be viewed as the result of the Christian church's bad karma and [past] evil deeds."[5]

Kudriavtsev also saw Theosophy as part of a larger Masonic conspiracy. This accusation is not quite as absurd as it first appears. The general syncretism of the age resulted in Masonic ideas and rituals being insinuated into numerous other occult trends; Masonic esotericism was certainly incorporated into the Secret Doctrine of the Theosophists (but then so were all other forms of occult thought that were at all suitable). Kudriavtsev's accusation is given additional weight by the visible affiliation of the French occultist par excellence, Papus, with Rosicrucian, Martinist, and Masonic organizations, where he had achieved the highest ranks. Papus had belonged to the General Council of the Theosophical Society, knew the principals, and was an influential member of the French Theosophically oriented Société Isis. He had visited Russia several times to found a Martinist Lodge in St. Petersburg (the Martinists were mystical Freemasons). Several influential Russian Theosophists had connections with Papus and the various organizations with which he was associated.[6] Moreover, Mme Blavatsky herself claimed Masonic ties: "I have been awarded the Order of Arch Auditor [the sixth degree in the Royal Oriental Order of Sat B'hai (Seven Brethren), a Masonic order incorporating Hindu elements] from the main Masonic Society in India. This is the most ancient of the Masonic lodges and it is said that it existed before the birth of Christ."[7] Mrs. Besant had also been initiated into various Masonic orders, as had C. W. Leadbeater and Rudolf Steiner; most high-ranking Theosophists held some Masonic post.

Kudriavtsev's most scathing criticism, however, was directed at Mrs. Besant and the recently created "Order of the Star in the East." Mrs. Besant had announced that her young disciple, Jiddu Krishnamurti (1895–1986) was an avatar of the new Messiah, a vehicle of the Christ. She had organized the Order of the Star in the East for the purpose of supporting him and his mission, which she proclaimed as the Second Coming. Membership in the international Order of the Star in the East was open to anyone, Theosophist or not. In Russia, however, one had to be a member of the Theosophical Society to participate; otherwise, the Order would need to be registered with the authorities as a separate religious organization. Even in the slightly less reactionary post-1906 period, no Russian authority would have granted a charter to an organization that recognized an unknown Hindu youth as the Christ. The Russian representative of the Order was Kudriavtsev's colleague at *Vestnik Teosofii*, V. N. Pushkina. Advertisements in the journal stated: "The Order of the Star in the East unites all who believe in the imminent coming of the Great World Teacher and desire to dedicate their efforts to preparing the way for Him."

This Order created much dissent within the worldwide Theosophical Society and finally resulted in a major schism. Mrs. Besant, who had herself converted to Brahmanism, did not seem to realize that her act would necessarily alienate Christian Theosophists, who, if they were good Christians, must view it as blasphemy. Kudriavtsev (with others) found

Mrs. Besant's position to be "a dogma contradictory to Christian doctrine."[8] Not only did it contradict the Christian Gospels, he meticulously pointed out, but it also ignored the Theosophical premise of evolutionary cycles (by the last Theosophical reckoning, the Second Coming was not to occur for another twenty million years).

Criticism of the Order was not limited to Kudriavtsev and a few apostate Theosophists. "A more horrible, a more blasphemous idea [than Mrs. Besant's] could not have been invented by anyone except Satan," wrote Vladimir Bykov, who had just then returned to the Orthodox church after several years as a Spiritualist and occultist.[9] And Bykov did not stop with calling the Krishnamurti affair a "satanic plot"; he went on to term it a Jewish plot and a Masonic plot as well. Lev Kobylinskii-Ellis, a friend of Andrei Belyi and a minor writer associated with the Musaget modernists, echoed the sentiments of the Symbolists when he criticized the "well-known scandal of Annie Besant and the false Christ, Krishnamurti."[10] Nor could Pavel Chistiakov, the critical editor of *Rebus*, let such a Theosophical tempest pass without making a comment:

> We will not try to give a name to this fantasy—it speaks for itself; but to those who seek spiritual peace in Theosophy, who seek a calm far from the tortured dissension between life and the contemporary forms of religious self-awareness, we can only say: "Don't hurry . . . take a good, close look before stopping at contemporary, modernized Hinduism: it is not what it claims to be or seems to be!"
>
> By the way, it is worth pointing out that our esteemed Theosophists have now raised the value of Christ a bit and say that he is no longer a "Great Disciple" and has become a "Great Teacher."[11]

While Kudriavtsev's criticism had the piquancy of being the criticism of a disaffected Theosophist, his voice did not cry alone in the wilderness. His critical pamphlet, supported by some parties within the occult community, by the clergy, and by other apostate Theosophists, heated up the polemical climate and supplied considerable ammunition for Theosophy's numerous critics. The Theosophists found themselves fending off attackers on three different fronts.

The Three Critiques of Theosophy

1. "Theosophy is Incompatible with Christianity"

Russian Orthodox critics ceaselessly bombarded Theosophists with accusations of being anti-Christian. Konstantin Kudriavtsev's thorough, "insider's" critique of Theosophy had reached the conclusion that Theosophy purposely sought to confuse the issue by "using the same terminology as Christianity, but imbuing it with a different content and thus leading its members into error: the 'Son of God,' according to Theosophical doctrine, is only one of the levels of 'initiation' into the occult school. This concept in no way corresponds to the Christian teaching about the 'Son of God'—it is fundamentally different, different in essence and in spirit."[12] Kudriavtsev precisely identified one of the elements that made the polemics between Theosophists and their Christian critics so provoking: each side spoke a superficially similar but doctrinally distinct language, the nuances of which were philosophically unacceptable to the other. In their attempt to convince the uninitiated, the Theosophists cited Theosophical texts as "proof" of the correctness of their position; such proofs could not possibly convince doctrinaire Christians, since, in their terms, the proffered proofs were based on pagan and heretical texts. The Christian faction quoted scriptures back at the Theosophists, but their scriptural "proofs" were simply absorbed by and dissolved in the all-embracing Theosophical doctrine. The Theosophists redefined basic concepts broadly, which they would cite as an example of Theosophy's "flexibility" and "tolerance." Christian critics, on the other hand, denounced such "flexible" thinking as syncretistic, reductive, ambiguous, and, ultimately, heretical.

The animosity between the church and the Theosophical Society was initiated by Mme Blavatsky herself, who pointedly promulgated an anti-Christian position. In *The Secret Doctrine* she wrote that Theosophy accepts all faiths and philosophies and "only refuses to accept any of the gods of the so-called monotheistic religions, gods created by man in his own image and likeness, a blasphemous and sorry caricature of the Ever Unknowable."[13] Never acclaimed for her verbal tact (Rudolf Steiner generously called her "audacious"), she tended to make extreme statements. She herself was prejudiced against Christianity (although she was occasionally indulgent toward Russian Orthodoxy) and flaunted her exotic Buddhist sympathies before sedate Christian critics. Bringing proof of her sinister mission, Kudriavtsev gleefully referred to her comments in the *Pall Mall Gazette* of April 26, 1884, in which, he alleged, Mme Blavatsky had stated that the goal of the Theosophists "is not to elevate Hinduism as much as it is to remove Christianity from the face of the earth."[14] Other Theosophists strove to soften this position, but such words, once said, were hard to "unsay."

In *The Key to Theosophy* Mme Blavatsky answered the question, "Do you believe in God?" in the following manner:

Theo. That depends on what you mean by the term.
Enq. I mean the God of the Christians, the Father of Jesus, and the Creator: the Biblical God of Moses, in short.
Theo. In such a God we do not believe. We reject the idea of a personal, or

an extra-cosmic and anthropomorphic God, who is but the gigantic shadow of *man*, and not of man at his best, either. The God of theology, we say—and prove it—is a bundle of contradictions and a logical impossibility. Therefore we will have nothing to do with him.[15]

The Theosophical concept of divinity, as already noted, is radically different from that of Christianity in that Theosophy does not recognize a personal God and denies the uniqueness of the Christian Revelation. Seeking God, the Theosophist looks within himself: God is not outside him, but is actually one in essence with the "Self." The Theosophists accepted *"Tat tvam asi"* ("That art thou"); this famous phrase from the Upanishads emphasizes the identity of the Self, *Atman*, with the Universe. Eventually, the individual will dissolve in the Godhead. There can be no personal God; there can be no individual immortality; there is no distinction between creature and Creator. In the eyes of the Christian critic this was hubris, and entirely incompatible with the concept of Christian humility. "The dissolution of the personality, of the unique individual, in a faceless divinity, in an abstract divine unity, is contradictory to the Christian idea of man and divine humanity," pointed out one of the leading philosophers of the Russian Religious Renaissance, Nikolai Berdiaev.[16]

The Theosophical position on God was unacceptable to Russian Orthodox critics, for whom the only Man who was "one in essence" with God was Christ. Theosophy, they said, encouraged the individual to believe in personal divinity; it elevated the human being and denigrated Christ; it was not Christianity at all, but pantheism. "Theosophical concepts, let us not speak of their veracity or lack of veracity," wrote one Russian critic, "are quite foreign to the concepts of Slavic-Byzantine Christian mysticism, and when they were transplanted to the soil of the cold north, it was impossible for them not to undergo considerable change. The Slavs have never been pantheists, while Theosophy is a doctrine of pantheism and, moreover, of panlogism [i.e., world as actualization of *Nous* or *Logos*]; neither the one nor the other fits well with the conceptions of Christian mysticism."[17]

The official Theosophical position on God was also unacceptable to the "Christian Theosophists" of the independent Smolensk Society. They differentiated between Christian and Hindu Theosophy as the products of different cultures from different parts of the world. Hinduism and Buddhism they found contradictory and clearly inimical to their own ecumenical Christianity. "The followers of Indo-Buddhist Theosophy call themselves simply Theosophists, and in this way appropriate for themselves the right to universality," wrote Vladimir Shtal'berg, president of the Smolensk Society. "Christ they accept only as one of the powerful prophet-teachers," but not as a divine revelation. "Hindu Theosophy generally rejects the unmediated revelation of God."[18] Shtal'-berg identified and rejected the "great logical error, committed by Indian Theosophists, in their attempt to make logical deductions and conclusions based on concepts that are incomprehensible to the human mind" [i.e., an infinite, absolute, limitless, eternal, and uncreated God].[19]

The accusation of anti-Christianity was a particularly bitter pill for the Russian Theosophists, who had a far stronger Christian profile than their European brethren in the Society. The Russian members continued to insist that Theosophy in no way excluded Christianity. Anna Kamenskaia wrote in all sincerity, "If we take Theosophy as a moral doctrine, as a philosophical system of thought, we will not find a single thing in it that is inimical to Christianity; on the contrary, many Christians find that Theosophical ideas provide help, throw light on many dark questions and make the Christian faith itself stronger and more spiritual."[20] In assuming this position, Kamenskaia followed the lead of the president of the Theosophical Society, Mrs. Annie Besant, as far as she could within the Russian context.

Many critics found fault with Mrs. Besant's understanding of Christianity. Brought up an Anglican, Mrs. Besant had passed through theism to atheism and Fabian Socialism before she became passionately involved with Theosophy and converted to Brahmanic Hinduism. In the eyes of Russian Orthodox critics, in particular, these credentials were inadequate to grant legitimacy to her sweeping pronouncements about the "obvious" compatibility of Theosophy and Christianity. They resented Mrs. Besant's reduction of Christianity to a moral doctrine and pointed out that her statements showed clearly to just what doctrinal dangers the reductivism of syncretic thought and immersion in oriental philosophy could lead.

A major point of disagreement was the understanding of the essence and role of Christ. Anna Kamenskaia daringly claimed that "more developed Christians are beginning to see Christ more and more as an ideal of that toward which all mankind must strive, as a promise of that which mankind will become, and least of all as an external Saviour, redeeming sins through Himself."[21] Mrs. Besant had explained that Theosophy's *exoteric* Christ was one in a series of "Divine manifestations which from age to age are made for the helping of humanity, when a new impulse is needed to quicken the spiritual evolution of mankind, when a new civilization is about to dawn."[22] He was an Adept, a Mahatma, a Master, a Teacher; He was everything that was good, but He was not the one Redeemer or a unique historical fact. An example of advanced Humanity, Christ came into Earth's current incarnational cycle to bring a portion of the Secret Doctrine to those who were ready for it.[23]

Orthodox critics were appalled. Theosophy "does not consider Christ to be God," wrote a shocked Archimandrite Varlaam of Poltava. Theosophy "places Him no higher than Buddha, Mohammed, and other founders of pagan religions." In Theosophy "all of the great and divine work of Christ is understood in a perverted sense, with complete denial of the divinity of Jesus Christ and his incarnation as God."[24] Theosophy is "a denial of the divine Saviour of the world, His passion, His divine resurrection; it is the replacement of the Holy Cross by . . . the Seal of Solomon," lamented Vladimir Bykov.[25] "It appears that Theosophy is a dangerous enemy indeed," wrote an anonymous author in the conservative Orthodox journal *Khristianin*. "And so a concerted struggle against it is necessary, if we wish to preserve our Orthodoxy, and even more, Christianity itself."[26] The objections were sincere. For anyone raised in a traditional Orthodox context, even if that person chose to embrace agnosticism or atheism, it was one thing to reject Christ as a personal Saviour or the Son of God, but it took a leap of faith of quite a different sort to accept Him then as an Adept, a Mahatma currently living with other great Masters in a secret lamasery in the Himalayas and from there guiding Earth's development.

Theosophy's *esoteric* Christ, according to Mme Blavatsky, corresponds (in part) to the Gnostic *Christos*, "a candidate for hierophantship; who, when he had attained it, through Initiation, long trials and suffering, and had been anointed (i.e., 'rubbed with oil,' as Initiates and even Idols of the Gods were, as the last touch of ritualistic observance), was changed into *Christos*—the 'purified' in esoteric or mystery language."[27] A major part of the gnosis received by this Initiate, now a "Son of God," is the knowledge that one's spiritual self is one with God, that the world of matter is illusory, that one's true home is with the Spirit. To the Initiate is revealed the eternal cosmic paradigm that informs one's finite material existence. Refining this idea in the more Western light of Anthroposophy, Dr. Steiner explained that the human monad "made a movement downward into matter, and that before the lowest stage was reached, there came the other Impulse which impelled it again upward in the opposite direction [toward Spirit]. This was the Christ Impulse."[28]

In his Russian translation of Mrs. Besant's "The Christ," Pavel Batiushkov added an explanatory note to the text, pointing out that "Theosophy distinguishes between the historical 'Christ' and the mystical 'Christ,'" the difference being that the latter is "Christ as a state of soul, and not as the God-man."[29] Mrs. Besant's elaboration of the mystical Christ in *Esoteric Christianity*, which appears to have been a much studied and important text for the Esoteric Section of the Russian Society, reveals the profoundly Gnostic dimension of her Theosophical conception of Christ.[30] According to her, "every man is a potential Christ" and undergoes Christ's sacrifice: "As he then touches the lowest depth of sorrow, the hour of his triumph begins to dawn. For now he learns that he must himself become the God to whom he cries, and by feeling the last pang of separation he finds the eternal unity, he feels the fount of life is within, and knows himself eternal."[31] Clearly this position of identification with divine being, echoes of which are found among heretical Russian sects (primarily the White Doves and the Flagellants), would be viewed as uncanonical and profoundly heretical by the traditional Orthodox church, although many Russian God-seekers of the time, fascinated by sectarian theology, found it seductive.

The Russian Theosophists interpreted Vladimir Solov'ev's God-man in this same way, although Solov'ev himself never identified man as a latent god, but spoke specifically of the "image of God" within man. The Theosophists felt that they and Solov'ev were working toward the very same goal and frequently cited him in support of their position. This superficial similarity of goals is not surprising, since Solov'ev's own work is permeated by the same vocabulary, the same religious concerns, and the same Valentinian Gnosticism (as well as the theosophy of Jakob Boehme, the Kabbala, and other speculative mysticism). Solov'ev held that man has not yet come to the end of his path of organic and spiritual development, that man's task is to develop his still-weak spirit, and that his strengthened immortal spirit will eventually immortalize the body; this corresponded on some points with the Theosophical anthropogenesis. Nevertheless, Solov'ev was careful in his definitions; he did not share the fundamental assumptions of the Theosophists or their antagonism toward the Church. He even warned his readers against Mme Blavatsky: as early as 1884 he wrote, "The man who wishes to achieve divine knowledge by himself, bypassing the Church—such an individual mangod is the incarnation of falseness, a parody of Christ, or Antichrist."[32]

"Deification" (or "divinization"), as a concept, does exist in Eastern Orthodoxy. "'In my kingdom, said Christ, I shall be God with you as gods.' Such, according to the teaching of the Orthodox Church, is the final goal at which every Christian must aim, to become god, to attain *theosis*, 'deification' or 'divinization.' For Orthodoxy man's salvation and redemption means his deification," explains Timothy Ware.[33] Deification in the Orthodox sense, however, is not understood in the same way as the Theosophists understood the Gnostic identification of man with God. In Orthodoxy,

the mystical union between God and man is a true union, yet in this union Creator and creature do not become fused into a single being. Unlike the eastern religions which teach that man is swallowed up in the deity, Orthodox

> mystical theology has always insisted that man, however closely linked to
> God, retains his full personal integrity. Man, when deified, remains distinct
> (though not separate) from God. . . . Nor does man, when he "becomes
> god," cease to be human. . . . Man does not become God *by nature*, but is
> merely a "created god," a god *by grace.*[34]

To identify with God, the Creator, and not with His creation, was heresy in the eyes of Orthodox theologians.

For the Orthodox Christian, salvation involves a greater divine grace
and a lesser human will acting in concert (synergy); Theosophy, however, does not share the Christian concept of grace. The Divine All-
Unity does not bestow grace; instead, the human monad engineers its
own spiritual return to the Godhead by acquiring spiritual knowledge
and self-awareness. Theosophy replaces grace with knowledge and justice. What is perceived as grace, Mrs. Besant pointed out, is no more
than the subtle working of karma, the law of retribution.[35]

Russian Orthodox critics immediately seized on this point. Theosophy *"is false in its very essence,* since it did not recognize the presence of
grace in the world and thus lost sight of this most sacred realm of religious experience," wrote Father Dmitrevskii.[36] Grace does exist, he insisted, even if it does not visit Theosophists. Writing a few years later,
the philosopher Nikolai Berdiaev concurred that "the Eastern doctrine
of *karma* is a negation of loving grace and creative abundance. Everything occurs and everything is given only by the measure of justice. But
divine love is not justice; through it one receives immeasurably more
than one should receive through justice. This is the mystery of Christ."[37]

Not all Theosophists rejected the Christ mystery and the Christian
notion of grace; debate within the Society on this doctrinal point was
one of the elements that contributed to the defection from the Society
of a significant body of members, including those who returned to the
church and those who turned to Anthroposophy, rejecting Theosophy's
oriental dimension and seeking a specifically *Christian* theosophy instead. Certain aspects of Rudolf Steiner's "Christ Impulse," already
mentioned, can be viewed as an attempt to accommodate the concept of
divine grace in an occult system that would seem to exclude it. This ac-
commodation appealed to many Russian Theosophists and accounted
for the popularity of the Steinerian variant within both the Russian
Theosophical Society and the independent circles.

The Russian Theosophists did not go nearly as far as Mrs. Besant and
the parent Society in their interpretation of Christ's role. In many cases,
Anna Kamenskaia's versions of Theosophical doctrine were in direct opposition to Mrs. Besant's. Where Mrs. Besant specifically stated that
Christ is a teacher, an adept, a founder of an historical church in which

all can potentially become Sons of God, Anna Kamenskaia softened the contours, leaving Christ with some of His divinity intact. No doubt Kamenskaia was constrained by what the Russian censor would most certainly reject for publication; surely other things were said in the meetings of the Russian Esoteric Section; but, in all likelihood, Kamenskaia was creatively reinterpreting, rather than entirely evading, Mrs. Besant's position in order to suit her Russian audience.

Many of the Russian Theosophists enthusiastically assumed the role of martyr vis-à-vis the Orthodox church. They accused their clerical critics of intolerance, of missing the point that Theosophy is "obviously" not inimical to any other religion, that Theosophy's goals of brotherhood and tolerance are to be admired. They themselves entirely missed the point the Christian critics were trying to make. Christianity *is* an intolerant religion; most religions are intolerant. Kamenskaia's repeated affirmation that all religions preach tolerance is patently untrue, as even a cursory glance at world history shows. From the Christian point of view, Theosophy constitutes heresy; its use of Christian terminology does not make heresy any more palatable, but only more insidious and dangerous.

The problem was further complicated by Theosophy's internal inconsistency. On the one hand, it claimed that Christianity was entirely compatible with Theosophy; on the other, it criticized Christianity for its "deadening dogmatism" and monotheism. The Russian Theosophists could have avoided some of the more virulent polemics with the Orthodox church had they not attempted to use Christian concepts and terminology to legitimize their position vis-à-vis Christianity.

Theosophy's most sympathetic Russian Orthodox critic, Father Dmitrevskii, noted the social power of Theosophy and was also ready to grant that science had by no means accounted for everything in heaven and earth. Presentiment, clairvoyance, prophecy, telepathy, he wrote, were recognized by science as fact and a human being was certainly more than the sum of five physical senses. The generous Father Dmitrevskii was able to find a place for many aspects of Theosophical doctrine within Christianity, but even he was unable to get past the problem that Theosophy, as a synthesis of all faiths, past and present, is left with no faith at all. "Its luxuriant religious-philosophical structure is transformed into a cold palace for the dead," he observed.[38] In the end, he found Theosophy to be profoundly materialistic in its attempt to make a doctrine, a science, and a philosophy out of religion. In place of living faith, Theosophy offered comparative religion, which he shrewdly characterized as no more than the history of dead faiths; in place of a religious impulse, he lamented, it offered Buddhist pseudoscience.

2. *"Theosophy is Neo-Buddhism"*

The second major criticism leveled at Theosophy was that its pantheism
and its worldview were overtly Buddhist. Theosophy was perceived not
only as distinctly anti-Christian, but also as militantly pro-Buddhist. A
typical comment is that of ex-Theosophist Lev Kobylinskii-Ellis, that
Theosophy is "not only a non-Christian, but a specifically anti-Christian
movement, a restoration of Brahmanism and Buddhism under the guise
of pan-religious truth."[39]

In 1893 Vladimir Solov'ev's brother, Vsevolod, who never denied
that he had fallen victim to Theosophy's seductive appeal, wrote that the
Theosophical Society was not the "universal brotherhood" it claimed to
be, but an orthodox and active advocate of Buddhism. "Such enmity
and hatred of Christianity by the Theosophical Society is understand-
able," he said, continuing his shattering critique, because

> Christianity does not deny the reality of life, and is thus capable of developing
> and civilizing society. Theosophy sees life as "Maya" (an illusion), and so the
> society that accepts Theosophy cannot develop and civilize itself, but must
> inevitably degenerate; a good example of this is India itself. Christianity
> strives toward life, Buddhism toward death. The teaching of Christ is true
> altruism, Buddhism is the embodiment of egoism, made into an ideal. The
> ideal of Buddhism is a man who is apathetic toward good and evil, a hard-
> hearted man, because only such a man creates neither good nor bad Karma,
> no longer desires to live, calls life a boring illusion, and retreats into
> Nirvana.[40]

Thus Solov'ev warned against the egoism, the passivity, the rejection of
this world that is characteristic of Theosophy's neo-Buddhism and, in
his view, inimical to Orthodox Christianity.

Other contemporary critics quickly identified the two basic premises
of Theosophy, reincarnation and karma, as fundamentally incompatible
with Orthodox Christian doctrine. The Theosophists, with their all-embracing, syncretic theories, saw no contradiction. They integrated reincarnation into Christian thought by distinguishing between the ephemeral mortal personality (*lichnost'*) and the eternal divine spark, or soul
(*individual'nost'*). Unchanging, the soul went through numerous personalities over the course of many reincarnations while seeking the Divine One, as the soul of the Christian seeks God. Christianity had obviously misunderstood its own gospels, Mme Blavatsky pointed out, while
Theosophy clearly comprehended that "resurrection" really meant the
"rebirth" of the Ego in another form, i.e., reincarnation.[41]

Russian Christianity, needless to say, had a profoundly different approach to the gospels. It could never accept the Gnostic view of the dualism of matter and spirit that makes the notion of reincarnation possible. Orthodoxy considers each human being to be unique; and any form of metempsychosis is excluded by the doctrines of the Incarnation, the Atonement, and the resurrection of the body.[42]

Karma posed an additional, even more complex problem. Despite the oriental origin of the concept of karma, much of Theosophy's understanding of that concept was inevitably refracted through the prism of the Western religious, ethical, and mystical traditions. Steiner, raised as a Catholic, and Mrs. Besant, raised as an Anglican, may have intuited an implicit parallel between the Western Church's emphasis on legalism and God's justice and the oriental concept of karma (as the law of divine retribution and justice). Neither legalism nor justice, however, are the central focus of the theology of the Eastern Church; rather than divine justice and retribution, Orthodoxy emphasizes mysticism and sinful man's transfiguration by divine grace and love.

Rudolf Steiner attempted to explain away the implacability of karma and return the concept of grace by uniting the concepts of karma and Christ. In his 1908 reflections on the Gospel of St. John, he claimed, "The idea of Karma is bound up with the idea of the Christ in its deepest sense." Focusing on the nonjudgmental, forgiving attitudes of Christ, Steiner explained, "When anyone fully understands the idea of Karma, he will understand it in this Christian sense":

> It means that no man should set himself up as a judge of the inner soul of another human being. Unless the idea of Karma has been understood in this way, it has not been grasped in its deepest significance. When one man judges another, the one is always placing the other under the compulsion of his own ego. However, if a person really believes in the "I AM" in the Christian sense, he will not judge. He will say, "I know that Karma is the great adjuster. Whatever you may have done, I do not judge it!"[43]

In this way Steiner reasoned that all the Christian virtues—Christian humility, Christian acceptance, Christian forgiveness, and Christian love, given freely even to one's enemies—all implicitly indicate the recognition that one's actions and the actions of others are karmic necessity and cannot be judged on the basis of one act in one lifetime.

Integrating the concept of karma into a Christian paradigm was not easy, and Steiner comprehended a good part of the problem:

> When karma is conceived as a necessity imposed on man in order that his wrong-doings may be redressed and his errors redeemed by an implacable

justice working over from one incarnation to another, the objection is sometimes raised that karma must do away with the role of Christ as Redeemer. In
reality, karma is a redemption of man by *himself*, by dint of his own efforts as
he gradually ascends to freedom through the series of incarnations. It is
through karma that man is able to draw near to Christ.[44]

In attempting an explanation that would allow him to retain both the
redemptive function of the Christ and karma in his system, however,
Steiner was forced to rely on the Theosophical-Gnostic concept of the
identity of man and God, thus once again moving toward pantheism and
away from any position acceptable to Christianity.

The emphasis on karma additionally raised the problem for Russian
believers of freedom of will. Orthodox Christianity is not interested in
predestination; it rejects anything that infringes on the individual's free
will. Orthodox critics charged that Theosophical doctrine denied not
only the individuality of a human being (through reincarnation) but also
freedom of will (through karma): "If an individual is bound by a karmic
necessity created during a sequence of previous lives (the specifics of
which one does not know in this life), where is free will?" they asked.

Mrs. Besant never achieved an especially coherent understanding of
the problem of free will. Her response only succeeded in making a
murky subject opaque: "Man by the exercise of free will gradually creates necessities for himself, and between the two extremes lie all the
combinations of free will and necessity which make the struggles within
ourselves of which we are conscious."[45] This would hardly fit comfort-
ably into Russian Orthodoxy, and it certainly did not satisfy thoughtful
God-seekers like Nikolai Berdiaev, who felt that Theosophy's fundamental doctrinal points crushed not only free will, but any form of free
spiritual activity.[46]

To an Orthodox believer, Steiner's more "Christian" explanations of
the liberating aspect of karma leaned toward paradox. He explained that
it was specifically "the Christ Impulse [that] transforms implacable Law
into Freedom, and the source of this impulse is the person and example
of Christ Jesus." Steiner rejected any notion of fatalism (latent in any
Western conception of karma) and refused to identify the notion of
karma as essentially "fatalistic." Karma, he declared, was "an instrument
essential to the attainment of that supreme freedom which is life in
Christ—a freedom attained not by defying the world order but by fulfill-
ing it."[47]

The Universal Brotherhood of the Mahatmas, based on the oriental
concept of "teachers," or gurus, was another major stumbling block to
general acceptance of Theosophy. Many who were ready to accept the
Gnostic, pantheistic basis of Theosophy balked at accepting magical Ma-

hatmas, and yet the entire Theosophical doctrine appealed to the authority of the Mahatmas and rested on blind faith in them. Belief in the Mahatmas posited a faith every bit as nonrational as belief in Christ, but the Mahatmas were not even divine; they were simply Advanced Humanity. Theosophy had to establish the superiority of the Mahatmas to Jesus Christ in a "scientific" way if they were to be taken seriously. The Russian Theosophists, hoping to evade the issue entirely, had renamed the troublesome Mahatmas the "Unseen Forces Who Lead Us," but it was clear to everyone who these "Unseen Forces" were. Chistiakov, sniping from the pages of *Rebus*, did not conceal his aversion to the "nonsensical dogma of faith in those invisible and immortal ancients, the Mahatmas":

> This dogma, unless it is a hidden symbol, is naive and silly; moreover, it has always remained a vexing and irritating point of contradiction and has frequently precipitated unpleasant disagreements between Theosophists and people who are sympathetic to their activity, but wish to see Theosophical concepts based not on fables about invisible holy Mahatmas, but on a more rational foundation. . . . The fable of the Mahatmas has only inspired mistrust of the Society and forced many to think that it is unconsciously and secretly affiliated with political Freemasonry.[48]

Again, when Kudriavtsev attacked Theosophy, it was this gullible and unquestioning acceptance of the "obvious fairy tale" about the Mahatmas that he despised most.

The extent to which Russian Theosophists seriously embraced Buddhist and Hindu thought is difficult to establish, although the external trappings of Eastern tradition are everywhere visible. Theosophical texts are full of Buddhist vocabulary, for example. The Theosophists peppered their texts with words like *chela, manvantara, devachan, Gupta Vidya, kamaloka, maya, paranirvana*, and numerous other borrowings.[49] Mikhail Petrovo-Solovovo, a frequent contributor to *Rebus*, observed on more than one occasion that Theosophical vocabulary seemed invariably saturated with "more than a few unintelligible Hindu terms, for which Theosophists have a particular weakness."[50]

The Russian Theosophists were also much taken with Indian material culture. The Indian motif was a large part of their image: they decorated their Theosophical salons with Indian textiles and art objects, sold Indian souvenirs to raise money, and used Indian jewelry, textiles, and design in their own dress. Several Russian Theosophists became respected specialists in oriental culture and literature. On her trip to Adyar to visit Theosophical Headquarters in 1916, Anna Kamenskaia, who learned Sanskrit and eventually became a specialist on Hindu sacred texts, was entrusted with the collecting of objects of Indian material culture for the

Academy of Science's Museum of Anthropology and Ethnography in St. Petersburg. The more enthusiastic St. Petersburg Theosophists spoke of building their own Buddhist temple in St. Petersburg, although there is no indication whatsoever that large numbers of Russian Theosophists ever converted to Buddhism.

The Theosophists also translated and paraphrased various Hindu and pseudo-Buddhist texts into Russian, and popularized them. Vera Johnston, Mme Blavatsky's niece, published "Otryvki iz Upanishad" in *Voprosy Filosofii i Psikhologii*; Konstantin Bal'mont, a Symbolist poet and Theosophist, translated Asvagosha's *Life of Buddha*; Pavel Batiushkov translated parts of Mabel Collins's *Light on the Path*; Elena Pisareva was a prolific translator, not only of Mme Blavatsky's own invented "Buddhist" texts (such as the "Stanzas of Dzyan"), but also those of Mabel Collins (which she claimed were ancient Indian devotional texts transmitted to her by "Hilarion," her personal Mahatma). The works of Rama-Krishna, Yogi Ramacharaka, Swami Vivekananda, and Sri-Shankara-Acharya were also available in Russian.[51] There were several translations of the *Bhagavad Gita* (which constitutes one section of the Indian epic, the *Mahabharata*, and is the one work of Hindu metaphysics widely known in the West). The most popular Russian translation of this famous text was the work of Kamenskaia and her friend, Irma Mantsiarli. Few Russian Theosophists, however, could work with original Sanskrit texts (Anna Kamenskaia being a notable exception), and most Russian translations were based on English, German, or French translations of oriental texts, allowing numerous errors and mistranslations to creep in.

In spite of the prevailing passion for things Indian, Theosophy, in its Russian variant, substantially reduced the excessive Buddhist and Hindu element that Anglo-American and Indian Theosophy publicly embraced.[52] The Russian Theosophists played down both Mme Blavatsky's anti-Christianity and Mrs. Besant's pro-Hinduism. *Vestnik Teosofii* regularly commemorated Russian Orthodox holy days and made reference to Orthodox saints. Russian Theosophists looked as much to Tolstoi, Dostoevskii, and Vladimir Solov'ev for inspiration as to the *Bhagavad Gita* or the *Upanishads*.

Theosophy's introduction of the oriental component into Russian popular culture at the turn of the century resonated to the larger philosophical concerns of Russian society. While European Theosophy frequently wore its oriental trappings as fashionable and exotic garb that served to distinguish its members from the "common herd" and make them "interesting," Russian Theosophy's oriental trappings manifested the centuries-old ambivalence felt by Russian culture toward the East. Russian Theosophy actively participated in the larger expression of the psychic crisis that had been formulating itself in Russia since at least the time of Peter the Great: Did Russia belong to the East or to the West? This question was of paramount importance to the thinkers of the Russian Silver Age; it was asked over and over again by Dmitrii Merezhkovskii (who warned of the "Yellow-faced Positivists"), Nikolai Berdiaev (who feared oriental passivity and chaos), Andrei Belyi (who titled his projected literary trilogy "East or West?"), and other God-seekers of the period.

The formless, chaotic threat of pan-Mongolism and the Yellow Peril was certainly a psychic reality for the Russians (especially after the annihilating defeats of the Russo-Japanese War), and some part of the Russian mind intuitively feared the turn Eastward, feared the anti-individualism, passive self-contemplation, withdrawal from life, and rejection of material reality that lay at the root of Eastern thought. But another part of the Russian psyche rejected the regimented materialism of Western culture and sought some kind of spiritual alternative. Russian thinkers like Vladimir Solov'ev felt that the mystical theology of the Eastern Orthodox church would provide the proper platform for the synthesis of occidental materialism and oriental spiritualism. Russian Theosophists, aspiring to similar goals, were certain that Theosophy could best provide that platform. Father Dmitrevskii, one of the Theosophists' more objective and conscientious critics, noticed this very element in Theosophical thought:

> The Theosophists point to the particular place of Russia between the East and the West and to the mission of unification that stems therefrom. They say that Theosophy has grasped the religious thought of the great religions of the East and is under the influence of Christianity; as such, it is the child of various religious-philosophical trends; this is obvious from its literature, which bears the stamp of amazing profundity and breadth. . . . It is possible that no one has such an organic spiritual tie to ancient India as the Russians do: Russian mysticism and the religious philosophy of India have profound points of coincidence and who knows?—perhaps the culture of the future will be born of this fiery point of contact.[53]

It was tempting to see the Theosophical "marriage" of Christianity and Buddhism as an attempt to reconcile East and West. Such a reconciliation, the Theosophists assured their critics, was an integral part of Russia's cultural mission to the world:

> Carefully wiping the dust of ages from the treasures of the religious thought of the ancient East, Theosophy has evoked the Renaissance of India, but it did not do this in order to supplant Christianity and transfer the negative features of the East to the West. The unification of the spiritual creativity of the East and the West is necessary for both sides: for the East, so as to shift the passive

inertia of its social consciousness with the active energy of the European; and for the West, so as to spiritualize the material culture of the Europeans with the high idealism of the Hindus, so that our soulless and petty bourgeois culture, mad with the pursuit of paltry pleasures, can be inspired by the noble, subtly aristocratic spirit which permeates Hindu culture.[54]

The events of the First World War (essentially a Western war) pushed Russian Theosophy further in the direction of the Orient. An editorial in the fall 1915 issue of *Vestnik Teosofii* pointed out how similar the Russian mind was to the oriental mind. Quoting from a recent article on "National Types of Culture" that had appeared in *Severnye Zapiski,* the author pointed out that both the spiritual, ethical, and philosophical strivings of the Russian people and their rejection of materialism and bourgeois comfort make them similar to the Hindu, not to the Westerner.[55] "Of all the young races, the Slavs are closer to the East, the source of religious light, than any other. A new Renaissance will burst forth in Europe after a period of cleansing war. . . . It is difficult to go against the laws of history: now, again, tired of the false Teutonic culture, we who are plunged in darkness extend our supplicatory arms to the holy, radiant East."[56]

More than any other discrete group except, perhaps, the God-seeking philosophers, the Russian Theosophists helped to formulate the problem of East and West in Russian culture. Their voice spoke for the Orient in the popular intellectual debates of the period; it forced the intelligentsia to rethink its own assumptions and to clarify its own philosophical and religious positions. The intense animosity Orthodox critics felt toward Theosophy's Orientalism was proof both of the threat its neo-Buddhism potentially posed to Orthodox Christianity and the seductive power that oriental philosophy could wield over the Russian religious mind.

3. *"Theosophy is Pseudoscience and Materialistic Pantheism"*

According to another group of critics, at Theosophy's core lay an essentially materialist, not idealist, doctrine. Theosophy, these critics claimed, tried to make a religion out of the "science" of religion, i.e., the study of the foundations of religion; its scientific or pseudoscientific proofs, however, were powerless to replace religious faith. Theosophy provided a detailed cosmogony, but never generated a theogony; it reconstructed "ancient wisdom," but neglected (or was unable) to find God. Its critics charged that it produced a nebulous, spurious, and, ultimately, sterile pseudoscientific doctrine. "Theosophy wants a purely human, earthly religion. It wants only to satisfy the religious feelings of man, but without any thought of God, toward Whom the human spirit strives. Theosophy wants to trick the religious manifestation of conscience; instead of an animating faith in a Living God, it provides a soporific atheism. For Mrs. Besant, who is an atheist by conviction (see her *Autobiography*), this is a natural step, but for a Christian, this is unacceptable," complained Konstantin Kudriavtsev.[57] Since God did not exist, the Mahatmas had to be invented to fill the external role of God in the Theosophical religious paradigm. And so Theosophy focused on Buddhism, and not on Christianity: oriental pantheism allowed it to say that everything is divine. Unfortunately, concluded Kudriavtsev, this left the individual with no personal God; and a religious-philosophical doctrine "about" God, but "without" God, was pointless.

Theosophy's philosophical and logical errors were identified and catalogued not only by apostate Theosophists, philosophers, and ecclesiastical critics, but also by scholars and other representatives of the "scientific" point of view. These critics maintained that there was not and could not be anything "scientific" about a synthesis of religion, science, and philosophy; such a synthesis would, by definition, be superficial and reductive. Theosophy was seeking scientific explanations for metaphysical and mystical phenomena; such explanations could only be pseudoscientific and misleading. The empirical cognition of noumena, as Kant had pointed out, was impossible in a modern, scientific world. Vsevolod Solov'ev, one of Theosophy's more informed critics, wrote, "For those who are familiar with the contemporary moods of our society and who take them seriously, the damage that can be done by an attraction to a *profoundly materialistic* doctrine, painted over with various *superstitions* and *imaginary miracles* and bearing the splendid name 'Theosophy' and the 'Wisdom Religion,' is obvious."[58] And he was not alone in considering Theosophy to be "scientific superstition." The same conclusion had been reached by the ecclesiastical critics as well.[59]

The complaint that Theosophy was guilty of reductivism and syncretism was made repeatedly. Mme Blavatsky had pointed out that "esoteric philosophy reconciles all religions, strips every one of its outward, human garments, and shows the root of each to be identical with that of every other great religion."[60] But in her attempt to embrace the vast ground of human religious thought, she succeeded only in forming an artificial, composite doctrine built of the bits and pieces of other faiths. "It is not synthesis that we see in Theosophy, but syncretism: the mechanical combination of elements of Western and Eastern thought, artfully combined with a basic substratum of Buddhism," observed *Rebus* in an article marking the thirtieth anniversary of the founding of the Theosophical Society.[61]

Theosophical texts, especially the associative, hypnotic prose of Mme Blavatsky herself, are remarkable for the sheer scope of their eclecticism. Benefiting greatly from G. R. S. Mead's scholarly and competent editorial hand, Mme Blavatsky's major work, *The Secret Doctrine*, remains a tour de force within the huge body of occult literature. It most clearly reveals, however, the problems of syncretism. Mme Blavatsky quarries quotations from a multitude of sources; she misquotes and misinterprets, takes her material out of context, and pairs it with other seemingly similar material. There is no religious thinker, philosopher, or metaphysician, from Abelard to Zeno, whom she does not cite somewhere. The result is a work of epic syncretism, wide open to attack from clerics, specialists in comparative religion, philosophers, and scientists, as well as representatives of other occult movements.

Theosophy was the object of particular criticism from the eminent Oxford Orientalist Friedrich Max Müller (1823–1900), a specialist on the sacred books of the East, and Theosophy's archenemy. Although Müller was "quite willing to allow that Madame Blavatsky started with good intentions, that she saw and was dazzled by a glimmering of truth in various religions of the world, and that she believed in the possibility of a mystic union of the soul with God," he felt that she erred in her assumption that "it was incumbent on every founder of a religion to perform miracles." In the end, he came to consider the Theosophical Society harmful and the works of its founder inaccurate, misleading, and intellectually pernicious. Müller was particularly critical of Mme Blavatsky's ignorance of Sanskrit, Pali, and the classical languages. "Unfortunately," he observed, "she was without the tools to dig for those treasures in the ancient literatures of the world, and her mistakes in quoting from Sanskrit, Greek, and Latin would be amusing if they did not appeal to our sympathy rather for a woman who thought that she could fly though she had no wings, not even those of Icarus."[62] Müller's widely circulated critical remarks were quickly translated and eagerly shared with Russian readers by the editors of *Rebus*.

Orientalists repeatedly criticized the founders and leaders of Theosophy for their ignorance of Indic languages and their selective and superficial knowledge of the history of religion, especially Buddhism. The Theosophists countered by claiming that *their* Buddhism was not ordinary, garden-variety Buddhism, but *esoteric* Buddhism. Esoteric Buddhism was not the *exoteric* teaching of Guatama Buddha (that was for the masses); it was not contained in the canonical Buddhist texts. Theosophical Buddhism was "that religion signifying literally the doctrine of wisdom, and which by many ages antedates the metaphysical philosophy of Siddhartha Sakyamuni," pointed out Mme Blavatsky.[63] In this way she ensured that educated Orientalists, having never seen the hidden secret texts and having never met the completely inaccessible Tibetan Mahatmas, could not possibly criticize Theosophy's esoteric Buddhism. This ploy did not stop Müller from pointing out that Mme Blavatsky's "esoteric" Buddhist writings were aberrations, that "no traveler's tale was ever more audacious and more incongruous than this misrepresentation of Buddha and his doctrine."[64]

Even while fighting the accusations of being pseudoscientific, Theosophy was ironically unable to rise above the positivist mindset of its age. Thus Theosophists proudly announced that in Theosophy "the foundations of Eastern doctrines (the doctrine of reincarnation and the doctrine of karma) merge with the doctrine which forms the basis of all Western European science (the doctrine of evolution), and this merging provides the first completely rational and scientifically based foundation for the hypothesis of the immortality of the soul."[65] Theosophy might speak of astral planes and karma and Atman, but it still assumed the Darwinian idea of progressive evolution and human progress, even if this progress was achieved through reincarnation instead of in more conventional ways.

Indeed, various critics found Theosophy too materialistic, too lacking in spirit, grace, and love, too descriptive and insufficiently creative to offer much to the discriminating seeker. Berdiaev accused Theosophy of being no more than "expanded positivism," and not true "divine wisdom": it "transfers the laws of natural evolution to other planes and other worlds, into the life of the spirit." But that, he pointed out, is not mystery wisdom; it is a variant form of Darwinism. Berdiaev never denied, however, that although "Theosophy is not great in itself, it is connected with that which is great and a reflection of ancient divine wisdom does touch it."[66]

Many Theosophists tended to reify their doctrine's spiritual tenets, to accept them literally instead of metaphorically or symbolically. They drew blueprints of the cosmos, mathematically calculated cosmic infinitudes, plotted the life of the soul in their attempt to apply "scientific" methodologies to their metaphysics, turned karma into spiritual bookkeeping, and "replaced the unmediated perception of existence with a perception of the diagrams of existence."[67] The religious philosopher Ivan Il'in (1882–1954) was severely critical of the Theosophists' "scientific" pretensions:

They love to hide behind the word "science," but in actual fact they preach and implement some sort of ostensibly spiritual practice. In their crepuscular spiritual practice, which they conceive of, if not as wisdom, then at least as the true path toward wisdom, the pure light of philosophical knowledge grows dim and the conscious, intelligent life of the *spirit* dissolves in the cultivation of the more physical sides and abilities of the *soul*: such is their "clairvoyance," purchased at the price of meaninglessness and the rejection of free subjective intuition. In vain they speak of "science": their science has nothing in common with that science which objectively studies the subject, openly affirms and openly proves; their science is *magic*, and the content of their "doctrine"—a disturbing chimera.[68]

Il'in concluded that Theosophists and Anthroposophists were "enemies and distorters of true philosophy" and that their doctrine was "an unoriginal and eclectic confusion of no interest whatsoever."[69]

Theosophy, "the synthesis of science, religion, and philosophy," failed to satisfy completely either the intellectuals, or the scientists, or the mystics, or the philosophers, being itself neither science nor religion nor philosophy; its critics considered it no more than a fashionable syncretism that offered the gullible old wine in cracked bottles. "Theosophy is full of hopeless antinomies and contradictions," lamented Lev Kobylinskii-Ellis, "uniting the absolute stasis of Eastern religion with the limitless evolutionism of Western theories, themselves already superseded; Asian nationalism with Parisian modernism; esoteric magic with American advertising; and finally, claims to synthesis with vulgar ignorance."[70]

Nikolai Berdiaev, who, like Kobylinskii-Ellis, had flirted with Theosophy in his youth but eventually found it wanting, criticized both Theosophy and Anthroposophy for ignoring certain major trends in nineteenth-century culture. The Theosophists attempted to come to terms with the natural sciences, Berdiaev pointed out, but avoided the social sciences. Rudolf Steiner's Anthroposophy answered the biologist Ernst Haeckel (1834–1919) and his theory of materialistic monism (an easy target), but neither Theosophy nor Anthroposophy answered Karl Marx.[71] Yet, the perceptive Berdiaev pointed out, Theosophy and Marxism had a great deal in common. "Eastern Theosophy is typical Westernizing on Russian soil," he observed; it is an arcane form of Western positivism. Both are artificial, cosmopolitan, international movements with no indigenous, national roots.[72] Berdiaev even called Theosophical literature "party" literature and compared it to enthusiastic but opinionated and cliché-ridden social-democratic tracts. His opinion echoed that of Kobylinskii-Ellis, who also identified the strong "propaganda element" in Theosophical literature and termed it "party agitation."[73]

Theosophy and the Russian Intelligentsia

Theosophy took particular hold of certain members of the Russian creative and God-seeking intelligentsia—writers, critics, artists, and philosophers—evoking from them responses that were sometimes positive, sometimes negative, often ambivalent. The intelligentsia's attitude toward Theosophy was, of course, more complicated than an ingenuous acceptance of it as an answer to the nineteenth century's crisis of culture and consciousness, or a rejection of it on firm moral or religious grounds. Their polemic with Theosophy differed from that of the apostate believers, the traditional clergy, the theologians, and the scholars.

The Russian creative intelligentsia did not write the Theosophists off as crackpots, but took the dialogue with Theosophy seriously; either they viewed it as a legitimate voice in the larger dialogue on culture, religion, and philosophy, or saw it as part of turn-of-the-century society's general interest in oriental religions and cultures that was visible in Russian scholarship, literature, music, art, and even architecture. Theosophy was one of several unusual paths explored by the Silver Age intelligentsia in their various spiritual, philosophical, and aesthetic quests. The creative intelligentsia was quick to identify and respond not only to Theosophy's religious and philosophical dimensions, but also to the mythic, poetic, and aesthetic implications of Theosophical thought.

This was especially true of the Russian Symbolist writers, who drew inspiration from Theosophy and even used its cosmogenetic paradigm to justify their own theories that art was religious creativity, as Andrei Belyi did in his novels and theoretical articles. Numbered among the Symbolists were not only committed Theosophists, such as Konstantin Bal'mont, Nikolai Minskii, Max Voloshin, and Andrei Belyi, but also curious seekers who flirted with, but eventually left, Theosophy, such as Nikolai Berdiaev, Aleksei Remizov, Valerii Briusov, and Viacheslav Ivanov.

Certain Russian modernist painters (Nikolai Roerich, Margarita Sabashnikova, and Wasily Kandinsky, among others) felt that Theosophy helped them to enhance the spiritual and intellectual content of their painting. The composer Aleksandr Skriabin, a member of the Belgian Section of the Theosophical Society, based his theory that the creation of music was a theurgic act of divine play directly on Theosophical doctrine.[74] Like the literary Symbolists, Skriabin was concerned with Theosophy's concept of theurgy, the importance of incantation and rhythm as a profoundly "magic" act, *sobornost'* as mystical experience, art as a form of religious action, the synthesis of matter and spirit—all notions central to Theosophy. Theosophy certainly touched the interests of the religious and esoteric philosophers, like Nikolai Berdiaev and P. D. Uspenskii, who felt the psychological attraction of Theosophical thought and pursued it at a formative time in their lives, although they eventually moved beyond it.

The creative intelligentsia and the Theosophists spoke a mutually intelligible, if not identical, language. They used many of the same cultural catchwords. Like other intellectual movements of the early twentieth century, Russian Theosophy clearly reflected the apocalypticism of its age. Certain aspects of its doctrine played on the various eschatological fears and expectations of the Silver Age. Theosophical notions of world catastrophe, cleansing destruction, suffering, and the building of a new, superior culture in which Russia would play a leading role were variants on the same messianic theme dear to God-seekers and God-builders alike. Theosophy resonated not only to the religious visions of Nikolai Fedorov, Vladimir Solov'ev, and Dmitrii Merezhkovskii, but also to the theurgical aspirations of Maksim Gorkii, based on his personal transmutations of modern Theosophy and Slavic sectarian Gnosticism. Gorkii's vision of a New Nature and a New World (subsequently assimilated to its socialist expression as the Radiant Future) is fundamentally Theosophical.[75]

Many members of the intelligentsia, particularly among the modernist writers and religious thinkers, were also able to find common ground with the Theosophists because their own views of religion tended toward the unconventional. Like the Theosophists, they, too, were interested in ancient mystery cults, sectarianism, Gnosticism, and the history of religious thought. Such views were occasionally expressed at the meetings of the various religious-philosophical societies that formed in St. Petersburg, Moscow, Kiev, and other cities of the Russian Empire. The more intellectually inclined Theosophists also belonged to these societies and participated in their discussions. The names of the leading Russian idealist philosophers (Sergei Bulgakov, E. N. Trubetskoi, Sergei Frank, Nikolai Berdiaev, Vasilii Rozanov, Aleksandr Meier, Dmitrii Filosofov, and N. O. Losskii) frequently appeared in *Vestnik Teosofii*; their lectures and articles were regularly reported and reviewed in its pages.

Anna Kamenskaia found Vladimir Solov'ev's and Nikolai Berdiaev's thought particularly relevant and cited them often. In spite of their criticisms of certain aspects of Theosophy, Kamenskaia found no inconsistency in using their statements to buttress her own brochures and lectures.[76] Both Solov'ev and Berdiaev considered the Theosophical phenomenon to be culturally important. "Despite all of the Theosophical Society's theoretical and moral flaws," wrote Solov'ev, "it, either in its present form or in the form of the neo-Buddhist movement evoked by it, is apparently cast for an important historical role in the immediate future."[77] Berdiaev also conceded the importance of Theosophy and its variant form, Anthroposophy, for the growth of the Russian religious urge. He freely admitted that the role of Theosophy had grown in Russia and would continue to grow. "Closely observing the religious seeking of our time, one cannot pass by Theosophy, because for certain strata of contemporary educated society Theosophy has made it easier to come to religion," he pointed out.[78] Both thinkers, while generally critical of Theosophy, expressed their opinions of it with sufficient ambivalence to warrant Kamenskaia's use of their comments in certain contexts.

The Theosophists felt themselves in touch not only with philosophical God-seeking, but also with literary modernism, which had a strong religious-philosophical dimension. Poems by Max Voloshin, Konstantin Bal'mont, and Aleksandr Dobroliubov (a decadent poet who rejected contemporary society and founded his own religious sect), appeared in *Vestnik Teosofii*. The journal also made reference to other modernist writers, such as Aleksandr Blok, Andrei Belyi, Viacheslav Ivanov, and Georgii Chulkov. *Vestnik* often printed entire articles by and about Lev Tolstoi. The Theosophists created their own cult of Tolstoi, blending Theosophy, Tolstoyanism, and oriental thought into an exotic Theosophical version of the Russian Idea.

The Theosophists were much taken by Tolstoi, and he expressed interest in their ideas as well, although he was ambivalent about the Theosophical Society as an organization and felt that the well-meaning Theosophists frequently muddled what were originally good ideas. Tolstoi had first heard of Theosophy and Mme Blavatsky from his friend Nikolai Aleksandrovich L'vov (1834–1887), a well-known Moscow Spiritualist, early in 1884. "L'vov told me about Blavatskaia, the transmigration of souls, the powers of the spirit, the white elephant, and a new faith."[79] He heard of her again in May 1884, when his friend Leonid Dmitrievich Urusov wrote him from Paris, where Mme Blavatsky had just then arrived from India and was about to be investigated by the Society for Psychical Research. Tolstoi subscribed to several European Theosophical journals and became a reader of *Vestnik Teosofii* shortly before his death. He also read most of the materials on oriental religions published under the auspices of the Theosophical Society, from the *Bhagavad Gita* to the translations of the Swamis Vivekananda and Ramakrishna. He also read Mme Blavatsky with interest, and liked her devotional work, *Voice of the Silence*.

Tolstoi was acquainted with several of the leading Theosophists. He had first met Dmitrii Stranden, Kamenskaia's right hand, when Stranden had been tutor to the son of Vladimir Grigor'evich Chertkov, Tolstoi's friend and secretary. On June 29, 1908, Anna Kamenskaia and Elena Pisareva made a pilgrimage to Tolstoi's estate, Iasnaia Poliana, to discuss Buddhism and the fate of Russia.[80] Tolstoi also briefly corresponded with Elena Pisareva's husband, Nikolai.

The Theosophists had good reasons to be worshippers at Tolstoi's shrine, for there were indeed parallels between Tolstoyanism and Theosophy. Like the Theosophists, Tolstoi attempted to rationalize faith, to make religion into knowledge rather than accept a belief not founded in "fact"; like the Theosophists, he rejected the concepts of mystery and divine grace and focused on Christian ethics, not theology. He was much taken by certain Buddhist ideas, including rejection of the physical world, a consoling attitude toward death (which Tolstoi feared), and passivity in the face of emotion and action (from which comes Tolstoyan nonresistance to evil), and, like the Theosophists, he filtered these ideas through a Russian prism. In Tolstoi's modern Buddhism is the source of the latent pantheism and metaphysical impersonalism that characterizes much of his thought. Finally, Tolstoi expressed his concern for the fate of Russia in terms not dissimilar to those of the Theosophists. They saw in him a natural ally for their cause.

Theosophy was also a topic of heated discussion in the rarefied atmosphere of the Russian Religious-Philosophical Society in St. Petersburg. At the end of 1909 the Society devoted an entire session to an examination of Theosophy. On November 24 Anna Kamenskaia was the featured speaker at their meeting, chaired that evening by her colleague, K. D. Kudriavtsev. Her talk, "Theosophy and God-Building," created a great deal of controversy, with the religious syncretism of Theosophy being one of the chief objections voiced. Kamenskaia, who was acquainted with most of the regular members of the Religious-Philosophical Society and easily anticipated their criticisms, presented a defense of Theosophy, stressing the following points: Theosophy is *not* neo-Buddhism; Theosophy is *not* materialistic pantheism; Theosophy is *not* an artificially created, eclectic, religio-philosophical system; Theosophy *is* a universal scientific-religious synthesis, at the basis of which are the Doctrine of the Logos, the Doctrine of the Path, and Ethics.[81]

The religious scholar, Symbolist poet, and critic Viacheslav Ivanov was the first discussant in the lively session that followed her presentation. He stressed the difference between "theosophy" as mystic gnosis, for which he had great respect, and "Theosophy" as the doctrine of the Theosophical Society, of which he was wary. His major objection was that Theosophy as a doctrine was excessively syncretic; this was potentially dangerous, since mixing religions, observed this Russian writer who tried to revive the ancient Greek mystery cults in the twentieth century, succeeds merely in distorting all of them. Ivanov wanted to know whether or not the Theosophical Society considered itself to be a church. He feared that all Theosophists were actually Buddhists and that Mme Blavatsky was profoundly anti-Christian. The one Theosophist for whom he had a good word was the "Christian Theosophist," Rudolf Steiner, to whose point of view Anna Mintslova had recently converted Ivanov.

The next attack came from the religious thinker and writer Dmitrii Merezhkovskii, who had actually attended Theosophical lectures, had heard Rudolf Steiner lecture in Paris in 1906, and had participated in the Theosophical discussions held in Anna Filosofova's salon as the friend of her son, Dmitrii Filosofov. Merezhkovskii admitted that Theosophy did not interest him at all; he felt toward Theosophy only "a gloomy lack of curiosity"; as for the Theosophists themselves, well, he found them "mercilessly kind."[82] Typically, Merezhkovskii did not underrate or understate the importance of Theosophy as an intellectual force, but he was excessively condescending, calling it "a terrible trap." It certainly competed with his own version of neo-Christianity and deflected attention from himself. "I feel revulsion and hatred [toward Theosophy] in particular," he added; it is no more than "the inspiration of the commonplace. Everything is uncommonly true, but everything is also uncommonly old hat."[83] As usual, Merezhkovskii soon mounted and rode away on his own hobby horse, the problem of evil. This problem, he claimed, is central to Christianity, but only peripheral to Buddhism. Theosophy lacks the threat of eternal perdition, a threat that Merezhkovskii apparently found appealing, for he spoke of hell and damnation enthusiastically and at length. He, like Ivanov, feared that Theosophy was a "false church."

The Theosophical position was defended by Kamenskaia, Kudriavtsev, and Elena Pisareva. Pisareva answered that churches are based on exoteric dogmas created by human reason. Theosophy, on the other hand, synthesizes esoteric teaching, which is *one*, regardless of the outer, exoteric garments it assumes historically; hence syncretism plays no role. Neither can Theosophy be a "religion" or a "church," since it is "scientific."[84] Kamenskaia, a competent if uninspired speaker, defended Theosophy well, although she was unable to break through the problem of definitions. Kudriavtsev was an enthusiastic but unconvincing defender; his contribution was to point out that Dmitrii Merezhkovskii, as a religious thinker, was "unawakened."[85] Kamenskaia soothed her God-seeking audience with a last word that touched on the Russian Idea: "If we have admitted that the Russian people, the Slavs, really have a particular tendency toward mysticism, then we should allow that it is actually through us [the Russians] that a new word and a new revelation should go forth."[86] And who would do this better than the internationally connected and cosmopolitan Russian Theosophists?

The attitude of the God-seeking philosophers toward Steiner and his "Christian Theosophy" was considerably different from their attitude toward Mme Blavatsky and Mrs. Besant; that they respected the work of the German Theosophist became clear at the Religious-Philosophical Society meeting of November 24, 1909. Recalling his meeting with Steiner in Paris in the spring of 1906, Merezhkovskii, conveniently putting aside the tension his provocative behavior had generated, said: "He [Steiner] had said that he had much to do in Russia; that he had many hopes for Russia; and that our meeting was not accidental. The impression that Viacheslav Ivanovich [Ivanov] received from a more profound study of [Steiner's] works coincides completely with my own impression of Steiner. I felt that in Steiner I had met not only a Theosophist, but an occultist as well."[87] Viacheslav Ivanov, who was then taken with Steinerian Theosophy (through the influence of Anna Mintslova, Margarita Sabashnikova, and Andrei Belyi), had called the German's Theosophy "an independent Steinerian trend which seeks to define itself as Christian."[88]

Steiner offered the Russian intelligentsia much more than a "Christianized" alternative to the neo-Buddhism of Theosophy. His emerging esoteric system also focused on three areas not generally emphasized by the Theosophists but of great importance to a certain faction within the Russian God-seeking intelligentsia: German idealist philosophy, the Mystery of Golgotha (the Christ Impulse), and Goetheanism. By "Goetheanism" Steiner meant an attempt to comprehend the interrelationship of the spiritual and the scientific search, as represented by Goethe's literary and scientific studies. Steiner saw Goethe as a man who had learned everything that modern science had to teach him, and, at the same time, had not neglected to develop his own spiritual faculties: Goethe symbolized a merging, in fact, of the scientific and the spiritual. In Steiner's system, "the dualism between religion and natural science was to be overcome not through a fuzzy pantheism, but through precise research in spiritual science [*Geisteswissenschaft*]" on Goethe's model, explained Margarita Sabashnikova.[89] Thus did Steiner seek to avoid the accusations of pantheism and Orientalism that made dialogue between Theosophy and Christianity difficult at best.

The second-generation Symbolists (Andrei Belyi, Viacheslav Ivanov, Kobylinskii-Ellis, and others) were all permeated with German idealist thought.[90] Their worldview owed much to medieval German mystics, to Schopenhauer, Schelling, Nietzsche, Wagner, and the neo-Kantians. The idealist and religious philosophers came from similar backgrounds; with few exceptions they stemmed from academic or intelligentsia families. Many of them studied with German professors at Russian universities; others were educated in Germany; several trained as natural scientists but chose to devote their lives to the arts and philosophy; all were desirous of reviving their Christian faith—now seen in a larger, not strictly Russian context—in a post-Kantian world. All were cosmopolitan, but with a strong neo-Slavophile residue. Steiner's credentials as rigorously trained philosopher in the German style, his knowledge of European mysticism, his belief in the important role of the Slavic folk soul in human development, and his neo-Christianity made him a figure of immense interest to these circles.

Steiner's "Christianized" Theosophy, Anthroposophy, nevertheless did not escape criticism from the Russian God-seekers. Berdiaev recognized Anthroposophy as "Gnostic Christology" and identified the Anthroposophists as "Gnostic sectarians"; this was acceptable before the First World War, when Berdiaev was himself under the sway of the Gnostic heresy, but not later. The archpriest Georgii Florovskii immediately knew Anthroposophy for "a psychological relapse into Gnosticism." While Anthroposophy returned Christ to the religious equation, the role it assigned to Him did not suit many of the Russian neo-Christians any more than it suited traditional Orthodox clerics.

The major criticism leveled against Steiner by the more ambivalent Russian God-seekers was that the German occultist was insufficiently spontaneous and intuitive, hence anticreative. "Steiner's secret science gives the impression of being not intuitive knowledge, not an integral penetration into the mysteries of existence, but of being an analytical anatomization of existence," complained Berdiaev. "Clairvoyance such as this examines the world as cadaver."[91] True spiritual cognition should preserve the human dimension. "Man is called upon to be an active creator in cosmic life, and not a passive instrument of the cosmic process, the meaning of which is alien and unknown to him."[92]

Berdiaev relevantly pointed out that both Mme Blavatsky's and Dr. Steiner's doctrines were cosmocentric. One can emphasize the cosmos, one can emphasize God, or one can emphasize Man (and the God-man, Christ). Both Theosophy and Anthroposophy (the former regardless of its "God"-centered name and the latter regardless of its "Man"-centered name) are mired in extravagant cosmologies (with astral planes and the reincarnations of planetary chains and Atlantean and post-Lemurian epochs and Moon beings); they are little more than naturalistic taxonomies of cosmic events and have lost sight of both God and man. Even Christ, pointed out Berdiaev, is reduced to being a cosmic agent, a moment in the evolution of the cosmos. "Christianity in Anthroposophy is a cosmic, not a divine revelation."[93] This makes the doctrine profoundly anticreative and leads in the direction of fatalism. Theosophy is so weighted down by the tyranny of its own doctrine, claimed Berdiaev, that it ignored spiritual creativity, the very essence of mysticism and religion.[94] The one individual who succeeded in escaping this anticreative tyranny, observed Berdiaev, was Andrei Belyi.[95]

Berdiaev was an independent thinker who hovered for a time on the periphery of Steiner's sphere of influence. While he rejected Steiner's popularizing and pedagogical tone and could not agree with the German occultist's attempt to make a science out of mysticism, he nevertheless felt that Steiner was an important and significant thinker.[96] Berdiaev, however, was a loner, and he avoided joining groups and being associated with any one trend; nevertheless, he was seduced (if only temporarily) by the initial appeal of Theosophy's Gnostic pull. Because Berdiaev had felt these seductions, and withstood them, because he was, in his own words, a "mystical realist" by temperament, he is a sophisticated commentator on Russian Theosophy.

Berdiaev's knowledge of Theosophy, Anthroposophy, and occultism, in general, was vast. He had read all the major texts; he had attended meetings and lectures; he was personally acquainted with the members of occult societies. Berdiaev was so au courant that many contemporaries suspected him of being an occultist. Although not a traditional Christian, he also knew the Christian tradition well. Finally, he was a philosopher born, not made; he had a strong sense of intellectual integrity. All this makes Berdiaev an excellent field guide to the tangle of Russian occult paths. His observations are those of someone who understands, who has even admired this particular worldview, but who has grown beyond it.

The curious Berdiaev had gone to meet Steiner and hear his lectures on "The Occult Significance of the *Bhagavad Gita*" in Helsingfors, May 28–June 5, 1913, in which Steiner focused on achieving a balance between the materialism and fear of God characteristic of the West and the "passive surrender to a world of pictures" (maya) characteristic of the East. Steiner has frequently been described as an hypnotic speaker and a charismatic personality; the phlegmatic Berdiaev described their meeting in the following manner:

> I wanted to acquaint myself with Anthroposophy. Thanks to my acquaintance with some Anthroposophists [principally Andrei Belyi], I had the opportunity to hear a cycle of Rudolf Steiner's lectures, which he read in Helsingfors in the Anthroposophical Lodge. I observed many things there. The atmosphere was most alien to me and I struggled against it constantly. Steiner himself, with whom I became acquainted, made a complex impression on me, a rather agonizing one. But he did not give the impression of a charlatan. This was a man who convinced and hypnotized not only others, but himself as well. . . . Rarely has anyone impressed me as a person so untouched by divine grace, as Steiner. Not a single ray came from above. He wanted to achieve everything from below, to force his way, by sheer effort, into the spiritual world.[97]

Berdiaev's evaluation of the Anthroposophists themselves was not particularly positive, either. "Some Anthroposophists impressed me as people possessed, in a maniacal state. When they spoke the words, 'The Doctor (i.e., Steiner) said,' then the expression in their eyes changed, their faces became different, and it was impossible to continue the conversation."[98]

Despite his more critical views later in life, in the years before his exile from Russia in 1922 Berdiaev regarded "Western" Anthroposophy as being preferable to "Eastern" Theosophy, since he felt it was more relevant to Western man's psychic and religious experience. "Theosophy is moving from East to West," he wrote in 1916. "And the Christian West is again remembering its own forgotten Western legends, which connect it directly with the wisdom of Greece and Egypt. A Western occult tradition is beginning to manifest itself, the antithesis of the Eastern occult tradition. The existence of Christian esotericism is being discovered. The separation of Anthroposophy from Theosophy took place on this soil and the Steinerian trend became manifest."[99]

The Russian God-seeking intelligentsia and the Theosophists were, it turned out, searching for the same thing: religious feeling and a coherent, meaningful, systematized universe imbued with divine being. Theosophy (and Anthroposophy) represented a desire to return to a spiritual path and to a God from whom humanity had been violently separated by modern science and materialism. In its attempt to reconcile science, philosophy, and religion, Theosophy sought order in the chaos of modern thought and wholeness in a fragmented modern reality. If the Theosophists were occasionally simplistic and limited in their scope (here the God-seekers gave preference to Anthroposophy as more sophisticated and more "correct"), they nevertheless nurtured the desire and search for spirituality and prepared the way for a future revelation, for a creative gnosis, which they, like the God-seeking intelligentsia, identified with Sophiology, Tolstoyanism, "spiritual Christianity," and certain forms of Russian sectarianism. As a result, the God-seekers were Theosophy's least critical critics.

Point and Counterpoint

The most biting criticism came from the church and from disappointed ex-Theosophists. Archimandrite Varlaam refused to admit that Theosophy might have something to say to his contemporaries and opined, "Once one is acquainted with Theosophy, it is impossible not to see that in itself it is nothing new or unheard-of; moreover, it does not represent some higher philosophy, reconciling science and religion, faith and knowledge. To raise the old and outlived from the ashes of centuries does not mean to give the world something new; to resurrect Buddhism in an imitation of Christianity does not mean to create something unique, something original."[100] The Archimandrite's opinion was echoed by Lev Kobylinskii-Ellis, recently converted to Anthroposophy: "Historically, logically, and psychologically, it was inevitable that mankind, when losing its [Christian] religion, should again turn to magic and Theosophy, i.e., to the 'ancient wisdom,' to the surrogates of the past. . . . Contemporary Theosophy is only a new, more disguised repetition of old errors."[101]

The hopeless and poisonous essence of Theosophy, Vsevolod Solov'ev felt, was hidden from most of its adherents by its seductive attractions. "It attracts that mind which is sick, which has abandoned its previous faith and no longer knows or understands that faith, toward a tempting and mysterious distance and shows it golden mirages there." For him, Theosophy, with its message of passive hopelessness and masked pessimism, was a phantom rising from the death bier of materialism; it was vulgar materialism's "astral body."[102]

Nikolai Berdiaev, who devoted his life to developing a philosophy of freedom, objected to Theosophical occultism specifically because it taught not spiritual freedom, but cosmic necessity. "I have never seen freedom of spirit in people carried away by occultism," he observed in his autobiography.[103] Theosophy did not encourage or even tolerate such freedom, but enslaved humanity to its cosmic doctrine. It was cosmocentric rather than anthropocentric or theocentric; it emphasized the primacy of the universe and made human beings prisoners of cosmic events and cosmic hierarchies. In this it looked back to the early gnosis, not forward to Christian redemption.

The anti-Theosophical tracts of Konstantin Kudriavtsev, Father Dmitrevskii, and Archimandrite Varlaam, all published within a year of each other, as well as attacks in mainline Orthodox publications, such as *Khristianin*, gave the Russian Theosophical Society cause for concern. *Vestnik Teosofii* preserved partial silence, but Dmitrii Stranden, who had replaced Kudriavtsev as Kamenskaia's right hand at the RTO, answered the criticisms in *Teosofiia i ee kritiki*.[104] He found Father Dmitrevskii the least objectionable, since his "criticism," leaning heavily on Mrs. Besant's *Ancient Wisdom* and Mohini Mohun Chatterji's *Sacred Religious Philosophy of India*, consisted mostly of a conscientious catalogue of the fundamentals of Theosophy. Only in the last chapter, "Bezumie Teosofii," did Father Dmitrevskii offer a few pages of Orthodox Christian criticism, which Stranden brusquely dismissed as "definitely without foundation."[105]

Anna Kamenskaia and the Russian Theosophists felt particularly betrayed by Kudriavtsev's anti-Theosophical *Chto takoe teosofiia i Teosoficheskoe Obshchestvo*. *Vestnik Teosofii* reviewed Kudriavtsev's book in a rather restrained tone, saying only:

> Its center of gravity lies in its allegations that the Theosophical Society has secret, possibly revolutionary goals and is practically a branch of Masonry, and

in the accusation that Theosophy is inimical to Christianity. Of course K. D. Kudriavtsev, a former member of the Council from the time the Society was founded, knows very well that the Society does *not* engage in political activity and has *nothing* in common with Masonry. The question of the relationship between Theosophy and Christianity has been adequately elucidated in the Theosophical literature.[106]

Vestnik Teosofii made no attempt whatsoever to address one of Kudriavtsev's primary criticisms, which concerned Mrs. Besant's establishment of the Order of the Star in the East. Religious and Spiritualist critics, however, were generally pleased by Kudriavtsev's critique and his noisy return to the fold. P. A. Chistiakov, reviewing the second edition of Kudriavtsev's book in *Rebus*, felt that the ex-Theosophist had performed an important service and told his readers, "We vigorously commend this book to the attention of all persons who are just now beginning to take an interest in Theosophy."[107]

Stranden's answer to Theosophy's critics was typical of Theosophical response to criticism. He resorted to repeating Theosophy's credo as a self-evident answer to its critics:

> Theosophy is not inimical to any religion, since it sees in each of them an original expression of one and the same great spiritual truth; it seeks the root of all religions in one and the same source, the inner revelation of the Wisdom of God, in all ages and among all peoples revealed to those who are pure of heart, and who have achieved such heights of moral and spiritual perfection that they have become worthy of being bearers of the unmediated revelation of Divinity.[108]

Stranden referred those critics who were uncomfortable with the neo-Buddhist dimension of Theosophy to the "Christian Theosophy" of Rudolf Steiner (although Stranden was most certainly aware that Steiner had recently left the Theosophical Society after prolonged struggle against those very Buddhist and Hindu elements). Otherwise, Stranden's "proofs" consist of claims that "Theosophy is acquired by living, not by thinking," that Theosophy is scientific, unlike the unsupported, subjective ravings of its critics, and that Theosophy's critics were all intolerant, ignorant, and prejudiced. His major criticism, however, was reserved for Kudriavtsev, who had dared to wash the Society's dirty linen in public. Stranden devoted most of his energy to condescendingly (but alas, unconvincingly) dismantling Kudriavtsev.

The Theosophists, however well-meaning they may have been, were not able polemicists and their answers to their critics tended to be hysterical, philosophically flaccid, semantically uncertain, and even ignorant. Too many Theosophists, including Dmitrii Stranden, were doctrinally confused, not only about Buddhism (after all, they had not grown up in the context that informs Buddhism and is informed by it), but also about the Russian Orthodox tradition whence they came. They were unable to avoid the seductive pitfalls of their amateur and too often haphazard approach to the study of comparative religions. They were insufficiently erudite to evaluate seriously Mme Blavatsky's incredible etymologies and extravagant analogies. Finally, they were neither discriminating nor rigorous in their philosophical thought.

The Theosophists' shortcomings in polemics, however, in no way negate the importance of their contribution to the philosophical and cultural dialogue of fin de siècle Russia. They added a creative and necessary voice to the noisy and occasionally vituperative dialogue that characterized the Russian religious renascence. Traditional Orthodox Christianity was becoming less and less of a viable force in the lives of some elements within Russian educated society; Theosophy, competing with the neo-Christianity of Dmitrii Merezhkovskii, the God-building of Maksim Gorkii, the Sophiology of Vladimir Solov'ev, the Dionysianism of Viacheslav Ivanov, and other esoteric worldviews presented by Russian Symbolists, occultists, and amateur philosophers, offered to fill the void in such a way that the desired reconciliation between religion and materialism might occur. Unfortunately, Theosophy also proved to be unviable in the retort that was Russian Silver Age culture. Nevertheless, that Theosophy generated such a passionate fury of discussion in educated circles is itself an indication that on the eve of the First World War it touched the *"bol'nye mesta,"* the "painful places" of the Russian psyche and offered at least a temporary respite from the suffocation of a spiritual vacuum.

Seven

The Russian Theosophical Movement after 1917

IN MAY 1916 Anna Kamenskaia received an invitation from Mrs. Besant to visit the Theosophical Headquarters in Adyar that coming autumn. She left Russia at the end of September, traveling through Siberia to China and from there overland to India. Excited about her first visit to India and to the heart of the Theosophical empire, Kamenskaia reached the Society's Headquarters in Adyar, Madras, a month and a half later, on November 19, 1916. Because of this visit to distant Adyar, she would not witness the beginning of the incredible events that took place in her native land.

While Kamenskaia visited Mrs. Besant and strolled through the lush gardens of Adyar, the unbuttressed facade of the Russian Empire crumbled at last. As the Russian military campaigns of the First World War headed toward disaster, as Russian losses mounted, as the Russian economy disintegrated, social unrest and labor strikes spread. Public trust in the government evaporated. The continuing influence of the hypnotic Grigorii Rasputin, the sectarian monk, over the royal family further shrank the already deflated credibility of an ineffectual monarchy. On March 2, 1917, in the midst of chaos and insurgence, Tsar Nicholas II abdicated the throne of the Romanovs and the Russian Duma formally announced the formation of a Provisional Government.

In Russia, the Theosophists greeted the February 1917 Revolution and the Provisional Government with joy. Writing from India, Kamenskaia was equally enthusiastic. She immediately saw great possibilities for Theosophy in the current "great upheaval in Russia":

> What a great and all-encompassing mission has been assigned to our beloved Society!
>
> A free Russia will now take her honored place among enlightened peoples and soon will probably be called upon to play a great role in world history, having voiced her particularly "Russian word" on the questions of the reorganization of social, human, and international relations.
>
> Political and social questions will naturally come to the fore and the heated work of building wisely on new lines will attract all hearts, devoted to the Motherland. The Theosophists will of course participate in this work.[1]

If Russian messianism had found a peculiarly Theosophical expression with the advent of world war, the February Revolution brought a new messianic impulse, inspiring Tsetsiliia Gel'mbol'dt and Elena Pisareva, editors of *Vestnik Teosofii* in Kamenskaia's absence, to rhetorical flights. Surely the revolutionary events prophesied a crucial breakthrough in the higher spheres; surely this was the spiritual surge forward that Russian Theosophists had long been anticipating. Summoning up in its enthusiasm every cliché contained in the vocabulary of the Russophiles and God-seekers, an editorial in the February *Vestnik Teosofii* effused:

> A blinding and stifling gloom surrounded us . . . It shrouded something great, important, something necessary to us all, something without which it was impossible to continue living, something which terrified and troubled us with the riddle of its existence, its undivined visage. . . . The time came for us not to gaze at our own individual portraits, exposing our own souls, but to apprehend our own, greater *Visage*, the unchanging, eternal Essence of the Russian national soul. . . . The Visage of Holy Russia revealed itself to us. . . .
>
> We had no poet-prophet to turn to in our days of need, we had no leader, anointed by destiny. We had only the great Humility of the people, the centuries-long seeking, the craving for Truth [Pravda], and the Suffering of centuries—the stigmata of the Cross. . . .
>
> Now we have beheld, we have seen, and we can never forget. . . . That moment of contact with the true Visage of our Angel forever transfigured the popular element, sealed it with a new stamp, gave it a new existence. The transfigured People, having conquered the darkness, will also conquer themselves. . . .
>
> Russia has a heavenly mission and thus her responsibility to the world is enormous. Magnanimous and humble, with pure and unblemished hands she must undertake the building of the bright future for herself and for others.
>
> She will give the world a new religious consciousness, a divine revelation, apprehended in Brother-Man; she will realize in this world, together with Liberty and Equality, the forgotten ideal of Fraternity, exhorting the mighty and the powerful to sacrifice themselves in the service of the powerless.
>
> For a pure, virginal Spring of creativity has been revealed in the depths of the national soul and can never again be sealed up by anyone.[2]

For the Theosophists the movement of history in general and Russian history in particular was a sequence not merely of world events, but of cosmic events. History was a distorted and grotesque reflection in the imperfect phenomenal world of major realignments taking place in the noumenal world. Those individuals with developed "supersensible sight" could see the symbolic logic that stood behind seemingly illogical events unfolding in the world of maya. Echoing the expectations (and vocabulary) not only of Rudolf Steiner, but also of a particular segment within the Russian intelligentsia, Pisareva proclaimed, "A new influx is beginning, the seeds of a *new culture* are finally sprouting, a new culture which the Slavs are destined to provide for the sixth race of the future."[3] She urged that "Russia create new paths, and not repeat the errors of the West, which has concentrated all its powers on building the outer man and has completely forgotten about edifying the inner man."[4]

In their attitudes toward the February Revolution, the Theosophists surprisingly found common ground, tenuous though it might be, with the socialists. N. Plaksina, writing in "Revolution and Our Tasks," saw those tasks as the overcoming of egoism and complete self-abnegation through labor. "It is our responsibility," she wrote, "to augment and illuminate the socialist concepts of liberty, equality, and fraternity," since the socialists interpret these concepts in an overly materialistic way; Theosophy would add a "spiritual" dimension to the New Russia that socialist materialism alone could not supply.[5]

When Anna Kamenskaia eventually returned to Russia in May 1917, it was no longer the Russia she had left eight months before. Nevertheless, in spite of strikes, chronic paper shortages, physical hardships, and a second, Bolshevik revolution in October, she remained optimistic about the New Russia and continued to publish *Vestnik Teosofii*. Within months of the October coup, as the Bolsheviks began the consolidation of their political position, Kamenskaia's enthusiasm withered.

After the Revolution

In February 1918 *Vestnik* suddenly ceased publication when the Bolsheviks nationalized the paper supply and refused to issue paper to the Theosophical press, thus imposing a de facto censorship (censorship de jure would not be in place until the end of 1921). Each issue since February 1917 had been getting shorter and shorter. If the issues averaged 100 to 130 pages over the course of war-torn 1916, then the two issues of 1918 were sad little booklets by comparison, fewer than 55 pages, and printed on inferior paper. All regular features were gone; the reader was left only with the opening chapters of Annie Besant's *Esoteric Christianity* and a translation of the Upanishads. Neither work was completed in Bolshevik Russia.

Disillusionment with the new regime was soon widespread in the occult community. By government order, the Theosophists, Anthroposophists, and other mystical, occult, and religious groups were required to cease overt activities by the end of 1918. Some members were arrested; many more left the country while they could.

The October coup was immediately followed by civil war, and the Bolsheviks had little time to worry about enforcing their order against the occult societies as they struggled to remain in power. Emerging victorious in 1920, the Bolsheviks' first priorities were necessarily political and economic. As soon as they felt secure, however, the Bolsheviks turned their attention to the mystical, occult, and religious groups. All such groups were officially liquidated by a series of government decrees issued between June 1922 and July 1923.

In her memoirs, Kamenskaia described the immediate effect of Bolshevik rule on the RTO:

> Our press was closed, our savings were confiscated, our Society and even our private apartment were sealed. The Theosophical Society was unable to continue its work any longer. All meetings were forbidden. We made an attempt to work in the countryside. We were a group of nine members of the Theosophical Society; of these, four were members of the Council, leaders of the Movement. We opened a working commune in Vladimir province, and shared our knowledge with the local peasants. Our experience was eminently successful, but by spring the Red Wave had flooded the countryside, and we had to flee from there. . . . We returned to Petersburg. . . . Some of our colleagues were already in prison or in exile. We didn't know what to do next; the question, point-blank, was: should we remain under the new conditions in Russia and become martyrs, or escape and continue our work abroad?[6]

The solution to Kamenskaia's quandary arrived with a deputation of English workers on a visit to Moscow. They secretly carried a letter for Kamenskaia from Mrs. Besant. Kamenskaia made the decision to flee from Russia because "Annie Besant called me, and her word was law to me, and besides, I viewed events more optimistically, and thought that in a year or two we would be back in our native land":

> She asked me to come and stay with her. We called our Council together and decided that three of us, Ts. L. Gel'mbol'dt, V. N. Pushkina, and I would flee abroad, since there was no possibility of getting a passport to leave. We were fortunate enough to find an organization which helped refugees cross the border into Finland, and on the night of 1 June 1921 Ts. L. and I crossed the border. (V. N. fled a month later.) In spite of grave difficulties and dangers, we successfully made our way to Kuokkala and were soon hospitably received by the Finnish T[heosophical] S[ociety] in Helsingfors.[7]

By the end of July 1921 Pushkina was on her way to England, where she would work with the Theosophical service organization in London and continue as the Russian representative of the Order of the Star in the East, while Kamenskaia and Gel'mbol'dt were staying in Brussels with Theosophist friends. Kamenskaia was content to remain and work with either the Belgian or the Finnish Sections, but Mrs. Besant herself sent her to Geneva, where the Swiss Section had been having organizational difficulties. She was pleased to go to Switzerland, the scene of her childhood and youth. Back in Russia, with the departure of the RTO's leaders, the slowly disintegrating Theosophical Society was headed by Sofiia Vladimirovna Ger'e, the president of the Moscow branch. Already ill and bedridden, she died soon after the Society was officially liquidated in 1923, although Theosophical activity continued after her death, especially in the provinces.

The Russian Anthroposophists, although a considerably smaller group with a lower public profile, met a similar fate. After the organized activities of the Anthroposophical Society were officially curtailed, however, Anthroposophical ideas were not immediately extinguished by the changed cultural environment in Russia. This was largely due to the efforts of Andrei Belyi and the prestige of the Russian writers and critics interested in Steiner's thought.

Called up for Russian military service in 1916, Andrei Belyi had left Dornach and Steiner to return to Russia; he remained there through the years of revolution and civil war.[8] When he left Switzerland he had heard more than four hundred of Steiner's lectures and had attended Steiner's elite Esoteric School. Between August 1916, when he returned to Petrograd, and October 1921, when he again left Russia for Europe, Belyi was an active and influential participant in numerous artistic and philosophical endeavors. He also gave specialized lectures at meetings of the Moscow Anthroposophical Society and hosted unofficial discussions about Steiner and Anthroposophy; these attracted considerable numbers of people. Belyi's sincerity, depth of knowledge, and sense of conviction were inspiring; he made new converts to Anthroposophical thought after his return to Russia.

Belyi was a founding member of *Vol'fila* (The Free Philosophical Association, *Vol'naia Filosofskaia Assotsiatsiia*, Petrograd, 1919–1923), an organization of writers, philosophers, academics, and artists who met regularly to discuss literature and philosophy.[9] The Petrograd *Vol'fila* had a counterpart in Moscow, the Free Academy of Spiritual Culture (*Vol'naia Akademiia Dukhovnoi Kul'tury*, 1918–1922).[10] Many participants in these two organizations came from Theosophical and Anthroposophical backgrounds; still others were bound to Theosophy and Anthroposophy by ties of friendship and a mutual interest in speculative mysticism; almost all represented idealist philosophical tendencies. By 1920 the meetings of *Vol'fila* and the Free Academy attracted audiences as large as a thousand, while topics ranged from proletarian culture, Oswald Spengler's culturological theories, and the philosophy of Symbolism, to Campanella's *City of the Sun*, neo-Platonism, the philosophy of creativity, Russian literature, and Anthroposophy as a means of self-cognition. For four important years, from 1919 to 1923, Russian Anthroposophy had a platform in Petrograd and in Moscow from which its most visible adherents could influence the emerging intellectual profile of the new Soviet regime.

By 1922 the Russian Anthroposophical Society's activities had already been limited and many members fled south to find relief from the famine in the cities. Seeking strength in numbers, the Society (on Vera Anisimova-Stanevich's initiative) approached various spiritually inclined groups in an effort to organize the Free Association of Spiritual Trends *(Vol'noe Sodruzhestvo Dukhovnykh Techenii)*. Anisimova approached the Tolstoyans, the Theosophists, the Anarcho-Mystics, and the Christian Students Union, among others. The Free Association met several times at the Tolstoyans' vegetarian cafeteria in Moscow, but wilted after less than a year. By 1930 many of its members would be in exile or in labor camps.

In 1923 the occult and spiritual movements found themselves severely hampered by government disapproval. Moscow's Free Academy of Spiritual Culture was disbanded late in 1922 and its philosophers were exiled from Russia.[11] Petrograd's *Vol'fila* was closed early in 1923. The Theosophical and Anthroposophical Societies, the Russian Spiritualist Society, the Martinists, the Tolstoyans, and all other mystical and occult groups were permanently liquidated by official decrees in the first half of 1923. In her discreet memoirs, M. Zhemchuzhnikova, a younger member of the Moscow Anthroposophical Society, described how the members all felt "the closing of their Society to be inevitable. It was simple and matter-of-fact. A decree appeared, requiring all societies, unions, and organizations 'not having material benefit as their object' to register. Those denied registration would be subject to liquidation. It was quite clear that the Anthroposophical Society would not receive permission to register."[12]

Not all deplored the closing of the societies. Andrei Belyi, who remained a committed Anthroposophist to the end of his life, wrote in 1928 that the Anthroposophical Society had in fact been a dead and useless thing. "It was clear to me: Steiner is necessary, Anthroposophy is necessary, the Society is unnecessary." Belyi had left Russia in October 1921 and was in Germany when he learned that the Russian Anthroposophical Society had been closed.[13] "I was sad, but I was also glad; the 'A. S.' SHOULD NOT EXIST in Russia; the fate of Anthroposophy is different here. Anthroposophy should 'bedew' people, like dew moistens parched earth, and not simply remain on the surface, like a 'SOCIETY.'" For Belyi, Anthroposophy was inextricably bound up with his concept of culture and cultural renewal. Anthroposophy was a new, vital, spiritual culture; a society's rigid bureaucratic structure and mundane concerns only pulled each member away from the all-important spiritual task. He concluded, "It is good that there are neither members nor a Society in Russia."[14]

The Bolsheviks waged war against the occult movements for a period of twelve years. They closed the presses that published mystical and occult literature and confiscated their machinery. They removed occult books from bookstore and library shelves, sent them to inaccessible "special collections," and, in some cases, even destroyed them as part of their new campaign to eradicate remaining idealist, mystical, formalist, and "bourgeois intellectual" elements from their midst.[15] In spring 1922 the Bolsheviks opened a new "antireligious front" that published a series of books and journals calculated to "historicize" religion and "demystify" it. That fall, they exiled almost all the leading idealist philosophers associated with the Russian Religious Renaissance; those not exiled would be arrested in the 1930s. These actions coincided with attacks on mysticism by major figures of the new regime, such as Trotsky's virulent criticism of Freemasonry at the Fourth Congress of the Comintern in December 1922 and his attack on Anthroposophy and Andrei Belyi in *Literature and Revolution* (1923). The newspapers and popular press also ran numerous assaults on the occult societies. The official campaign against the "decadent bourgeois intelligentsia" signaled the end of the period of relatively open philosophical inquiry and the beginning of compulsory ideological conformity.

After *Vol'fila* and the occult societies were closed, the center of Anthroposophical activity shifted briefly to the experimental Second Studio of the Moscow Art Theater (MKhAT). Several of its leading members were Anthroposophists, including the well-known actor and director Mikhail Chekhov (1891–1955), who headed MKhAT's Studio I from 1918 to 1924 (when it was renamed Studio II), and from 1924 until 1928, when he emigrated in the wake of accusations that he was using the Studio to disseminate Anthroposophical doctrines inconsistent with MKhAT's worldview. Chekhov was responsible for the staging of Andrei Belyi's Anthroposophical drama, *Petersburg*, in 1925. He also staged two Anthroposophical plays by Nadezhda Nikolaevna Bromlei (1884–1966), poet, writer, dramatist, and actress at MKhAT: *Arkhangel Mikhail* (1922) and *Korol kvadratnoi respubliki* (1925). Chekhov also incorporated Steiner's concept of the "Higher Self" into his acting method. The MKhAT Studio II was an unlikely pulpit for the Movement, but Anthroposophical ideas managed to stay alive there until 1928.

The postrevolutionary legacy of Theosophy and Anthroposophy also survived in Russian art and poetry of the avant-garde. The twenties, despite the clouds of repression clearly gathering on the horizon, was a period of intense intellectual and artistic ferment. Occult concepts and images entered into this heady, experimental environment, often in unsuspected and round-about ways. Eastern literature and mysticism, the Theosophical philosophy of P. D. Uspenskii, and the continuing influence of major painters with Theosophical interests, such as Wasily Kandinsky and Nikolai Roerich, exerted an influence on Russian Cubo-Futurism, especially on the painting of Mikhail Matiushin (1861–1934) and Kazimir Malevich (1878–1935), and the poetry of Aleksei Kruchenykh (1886–1968). The poet Velimir Khlebnikov (1885–1922) also left a legacy of oriental thought in his arcane and esoteric literary works.[16]

Russian abstract art, highly ideological, strove to realize Uspenskii's suggestion that "from the fourth dimension it should be possible to see the cube simultaneously from all sides and from the inside, as if from the center, even though in three dimensions it might seem totally untransparent."[17] In developing his theories of the fourth and fifth dimensions (in which linear time and three-dimensional space are shown to be an illusion), Uspenskii was influenced not only by Charles Hinton, R. M. Bucke, and Friedrich Nietzsche, but also by Mme Blavatsky. His theory "proved" that the dimensions of time and space are the illusory products of maya, while eternity is another, higher dimension, visible to the "new man" with "supersensible sight," the man who realized his "higher self," the Theosophical Superman.

The Bolshevik regime's bans, regulations, and propaganda were ineffective in stopping occult activity in Soviet Russia as long as physical repression was minimal. When occult books were no longer openly available, occultists obtained them through a black market system of private dealers specializing in forbidden books. When some presses were closed, other presses printed texts in the underground, using false imprints and bootlegged paper. The police did not (indeed, could not) prevent small groups from gathering in private apartments. And while the Bolsheviks did not hesitate to liquidate occult circles with obvious political agendas and to arrest their members, actual liquidation was in fact an exception, not a rule. Dr. Aleksandr Aseev, an independent Russian occultist then living in Yugoslavia, observed that between 1923 and 1929 many circles were able to continue their work:

> Officially these circles could not, of course, be registered, but they actively functioned and were not in fact persecuted, although the well-informed GPU must have been aware of their existence. Of the older occult organizations, the Theosophists were quite active, even though the Revolution had deprived them of their most experienced leaders—almost the entire Council of the Russian Theosophical Society emigrated; the Theosophists regularly sched-

uled meetings to which they invited guests; they had solid libraries of occult books, and fearlessly corresponded with each other. . . . The Anthroposophists met almost openly as well. The Rosicrucians and some Masonic organizations also remained active, although they were considerably more conspiratorial; even some new occult organizations emerged.[18]

In the first twelve years that followed the Bolshevik revolution, while some individuals were arrested and some occult circles broken up, no serious mass repressions of occultists occurred and many organizations carried on their activities discreetly, but more or less openly, especially in the provinces.

The situation changed dramatically with the implementation of the First Five-Year Plan in 1929. In that year the Bolsheviks, spurred on by Stalin, launched a new campaign against the "remnants of the bourgeois intelligentsia," actively hunting down and arresting members of occult groups on a large scale and confiscating their libraries and archives. After 1929 those Theosophists, Anthroposophists, and other occultists who remained free went underground or ceased their activities altogether. Arrest for "occult propaganda" after 1933 inevitably meant exile and frequently meant execution.

The destruction of the occult societies by decree, arrest, exile, and execution did not destroy Russian interest in occultism, especially in its more vulgar forms. Spiritualism, mediumism, parapsychology, and the supernatural continued to attract many Russians even after 1929. Table-rapping and hypnotism remained particularly popular. "A great attraction to spiritism has been observed in Moscow," lamented a Moscow newspaper, "and in spite of the ban, public seances of mass hypnotism are being held in one of the workers' clubs."[19]

Neither did political repression terminate the sense of mission shared by the occultists who had escaped arrest. Many continued their studies individually or bravely lectured to small, trusted groups in the Russian spiritual underground; they produced new translations of materials that occasionally seeped in from abroad; they copied and recopied existing materials to prevent the loss of texts when their tiny private libraries were periodically confiscated and their members taken away by the secret police.

After Stalin's death, exiled members of the Theosophical, Anthroposophical, and some other occult societies were allowed to return to Moscow and Leningrad. When those who had survived the purges finally did return to the capitals, they organized in small circles that the uninitiated could not penetrate and began to rebuild their libraries and their movements. Theosophical and Anthroposophical texts circulated among them in precious prerevolutionary editions and in manuscript copies that had been preserved at great risk through the years of Stalinist terror and world war.

Theosophical and Anthroposophical circles have flourished in post-Soviet Russia (as have numerous other occult groups, from Rosicrucians to the disciples of Nikolai Roerich). The changes that began in Soviet society in the second half of the 1980s as a result of Mikhail Gorbachev's policy of *glasnost'* have brought these Societies out of their semidormant state and allowed them to enter, albeit tenuously, the dialogue about spiritual renewal in Russia. Zhemchuzhnikova, writing in 1975, anticipated that the Russian Anthroposophical movement would send out new shoots once the Russian spiritual renaissance came, and that "the Soul of the Russian people would be arrayed in them when, having passed through its tragic purgatory, it would appear in all the greatness of its historical mission."[20]

The "Russian Theosophical Society Outside Russia"

While Theosophy and Anthroposophy appeared to have little future in the further evolution of Soviet Russian culture after 1929, Anna Kamenskaia succeeded in restoring the fortunes of the Russian Theosophical Society Outside Russia within an amazingly short period. Between 1922 and 1924 she tracked down the Russian Theosophical diaspora and managed to make contact with many Russian Theosophists who had been scattered throughout the world after the October Revolution. Many Russian Theosophists had taken refuge with the national sections of other countries. Thus a Russian Theosophical circle in Reval (Tallinn), headed by an old RTO member, Professor N. I. Erassi, was formed by the fall of 1921 and was affiliated with the English Section in May 1922. Three separate Russian circles were chartered by the Finnish Section between 1920 and 1924.[21] Similar circles reported in from the Far East (from Vladivostok, Tiantsin, Shanghai, Hankow, and Hong Kong), from Berlin, Paris, Lyon, Florence, Turin, Constantinople, San Francisco, Brooklyn, Batavia (Djakarta), and various cities in South America. Kamenskaia received news of all their activities.

In the summer of 1924 Mrs. Besant and the Theosophical Council gave Anna Kamenskaia permission to organize a Russian Association *(Russkoe Ob"edinenie)* under the auspices of the parent Society as a preliminary step toward officially chartering a Russian Theosophical Society Outside Russia. Mrs. Besant named Kamenskaia chair of the Russian Association and fully empowered her to act for the Theosophical Society. Membership in the Russian Association was not by application, but by recommendation. Russian Theosophical circles already associated with other national sections were encouraged to maintain their affiliations and simultaneously participate in the Russian Association. There were no membership dues; in most cases the destitute Russian émigrés would not have been able to afford them anyway.

Having lost one organization to the tidal wave of history, the determined and well-organized Kamenskaia succeeded in establishing another. At the Fiftieth Anniversary Congress of the Theosophical Society in Adyar, Madras, on December 24–31, 1925, the General Council of the Theosophical Society approved the Russian Association's petition to be recognized once again as the Russian National Section. On the first of the year (January 1, 1926) Kamenskaia received the charter, signed by Mrs. Besant, authorizing the "Russian Theosophical Society Outside Russia" *(Rossiiskoe Teosoficheskoe Obshchestvo vne Rossii;* RTOvR). The charter allowed the Russian Society to retain its historical status as the fourteenth national section chartered by the parent Society (forty-one national sections had been chartered by 1925). At the time of this second charter, the Russian Theosophical Society Outside Russia had 10 lodges, 20 centers, and 175 registered members.[22] The Russian Section was the only national section without a homeland, and so it enthusiastically participated in international activities.[23]

Kamenskaia's primary tool in the renewal of the RTOvR was her new journal *Vestnik: Satyat Nasti Paro Dharmah* ("There is no religion higher than truth). The first issue, approved by the Theosophical Society and financed by the European Federation (the organization of European national sections) and private donations, appeared in April 1924. A spare magazine of about a dozen pages, it was printed in Brussels and distributed free of charge. The journal quickly doubled in size. Its format was essentially that of its St. Petersburg predecessor: it began with Kamenskaia's editorial column, "On Watch," and included short original articles by Russian members; poems by Vladimir Solov'ev, Konstantin Bal'mont, Max Voloshin, Aleksandr Pushkin, and others; gems of oriental and occidental wisdom; translations of Western Theosophical classics and speeches by the president; and a chronology of the Theosophical Movement. Kamenskaia and Gel'mbol'dt edited it together and were its primary contributors.

"I receive letters and inquiries from almost all the countries of Europe," wrote Kamenskaia in her first editorial column; "they also come from the Americas and China. And all of them tell of terrible spiritual isolation and an acute hunger for books."[24] Russian Theosophists from all over the world complained of the dearth of classic Theosophical texts in Russian, of having to copy and share books preserved from the Revolution, of the lack of discussion materials. Clearly the establishment of a Russian press to print Theosophical books was of paramount importance to the strengthening of the new Society. And it was imperative that precious resources be husbanded: translating and publishing efforts had to be coordinated to avoid duplication and waste. No one was better placed than Kamenskaia, in Geneva, to oversee this activity. Eventually she coordinated the publishing work of three major Russian Theosophical presses in Brussels, Geneva, and Tallinn. Smaller presses existed in China, Prague, and Paris.

The Geneva *Vestnik* was a pale imitation of the St. Petersburg publication. No interesting original thinker of the caliber of P. D. Uspenskii or Pavel Batiushkov emerged from the Theosophical emigration; even the translated articles were of minimal interest. The best mind represented in the journal was Anna Kamenskaia's, and she was occupied almost exclusively with holding the Movement together: she published *Vestnik*, corresponded extensively, traveled a great deal, and lectured frequently. Spiritual sentimentality and émigré nostalgia reigned on *Vestnik's* pages.

Kamenskaia and the faithful Ts. L. Gel'mbol'dt continued the traditions of the Russian Theosophical Society that they had helped to establish in St. Petersburg. They were joined by Elena Pisareva, who, after great difficulty, managed to leave Soviet Russia in the fall of 1922 and go to her daughter in Udine, in northern Italy. All three women were involved in philanthropic and international relief work. The Geneva Theosophists, especially Anna Kamenskaia, were involved in various relief projects sponsored by the League of Nations, which they enthusiastically supported; they coordinated their Theosophical relief work with the League's Nansen International Office for Refugees, based in Geneva. Many Russian Theosophists were associated with various charitable and public-spirited groups; they worked for labor, peace, human rights, animal rights, education, philanthropy, and vegetarianism.

Kamenskaia took on many public responsibilities, both for the Theosophical Society and for the numerous social organizations with which she was affiliated. In addition to her other duties, she ran the International Theosophical Centre in Geneva (sponsored by the European Federation) from its founding in 1928 to its dissolution a decade later. Nor did she neglect her own intellectual growth: on June 17, 1926, Kamenskaia defended a doctoral dissertation, "La Bhagavad-Gîtâ, son rôle dans le mouvement religieux de l'Inde et son unité," at the University of Geneva. For the next twenty-five years she taught at the university as a *privat-docent;* her specialty was Hindu philosophy.

Kamenskaia lived and worked together with Gel'mbol'dt, her girlhood friend; their Geneva apartment in the *rue Cherbuliez*, No. 2, dou-

bled as the headquarters of the RTOvR. Gel'mbol'dt helped her edit
Vestnik and directed "Giordano Bruno," the Russian Theosophical
Lodge in Geneva. By 1933 they were joined in Geneva by Elena
Pavlovna Solovskaia, an Odessa Theosophist who had participated in the
establishment of the "Iaroslav Mudryi" Lodge in Belgrade, where there
was a large and active Russian community of occultists.[25] As the ailing
Gel'mbol'dt became increasingly bedridden, Solovskaia took over her
many duties. The three women lived together in their Theosophical
apartment, which Solovskaia called "the occult nunnery."

Over the course of its fifteen-year existence, the optimism of *Vestnik*
about Russia and the future of Theosophical work in Russia never wa-
vered. The dedicated members of the RTOvR believed that everything
they were accomplishing in exile was only preparation for the great role
they would soon be called on to play in their homeland as the time approached when they would return and lead the Revolution of the Spirit.
Again history was explained in accordance with the principles of Theosophical cosmology: "The European war, the Russian Revolution, the
extraordinary dimensions of the world catastrophe which played itself
out before our very eyes," wrote Elena Pisareva, "evoked in my imagination the image of a cosmic *'pralaya'* which separates one *manvantara*
from another."[26] World war, revolution, civil war were all perceived as
reflections in the material world of a cleansing catastrophe that heralded
the end of one cycle and, after a period of obscuration, the beginning of
a new, superior cycle in which Russia would fulfill its dharma, the
"higher truth" that informs its cosmic mission, and finally give voice to
its spiritual "word."[27]

All this had been predicted by Mme Blavatsky, Mrs. Besant, and
Rudolf Steiner (well before 1917, he had made several predictions about
the catastrophe that would overtake Russia). The Slavs were to be the
people of the next (sixth) sub-race; theirs was a brilliant future. Clearly
the world catastrophe only heralded the end of the fifth sub-race, the
Aryan race that had so long dominated world evolution. Following the
cosmological pattern, the brief period of obscuration would be followed
by the rise of the Slavs and the fulfillment of their cosmic mission. The
Theosophists, blending fin de siècle Russian millennialism and messianism with Buddhist cosmology, knew what that mission was to be.

It was not to be bolshevism, of that they were certain. The Bolsheviks
were an evil force let loose by the Russian nation's bad karma to ravage
a sinful and guilty Russian land. But bolshevism was only a temporary
chimera whose karma would run its course; meanwhile, "enormous
possibilities" still lay dormant in Russia. The Theosophists saw the Bolsheviks as unconsciously working for the mission of Russia and even
interpreted the Soviet hammer and sickle as hidden symbols of the

blacksmith's art, hinting at future transmutation and transformation.[28] Bolshevik rule would be the cleansing fire out of which a new, pure Russia would be forged.

The salvation of Russia lay in its recognition of the higher truth and fulfillment of its cosmic mission, or duty (dharma). The Russian Theosophical perception of this duty had not changed since the founding of the Society: Russia's duty was to become the bridge between the East and the West. "We, the Slavs, the wall between the East and the West, must sing our original song, which pours from our soul, and thereby build a bridge across which shall come the nations of the Orient and the Occident, and merge into one great, friendly, universal family," exclaimed Kamenskaia.[29] The image of Russia as the bridge between East and West became the central metaphor of Russian Theosophy in the emigration.

A key text for the Russian Theosophists abroad was Anna Kamenskaia's speech at the Vienna Theosophical Congress, "The International Mission of the Slavs"; it was reprinted in *Vestnik* in early 1925 and closely perused in the various Theosophical study groups, becoming prescriptive for the Movement. "The Slavic race does not know its fate, it lives in expectation, it belongs to the future," Kamenskaia wrote, playing to the hopes and longings of the emigration. "The very name of the Slavs is surrounded by mystery, for on the one hand it evokes the eternal Karma of suffering and slavery *(esclave)*, while on the other it seems to herald a glorious *[slavnoe]* future."[30] Kamenskaia further related Slavdom and "glory" *(slava)* with "the word" *(slovo)*, thus creating an almost mythic trinity of concepts that spoke to the nationalist and messianic dreams of the Russian emigration (such triune formulations were characteristic of the Russian religious renaissance). She concluded with a paean to the mysticism, intuition, enthusiasm, love, and spirituality that she considered an integral part of the Slavic soul.

Kamenskaia praised Slavic contempt for material goods. This very contempt for materialism allowed many Russian intellectuals to see their property confiscated, and to see in that confiscation a just act, and the beginning of a new era, she pointed out. "One must become a new man, free of the bonds [of material desires and of the past], in order to freely build the Temple of the future," she wrote, sounding oddly like Lenin. "Between the West, which seeks the Good, and the East, which strives for Truth, will it not be the Slavs who build the bridge across the Beautiful, which they revere?"[31] Kamenskaia, herself passionately devoted to Indian culture, felt certain that in the Slavs "still live the ancient Aryan traditions and the spirit of the Vedic heroes." The Slavs are a young race, she felt, and they still have much to learn, but they will eventually understand the responsibility of their freedom, achieve self-awareness, and comprehend their destiny, their dharma, which they are collectively fated to fulfill. "In this hour," she predicted, "crucified Russia will come down from the Cross to which it has been nailed during these years of indescribable suffering" and build the long-awaited bridge uniting East and West.[32]

If Kamenskaia had a criticism of the Slavic soul, it was in its undiscriminating idealism and expansiveness of character. She warned against the tendency of the Slavs to endeavor to realize concretely their own truth, to create heaven on earth in their own image, no matter what the cost. No guarantee existed, however, that what the Slavic soul embraced with such passion was indeed the truth (unless, of course, it embraced Theosophy); one had only to look at the results of Lenin's attempt to create a socialist utopia in the Soviet Union.

The Russian Theosophists saw their historical fate as a great trial, an initiation, during which they had to prove themselves worthy of the formidable task at hand. They explicitly identified themselves and the fate of their country with the *imitatio Christi* (as did Andrei Belyi, and as did the philosophers of *Vekhi*, then also in exile). Writing about her reception as a Russian expatriate in England in 1924, Kamenskaia even used the imagery of the Passion: everywhere she was "met as the representative of an eminent and enigmatic land, passing through the Golgotha of the historical cross toward a great future."[33] The vocabulary of the Passion was everywhere present in the Theosophical prose of *Vestnik*: "crucifixion," "Golgotha," "nailed to the cross," "suffering," "crown of thorns." At the end of the narrow way, however, always lay a future as bright as, or even brighter than, that promised by the Bolsheviks.

In an effort to help Russians achieve self-awareness and discover their dharma, Elena Pisareva founded the "Union of Service to Russia" *(Soiuz sluzheniia Rossii)* in 1924. Branches of this Union soon formed in London, Brussels, Prague, Berlin, Reval (Tallinn), Belgrade, Geneva, and other cities. The Union's credo was: "I believe in God, I believe in the victory of the Good, I believe in the Resurrection of Russia." The Union touched on every mythic moment, every archetypal perception, every emotional tie that bound the emigration to its homeland. It encouraged Russian handicrafts, the study of Orthodoxy, Russian folklore, art, literature, and music. "What else can Russian exiles, forced out into strange lands, think about, dream about, and speak about, if not about our dear, suffering, great Mother-Homeland?" asked Pisareva.[34] The "Union of Service to Russia" did everything it could to encourage the preservation of Russian culture so that when the time came to return to Theosophical work in the homeland, the Theosophists could restore to their native land the Russian culture destroyed by the Bolsheviks.

The RTOvR was not cut off from other emigration movements or from independent Russian Theosophists abroad.[35] Kamenskaia stayed in touch with Russian religious philosophy of the emigration and occasionally debated with its representatives on the pages of *Vestnik*. She took issue, for example, with articles and lectures by Nikolai Berdiaev, Dmitrii Merezhkovskii, Boris Vysheslavtsev, and other figures of the Russian religious renaissance in the emigration. She was appalled that although more than twenty years had passed since their initial confrontation in the Religious-Philosophical Society, "we are forced to observe, with a certain incomprehension, that the Theosophical doctrine, with which it has certainly been possible to become better acquainted, is still being treated by a well-known faction with that same puerile lack of thought and that same superficial criticism which astounded us in the past."[36]

The Russian Theosophical Society's sense of mission did not wane in the emigration; on the contrary, it grew ever stronger. Kamenskaia, writing thirteen years after the founding of the Union of Service to Russia, continued to extend the metaphor, using the imagery characteristic of the God-seeking intelligentsia:

> Specifically here, abroad, where our visage is not distorted, where it can freely manifest itself, specifically here we are given an important task: to preserve our native values and to bring them carefully through all storms and ill winds, in order to place them reverently at the altar of our resurrected homeland. We must do more than just bring these spiritual values in all their inviolability as an offering, but we must also prepare ourselves, as knights bearing the Light, the builders of a future free Russia.[37]

The last issue of the Geneva *Vestnik* appeared at the end of 1940. In 1939 there had been some concern that the Council of the Theosophical Society might choose not to continue the charter of the RTOvR, since the Russian Section had ceased to grow. Several of the Russian lodges had disintegrated as their aged members, those who had been affiliated with the original Russian Section in St. Petersburg, moved away or died. *Vestnik* was a financial drain (it had been in the red for most of its existence, and Kamenskaia constantly begged for contributions). Like the first *Vestnik*, also a victim of historical catastrophe and war, the second *Vestnik* ceased publication without notice.

During the Second World War, Kamenskaia worked for the peace movement and war relief efforts. She sent Theosophical texts and old copies of *Vestnik* to Russian prisoners of war. After the war, she worked with displaced persons. She continued to teach at the University of Geneva, fielded inquiries from Theosophists around the world, and distributed her dwindling stockpile of Russian Theosophical texts. When she finally died on June 23, 1952, just two months before her eighty-sixth birthday, the obituary in the *Journal de Genève* observed that she was "devoted to an ideal and ardent in the service of all noble causes."[38]

Kamenskaia's zealous and tenacious personality was the driving force behind the existence of the Russian Theosophical Society from the very beginning. Anna Kamenskaia *was* the RTO. It is appropriate that she was repeatedly and unanimously reelected to the presidency of the RTO; no one else ever held that post at any time during the Russian Society's entire existence. She saw the Russian Society through the traumas and setbacks of the years in exile; through Krishnamurti's unexpected dissolution of the Order of the Star in the East in 1929 and his resignation from the Theosophical Society the next year; through the decimation of the Russian Society by the deaths of its leading members; through Mrs. Besant's turn toward "evangelical occultism" and her proclamation of the "New Era," which could not have been entirely to the Russians' taste. The RTO lived as long as Kamenskaia stood "On Watch" and fought the Russian tendency toward fragmentation and ideological division; it was fed by her strength of will, her organizational competence, her health, and her complete devotion to the organization. When she died, the RTO died.

After Anna Kamenskaia's death the Russian Theosophical Movement inevitably dissolved because there was no longer a need for it. She had outlived her entire generation. If she failed to build a Theosophical bridge between East and West, she succeeded in creating another bridge that led the émigré Russian Theosophists from an old world to a new one; she was their reliable anchor in a disintegrating universe. Now her generation was gone. Its children, if they remained Theosophists, melted naturally into the national sections of other countries, whose language they had accepted and into whose culture they had begun to assimilate. This second generation was already cut off from Russian soil; the call to return to Theosophical work in Russia did not come in their lifetime. Modern history made it impossible for them to share their parents' optimistic and messianic expectations.

Afterword: Theosophy's Impact on
Fin de Siècle Russian Culture

FOR HISTORIANS of thought and culture to dismiss as superficial and peripheral the role that Theosophy and other occult movements played in the crisis of culture and consciousness experienced by fin de siècle Europe and Russia would be a profound error. The psychologist Carl Gustav Jung, speaking of the proliferation of such religious and quasi-religious movements at the turn of the century, pointed out that "the world has seen nothing like it since the end of the seventeenth century. We can compare it only to the flowering of Gnostic thought in the first and second centuries after Christ." Jung was profoundly aware that "the spiritual currents of our time have, in fact, a deep affinity with Gnosticism. . . . The most impressive movement numerically is undoubtedly Theosophy, together with its continental sister, Anthroposophy; these are pure Gnosticism in Hindu dress."[1] Nikolai Berdiaev, an ambivalent seeker who was no friend to Theosophy in the latter part of his life, nevertheless realized that "in spite of the charlatanism with which it is so often associated, Theosophy is not to be taken lightly and we must recognize it as an important symptom. Its growing popularity is bound up with the crisis which has overtaken both science and Christianity. It is symptomatic of a profound unrest in man and of a return to the spiritual. Moreover, neither science nor the official church are attaching sufficient importance to Theosophy and the occultism connected with it."[2]

That occult philosophy has long been considered incompatible with the prevailing worldview and "establishment culture" (and therefore intellectually unrespectable) in no way diminishes its enduring popularity or its importance to the history of ideas. James Webb, in the introduction to his chronicle of nineteenth-century esoteric trends, *The Occult Underground*, concludes, "To ignore the occult revival of the nineteenth century is to ignore a large slice of modern intellectual development"; he goes so far as to suggest that "the proper understanding of the workings of the occult mind explains much which has been puzzling commentators on the history of the last fifty years as well."[3] Theosophy was an organic part of a broad and at times frantic search for new values and a new world conception. This search, or quest (to use a more romantic term), was symptomatic of the prewar world, and if many chose to seek this world conception in Theosophy (and its brother doctrine, Anthroposophy), it should come as no surprise, for this Movement was one of the few complete "world conceptions" presented during a period of intense intellectual and spiritual upheaval, and many of its aspirations and basic premises have affected the way we think today.

This study has described Theosophy's role as an influential force in Russian middle-class and popular culture of the Silver Age. It has outlined the history of Theosophy in Russia and abroad and has traced its reception in Russia among the clergy, the middle and gentry classes, and the God-seeking intelligentsia; it has presented the general features of its doctrine. This book has indicated that the passionate interest in Theosophy and other forms of occultism among the Russian middle and gentry classes was an expression of that group's participation in the Russian religious renaissance that ended the preceding period of "*Bezvremenn'e*," when little of vital cultural importance happened and intellectuals felt trapped in a spiritual void. The study would not be complete, however, without some indication of Theosophy's influence on the Russian creative intelligentsia and speculation about the possible ramifications that an understanding of Theosophy has for the understanding of Russian fin de siècle art and culture.

Nowhere was the overt and covert influence of Theosophy as profound as among those members of the Russian artistic elite (painters, philosophers, writers, and composers among them) who turned to that esoteric doctrine. These sensitive and talented individuals were particularly predisposed to see Theosophy as a means of exploring psychic and spiritual states that defy rational ("positivist") comprehension. In Theosophy they found a new vocabulary for discussing topics that could no longer be spoken of in the existing terminology of theology or science. In Theosophical images they found a translogical meaning that moved far beyond the limiting Kantian categories of time, space, and causality. They related to Theosophy's use of metaphor and symbol as the primary means of conveying meaning and agreed with Theosophy's claim that image has primacy over concept (Andrei Belyi termed this "the primacy of creativity over cognition"). Finally, they found in Theosophy the same identification of aesthetic and religious action at which they themselves had arrived. They had as examples before them the cosmogenetic power of certain Theosophical literary works, such as Mme Blavatsky's highly poeticized "Seven Stanzas from the Book of Dzyan" and her meditative *Voice of the Silence*.

At the same time, the majority of Russian *intelligenty* with Theosophical interests were remarkably independent. They distinguished between Theosophy as an organized movement and Theosophy as a religious-philosophical doctrine, and so were "Theosophists" without necessarily being dues-paying members of the Theosophical Society; they disdained the Society's exoteric Theosophy, intended not for them, but for the "common herd." As creative artists they hesitated to submit themselves to the constraining atmosphere of a structured Society and preferred to work independently and selectively, or even to create their own alternative circles. They were neither followers nor joiners, unless they themselves happened to be leaders of the group. But Theosophical ideas were "in the air," and the syncretic and diffuse nature of Theosophy encouraged selective and at times irresponsible borrowing. Theosophy was taken seriously as religious philosophy by many in its time, and not a few artists felt the enormous archetypal power of its basic images.

In determining the specific influence of Theosophy on literature and the arts, it is impossible in most cases (and pointless as well) to identify mechanically the specific allusions to Theosophy in the cultural realm. Many artists accepted Theosophical ideas selectively and, as creative personalities, built on or strategically altered those ideas. In some cases they may have expanded them far beyond the possibilities offered by the original material. Some merely read a few Theosophical texts in areas of interest to them and borrowed a concept or two. Others picked up Theosophical ideas in fashionable salons without knowing what it was they had found. What is important, however, is that many writers and artists, especially among the Russian Symbolists, did encounter Theosophy in Viacheslav Ivanov's Tower, at Margarita Morozova's exclusive intellectual soirées, at meetings of the Religious-Philosophical Societies, at public lectures, and in many private salons. They found there theories of creativity that complemented their own understanding of the creative act and a neo-Platonic world conception compatible with their notion of "Symbolism as a worldview" (as defined for the Silver Age by Andrei Belyi, one of Symbolism's leading thinkers and theoreticians, but echoed by Pavel Batiushkov, Lev Kobylinskii-Ellis, and others). These artists and writers did not compartmentalize their world conception and their art in different pigeon holes; the very concept of Theosophy precluded it, since a world conception cannot be separated from art (or art from a world conception), aesthetics being necessarily part of a "total worldview."

The modern critic should, however, be sufficiently acquainted with the popular occult movements of the fin de siècle to discern evidence of the contact of the creative personality with Theosophy, when valid, and to consider the possible influence of a Theosophical world conception or the use of key Theosophical imagery and vocabulary in the artist's work. Some knowledge of Theosophy can be particularly productive, for example, in dealing with modernism in Russian literature and abstraction in Russian painting. Sixten Ringbom, writing about the tremendous social and intellectual changes that occurred during the fin de siècle, points out that it is no coincidence that "abstract art [and, we might add, modernist literature] emerged by the end of the first decade of our century, the same decade that saw the publication of theosophical works describing the non-objective worlds in texts and illustrations." He goes on to say that Theosophy was "the creed that contained, as it were, a built-in link between the spiritualistic world conception and its materialization in an image."[4] In the case of Kandinsky and Piet Mondrian, both of whom read Annie Besant's, Charles W. Leadbeater's, and Rudolf Steiner's creative descriptions of life on higher planes and in different forms of refined matter, their abstract art clearly emerged from a desire to portray spiritual and psychic realities rather than from boredom with figurative painting or the experience of alienating angst (although that may have come later, and was probably exacerbated by the subsequent loss of the spiritual that the first generation of abstractionists was seeking to avoid). When the two painters, both attracted by Theosophy, used words like "mystic" and "spiritual" to describe their art, they had specific connotations in mind.

This thought can be pursued into the realm of modern literature as well. The resonance between the abstract paintings of Kandinsky and the modernist novels of Andrei Belyi is suggestive. Both Kandinsky and Belyi were highly creative personalities, both had rigorous academic training, both were seriously interested in Theosophy. Belyi was philosophically and aesthetically saturated with Theosophical doctrine; Kandinsky was more selective, as his and Gabriele Münter's personal occult library shows. Yet, in both cases, the notion of the modern that emerges in their work is one based on the supersensible perceptions of a higher reality, on the representation of that which occurs beyond the plane of gross matter, where spiritual "forms" need not resemble the forms of physical matter found in this world at all. Their works strive for an intellectual and spiritual dimension that is simultaneously personal and universal. Like the Theosophists, these artists strip away the "outer garments" of their historical period and their own personalities to reach the eternal and spiritual in art. It is no coincidence that the same phenomenon is present in Aleksandr Skriabin's music theory, where he defined the concept of "Ecstasy"—a concept central to his creative philosophy and to his worldview—as "seeing on the higher planes of nature." Again, such terminology is specific, not vague, in Theosophical terms.

Theosophy and other occult systems did not introduce, but they certainly popularized, the question of *what is really real* at the turn of the century. If, as the esotericists proclaimed, the noumenal, spiritual realm is more real than the illusory phenomenal world of physical reality (Ivanov's *a realia ad realiora*), if matter is degraded spirit, and spirit is refined matter, then the "true" artist will find that figurative and representational forms, which depict only gross physical matter, are invalid for the transmission of the higher reality. Naturalism and vulgar realism are to be despised, for they are blind to *real*, spiritual reality. A true artist must find other means of expression. In their modernist works, Kandinsky and Belyi were in fact being realistic, as they understood "realism"; they accurately depicted the refined matter of the astral, mental, and spiritual planes. And while such concepts of reality were not exactly new in the history of human ideas (they date back to Neoplatonism and form the root of Gnosticism), it was Theosophy that made them a popular topic in intellectual salon discussions of the fin de siècle.

While no one would insist on Theosophy as a single cause in the development of modernism (and it is not the aim of this discussion to do so), the critic should consider seriously the world conception promulgated by occult doctrines as one of the factors in the development of modernism, especially given the popularity of the occult among intellectuals at the turn of the century and the respect that certain occult doctrines enjoyed at that time, if not today. The general arena in which Theosophy and occult thought played their particular role is a larger one. In painting, abstraction emerged as a rejection of the rational and representational; in literature, the elusive, enciphered modernist novel offered an alternative to traditional realism. These cultural developments had their counterpart in other aspects of the intellectual history of the period: philosophy's rejection of positivism and rationalism for new forms of idealism and religious philosophy; the emergence of analytical (depth) psychology from empirical and experimental psychology; science's exponential development from classical mechanics to modern theoretical physics, with all the mind-boggling implications that subatomic particles, x-rays, and cinematography had for an understanding of reality and matter.

The specific implications these massive shifts in consciousness have for modern culture have yet to be completely catalogued; this study is merely a part of the ongoing examination of that critical period. In the course of this study, every effort was made to identify those areas where Theosophy has impinged on the thought of Russia's Silver Age, but it cannot be the purpose of this preliminary historical survey to examine in detail the transmutation of Theosophical ideas into the specific literary or artistic text; that work lies in the future. To illustrate Theosophy's particular impact on the culture of its time, however, it may be appropriate to examine two very different representatives of Russian fin de siècle culture whose life paths and subsequent influence were configured by their contact with Theosophical thought. The two representative figures selected are Nikolai Roerich and Andrei Belyi, although Maksimilian

Voloshin, Aleksandr Skriabin, Wasily Kandinsky, or any one of the other leading cultural figures mentioned in these pages could have served the purpose as well.[5]

Orientologist and Painter: Nikolai Konstantinovich Roerich (1874–1947)

One of Theosophy's least acknowledged contributions to Russian culture was its encouragement of interest in the East and in oriental studies, especially in Eastern religions and literary texts. European interest in the Hindu East began late in the eighteenth century, when the *Bhagavad Gita* first became available in Western translations. Eastern thought was also popular among the romantics, notably Schelling, Novalis, and, of course, Schopenhauer. The mid-nineteenth century saw an increase in both translations of texts and scholarship addressing oriental religion, philosophy, and art. By the end of the nineteenth century, the Theosophists' neo-Buddhist gospel found itself competing for public attention not only with translated texts and Indian arts and artifacts, but also with visiting swamis and gurus, oriental sectarians, enthusiastic Western converts to oriental faiths, American Vedantists, and the newly founded Baha'is. Less quick to permeate the closed borders of Russia than those of Europe and America, these oriental influences were encouraged by the Russian Theosophical Society.

Several fine Orientologists emerged in Russia during the fin de siècle (not least among them Anna Kamenskaia herself), producing Russian translations of Buddhist and Hindu texts, as well as competent commentaries. They included I. Minaev, S. F. Ol'denburg, F. I. Shcherbatskoi, O. Rozenberg, and V. P. Vasil'ev. Work on the East was carried on by the Oriental Division of the Russian Archaeological Society and by the Imperial Academy of Sciences. Popular articles about Oriental thought came from the pens of V. V. Lesevich, A. I. Vvedenskii, V. A. Kozhevnikov, and others; they were read by the subscribers of *Russkaia Mysl'*, *Russkii Vestnik*, *Voprosy Filosofii i Psikhologii*, and other journals catering to the intelligentsia. This scholarship, which coincided with the popularity of Theosophy, helped to disseminate information about Eastern thought and made Theosophy less "exotic" than it might otherwise appear.

The Orient appealed to more traditional scholars as well. The influential Russian art and music critic and member of the St. Petersburg Academy of Sciences, Vladimir Vasil'evich Stasov (1824–1906), was greatly respected for his work in art and music history, archaeology, ethnography, and philology. Stasov held to the theory, shared by several Russian

Orientologists and later picked up and promulgated by the Russian Theosophists, that the ancient Slavic and ancient Indian cultures were closely interrelated. Stasov felt, for example, that the Indian epic, *The Mahabharata*, had a definite influence on Russian epic genres.[6]

Stasov's theory of the closeness of India and Russia was shared by a young artist whom he served as mentor: Nikolai Konstantinovich Roerich (1874–1947). A member of the "World of Art" and personal friend of many leading Symbolist writers, Roerich was fascinated by the ancient Slavic past, apocalypticism, and Eastern ethnology and religion. He was convinced that the Slavic and Indian cultures shared a common origin and that the destiny of Russia was tied to this relationship. A prominent artist, critic, stage designer, and decorator, he did more in his paintings, articles, and lectures than any other single individual to popularize Indian art and culture among the Russian creative intelligentsia.

Roerich and his wife, Elena Ivanovna Shaposhnikova-Roerich, quickly discovered Theosophy and were much taken with its neo-Buddhist dimension. They read the *Bhagavad Gita* and studied the works of Ramakrishna and Vivekananda, all available in Russian translation. Claiming a "karmic tie" to H. P. Blavatsky, they became members of the Theosophical Society and continued their connection with the Theosophists and with independent Russian occultists even after the Roerich family left Russia following the February Revolution, first for Finland, then for New York and the Far East.

Between 1916 and 1921 Roerich wrote many of the poems, with their strong Theosophical subtext, that comprise the anthology *The Flowers of Morya* (*Tsvety Morii*), while his wife worked on a translation of Mme Blavatsky's *Secret Doctrine*.[7] Roerich considered the poems in *The Flowers of Morya* to be programmatic, to reflect the essence of his own creative path. Like his paintings, the poems are deceptively simple, filled with archetypal symbols, mystically ambiguous, even elusive. "We go in search of sacred signs," says one of the poems, introducing the leitmotiv of Roerich's collection and his life. The reader encounters the light, the path, the forest labyrinth, the flower, water, mountains, and eternity as he searches for the sacred. Much of Roerich's free verse is reminiscent of Mme Blavatsky's poetic moments in "The Stanzas of Dzyan" and *The Voice of the Silence*, including her prophetic, impersonal tone. The volume's title is also suggestive; Master Morya was Mme Blavatsky's Mahatma contact and Roerich believed in the Mahatmas. Many of Roerich's later writings are present *in potentio* in this slim volume of poeticized oriental wisdom, which was appreciated and praised by admirers as diverse as Rabindranath Tagore, Leonid Andreev, and Maksim Gorkii.

In late 1924 and throughout 1925 Nikolai Roerich undertook a major cultural expedition to Central Asia where, like many occultists of the time, he felt he might find traces of the origins of human culture. In the course of the expedition he detoured to the Theosophical Head-quarters in Adyar and donated his painting "Vestnik" ("The Messenger") to the Blavatsky Museum there.[8] In a ceremony at the recently founded "Adyar Art Centre," Roerich himself unveiled the deep red, violet, and golden painting, depicting a dark oriental temple, from within which a young woman opens a door to admit "The Messenger," a young man bearing the Light of the World. It was the first painting contributed to the Adyar Collection of Spiritual Art.

During the 1920s and 1930s, the Roerichs drew on their Theosophical foundation to compile their own doctrinal variant, called Agni Yoga, a synthesis of Eastern and Western thought heavily based on Theosophical doctrine. This creative aspect of their Theosophical activities complicated the Roerichs' relations with the more traditional Russian Theosophical Society Outside Russia. But they maintained a cordial correspondence with Elena Pisareva and several other members who tried to make peace between them and the strong-willed, dogmatic Anna Kamenskaia as the two camps tried to position themselves as acknowledged leaders of the occult emigration.[9] The thirteen volumes of the *Agni Yoga* series, written over a period of twenty years and published in English, Russian, French, Polish, Latvian, Bulgarian, and other European languages, have continued to be popular, both in the Russian emigration and in the Soviet Russian underground.

The legacy of the Roerichs in the area of Theosophical culture is considerable. Roerich and the international Society that bears his name were dedicated primarily to the ideas of Beauty and Culture as inspired by religious philosophy; Roerich defined his own personal mission in these terms. In 1922 he founded the *Corona Mundi*, International Art Center, which recognized Beauty as the Crown of Human Existence; the Center was "dedicated to widening the appreciation of art, of beauty, of culture among all peoples."[10] The Society Roerich founded, inspired by his theosophical vision (without being overtly "Theosophical"), has touched on nearly every aspect of cultural life worldwide. It has sponsored schools, study of the arts (music, art, architecture, ballet, drama, languages and literature), libraries, lectures, adult education programs, museum exhibits, concerts, performances, archaeological and scientific expeditions, working with the blind and physically handicapped, the arts for children, women's groups, and a broad variety of international organizations. In this way the Roerich Society continues the social mission that was an important dimension of Theosophical activity.

During the period between the First and Second World Wars Nikolai Roerich received many of the world's highest honors: he was recognized for his promotion of world peace and culture by the League of Nations, the Vatican, heads of state of European, American, and Asian governments, numerous national academies of sciences and the arts, and other cultural organizations; he was nominated for the Nobel Peace Prize; he was honored as the founder of the Roerich Peace Pact and Banner of Peace, advocating "Peace Through Culture" (*Pax Cultura*) and seeking to protect cultural treasures in times of war and destruction.

The influence of Roerich's thought, molded by the Theosophical Movement, is international and enduring. Echoing the Theosophical credo, today's Roerich Movement asserts the pantheistic unity of man, world, and God; it advocates tolerance and the Brotherhood of Man; it strives for the synthesis of religions. Roerich never abandoned his youthful belief in the spiritual affinity of Russia and the East, and in his system the Slavs continued to play a central role as the future advocates of peace, spirituality, and culture in the world. The spirituality of Russian Orthodox icons merge in his art with Tibetan and Indian religious motifs, and his drive toward Theosophical synthesis is apparent in his many mystical paintings (they have never been exhaustively cataloged, but there are more than seven thousand works). Like many spiritual paintings, Roerich's canvases frequently evoke either adulation or dismissal, but they invite all viewers to enter a clearly sacred space.

The Roerichs' Theosophical ideas have taken particular hold in the Russian occult underground, and the idea of his *Pax Cultura* has appealed to the Russian government. With *glasnost'* the Roerich Movement has openly become part of the resurgence of Russian interest in Eastern philosophy and mysticism; with the current renewed interest in the Russian religious renaissance, the Silver Age, and H. P. Blavatsky, it may well lead to a renascence in Russian Theosophical thought. The Roerich Center in Riga, established during the interwar period but dormant since the Soviet occupation of the Baltic countries, was revived at the end of the 1980s and began almost immediately to issue the popular *Agni Yoga* series in Russian.

Roerich's influence continues in Russia today. One of his sons, Iurii Nikolaevich Rerikh (1902–1960) returned to live in the USSR in 1957; he was considered a leading Soviet Orientologist. His other son, the portraitist Sviatoslav Roerich, has been a frequent visitor to Russia and has assisted in furthering his father's mission by arranging immensely popular exhibits of his art work there. Recently he donated the entire Roerich legacy to the Roerich Fund and Roerich Center in Moscow.[11]

If Nikolai Roerich's particular brand of Theosophy generated a religious, ethical, and social legacy, focused outward and expressed by an essentially figurative if exotic art style accessible to almost any viewer, then the interest in Theosophy of the abstract painter Wasily Kandinsky (1866–1944) led in a very different direction, toward a subtle application of Theosophical ideas that ultimately made his "spiritual art" accessible to only a few. Like many intellectuals of his day, Kandinsky lived in the hothouse of avant-garde culture. He had close connections to the German avant-garde, many of them taken with Dr. Steiner, and to the "Theosophized" Russian Symbolists. He was also acquainted with Aleksandra Unkovskaia, a prominent Russian Theosophist, and had read her Theosophical synesthetic study, "The Method of Color-Sound-Numbers."[12]

Kandinsky's knowledge of Theosophy and acquaintance with Theosophical texts have been documented in the secondary material on this important artist. He was familiar not only with several fundamental works of Mme Blavatsky, Mrs. Besant, Charles Leadbeater, and Rudolf Steiner, but he had also attended Steiner's lectures at the *Architektenhaus* in Berlin in 1907 and 1908. Despite his enthusiasm, Kandinsky browsed selectively among occult offerings. He was interested in alternate planes, depiction of subtle emotions, especially as expressed through the aura, and synesthesia. Anything that touched on his own passion, the eternal in art, commanded his attention.

Among the most provocative Theosophical works for Kandinsky, as for many other European and Russian writers and artists, was Mrs. Besant's and Charles Leadbeater's *Thought-Forms*.[13] The book was devoted to the mysticism of form and color and to the use of color and abstract forms as shorthand for emotions, thoughts, and feelings projected onto the astral plane. Much of the material in the volume had been presented earlier in Mrs. Besant's *Ancient Wisdom*, but *Thought-Forms* lavishly illustrated the thought forms in vibrant color. The volume defines thought form as a mental projection, thought, or idea, too subtle to be seen in gross physical matter, but that manifests itself in refined astral matter. While it may assume the forms of physical matter, it more commonly assumes a more abstract form natural to the astral or mental plane, and such a form would have nothing in common with its physical variant. The book contains illustrations of such thought forms: geometric figures, starbursts, hazy clouds, even protocomputer graphics, all highly suggestive of later abstract art.

Widely available and advertised, *Thought-Forms* was closely read by the avant-garde art community. Kandinsky owned the 1908 German translation and familiarized himself with it before publishing his own major essay, *Über das Geistige in der Kunst*.[14] In Russia Theosophists

and occultists read it in English, in German, or in the popular and frequently reprinted Russian paraphrase of Elena Pisareva. One of those
who read it (as well as *Ancient Wisdom*) was the Symbolist writer
Andrei Belyi.

Theorist, Philosopher, and Writer: Andrei Belyi (1880–1934)

If Nikolai Roerich came to Theosophy primarily because it provided
a vocabulary for his feelings for Indian culture and religion and inspired
his art and his sense of mission to the world; if Kandinsky selectively
took from Theosophy those concepts that allowed him to express the
inexpressible through his art; then Andrei Belyi came to Theosophy because it offered a total world conception. Russian literature has traditionally carried a great deal of philosophical baggage. Critics have little
trouble dealing with such baggage when it is Marxist, Freudian, or Populist, but they usually detour around occultism. Yet, any factor that fundamentally determines an author's worldview will profoundly affect the
world of the novel. And exploring the building blocks of the author's
worldview, especially when that worldview deviates considerably from a
culturally accepted ideological or religious norm, not only provides insight into the artistic merits of the work, but also enhances the reader's
understanding of it. In Belyi's case, Theosophy and Anthroposophy
serve as the key to many of his literary texts, and a case can be made that
many of the elements critics consider to be "modern" or "enigmatic"
about his work are in fact "occult."

Belyi first became interested in Theosophy when only sixteen, in
1896. His was a commitment that would last a lifetime, for in Theosophical doctrine he discovered a mode of thought and a vision of reality
that corresponded to his own independently discovered world perception. Extensive critical and autobiographical materials, documenting his
complex spiritual and philosophical evolution, reveal an intimate knowledge of the major texts of Mme Blavatsky, Mrs. Besant, Edouard
Schuré, Charles Leadbeater, and Rudolf Steiner. Steiner and Anthroposophy did not drop into Belyi's life like a thunderbolt 1912; Belyi had
been hearing about Steiner from two of his "Theosophical ladies" (Anna
Mintslova and Elena Pisareva) since 1905. Belyi came to prefer Steiner's
rationalized and Christianized Theosophy to Mme Blavatsky's and Mrs.
Besant's neo-Buddhistic variant, but the fundamental cosmology and
the language of metaphor, image, and symbol did not change.

Belyi's mature works, especially *Serebrianyi Golub'* (*The Silver Dove*,
1909) and *Peterburg* (*Petersburg*, 1913), the two completed novels of

the unfinished trilogy, "East or West," are permeated with Theosophical content but are not yet tendentiously Anthroposophical. This is not to say that Theosophy is the only or even the most important informing element of these intricate and multidimensional literary works. The novels build on the tradition of Russian literature and can be read as philosophical, psychological, historical, satirical, or fantastic novels. But, in addition, both *The Silver Dove* and *Petersburg* incorporate a profoundly Theosophical worldview, and without an appreciation of this they remain only partially accessible to the reader.

On a superficial level, the two novels are concerned with Russia's destiny during the fateful days of the Revolution of 1905. *The Silver Dove* is set in the countryside and narrates the story of Petr Dar'ial'skii, a young *intelligent* engaged to an attractive lady who lives with her grandmother on their country estate. Dar'ial'skii becomes infatuated with a pock-marked peasant wench and leaves his aristocratic fiancée to live with the peasant woman and a sectarian carpenter. He enters into their peasant life, but, coming from a different world, is ultimately unable to establish genuine contact with them: the common people and the intelligentsia remain divided. In the end the sectarians murder him. In contrast to this rural apocalypse, *Petersburg* depicts revolutionary events in the capital. The highly placed Senator Ableukhov is the object of an assassination plot involving his son, Nikolai, and two terrorists, Dudkin and Lippanchenko. The plot fizzles, the Senator retires from government service, and Nikolai goes to Egypt to seek esoteric knowledge. Critics have been attracted by the innovative language, imagery, and structure of the two novels, but some aspects of the text remain obscure. Here an acquaintance with Theosophy can assist the reader.

Many of the Theosophical and occult images in the novels are easily identified when one knows the vocabulary and the imagery. For example: Petr Dar'ial'skii, the hero of *The Silver Dove*, is literally trapped by Maya in a spiderweb (the world illusion) spun by the villainous sectarian carpenter; this web surrounds the hero and attempts to ensnare him eternally on the physical plane. The plot literally realizes the mystery drama of the Pilgrim-Soul who descends from his spiritual home into the "labyrinth" of matter, becomes entangled there, but hears the "Call" and awakens from the "dream of this life" to return to the "real" realm of spirit; the novel uses these Theosophical terms in the text. The neurotic student Chukholka is a spiritualistic "medium" for dark and evil forces that wish to harm Russia; the mysterious Schmidt is an adept and Dar'ial'skii's guru. The work itself is Theosophically structured: the novel (One, the Unity) is divided into two parts (Two, Duality of Matter and Spirit); the first part is divided into four chapters (Four, the square, is the number of Matter and Evil); and the second part consists of three chapters (Three, the triangle, is the number of Spirit and Good). At its center is a horoscope which, when deciphered, is found to contain the plot, imagery, and verbal texture of the novel. *Petersburg* contains a similar menu of overtly Theosophical images and vocabulary.

More intriguing than the overt Theosophical images and terms used in the two novels is that the novels express two fundamental and related generative principles that lie at the root of Theosophical cosmogenesis. The first is the generative principle that produces the novels themselves: *theurgy*. Theurgy is the belief in the magical power of words and sounds (prayer, incantation, Logos, and so forth) and forms one of the cornerstones of Andrei Belyi's theory of symbolism as a worldview. In esoteric philosophy, the Word is the fundamental creative category that gives shape, form, and reason to chaos, transfiguring chaos into cosmos. Theurgy in Theosophy is associated with the creative, Spermatic Word. In Andrei Belyi, it becomes "the creative word [that] creates the world," the union of mysticism and art.[15] The excessive focus on sound in Symbolist literature is not accidental, but esoterically motivated; sounds have magical potency. Belyi's friend, the poet Aleksandr Blok, agreed that art is magic: "From the beginning the Symbolist is a theurgist, i.e., the possessor of occult knowledge, behind which stands occult activity."[16] Analogically, poets create their literary and personal world as the Divinity creates the universe. Thus Belyi creates *The Silver Dove* from the sounds of the ancient Alphabet of the Magi, said to contain the original sounds of the cosmos, as enciphered in the horoscope of the novel's hero.[17]

The occult generation of *Petersburg* is based on an allied occult principle, the concept that *consciousness creates form*. Unlike scientific positivism (the archenemy of Belyi and Theosophy), which claims that matter creates thought (thought defined as electric impulses caused by chemical reactions in the matter of the brain, for instance), this fundamental principle of many occult systems claims that, on the contrary, it is thought that creates matter: the sheer power of Will can create palpable objects. This concept was not invented by Belyi. It is much older than Russian Symbolism, but it was concisely formulated by Mme Blavatsky in *Isis Unveiled*:

> As God creates, so man can create. Given a certain intensity of will, and the shapes created by the mind become subjective. Hallucinations, they are called, although to their creator they are real as any visible object is to anyone else. Given a more intense and intelligent concentration of this will, and the form becomes concrete, visible, objective; the man has learned the secret of secrets; he is a MAGICIAN.[18]

The implications for the author-magician, the theurgist who parallels God in the creation of an entire alternative universe by thinking, willing, and speaking, are clearly manifold. This is the source of what Belyi defines as *mozgovaia igra* ("cerebral play") in his novel *Petersburg*. The characters "think" each other into being exactly as the author "thinks" the characters into being. In *Petersburg* Belyi's description of Senator Ableukhov mentally generating the terrorist Dudkin is actually a "scientifically" concrete description of the generation of thought-forms onto the astral plane as described by Mrs. Besant and Charles W. Leadbeater in their influential book, *Thought-Forms*.

In *Petersburg*, Senator Ableukhov himself is not consciously aware of what is actually happening, because he is an unenlightened prisoner of scientific positivism. The Senator reads Auguste Comte, whose work Mme Blavatsky considered positivism carried to absurdity. His positivistic inclination is clear in that his house (a traditional metaphor for the brain) is yellow. Yellow, in Theosophical color theory, is the color of pure intellect, untempered by any other quality. (Other elements of Theosophical color theory, explicated in *Thought-Forms*, are also present in the novel.) And the Senator clearly believes that matter generates thought: poor Senator Ableukhov, the novel's narrator tells us, regards perception as "an irritation of the cerebral membrane, if not an indisposition of the cerebellum." But physical senses and sensations are not the measure of reality, and cannot be, in Theosophy; Theosophy subscribes to the idea that the physical plane of existence is just one of several, and the lowest and coarsest at that. There are other, more subtle planes of existence, including two that are accessible to some human minds and several that are not. Accessible are the astral and the mental planes.

The various planes of existence, Mrs. Besant points out, are "concentric interpenetrating spheres, not separated from each other by distance, but by difference of constitution."[19] They exist simultaneously and are, in fact, differing dimensions, or states of consciousness (Steiner). They are invisible to the average human being, but can be contacted by those who are spiritually trained, mentally ill, or in a dreaming state. The world of the astral plane exists simultaneously with the physical world and looks much like it. "Astral world scenery much resembles that of earth in consequence of its being largely made up of the astral duplicates of physical objects," explains Mrs. Besant.[20] Some Theosophists have called the astral plane the fourth dimension. It is inhabited not by human beings, but by all the thoughts, feelings, fears, desires, wishes, and impulses human beings feel. On the astral plane thoughts take on visible, concrete form and become a living force. "While they maintain a separate existence they are living entities, with bodies of elemental es-

sence and thoughts as the ensouling lives, and they are then called artificial elementals, or thought-forms," Mrs. Besant explains.[21]

"Thought and action, will and deed, are one and the same thing" in
the astral world, continues Mrs. Besant. The thought on the physical
plane becomes the deed on the astral plane. The physical and astral
worlds interact. Once thoughts and feelings take on an astral existence
of their own, they in turn influence events that happen on the physical
plane. Astrally inspired incidents on the physical plane may *appear* arbitrary and incomprehensible, but they have their own ineluctable logic in
the cosmic scheme of things if one knows how to read the world as a
mystic text (as Theosophists and Symbolists thought they did). Thus the
Senator, a thought-form produced by the author's mind, or Dudkin, a
thought-form produced by the Senator's mind, live separate lives and
affect events and people—as senator and revolutionary on the physical
plane; as ancient Turanian destroyer and avenging Horseman on the astral plane.

Astral matter, or elemental essence, has considerable fluidity. It is perceived as fogs and shadows and as continually changing shapes that appear and disappear as human thought-impulses constantly massage the
elemental essence; the city of Petersburg is so described in Belyi's novel.
Belyi's shadows appear from and disappear into the St. Petersburg fog,
echoing Mrs. Besant's description, found in *Man and His Bodies* (the
book one of the characters is reading in the novel), of the astral world as
"full of continually changing shapes; . . . vast masses of elemental essence from which continually shapes emerge and into which they again
disappear." "An astral entity will change his whole appearance with the
most startling rapidity," Mrs. Besant explains, "for astral matter takes
form under every impulse of thought, the life swiftly remoulding the
form to give itself new expression."[22] And this is one reason why
characters in *Petersburg* constantly change into other people: the Se-
mitic-Ukrainian Mongol, Lippanchenko-Mavrokordato, Shishnarfiev-
Shishnarfne-Enfranshish, Voronkov-Morkovin, the Bronze Horseman-
Dutchman-sailor-Bronze Guest; this is why metaphors are realized and
why slippers and wallpaper come alive and suitcases reshape themselves.
They are all astral entities, constantly being remolded by the overactive
brains of Russians thinking and feeling on the physical plane of October
1905.

During the lectures he read for the Russians in Paris in 1906, Steiner
added his own footnotes to Mrs. Besant's entertaining travelogues of
the astral world. He explained that the astral world is, additionally, the
"inverse unraveling of things," that it is the mirror image of the physical
world. Everything that happens in the physical world plays backward in
the astral world. This is incorporated into the novel in its mirror and

reflective imagery, in the detail that number 1000 is really 0001, that Enfranshish is Shishnarfne; the Senator is his son, and the son is the father. History also runs backward. Cause follows effect, not effect the cause, thus making the goal, the aim, appear to be the cause, and proving, as Steiner asserts, that aim and cause are ultimately the same thing.

And this is not idle play on Belyi's part, for these last two points are essential to the main thrust of the novel, the fate of Russia. If history, *Russian* history in the novel, runs backward, then a reverse chronological sequence of effects should lead back to a cause. The novel constantly returns to the past, to the two mythic turning points in Russian history: to the Mongols and their "mission of destruction," and to Peter the Great and the astral city he built. (Shishnarfne identifies it as *"our* capital city," the capital of the "Shadowland.") "Petersburg has not three dimensions but four; the fourth dimension is subject to ambiguity and is not indicated on maps at all, except, perhaps, by a point, for a point is the place at which the plane of this [physical] existence touches the spherical surface of the enormous astral cosmos."[23]

We are told that Petersburg will sink into the swamp (reversing the process of its building). "Petersburg, Petersburg! Precipitating out of the fog, you have pursued me with idle cerebral play. Hard-hearted tormentor! Restless specter!" observes the narrator.[24] The Mongol cause was destruction through immutability. The Petrine cause was destruction by division and change. By creating his city in the swamp by force of conscious will, Peter "doomed Russia irrevocably." He created the destructive duality between East and West, *narod* and intelligentsia, Slavophile and Westernizer, God-seeker and God-builder, Muscovite and Peterburgian: "From that pregnant moment when the metallic Horseman first galloped to the banks of the Neva, from that moment, pregnant with days, when he had flung his steed upon the gray Finnish granite, Russia was divided in two, and the destiny of the Fatherland was divided also in two [hence "East or West?" as the name of the projected Trilogy]; suffering and weeping, Russia was divided in two until the final hour."[25] The cause—Peter—and the aim—division—were identical.

Thus the city of Petersburg becomes the astral center of the Russian universe. This city, the "most intentional and rational city on earth," in the words of Dostoevskii, is *willed* into existence by Peter the Great. His intensity of will created simultaneously a physical and an astral city. Since that time, the thoughts and feelings of the Russian national consciousness have molded and remolded the city's astral image, inhabiting it with strange and dangerous thought-forms, ensouled by revolutionary and dangerous ideas; this astral capital is more real than the physical Petersburg. The Revolution of 1905, a turning point in the consciousness of the Russian intelligentsia, was precipitated onto the physical plane by all the negative forces that Russian history had projected into the astral plane over the centuries. Those events were inevitable, they had their own inexorable cosmic logic: they were the expression of the negative collective karma of the Russian people, and this karma had to be expiated before Russia could fulfill her destined role as the savior of Europe.

Belyi consciously embedded the most important intellectual point of his novel into a Theosophical framework. Many of the more ambiguous and puzzling aspects of the novel take on meaningful, if complex, referents when considered in this Theosophical context. *Petersburg*, generally regarded as an inaccessible and eccentrically subjective novel, is, in fact, an "astral" novel, as Belyi's contemporaries were quick to notice. Nikolai Berdiaev, who even titled his review of *Petersburg* "Astral'nyi roman" (An astral novel), took Belyi's Theosophical format as given and perceptively noticed the striking parallel between what Belyi achieved in *Petersburg* and the painting style of cubism.[26] Belyi's aim was not to be obscure or elitist in this quintessentially Symbolist novel, but to make sense of the Russian crisis of culture and consciousness. To this end he used a Theosophical world perception and its vocabulary as a form of philosophical shorthand that his readers would understand; sound and image he employed not in a purely formalistic way as literary device, but in a mythic way as a potent magical symbol that makes accessible the realiora that inform the realia of historical events, thereby transforming chaos into cosmos.

In his subsequent work Belyi became fixated on his own biography, in both fictional and nonfictional genres, but it was not biographical material in the traditional sense that fascinated him. His autobiographical works were, in fact, spiritual autobiographies. His unpublished and unknown magnum opus, "Istoriia stanovleniia samosoznaiushchei dushi" (The history of the formation of the consciousness soul; a Steinerian term for the fifth principle of man), strove to summarize the development of the entire history of human thought and consciousness. This mammoth work of more than a thousand manuscript pages is not merely a history of human culture and philosophy seen through Steiner's Anthroposophical prism, but a macrocosmic version of the microcosmic individual biography. As his biographical materials traced the physical, mental, and spiritual development of Boris Bugaev (and his aesthetic alter ego, "Andrei Belyi"), so "Istoriia" traces the spiritual development of mankind.

Theosophy and subsequently Anthroposophy appealed to Belyi primarily because they offered a seemingly coherent explanation of apparently chaotic events and provided a vocabulary for discussing psychic states for which no vocabulary existed. Knowledge of Theosophy suggests that much of what may seem startling, innovative, and opaque in

Belyi is actually mainline Theosophy. And why Theosophy? Because
Belyi thought it might be that system for which he searched all his life,
a system that *explained it all*, a system that allowed him to conquer the
chaos that modern life had become and resolve the crisis of culture and
consciousness he and his generation experienced so poignantly.

In Conclusion

The Russian intelligentsia, from the moment it became conscious of
its separate and unique identity sometime in the first quarter of the nineteenth century, has searched for a system, something to organize and
make coherent Russia, the Russian mind, and the universe. This search
for a system under threat of chaos has always been highly ideological and
hampered by the general Russian conviction (from wherever it springs)
that there can be only one Truth (*istina*), and that man exists to seek It.
This Truth, however it might be conceived at any given historical moment, must be all-encompassing. When this quest for Truth took a religious form, as it did in the Russian Middle Ages, religion struggled to
subordinate the Russian secular world to its vision. When the quest took
a secular form, as it did during the Soviet period, it struggled to subordinate the religious impulse to itself.

One of Theosophy's greatest temptations for certain idealist elements
within the Russian intelligentsia was its promise of the Great Synthesis:
of science, religion, and philosophy, of matter and spirit, and of East and
West. For these idealists Theosophy was, first and foremost, a particular
view of the world, of life and death, of God and man, of good and evil,
and of the purpose of human existence. It was neither a faith nor a science (both had been discredited), but it seemed to have already achieved
the unification of the secular and the religious spheres into one
enormous, sublime, and glorious system that reconciled all contradictions between sacred and profane and expressed *the Truth*. In the area of
religion, Theosophy claimed to show the derivation of all world religions from a single divine source; in science, Theosophy claimed to
prove the contiguity of the material and physical worlds; in art, Theosophy united all art under the aegis of a single and eternal concept of
beauty, emphasizing the symbiotic interrelationship of architecture, poetry, dance, music, literature, and the graphic arts, and identifying aesthetic creativity with religious creativity; in the social sphere, Theosophy
promised a single brotherhood uniting all humanity, a global utopia.

Furthermore Theosophy, as an all-encompassing, cosmopolitan Movement seemingly without disciplinary or political boundaries, easily made
room for all of the major concerns of the Russian intelligentsia. God-

seeking, Pan-Slavism, eschatological ahistoricism, messianism, and the Russian Idea (regardless of whether it was expressed as destiny, karma, or mission), mystical populism, and the Gnosticism underlying many Russian mystical sects were all subsumed under its syncretic aegis. Theosophy revealed the Path of Russia's destiny as bringer of spiritual values to the West. This sense of destiny was visible in the role of Mme Blavatsky herself, a Russian woman who carried spiritual values to the rest of the world through Theosophy. Her appropriation of Buddhist thought from the East and her dissemination of it in the West became a potent mythologem. Theosophy's implicit social agenda, its answer to the question "How should we live?" was also attractive to the Russian intelligentsia. Its program dealt with everything from tolerance of race and religion to vegetarianism.

Finally, Theosophy affirmed the intelligentsia's spiritual and intellectual understanding of human evolution and humanity's central role in the universe. Its complex cosmology provides "proof" that human consciousness and human culture were destined to evolve and were, in fact, evolving at that very moment in the direction of the spiritual. Humankind had passed through the worst, most material stage of its development and was already on the Path upward toward Spirit. This spiritual Darwinism of the Theosophists easily found an echo in the views of the Russian God-builders and the idealistic socialists.

Theosophy was forcibly evicted from Russian soil by political events, and its credibility was further diminished in the late 1920s and 1930s because it continued, in the face of a profoundly material and technological twentieth century, to deny matter as illusory. Steeped in pantheistic monism, it also denied individualism, the very basis of post-Enlightenment societal structure (although this aspect concerned Western European Theosophy more than its Russian variant). Psychologists, recognizing the widespread interest in Theosophy and its kindred phenomena, warned against their seductions. Perhaps Theosophy turned out to be part of the darker side of spiritual searchings of the Russian Silver Age, but, as the intellectual historian S. A. Levitskii pointed out, periods of "creative inspiration are frequently associated with temptations and heresies."[27] Perhaps it was only a pseudointellectual pseudosystem after all, a pseudoreligion, a pseudophilosophy. Perhaps, in the end, neither Mme Blavatsky's Eastern Theosophy (with its neo-Buddhism) nor Dr. Steiner's Western Anthroposophy (with its Rosicrucianism) was able to satisfy the quest of the Russian spirit for its Russian Truth. But for some highly visible individuals—Nikolai Roerich, Konstantin Bal'mont, Margarita Sabashnikova-Voloshina, Maks Voloshin, Asya Turgeneva, and Andrei Belyi among them—Theosophy apparently provided some much needed answers, gave structure and significance to their life, and found expression through their work. It served to enhance, not impede, their creative impulse. Even those who subsequently rejected Theosophy— Viacheslav Ivanov and Lev Kobylinskii-Ellis, both of whom converted to Catholicism, or Nikolai Berdiaev, who followed his own philosophical imperative—evolved as they did in the context of their encounter with Theosophy.

Theosophy did not pass through Russian culture and thought without a trace. If it had, God-seekers and Orthodox theologians would not have felt the need to continue to discuss Theosophy and Anthroposophy, to refute its doctrine, and to criticize its practitioners for the rest of their lives in the emigration. Nikolai Berdiaev devoted an entire section to "Theosophy and Gnosis" in *Filosofiia svobodnogo dukha* (1927), arguably his most important single work. He was answered in the émigré journal *Put'* by Nataliia Turgeneva, the Paris Anthroposophist and sister of Andrei Belyi's first wife, the Anthroposophical artist, Asya Turgeneva.[28] In 1935 Berdiaev, Semen Frank, Vasilii Zenkovskii, Boris Vysheslavtsev, and Father Georgii Florovskii published in Paris a small but interesting volume, *Pereselenie dush; problema bezsmertiia v okkul' tizme i khristianstve*, which continued to address the perceived importance and potential threat posed by the occult, neo-Buddhist thought of Mme Blavatsky and Dr. Steiner on the philosophy of the Russian religious renaissance.

Today it is still difficult for critics to take seriously the occult movements of the fin de siècle and their influence or to evaluate that influence objectively. It is far easier to lampoon or deride the occult's more notorious or bizarre manifestations. But in their time such movements nevertheless attracted many intelligent, serious, and respected individuals—scientists, scholars, artists, and writers. The adherents of these movements, except in the more extreme cases of Bohemian excess, were not viewed as a lunatic fringe; most of them stemmed from the middle and gentry classes and enjoyed social acceptability, even prestige. It is not unusual in the legitimate and popular philosophical, religious, and scholarly literature of the period to see the works of Mrs. Besant, Rudolf Steiner, and Edouard Schuré listed in bibliographies and cited as sources.

It may be true that, like the characters of Umberto Eco's modern occult novel, *Foucault's Pendulum*, Theosophy ultimately invented nothing new; but it is also true that, like those same characters, it rearranged the old pieces and, merely by doing so, rewrote history and changed reality. The conflation of time and space, the blurring of historical epochs and geographical locations, the frequently specious analogies characteristic of modernist and postmodernist art may well have their roots in the analogical syncretism that Theosophy (and other occult movements) disseminated in their time as an antidote to logical, linear thought. The occult mind is driven by analogy and by symbol, not by the principle of cause and effect or the concept of "fact." Theosophy was the widest promulgator of the analogical and synthetic, rather than the logical and analytic, mode of thought in its time. It had been called into existence because of a perceived need for an alternative to scientific positivism. Perhaps Theosophy did not appeal to everyone; perhaps it did not succeed in solving the Great Mystery of the Universe; but many preferred it to the existential thought that no Mystery exists, and that at the end of the Path lies nothing.

Notes

Introduction
The Esoteric Tradition and the Russian Silver Age

1. Otets Ioann Dmitrevskii, *Teosofiia—religioznaia filosofiia nashego vremeni* (Khar'kov: 1911), 1. Ironically, Father Dmitrevskii might well be describing Soviet Russian book kiosks during the heady days of *glasnost'*.

2. L. E. O., "Religiozno-misticheskie brozheniia v sovremennoi Rossii," *Rebus* 8/9(1906): 4. There was a more sinister side to the occult phenomenon as well. Anatolii B., writing on "Peterburgskie satanisty" in *Rebus* 8(1913): 5, pointed out that the capital was full of "Satanists, Luciferians, fire-worshippers, black magicians, and occultists" (his article was reprinted from *Golos Moskvy* 34 [1913]). And they were everywhere: among the court pages, in the medical academies, in the schools, and in the elegant salons of Petersburg's *beau monde*. The darker side of Russian occultism was frequently associated with narcotics, suicides, confidence games, and the occasional Black Mass. Several foreign occultists (such as the notorious Czeslaw von Czinski) were told to leave Russia and never return.

3. Ivanov-Razumnik, "Andrei Belyi," in S. A. Vengerov, *Russkaia literatura xx veka*, vol. 3, pt. 2 (Moscow: Mir, 1916), 59. "Zheorzhii Nulkov" is a character from Belyi's fourth "Symphony," *Kubok metelei* (1908); he is a parody of the mystical anarchist and second-rate Symbolist writer, Georgii Chulkov (1879–1939).

4. Nikolai Berdiaev, *Samopoznanie* (1949; 2d rev. ed. Paris: YMCA, 1983), 224–25.

5. H. P. Blavatsky, *Isis Unveiled* (New York: J. W. Bouton, 1877), vol. 1, xxxvii.

6. *Mystic* and *mystery* from Greek *musterion*, secret rites, and *mustes*, one initiated into secret rites; from *muein*, to initiate, and *muein*, to keep silence; *occult* from Latin *occulere*, to cover, conceal.

7. Gershom Scholem, *On the Kabbalah and Its Symbolism* (New York: Schocken Books, 1965), 9. Scholem is speaking theoretically on the nature of mysticism in general.

8. A. E. Waite, *Lamps of Western Mysticism* (1923; Blauvelt, N.Y.: Rudolph Steiner Publications, 1973), 66.

9. Andrew Seth, quoted in William R. Inge, *Christian Mysticism* (1899; London: Methuen, 1948), 339.

10. Inge, *Christian Mysticism*, 5.

11. Ibid., 339.

12. E. Barabash, "Teosofiia i teosofy," *Rebus* 43(1884): 395.

13. Additional information on Russian Anthroposophy is available in the recent book by the Anthroposophist Victor B. Fedjuschin, *Russlands Sehnsucht nach Spiritualität* (Schaffhausen, Switzerland: Novalis Verlag, 1988).

Chapter One
A Historical Survey of Russian Occult Interests

1. See A. N. Pypin, "Lozhnye i otrechennye knigi russkoi stariny," in *Pamiatniki starinnoi russkoi literatury*, ed. G. Kushelev-Bezborodko, pt. 3 (St. Petersburg: 1862), 161–66; Count Kushelev-Bezborodko was a leading occultist and Spiritualist; see also M. N. Speranskii, "Iz istorii otrechennykh knig," in *Gadaniia po psaltyri* (1899), also his "*Aristotelevy Vrata i Tainaia tainykh*," in *Sbornik statei v chest' A. I. Sobolevskogo* (SORIaS CI:3) (Leningrad: 1928); A. N. Veselovskii, "Gadatel'nye knigi na Zapade i u nas," in *Vestnik Evropy* 4(1886); A. A. Turilov, V. Chernetsov, "*Rafli—iazycheskie sviatsy* Ivana Rykova," in *Pamiatniki kul'tury 1984* (Leningrad: Nauka, 1986), 20–28.

2. For discussion of Russian Freemasonry, see A. N. Pypin, *Russkoe masonstvo XVIII i pervaia chetvert' XIX v.* (Petrograd: 1916); [E. N. Berendts], *Masonstvo, ili velikoe tsarstvennoe iskusstvo bratstva vol'nykh kamen'shchikov* (St. Petersburg: 1911); *Masonstvo v ego proshlom i nastoiashchem*, 2 vols. (Moscow: 1914); A. V. Mezier, *V poiskakh pravdy i smysla zhizni* (Petrograd: [Stranstvuiushchii entuziast], 1919); *Ocherk iz istorii russkogo masonstva* (St. Petersburg: 1906); Tira O. Sokolovskaia, *Russkoe masonstvo i ego znachenie v istorii obshchestvennogo dvizheniia.* (St. Petersburg: 1908); Vl. Tukalevskii, *Iskaniia russkikh masonov* (St. Petersburg: 1911).

3. Both Cagliostro and his occult contemporary, the charismatic Comte de Saint-Germain, continued to be a subject of interest in Russia; Saint-Germain taught the old Countess the trick of the cards in Pushkin's "Pikovaia Dama"; Cagliostro was the subject of an entire novel by Mikhail Kuzmin, *Chudesnaia zhizn' Iosifa Bal'zamo, Grafa Kaliostro* (Petrograd: 1919). Both names frequently appear in the supernatural fiction of the nineteenth century when a "mysterious foreigner" is required by the plot.

4. Representative eighteenth-century translated occult classics include: *Khrizomandr* (Moscow: Lopukhin, 1783); *Dragotsennyi magicheskii kamen'* (Moscow: 1783); *Krata Repoa* (Moscow: 1784); *Kolybel' kamnia mudrykh* (Moscow: Lopukhin, 1786); Paracelsus, *Khimicheskii psaltyr', ili filosofskaia pravda o kamne mudrykh* (Moscow: 1784); *O drevnikh misteriiakh ili tainstvakh* (Moscow: 1785); [St.-Martin], *O zabluzhdeniiakh i istine* (Moscow: Lopukhin, 1785); *Dolzhnost' brat'ev Z.-R. K. [Zlato-Rozovogo Kresta]* (Moscow: 1786); *Bagvat Geta* [Bhagavad Gita] (Moscow: Novikov, 1788).

Representative works by Eckartshausen include: *Vazhneishie ieroglify chelovecheskogo serdtsa* (St. Petersburg: 1803); *Nauka chisl*, 2 vols. (St. Petersburg: 1815); *Kliuch k tainstvam natury*, 4 parts (1804; 2d ed. 1821); Halle, *Magiia ili volshebnaia sila prirody*, 9 vols. (Moscow: 1784–1802).

5. Michael Florinsky, *Russia; A History and an Interpretation*, vol. 2 (New York: Macmillan), 638–46.

6. Christopher McIntosh, *Eliphas Lévi and the French Occult Revival* (New York: Weiser, 1972), 141.

7. For an informative description of the French manifestation of the occult revival, see "Religious Unease," in Jean Pierrot's *The Decadent Imagination 1880–1900*, trans. Derek Coltman (Chicago: University of Chicago Press, 1981), 79–118.

8. Bulwer-Lytton's major occult novel, *Zanoni*, was translated into Russian as *Prizrak* (St. Petersburg: 1879).

9. *Revue illustrée*, February 15, 1890; cited in Mircea Eliade, *Occultism, Witchcraft, and Cultural Fashions* (Chicago: University of Chicago Press, 1976), 51.

10. Nina Berberova, *Liudi i lozhi; russkie masony xx stoletiia* (New York: Russica, 1986), 20.

11. To Hermes Trismegistus, the "Thrice-Greatest Hermes," were attributed an eclectic compilation of Neoplatonic, Kabbalistic, and Gnostic sacred texts from the third century B.C. to the third century A.D. Hermes-Thoth was supposedly a sage-adept who preserved the ancient mystery wisdom of the Egyptian Magi; he shares his name with the Egyptian god of wisdom and learning. The medieval alchemists used the term *hermetic* to refer to books of mysticism and occult wisdom; they, in turn, were called "Hermeticists." The term *hermetic* thus refers both to this ancient, Gnostic trend and to medieval philosophical alchemy, which claimed to be a continuation of the ancient tradition.

12. Tukholka's book was in a fourth edition by 1917 and widely read; this was her most successful book, but she also wrote on occult healing, the witch trials, and animal magnetism. Zapriagaev's version of Thomas Henry Burgoyne's *The Light of Egypt* (1889 and subsequent eds.) became an occult bestseller in Russia (*Svet Egipta, ili nauka o zvezdakh i dushe* [Viaz'ma: 1906; 2d ed. 1910]); Zapriagaev also published astrological ephemerides and occult "how-to" texts.

13. Emma Hardinge Britten, *Nineteenth Century Miracles; Spirits and Their Works in Every Country of the Earth* (New York: Lovell, 1884), 349, 356. See also "Kratkii ocherk razvitiia spiritualizma v Rossii," *Rebus* 20(1887): 207–10.

14. D. D. Home and the Spiritualism he helped introduce into Russia also found their way into Russian literature. L. N. Tolstoi met D. D. Home in Paris in 1857 and used him as the model for the medium Landau in *Anna Karenina*. Tolstoi also parodied the passion for Spiritualism among the upper classes in his play, *Plody prosveshcheniia* (1891). N. V. Davydov had arranged for Tolstoi to attend a seance at the home of the well-known Moscow Spiritualist Nikolai Aleksandrovich L'vov (1834–1887) sometime in the mid-1880s. Tolstoi's satiric play was based on his experiences in the L'vov home.

15. Some additional material on spiritualism in Russia is available in Thomas Berry, *Spiritualism in Tsarist Society and Literature* (Baltimore: Edgar Allan Poe Society, 1985). Prof. Berry's study, however, is preliminary, with many lacunae.

16. An insightful account of this episode may be found in V. I. Pribytkov's *Vopros o spiritizme v Rossii* (St. Petersburg: Izdatel'stvo *Rebusa*, 1901); for more general information, see Arthur Conan Doyle, *History of Spiritualism* (London: George H. Doran, 1926), 2 vols.; for a Russian point of view, see V. S. Akatov, *O pozitivnykh osnovakh noveishego spiritizma* (Moscow: 1909).

17. *Rebus* 1(1894): 4.

18. Thomas Berry, *Spiritualism in Tsarist Society and Literature*, 112. For more information on the formative years of *Rebus*, see the Jubilee Number 1000 (9[March 4, 1901]; also issued separately as a book).

19. See *Trudy pervogo vserossiiskogo s"ezda spiritualistov* (Moscow: 1907, 1908).

20. On December 6, 1908, *Russkie vedomosti* and other newspapers carried an advertisement that offered the following premiums to new subscribers: an Aksakov-approved ouija board, a black *boule* for developing clairvoyance, and a "Palmograph" to help with automatic writing. New subscribers also had the right to submit up to three questions a month to be asked at seances held under the auspices of *Ottuda*'s editorial board.

21. At which point Bykov brutally attacked Spiritualism as a satanic, Masonic, and Jewish conspiracy in *Spiritizm pod sudom nauki, obshchestva, i religii* (Moscow: Izdanie E. I. Bykovoi, 1914).

22. V. P. Bykov, *Spiritizm pod sudom nauki, obshchestva i religii,* 77–78.

23. Andrei Belyi, letter to Aleksandr Blok of December 18 or 19, 1904, in *Andrei Belyi—Aleksandr Blok. Perepiska* (Moscow: 1940; reprinted Munich: Fink Verlag, 1969), 116.

24. *Spiritualist* 1(1909): 32–33.

25. That both Spiritualism and Theosophy originated in the New York area is not as coincidental as it may first appear. New York was the heart of the so-called burned-over district, an area of the American Northeast through which most immigrants were channeled. The "burned-over district" became famous for its revivalists, free thinkers, dissenters, and religious eccentrics of every conceivable stamp. The Seventh Day Adventists, Jehovah's Witnesses, Joseph Smith's Mormonism, and Mary Baker Eddy's Christian Science all emerged from this area, as well as the Transcendentalists and a variety of social utopian groups. That Mme Blavatsky gravitated toward this area and that both Spiritualism and Theosophy had their beginnings there is not to be wondered at.

26. Mrs. Annie Besant, *The Ancient Wisdom* (1897; Adyar: The Theosophical Publishing House, 1977), 4–5.

27. Ibid., 1.

28. Mme Blavatsky, *The Secret Doctrine* (New York: The Theosophical Publishing Co., 1888), vol. 1, xx.

29. Edouard Schuré, *The Great Initiates*, vol. 1, trans. Fred Rothwell (1889; London: 1913), xx, xxi.

30. Mme Blavatsky, *The Secret Doctrine*, vol. 1, xxxiv.

31. Mrs. Besant, *The Ancient Wisdom*, 3.

32. Ibid., 41.

33. Schuré's preface to Steiner's *An Esoteric Cosmology* (Blauvelt, N.Y.: Spiritual Science Library, 1987), 5; lectures read in Paris May 25–June 14, 1906.

34. V. Gol'dberg, in *Antroposofskoe dvizhenie i ego prorok* (Berlin: 1923), went so far as to call Anthroposophy "the Protestantization of Indian wisdom" (33).

35. Mme Blavatsky, *The Secret Doctrine*, vol. 1, viii.

36. A. P. Sinnett, *Esoteric Buddhism* (London: Trübner, 1883), 22, 29.

37. Mrs. Annie Besant, *The Ancient Wisdom*, 302.

38. Andrei Belyi, Notebook from 1901, Manuscript Division, Lenin Library, Moscow, MS# 25;1;4, fol. 80a.

39. E. M. Butler, *Myth of the Magus* (Cambridge: Cambridge University Press, 1948), 216.

Chapter Two
The Early Days of Theosophy in Russia (1875–1901)

1. For information on Mme Blavatsky's early life, see Vera Zhelikhovskaia, "Elena Petrovna Blavatskaia (biograficheskii ocherk)," *Russkoe obozrenie* 11(1891): 242–94; 12(1891): 567–621; Elena Pisareva, "Elena Petrovna Blavatskaia," in *Voprosy teosofii; sbornik statei*, pt. 2 (St. Petersburg: 1910), 7–52; both are panegyrical and hagiographical. Much conflicting material comes from Mme Blavatsky's aunt, Nadezhda Andreevna Fadeeva, three years her senior and an intimate friend and defender, and Mar'ia Grigor'evna Ermolova, the wife of the governor of Tiflis, who knew the Fadeev family well. Elena Petrovna's sister, Vera Zhelikhovskaia, also wrote memoirs of her youth, "Kak ia byla malen'kaia" and "Moe otrochestvo," with considerable material about Elena Petrovna; Zhelikhovskaia also kept a diary. I have not been able to locate these last materials.

Numerous biographies exist for readers who want more details of Mme Blavatsky's career; read with care. See: Henry Steel Olcott, *Old Diary Leaves* (New York: G. P. Putnam's, 1895), and A. P. Sinnett, *Incidents in the Life of H. P. Blavatsky* (1886; New York: Ayer, 1976), two works written by contemporaries and fellow Theosophists; Countess Constance Wachtmeister, et al., *Reminiscences of H. P. Blavatsky and the Secret Doctrine* (1883; Wheaton, Ill.: The Theosophical Publishing House, 1976); Charles Ryan, *H. P. Blavatsky and the Theosophical Movement* (1937 2d rev. ed. Pasadena: Theosophical University Press, 1875); Marion Meade, *Madame Blavatsky: The Woman Behind the Myth* (New York: G. P. Putnam's, 1980). Meade's book, the least flattering of those listed, is readable and informative; while it presents the "mythology" of Mme Blavatsky, as well as substantiated facts, it does not integrate the mythology unquestioningly into the biography. Meade seems to have missed, however, the charismatic dimension of Mme Blavatsky's character, a necessary point if one is to understand how a single woman impressed, convinced, and inspired so many people, given the more incredible aspects of her Theosophy (and her trying personality). For a very different view of Mme Blavatsky, see Sergei Witte's *Memoirs of Count Witte* (Garden City, N.Y.: 1921). Other Russian material includes Zinaida Vengerova and Vladimir Solov'ev, "Blavatskaia, Elena Petrovna," in S. A. Vengerov's *Kritiko-biograficheskii slovar'* (St. Petersburg: Semenovskaia tipografiia, 1892), and Vsevolod Solov'ev, *Sovremennaia zhritsa Izidy* (St. Petersburg: Obshchestvennaia Pol'za, 1893). Other materials are listed in the general bibliography.

2. Pisareva implies that Prince Golitsyn was somehow involved in Elena Petrovna's disappearance from home for several days, and that the hasty marriage with the socially unsuitable and unloved Nikifor Blavatskii was arranged to save her reputation. Elena Petrovna was married in 1849, not 1848, as most biographies state.

3. Geoffrey Barborka, *H. P. Blavatsky, Tibet, and Tulku* (Adyar, Madras: The Theosophical Publishing House, 1974), 24–25.

4. "Pravda o E. P. Blavatskoi," *Rebus* 40–41, 43–44, 46–48(1883).

5. Mme Blavatsky's later descriptions of life in Tibet bear a more than coinci-

dental resemblance to classic travel texts of the period; she herself admitted re-
sorting to contemporary travel guides when writing her Indian travelogues in
the late 1870s and early 1880s, and probably did the same for her Tibetan "adventures." Her narratives include no unique experiences or descriptions that
would indicate that she had in fact penetrated or even reached Tibet, which at
the time permitted almost no foreigners, and no white women, to cross its
borders.

6. The spying accusation possibly has foundation in fact. On December 26,
1872, Mme Blavatsky wrote from Odessa to the Director of the Third Section
offering her services as an agent: "During these twenty years I have become well
acquainted with all of Western Europe, I zealously followed current politics not
with any goal in mind, but because of an innate passion; in order better to follow
events and to divine them in advance, I always had the habit of entering into the
smallest details of any affair, for which reason I strove to acquaint myself with all
the leading personalities, politicians of various nations, both of the government
factions and of the far Left." After recommending herself to the Director by
referring to her Fadeev connections, she went on: "As a Spiritualist, I have a
reputation in many places as a powerful medium. Hundreds of people undoubtedly believed and will believe in spirits. But I, writing this letter with the aim of
offering my services to Your Excellency and to my native land, am obligated to
tell you the entire truth without concealment. And thus I must confess that
three-quarters of the time the spirits spoke and answered in my words and out
of my considerations, for the success of my own plans. Rarely, very rarely, did I
fail, by means of this little trap, to discover people's hopes, plans, and secrets."
Mme Blavatsky followed her offer with a list of all the military secrets she had
managed to discover while in Cairo the previous year. The Third Section did not
accept her kind offer, although she quite accurately told them: "I have played
every role, I am able to represent myself as any person you may wish" (TsGAOR
[Central State Archive of the October Revolution], MS# 109;3;22; cited in *Literaturnoe obozrenie* 6[1988]: 111–12.) Probably genuine, this letter, which is
alternately boastful and obsequious, is suggestive of her personality.

7. Radda-Bai [pseud. of H. P. Blavatsky], *Iz peshcher i debrei Indostana;
pis'ma na rodinu*, Addendum to *Russkii vestnik* 1–8(1883); second series
11(1885), 2–3, 8(1886); *Zagadochnye plemena. Tri mesiatsa na "Golubykh Gorakh" Madrasa*, in *Russkii vestnik* 12(1884), 1–4(1885); separate edition, *Iz peshcher i debrei Indostana. Zagadochnye plemena na "Golubykh Gorakh." Durbar
v Lagore* (St. Petersburg: V. I. Gubinskii, 1893). The work contains a biography
of Mme Blavatsky by V. P. Zhelikhovskaia. A second, illustrated edition was
published by Suvorin in 1912, under the name E. P. Blavatskaia, not Radda-Bai.

8. Founded in 1882, the Society for Psychical Research had many prominent
members, including Edmund Gurney, Frederic Myers, Henry Sidgwick, Sir William Barrett, and Alfred Russel Wallace; its more illustrious "affiliates" from the
Royal Society represented the acme of the worlds of politics, letters, and philosophy: Prime Minister Gladstone, Alfred, Lord Tennyson, John Ruskin, and William James.

9. Marion Meade, *Madame Blavatsky: The Woman Behind the Myth* (New
York: G. P. Putnam's, 1980), 289.

10. Society for Psychical Research, "Report of the Committee Appointed to Investigate Phenomena Connected with the Theosophical Society," *Proceedings of the Society for Psychical Research*, no. 3 (December 1885), 207.

11. A leading Theosophist who was residing at the Adyar Headquarters during the Mahatma scandal, Franz Hartmann, wrote a short work entitled *An Adventure Among the Rosicrucians* (1887), in which a traveler is taken to one of the outposts of the Brotherhood in the Alps, and there meets an adept named "Ellen" and hears astral bells (one of Mme Blavatsky's most frequently produced phenomena). A popular translation into Russian was serialized in *Rebus* between November 21, 1904, and May 8, 1905.

12. *The Secret Doctrine*, 2 vols. (London: The Theosophical Publishing Co., 1888); almost all of Mme Blavatsky's major works underwent considerable revision and editing by her colleagues and disciples; the success of *The Secret Doctrine* rests largely on the magnificent editing job and revisions made by the religion scholar G. R. S. Mead and the competent Archibald and Bertram Keightley.

13. Mme Blavatsky's letters to Vera Zhelikhovskaia (those few that have been published in various Theosophical journals) indicate that this correspondence might be informative indeed. Soviet archives have not released any personal materials, although any remaining Blavatsky papers are probably scattered throughout various archives.

At least part of Mme Blavatsky's library also went to her sister. *Russkie vedomosti* announced on January 18, 1908, that Mme Blavatsky's Theosophical Library, donated to the Rumiantsev Museum in 1907 by Vera Vladimirovna Zhelikhovskaia, Mme Blavatsky's niece, was cataloged and ready for use. The library consisted of three hundred volumes. (The newspaper article identified Mme Blavatsky as "avantiuristka-teosofka.")

14. Theosophy admitted the reality of mediumistic phenomena. It did not agree, however, that these phenomena were caused by the spirits of the dead; mediumistic phenomena, according to Theosophy, are either psychically induced or, in the worst case, are the work of disintegrating astral bodies and elementals, the projection of unconscious thoughts and wishes through the magnetic field into astral matter. These last are potentially very dangerous. Since elementals have no will or intent, spiritualistic communications are frequently absurd and irrelevant; the elementals, conclude the Theosophists, are simply making a game of gullible Spiritualists.

15. "Teosofiia i spiritizm," *Rebus* 7(1886): 79.

16. "Pravda o E. P. Blavatskoi," see note 4; this series, together with Zhelikhovskaia's "Neob"iasnimoe i neob"iasnennoe" in *Rebus* 4(1885) were separately published as a small book entitled *Neob"iasnimoe i neob"iasnennoe* in 1885.

17. *Rebus* 16(1884): 156.

18. Vera Zhelikhovskaia, "E. P. Blavatskaia i teosofisty," *Odesskii vestnik* 123(June 5, 1884): 1–3; reprinted in *Rebus* 28(1884): 263–65, 29(1884): 274–75; "V oblasti okkul'tizma i magnetizma," *Odesskii vestnik* 166, 172, 181, 184(1884); recapped as "Phenomeny okkul'ticheskoi sily g-zhy Blavatskoi" in *Rebus* 50(1884): 465–67; "Pis'ma iz-za granitsy," *Novorossiiskii Telegraf*, no. 2789(June 6, 1884).

19. "E. P. Blavatskaia i teosofisty," *Rebus* 28(1884): 263; excerpted from a letter by Vera Zhelikhovskaia to the editor of *Odesskii vestnik* (written from Paris, May 25/June 6, 1884). The reference is to an interview with Mme Blavatsky in the London *Pall Mall Gazette* of April 26, 1884, in which Mme Blavatsky claimed that the first goal of her Theosophical Society was "the restoration of Buddhism to its original purity"; she also had unkind words for Christianity as an institution (*Gazette*, 4). She said nothing in that particular interview about building Buddhist temples, but she gave many other interviews at the time, and the patently outrageous claim about destroying Christianity and building Buddhist temples would not have been out of character.

20. E. Barabash, "Teosofiia i teosofy," 41(1884): 375; the article ran for three issues, 41–43(1884).

21. "Spiritizm v istorii," *Rebus* 20–38(1885).

22. "Noveishie dvizheniia v Buddizme," *Russkaia mysl'* 8(1887): 17, 2d pagination. Lesevich's article served as an introduction for Colonel Olcott's "Buddhist Catechism" and Edward Arnold's *India Revisited*, published in the same issue. Edward Arnold was popular in Russia (as well as in Europe), and his *Light of Asia* (*Svet Azii* [St. Petersburg: 1893]), translated into Russian by Margarita Sabashnikova's uncle, Ivan Sabashnikov, went through numerous editions.

23. Vladimir Solov'ev, *Russkoe obozrenie* 8(1890); also in his *Sobranie sochinenii*, ed. E. L. Radlov and S. M. Solov'ev, vol. 6, 2d ed. (St. Petersburg: Prosveshchenie, 1911–1913), 287–92.

24. Vl. Solov'ev, *Sob. soch.* vol. 6, 287.

25. Ibid., 289, 291.

26. Vladimir Solov'ev, "Blavatskaia, Elena Petrovna," in S. A. Vengerov's *Kritiko-biograficheskii slovar'* (St. Petersburg: Semenovskaia tipografiia, 1892), vol. 2, 315–19; printed together with Zinaida Vengerova's biographical sketch, 301–15. Also in Solov'ev's *Sob. soch.*, vol. 6, 394–98, under the title "Zametka o E. P. Blavatskoi"; a reprint of Solov'ev's "Zametka o E. P. Blavatskoi" (under the title "V. Solov'ev o teosofii") was begun in *Rebus* 4(1915): 1–2, but never completed.

27. Vengerov, 315.

28. Ibid., 318.

29. Ibid., 319.

30. Pisareva, "E. P. B." (Boston: Alba, 1966), 9; hectograph.

31. Alba, "Zadachi Teosofii," *Rebus* 6/7(1907): 6.

32. *Russkii vestnik* 2–5, 9–12(1892); St. Petersburg ed.: 1893; subsequent editions.

33. Translated by W. Leaf, a member of the Society for Psychical Research, and published in London in 1895.

34. Vs. Solov'ev, "Interesnyi fenomen," *Rebus* 26(1884): 243; letter to the editor from Paris, dated June 10/22, 1884.

35. Meade, 367; also Vs. Solov'ev, *Sovremennaia zhritsa Izidy*.

36. Vs. Solov'ev, *Zhritsa*, 217; all citations from St. Petersburg 1904 ed.

37. Ibid., 236.

38. Zhelikhovskaia's effort must have been worth it, because after the Revolution, the Theosophical Society pensioned two of Mme Blavatsky's nieces (Nadezhda Vladimirovna, the childless widow of General Brusilov, whom she had met while working with the Red Cross on the Galician front, and Elena Vladimirovna, a children's writer who never married) and supported them for the rest of their lives; they lived in Czechoslovakia. The third niece, Vera Vladimirovna, married the Irish Theosophist and Orientalist Charles Johnston.

39. Vs. Solov'ev, *Zhritsa*, 252.

40. Pisareva, "E. P. B.," 10.

41. Vs. Solov'ev, "Chto takoe 'doktrina teosoficheskogo obshchestva,'" *Voprosy filosofii i psikhologii* 18(May 1893): Book 3, 41–68, 2d pag.

42. Ibid., editorial footnote, 41.

43. N. F., "Dva novye inostrannye otzyva o g-zhe Blavatskoi," *Rebus* 38(1894): 361.

44. *Rebus* 18(1895): 181–83.

45. "Istoricheskii ocherk vozniknoveniia i rasprostraneniia noveishego spiritualizma," *Rebus* 14(1894): 145–46.

46. "Maks Miuller o noveishei teosofii i ee rasprostraniteliakh," from *Spiritualistische Blätter* 4(1894), in *Rebus* 21(1894): 213. The article borrows freely from Müller's entertaining and sincere essay, "Esoteric Buddhism," from *The Nineteenth Century* (London), 33:195 (May 1893), 767–88.

47. *Rebus* 38(1894): 362.

48. Radda-Bai, "Peshchera Ozerkov," *Rebus* 1–3(1886); modified Russian version of her "Cave of the Echoes."

49. Vs. Solov'ev, *Zhritsa*, 279. Mme Blavatsky's travel notes were never completed in *Russkii vestnik* although a continuation was promised. It is entirely possible that Vs. Solov'ev, who had influence with Mihkail Katkov, the journal's owner, encouraged him to have nothing more to do with the notorious Mme Blavatsky.

50. Stranden, *Teosofiia i ee kritiki* (St. Petersburg: Stasiulevich, 1913), 35.

51. E. Pisareva, "Missiia E. P. Blavatskoi," *Vestnik teosofii* 1(1913): 15.

Chapter Three
The Theosophical Society in Russia (1901–1917)

1. Anna Kamenskaya, "Theosophy in Russia," *Theosophic Messenger* 6(March 1909): 234.

2. Nina Gernet contributed several popularizing articles on Russian and ancient Slavic mysticism, Russian Freemasonry, Russian folklore and legends, and so forth, to the London-based *Theosophical Review*. Some were misty, moody pieces describing "Helena Blavatsky's Russia." Her articles were frequently signed "A Russian" and go back to at least 1898. Her longest work was "The Rosy Cross in Russia," in the *Theosophical Review* 38(1906): 489–501; 39(1907): 9–20, 138–44, 201–11, 304–6; the articles contain little substance.

3. Anna Kamenskaya, "Theosophy in Russia," *Theosophic Messenger* 6(March 1909): 234.

4. Ibid.

5. "Anni Bezant (Vospominaniia A. Kamenskoi)," *Vestnik: Satyat Nasti Paro Dharmah* (Geneva) 1937 (October), 5.

6. Maria von Strauch-Spettini (née Maria Magdalena Speckien; Spettini was her stage name) was one of the first serious Theosophists in Russia. She was born in Königsberg in 1847. An actress by profession, she appeared on the German and Russian stage, but retired after marrying Evgenii Fedorovich fon Shtraukh, a state councillor in St. Petersburg. An intimate friend and mentor to Marie von Sivers (subsequently Mme Steiner), she had close ties to Rudolf Steiner and the German Section of the Theosophical Society. Marie von Sivers had lived in St. Petersburg; her sister Olga continued to reside there. Maria von Strauch died unexpectedly of pneumonia on December 28, 1904, not long after founding the circle.

7. Hella Wiesberger, ed., *Aus dem Leben von Marie von Sivers; Biographische Beiträge und eine Bibliographie* (Dornach: Rudolf Steiner Nachlassverwaltung, 1956), 159–60.

8. Hypatia of Alexandria (370–415) was a mathematician, astronomer, and Neoplatonist philosopher. She was killed by fanatic Christians. Hypatia figures in Mme Blavatsky's *Isis Unveiled* in her attack on Christianity; see vol. 2, 53. Kamenskaia's mentor, Mrs. Besant, claimed that she was Hypatia in a previous incarnation.

9. Pisareva, *Vestnik teosofii* 7/8(1912): 15.

10. Anna Filosofova apparently did not thrill the spiritualist public, because P. A. Chistiakov, the editor of *Rebus*, subsequently reported that "at the recent Congress the Theosophical doctrine was rather weakly represented; the reasons for this are twofold: the first, our friends the Theosophists did not prepare suitable materials in time after their summer holidays; and the second, I, as the chairman of the organizational committee, did not find it possible to pass several items submitted to the Congress because of their rather specialized terminology and a certain dogmatism" (*Rebus*, 43/44[1906]: 8–9). Filosofova read "Etiudy po teosofii" on October 25, 1906.

11. *Rebus* 3(1908): 4. The cryptic comment about *Vestnik teosofii*'s "relation to the European Theosophical Movement" refers to splinter group loyalties. By no means did all Russian Theosophical circles represented at the January meeting wish to enter into the proposed Russian Theosophical Society, which would be loyal to Mrs. Besant. Many circles continued to function independently, especially in Moscow; these represented a group at least as large, if not larger, than the Russian Section.

12. "Khronika," *Russkii Frank-mason* 1(1908): 22.

13. As soon as feasible, the St. Petersburg circles began finding like-minded individuals in other Russian cities. The Theosophical Society required that seven branches exist before a national Section could be opened. This requirement also contributed to the late start in chartering the Russian Section. Meeting Russian regulations was only half the problem; Theosophical Society regulations had to be met as well.

14. The Reverend Charles Webster Leadbeater (1847–1934) was a British clergyman who embraced Theosophy in 1884; he was charged on several occa-

sions with immoral practices involving young boys and was forced to resign from the Society in 1906. Leadbeater had considerable influence over Mrs. Besant, and she allowed him to return to the Society in 1909 over the protest of many members. Leadbeater's reinstatement led to the resignation from the Society of G. R. S. Mead (then editor of the Society's major organ, *The Theosophical Review*) and more than seven hundred members of the British Convention alone. The situation became more complicated when Leadbeater was given responsibility for the tutoring of the young Jiddu Krishnamurti (1895–1986), whom he and Mrs. Besant proclaimed the "vehicle of the Christ" and the new Messiah. Mrs. Besant organized the Order of the Star in the East to sponsor Krishnamurti. This may have been acceptable to converts to Buddhism (such as Leadbeater and Mrs. Besant), but it was considered blasphemy by many Christians, both within and outside the Theosophical Society. Krishnamurti eventually rejected the role prepared for him and left the Theosophical Society in 1929; his departure was a tremendous blow to Mrs. Besant.

15. *Rebus* 51/52(1907): 1.

16. *Vestnik teosofii* 5/6(1914): 78–79. Another indicator of participation is the number of Russian Theosophists attending International Congresses. In 1906 about a dozen Russian delegates attended the Theosophical Congress in Paris; in 1913 the Russian delegation to the Congress in Stockholm numbered sixty-five. Russian Theosophy was growing fast enough for Mrs. Besant to agree to have the 1914 World Theosophical Congress in Russia. Russian Theosophists were busy making necessary arrangements when the war changed everyone's plans. See *Vestnik: Satyat Nasti Paro Dharmah* (Geneva) 2(March 1938): 4.

17. The official figure for Russian membership in 1912 was 225; in 1910, 170.

18. L. N. Tolstoi's daughter-in-law, Countess Sof'ia Nikolaevna Tolstaia (d. 1934 in Prague; wife of Tolstoi's second son, Il'ia), a friend of Anna Kamenskaia and member of the Kaluga branch; Varvara Pushkina, née Princess Golitsyna; Princess Ada Trubetskaia; Prince Sergei Mikhailovich Volkonskii (1860–1937), the Director of the Imperial Theatre; Princess Sofiia Vladimirovna Urusova, who was first secretary, later president, of the Moscow branch, et al.

19. Addresses: St. Petersburg branch, Ivanovskaia, 22; Moscow branch, Arbat, Starokoniushennyi pereulok 19; after October 19, 1914, Bol'shoi Uspenskii pereulok, Dom No. 8; public meetings of Moscow branch were held on the Znamenka, at E. Kirpichnikova's gymnasium; Kiev branch, Bol'shaia Podval'naia, 26; Kaluga branch, Voskresenskaia, dom N. V. Pisareva, also the Pisarev estate, Podborki; Rostov-na-Donu branch, Nakhichevan, 4-aia liniia, d. 12.

20. *Izvestiia RTO* 1(1914).

21. Working with a ratio of three to one, we could posit nine hundred Russian Theosophists of the Adyar persuasion. The number of serious independent Russian Theosophists would easily double that figure; add to that figure casually interested individuals who bought Theosophical brochures and occasionally attended lectures, and the number might double again or even triple. That *Vestnik teosofii* was selling seven hundred copies monthly in 1911, when official membership hovered around two hundred, is also suggestive.

Theosophy was not always as well tolerated in the provinces as in Moscow and St. Petersburg. In March 1914 the Theosophists encountered trouble with the authorities in Yalta about the opening of the new branch. The police arrived to break up an "unauthorized meeting" of dangerous Theosophists at Elizaveta Rodzevich's home and to arrest the conspirators; the "meeting" was a tea party, hosted by Rodzevich for Kamenskaia and two other ladies (*Vestnik teosofii* 5/ 6(1914): 53).

22. Optina Pustyn' was a monastery founded in the fourteenth century; a hermitage was added in 1821. Noted for its mystical practices and Hesychast traditions, Optina Pustyn' was a spiritual Mecca for many mystically inclined Russians, including Ivan Kireevskii, Nikolai Gogol', Fedor Dostoevskii, Lev Tolstoi, and Vladimir Solov'ev.

Many Theosophists, in spite of important doctrinal divergences, were active members of the Russian Orthodox church and had close ties with certain church mystics and elders. Nikolai Berdiaev pointed out in his autobiography that "not only the neo-Christians revered the elders, but also the Theosophists and Anthroposophists, who really had little in common with the church. They saw the elders as 'initiates'" (*Samopoznanie* [Paris: YMCA, 1983 (1949)], 214).

23. *Vestnik teosofii* 12(1913): 57.

24. Several Russian Theosophists (notably Elena Pisareva and Anna Mintslova) had close ties to the German Section and to Dr. Steiner in particular. They brought his lectures and materials back with them and shared them with their colleagues. Thus, for example, Elena Pisareva read several of Steiner's lectures at Anna Filosofova's casual salon in a Moscow hotel during the Congress of Spiritualists in October 1906 ("Knowledge of the Supersensible in our Time," "Blood is a Very Special Fluid (on *Faust*)," "The Relation of Precious Stones to the Human Senses," and "The Relation of Human Senses to the Surrounding World"). Two weeks earlier Pisareva had returned from Steiner's lectures in Berlin.

25. A. V. Tyrkova, "A. P. Filosofova i ee vremia," *Sbornik pamiati A. P. Filosofovoi*, vol. 1 (Petrograd: 1915), 443.

26. Other members of the Kaluga branch included Iraida Chulitskaia (d. 1913), one of the founding members of the RTO, later secretary of the Moscow branch; M. F. Vasil'eva, and Countess S. N. Tolstaia, an active philanthropist.

27. The titles of these lectures were taken from the January and February 1914 schedule of the RTO; these and eleven other lectures were read publicly in St. Petersburg, Moscow, Kiev, Kaluga, and the Crimea between January 17 and February 18, 1914. Additional lectures were read in closed meetings. See *Vestnik teosofii* 3(1914): 81–82.

28. Chistiakov, *Rebus* 16(1910):3; a year later, in *Rebus* 37(1911): 6, Chistiakov would add, "This unrestrained visionary [Leadbeater] has greatly discredited the Theosophical doctrine in the eyes of many with his hilarious visions."

29. The notion of an Esoteric Section was the brainchild of Mme Blavatsky, who formed it to prevent serious occultists, bored by the well-meaning but unsophisticated middle-class Theosophists who embraced the Movement, from leaving Theosophy to start their own circles; her Esoteric Section was called "Dzyan" and worked on practical occultism and *raja-yoga*.

Vl. Solov'ev, writing about the structure of the Theosophical Society in his review of Mme Blavatsky's *Key to Theosophy*, added: "Members of the Society employed in exoteric tasks, specifically philanthropy and the study of Eastern doctrines, are called lay members; those who devote their lives to the mastery of secret doctrines and forces are called initiates" (*Sob. soch.*, vol. 6, 288).

I was unable to discover who ran the Russian Esoteric Section and who were its members. There are only occasional veiled references to its existence, and it may even have been kept secret from the majority of the RTO membership because of possible problems with the authorities.

30. *Vestnik teosofii* 4(1912): 82–83.

31. It is impossible now to determine how many Russian Theosophists actually followed the example of Mme Blavatsky, Colonel Olcott, Mrs. Besant, A. P. Sinnett, C. W. Leadbeater, and other prominent Theosophists and actually converted to Hinduism. Talk of building a Buddhist temple in St. Petersburg, however, speaks of more than a casual interest.

A Buddhist temple was built in St. Petersburg, but for Buddhists, not for Theosophists. The "Buddiiskaia pagoda" was located just outside St. Petersburg, in Staraia Derevnia, on the Bol'shaia Nevka River.

32. When the charter of the RTO was legalized, *Rebus* congratulated the new Theosophical Society and wished them luck, then added that *Rebus* hoped that "in the new Society brotherly tolerance and the absence of dogmatic prejudice toward related movements, schools, and trends would really blossom." The article went on: "We express this second wish because the majority of the Russian representatives of the Theosophical world view do not distinguish themselves by adequate tolerance and broad views and tend very much toward dogmatic narrowmindedness and self-adoration" (*Rebus* 32[1908]: 3).

33. N. T[rofimenko-Dmitrieva], "Teosofiia i zhenskoe dvizhenie," *Vestnik teosofii* 12(1915): 24–25.

34. See the following representative pamphlets: Alba (Kamenskaia), *Voprosy vospitaniia v sviazy s zadachami dukhovnoi kul'tury* (St. Petersburg: 1912); *Vekhi: Pervoe semiletie rebenka. Reziume rabot Pedagogicheskogo Kruzhka RTO 1910–1915* (Petrograd: 1918).

35. Otets I. Dmitrevskii, *Teosofiia—Religioznaia filosofiia nashego vremeni* (Khar'kov: 1911), 2.

36. *Vestnik teosofii* 1(1915): 11.

37. *Vestnik teosofii* St. Petersburg: January 7, 1908–1918; publ. and ed. Anna Alekseevna Kamenskaia, later Kamenskaia and Ts. Gel'mbol'dt, on the seventh of every month), no. 5/6 (May 7); no. 7/8 (August 7).

By 1914 the RTO had grown large enough to justify a second publication: *Izvestiia Rossiiskogo Teosoficheskogo Obshchestva* (St. Petersburg, 1914–1917; publ. and ed. Ts. L. Gel'mbol'dt). The *Izvestiia RTO* were published two to four times a year, as material permitted. They contained the reports of the various circles, chronicles of events, letters.

38. London; founded by H. P. B. in 1887 under the title *Lucifer*, vols. 1–43 (September 1887–February 1909). In February 1909 the editor, G. R. S. Mead, resigned from the Theosophical Society and shut down the journal. See note 14.

39. See "Bibliography of Theosophical and Related Works Published in Russia Between 1881 and 1918"; the one major Theosophical work, in addition to Mme Blavatsky's *Secret Doctrine*, which was not published in Russia in its en-

tirety, was Mrs. Besant's *Esoteric Christianity*, because of the same censorship objections (strongly anti-Christian bias).

40. Bookstores selling Theosophical books include: in Kiev, "Knizhnyi magazin N. Ia. Ogloblina," Kreshchatik 33; in St. Petersburg, "Dobroe Delo," Basseinaia 4, and "Knizhnyi magazin Karbasnikova" in Gostinnyi Dvor; in Moscow, "Knizhnyi magazin Karbasnikova" on the Mokhovaia, across from the University, "Biblioteka Skibnevskoi" on Malaia Bronnaia, "Posrednik" on the Petrovskie Linii; Odessa: "Trud" and "Odesskie novosti," both on Deribasovskaia. Russian and East European Theosophical books were also available by mail and from the editorial offices of *Vestnik teosofii*.

41. Letter from von Strauch-Spettini to von Sivers, St. Petersburg, April 3, 1903; Wiesberger, *Aus dem Leben*, 162.

42. From *A Further Record of Extracts from Meetings Held by P. D. Ouspensky Between 1928 and 1945* (Capetown: Stourton Press, 1952); cited in Merrily Taylor, *Remembering Pyotr Demianovich Ouspensky* (New Haven: Yale University Press, 1978), 11.

43. Berdiaev, "Tipy religioznoi mysli," *Russkaia mysl'* 11(1916): 1 (2d pagination).

44. P. D. Upsenskii, *Chetvertoe izmerenie* (St. Petersburg: Trud, 1910), 95.

45. *Izvestiia RTO*, 1(1915): 35.

46. J. H. Reyner, *Ouspensky: The Unsung Genius* (London: George Allen and Unwin, 1981), 28; the "inner circle" refers to the Esoteric Section of the Theosophical Society.

47. See "Bibliography of Theosophical and Related Works," for Uspenskii's Russian publications.

Even during the bleakest days of the "Period of Stagnation," Uspenskii's books continued to sell in Soviet second-hand bookstores for 150 to 400 rubles a volume. Sold discreetly and only to known clients, prerevolutionary Russian occult texts of all kinds have always been available in the Soviet Union.

48. *Vestnik teosofii* 1(1915): 10–11.

49. *Izvestiia RTO* 2(1916): 5–6.

50. A. Bezant, "Bratstvo i voina," *Vestnik teosofii* 10(1915): 8–20.

51. *Vestnik teosofii* 7/8(1915): 1–2.

52. Ibid., 14.

53. Ibid. 5/6(1915): 14–15.

54. Ibid. 4(1915): 12.

55. Ibid. 5/6(1915): 11.

56. *Landmarks; A Collection of Essays on the Russian Intelligentsia 1909*, trans. Marian Schwartz (New York: Karz Howard, 1977), 9, 44.

57. *Vestnik teosofii* 10(1917): 12.

Chapter Four
Other Russian Theosophical Movements

1. The Society was planned and organized during the summer of 1907. It was advertised by flyers that members handed out and was mailed to publishing houses. By fall the new Society had won some local approval by organizing a

philanthropic circle, helping needy Smolensk families, and assisting with flood relief.

2. *Teosofskaia zhizn'* 1(1907): 13.

3. L. E. O., "Teosoficheskoe obshchestvo v Smolenske," *Rebus* 39(1907): 4.

4. *Rebus* 39(1907): 4–5.

5. *Teosofskaia zhizn'*, 2(1907): 4.

6. Ibid. 9(1908): 47–48.

7. N. Mariupol'skii [I. G. Aivazov], "Pravoslavnyi arkhimandrit—uchreditel' 'Teosofskogo Obshchestva,'" *Kolokol* 681(May 21, 1908): 4.

8. *Teosofskaia zhizn'* 5(1908): 2.

9. *Rebus* 5(1907): 4.

10. *Teosofskaia zhizn'* 1(1908): 1–5.

11. [Anonymous], "Protiv rozhna," *Teosofskaia zhizn'* 10/11(1909): 412.

12. See, for example, her *Eliksir zhizni, Magi, Gnev Bozhii, Smert' planetov,* and *V inom mire,* among many others, that were published both in Russia and in France under her pseudonym, "Rochester."

13. "Ot redaktsii," *Teosoficheskoe obozrenie* 1(1907): 3.

14. Ibid., 4.

15. *Rebus* 5(1908): 4.

16. Evgenii Viktorovich Radvan-Rypinskii, a "professor" of Esperanto in St. Petersburg and an active proselytizer. He was affiliated with the "Espero" Society and their journal, *Ruslanda Esperantisto.* Many Theosophists, European and Russian, were interested in Esperanto, given the international nature of Theosophy, and studied it with enthusiasm. Radvan-Rypinskii published a compact grammar and dictionary of Esperanto in installments in *Teosoficheskoe obozrenie.*

17. *Teosoficheskoe obozrenie* 1(1907): 44.

18. Ibid. 5(1908): 388.

19. After the death of William Q. Judge, Katherine Tingley (1847–1929) took over the enormous American Theosophical Society, which had seceded from the Adyar-based parent Society during the power struggle that followed Mme Blavatsky's death in 1891. Influenced by the Social Gospel and late-nineteenth-century American utopianism, Tingley's vision was to combine humanitarianism, social reform, and occult philosophy. The culmination of her experiment in applied Theosophy was a Theosophical utopian community at Point Loma, California.

20. *Rebus* 50(1908): 2.

21. A. R. Mintslova's father, Rudol'f Rudol'fovich Mintslov (1845–1904), was also a well-known bibliophile and journalist; her brother, Sergei Rudol'fovich Mintslov (1870-1933) was an archaeologist (who specialized in Russian country houses), a bibliophile, and a writer; he was fascinated by the supernatural. The Mintslov family had entrée to the musical and literary salons of both St. Petersburg and Moscow.

22. Andrei Belyi, *Mezhdu dvukh revoliutsii* (Leningrad: Izdatel'stvo pisatelei, 1934), 355. Margarita Sabashnikova, who knew Mintslova well and even lived with her for a time in St. Petersburg, left a similar description: "Her figure was without form, her forehead was overlarge, as often depicted on angels in old German paintings, her protuberant blue eyes were very shortsighted—neverthe-

less, she had a glance that saw into horrendous distances. Her red-blond hair was parted in the middle and its frizzy waves were in disarray, her bun threatened to come apart, and she constantly rained hairpins everywhere. Her nose was coarsely formed, and her entire face was sweaty and bloated," and so forth. Like Berdiaev, Sabashnikova was much taken with Mintslova's fascinating hands and tapering fingers, on one of which she wore an amethyst ring, which Andrei Belyi subsequently claimed she gave him (*Die grüne Schlange* [Frankfurt am Main: Fischer Verlag, 1982], 144).

23. Nikolai Berdiaev, *Samopoznanie* (1949; 2d rev. ed. Paris: YMCA, 1983), 221.

24. See Belyi's "Kasaniia k teosofii," Manuscript Division, Lenin Library, Moscow, MS# 25;31;2; 16 fols.; also his "Nachalo veka" (1928–1930) Manuscript Division, Saltykov-Shchedrin Library, St. Petersburg, MS# 60;13, fols. 29, 32ff. Steiner's *Kak dostignut' poznaniia vysshikh mirov* was serialized in *Vestnik teosofii* over the course of 1908 and 1909.

25. Although Belyi did not become a devoted Steinerian until 1912, everything about his Theosophical experience conspired to bring him inevitably to Steiner: the influential Pisareva was a member of the German Section and had known Steiner and popularized his works in Russia since 1903; Mintslova, who mesmerized Belyi with her promises of occult superiority, fed him Steinerianism, claiming it was her own brand of occultism; Mikhail Ertel' was Steiner's disciple; Grigorov, initially a student of Ertel's, eventually went abroad to work with Steiner directly.

26. Andrei Belyi, "Nachalo veka," fol. 40–41; emphasis in original. The two women played to Belyi's sense of self-importance and spiritual superiority, taking advantage of his neurotic, unstable, and overworked state. The writer had a nervous breakdown early in 1909, hastened and exacerbated, no doubt, by Mintslova's occult hysteria.

27. Ibid., fol. 72.

28. For further details of Mintslova's relation to Belyi and Ivanov, see Maria Carlson, "Ivanov-Belyj-Minclova: The Mystical Triangle," in *Cultura e Memoria; Atti del terzo Simposio Internazionale dedicato a Vjaceslav Ivanov*, ed. Fausto Malcovati, vol. 1 (Firenze: 1988), 63–79.

29. In her book *Liudi i lozhi* (New York: Russica, 1986), Nina Berberova writes that "the Lucifer Lodge, which was close to the Martinists [a Masonic-Rosicrucian organization], was formed about 1910 and lasted only a short time. According to not entirely reliable documentation, several Symbolist poets belonged to it, including Viach. Ivanov, Briusov, Belyi, and Belyi's friend A. Petrovskii" (24). Clearly this refers to the Rosicrucian "Order" Mintslova was trying to create with Belyi and Ivanov. Briusov, who was acquainted with Mintslova, would have been an occasional visitor. Mintslova was dreadfully disappointed when Ivanov and Belyi refused to travel to Italy to be "initiated" into the Order at a Martinist-Rosicrucian Congress planned for early 1910.

Steiner himself was briefly connected with various Masonic groups, including the Martinists (as was Mintslova, for the Martinists initiated both men and women); he shared their Rosicrucian dimension. Steiner's German Theosophical journal was called *Lucifer*.

30. The last member of Musaget, Belyi's old friend Lev Kobylinskii-Ellis, was excluded at Mintslova's request; she felt he was a medium who was unable to control the passage of dark forces through himself and could therefore jeopardize the "mission." Ellis was offended, of course.

31. Andrei Belyi, "Nachalo veka," fol. 117.

32. Andrei Belyi, *Vospominaniia o Bloke, Epopeia*, vols. 1–4 (Moscow-Berlin: 1922-1923; reprinted as *Vospominaniia ob A. A. Bloke* [Munich: 1969]), 195 [675].

33. "Belyi, promise me, really promise me that you will not go to Steiner," Belyi later claimed she said to him; "remember, they won't understand you there; you are completely different" ("Nachalo veka," fol. 55).

34. Belyi, "Nachalo veka," fol. 101.

35. Berdiaev, *Samopoznanie*, 222.

36. Rudolf Steiner attended the Oberrealschule in Wiener Neustadt, then studied at the Technische Hochschule in Vienna; he defended his doctoral dissertation, "Wahrheit und Wissenschaft," at the University of Rostock in 1891.

37. When Andrei Belyi requested an interview with Rudolf Steiner in May 1912, he wrote first to Marie von Sivers, using Anna Mintslova's and Kleopatra Khristoforova's names as references to commend himself to von Sivers and Steiner (letter from Andrei Belyi to Marie Steiner-von Sivers, in *Andrej Belyj und Rudolf Steiner; Briefe und Dokumente*, ed. Walter Kugler and Victor Fedjuschin. Beiträge zur Rudolf Steiner Gesamtausgabe 89/90[Dornach: Steiner Nachlassverwaltung, 1985], 10).

38. Marie von Steiner, in *Aus dem Leben von Marie Steiner-von Sivers*, comp. Hella Wiesberger (Dornach: Rudolf Steiner Nachlassverwaltung, 1956), 43; also cited in Rudolf Steiner and Marie Steiner-von Sivers, *Correspondence and Documents 1901–1925* (London: Rudolf Steiner Press, 1988), 278–79.

39. Schuré and Steiner met for the first time at this lecture cycle. Schuré's resumé of the lectures was originally published in French and English in 1928; a new edition appeared in 1987: Rudolf Steiner, *An Esoteric Cosmology* (Blauvelt, N.Y.: Spiritual Science Library, 1987).

40. Woloschin [Sabashnikova], Margarita, *Die grüne Schlange* (Frankfurt am Main: Fischer Verlag, 1982), 163.

41. In her brief biography of Filosofova, for example, Pisareva mentions that she read Steiner's Berlin lectures in Filosofova's hotel room in Moscow to interested members during the Spiritualist Congress ("Pamiati Anny Pavlovny Filosofovoi," *Vestnik teosofii* 5–8[1912]).

42. Rudolf Steiner, *Theosofiia*, trans. A[nna] M[intslova] (St. Petersburg: 1910); a translation of the 2d ed. of *Theosophie; Einführung in übersinnliche Welterkenntnis und Menschenbestimmung* (1908; 1st ed. 1904).

43. Steiner again planned to visit Russia in 1912 and 1913, but was denied permission; he lectured in Helsingfors instead. Steiner never visited Russia.

44. Rudolf Steiner, *An Autobiography*, trans. by Rita Stebbing (Blauvelt, N.Y.: Rudolf Steiner Publications, 1977), 363.

45. Ibid., 362–363.

46. Alba [A. A. Kamenskaia], "Khronika Teosoficheskogo dvizheniia," *Vestnik teosofii* 2(1913): 63.

47. Other prominent Russian Anthroposophists, Margarita Sabashnikova, Ekaterina Bal'mont, Klavdiia Nikolaevna Vasil'eva (1886–1970; she would become Belyi's second wife), her first husband, Dr. Pavel Nikolaevich Vasil'ev (d. 1976), Boris Lehmann (who would head the St. Petersburg branch), Ol'ga Nikolaevna Annenkova (d. 1949), and several other Russian seekers, although acquainted with and influenced by Mintslova, found their own, separate way from Theosophy to Steiner.

48. When Margarita Sabashnikova met Steiner in Berlin in 1908, he had already heard about Viacheslav Ivanov from Mintslova; he asked Sabashnikova for more information (Woloschin, *Die grüne Schlange*, 195): "He was particularly interested in what I thought Ivanov's cultural mission was. I said, in the fact that he was able to unite the natural intellectuality of antiquity with Christianity; I also spoke about his works and his ability to awaken the creative instinct in those individuals with whom he comes in contact." Sabashnikova had just returned from visiting Ivanov. "'When I saw you last, you were more creative and richer than now,'" Steiner said laconically to Sabashnikova. He evidently concluded, for whatever reasons, that Ivanov did not have the right approach or attitude toward the secret science.

In 1912, when Viacheslav Ivanov visited Belyi in Basel (the latter had gone with a group of Russians to hear Steiner's lecture series on "The Gospel of St. Mark" between September 15 and 24), Steiner rejected Ivanov's request to attend the lecture courses for members only. Belyi reported that Steiner said, "I do not think that my courses would be of any use to Mr. Ivanov at this time" (Belyi, "Nachalo veka," fol. 170). In her memoirs Belyi's first wife, Asya Turgeneva, recalled that Ivanov "wanted to join the Society and asked us to arrange a meeting for him with Steiner, but Steiner directed us to advise Ivanov against this" (A. Turgeneva, "Andrei Belyi i Rudol'f Steiner," *Mosty* 13/14[1967–1968], 245). Shortly thereafter Steiner forbade Belyi and Sabashnikova to share materials from the private lectures with Ivanov.

49. Cited in Kudriavtsev, *Chto takoe teosofiia i teosoficheskoe obshchestvo*, 2d rev. and exp. ed. (St. Petersburg: Gorodskaia tipografiia, 1914), 27.

50. Woloschin, *Die grüne Schlange*, 271.

51. Rudolf Steiner, *The Destinies of Individuals and of Nations*, trans. Anna R. Meuss (London: Rudolf Steiner Press, 1986), 75; originally this was a course of fourteen lectures given in Berlin between September 1, 1914 and July 6, 1915. While Steiner gave 1879 as the year in which the Michaelic Spirit became the guiding force, the year 1912 (when the decision was first taken to create the Anthroposophical Society) is also important, because 1912 was 1,879 years *after* the birth of the "I AM" (i.e., 1,879 years after the crucifixion and resurrection of Christ). The number 1,879 reduces, according to the primary numerological principle, to seven, *the* occult number.

52. M. Zhemchuzhnikova, "Vospominaniia o Moskovskom Antroposoficheskom Obshchestve 1917–1923," 1975 ms. in private hands, fol. 44.

53. Margarita Sabashnikova was struck by this coincidence, and observed that it was "a remarkable stroke of fate, that at the very hour when we assembled in Moscow to celebrate the founding of our Anthroposophical Society, the laying of the cornerstone of the building on the hill in Dornach took place." Tying

the fate of the Russian Anthroposophical Society to the fate of the first Goetheanum, Margarita Sabashnikova pointed out that "when the [Goetheanum] building fell victim to fire [it was completely destroyed on the night of December 31, 1922–January 1, 1923], it was at about the same time, in 1922 or 1923, that the Russian Anthroposophical Society was banned by the Bolsheviks" (Woloschin, *Die grüne Schlange*, 273).

54. Steiner wrote four mystery dramas: *Pforte der Einweihung—ein Rosenkreuzermysterium* (1910), *Die Prüfung der Seele* (1911), *Der Hüter der Schwelle* (1912), and *Der Seelen Erwachen* (1913). He had produced Edouard Schuré's mystery dramas, *Das heilige Drama von Eleusis* and *Die Kinder des Luzifer* (translated into German by Marie von Sivers) in 1907 and 1909, respectively. Both Schuré and Steiner were as strongly influenced by the aesthetic vision of Richard Wagner as by the dramatic rituals of ancient mystery cults. In 1906 Steiner explained the importance of the mystery drama to spiritual science in a lecture given in Berlin: "The Mystery is the true birthplace of Art. The mysteries were real and alive in astral space. In them is the synthesis of truth, beauty, and religious feeling" (Lecture of October 21, 1906, Berlin; cited in *Rudolf Steiner: Im Mittelpunkt der Mensch; eine Einführung in die ausgewählten Werke Rudolf Steiners*, ed. Hella Wiesberger and Walter Kugler [Frankfurt am Main: Fischer Verlag, 1985]). Steiner's emphasis on the importance of the mystery drama found particular resonance in Russia in the literary work of Viacheslav Ivanov and Andrei Belyi.

55. April 3–19, 1912: Lecture series on "Spiritual Beings in the Heavenly Bodies and in the Kingdoms of Nature"; in this sequence Steiner emphasized the "symphonic" structure of the world, showing how man himself, the beings who have already passed through the earth incarnation and are more spiritually developed than man, and some nature and elemental beings which are below man in spiritual development, all interrelate. The 1913 sequence took place between May 28 and June 5; it addressed "The Occult Foundations of the *Bhagavad Gita*."

56. Matvei Mikhailovich Troitskii (1835–1899): professor of philosophy, Moscow University, first chairman of Moscow Psychological Society, author of *Nauka o dukhe*, 2 vols. (Moscow: 1882); Eduard von Hartmann (1842–1906): psychologist who postulated the unconscious and then proposed that it was the source of all occult phenomena, author of *Philosophie des Unbewussten*, 3 vols. (1869; Russian ed. 1873); Wilhelm Windelband (1848–1915): pre-eminent German historian of philosophy, idealist philosopher whose major works appeared in Russia where he was well known; Wilhelm Wundt (1832–1920): German philosopher and psychologist whose work on mythopoesis and the psychology of myth, *Mythos und Religion* (1905), was of interest to the Symbolists; Harald Höffding (1843–1931): Danish philosopher, psychologist, and specialist in the philosophy of religion who proposed a theory of "critical monism" (form of idealistic monism). Carl Gustav Jung (1975–1961), who was interested not only in depth psychology but also in mythology and the history of occult thought, came out of this same German psychological tradition. Rudolf Steiner was acquainted with the work of both Jung and Sigmund Freud; Jung was aware of Steiner's philosophy as well.

Belyi, in particular, deplored Theosophy's lack of methodology: "The Theosophy we have today disregards methodological criticism: consequently, many valuable propositions put forward by contemporary Theosophy have no cognitive value behind them; a striving toward the synthesis of science, philosophy, and religion without methodological criticism dooms contemporary Theosophy to sterility" (Andrei Belyi, commentaries to the article "Emblematika smysla," in his *Simvolizm* [Moscow: Skorpion, 1910], 505).

57. Nikolai Belotsvetov, *Religiia tvorcheskoi voli* (Petrograd: F. F. Tum, 1915), 10. This desire to find or to be the synthesis of two antithetical theses also appears in Theosophy; it is a leitmotiv of Silver Age culture in general. It appears even in the futuristic dreams of the Russian socialists.

58. D. Filosofov, "Zashchitniki kul'tury," *Rech'*, July 14, 1914.

59. Victor Fedjuschin, *Russlands Sehnsucht nach Spiritualität* (Schaffhausen: Novalis Verlag, 1988), 112.

Chapter Five
Theosophical Doctrine: An Outline

1. Alfred Percy Sinnett, *Esoteric Buddhism* (London: Trübner, 1883), vi.

2. The words *gnosis* and *Gnosticism* are used frequently in this discussion and merit some definition. *Gnosis* (literally, *knowledge*) came to refer to the esoteric knowledge of a higher spiritual truth (i.e., self-knowledge, insight, or intuition, rather than faith or revelation) claimed by numerous sects, both pagan and Christian, in the Hellenized East during the first centuries of the new era. The roots of the gnosis lie unmistakably in the pre-Christian mystery religions. The forms of its expression are considerably diverse.

A highly syncretic Gnostic worldview *(Gnosticism)* grew out of the pagan mystery religions; in many cases it merged with early Christian doctrine. Gnosticism posits spiritual monism and material dualism, and strives for the transcendence of matter (spirit having a positive valence, and matter a negative one). An essentially cosmocentric (rather than theocentric or anthropocentric), emanationist doctrine, Gnosticism has an extensive and complex cosmology. The universe emanates from an unknowable God; in the process of emanation a portion of the Divine Spirit (light, Good) falls into matter (darkness, Evil) and must be redeemed. The earth and mankind were created by a Demiourgos to facilitate this redemption. The Christ is an emissary of the original Divine Being; he descends from Spirit into Matter in order to bring the gnosis to an elite group of spiritual seekers and thereby provide humanity with the knowledge it needs to achieve the redemption of spirit.

Although criticized by the Christian church as heretical, Gnostic thought has never lost its psychological appeal. Gnosticism was rediscovered and popularized in the second half of the nineteenth century as archaeological discoveries and new research in the history of religions made texts available to general readers for the first time. Both Theosophy and Anthroposophy are modern variants of the gnosis.

For an excellent summary overview, see: Hans Jonas, *The Gnostic Religion; The Message of the Alien God and the Beginnings of Christianity*, 2d rev. ed.

(Boston: Beacon, 1963). For materials that influenced Theosophical thought, see: Charles William King, *Gnostics and Their Remains, Ancient and Medieval* (1887; Minneapolis: Wizards Bookshelf, 1973); G. R. S. Mead, *Fragments of a Faith Forgotten* (1900; New Hyde Park, N.Y.: University Books, 1960), and his *Pistis Sophia: A Gnostic Gospel* (1921; Blauvelt, N.Y.: Spiritual Science Library, 1984). The scholar G. R. S. Mead was for several years Mme Blavatsky's personal secretary. Before the Nag Hammadi cache of Gnostic manuscripts was discovered in 1945 (a discovery that revolutionized many aspects of the field), Mead was considered a leading authority on Gnostic texts.

3. "The Stanzas of Dzyan," from Mme Blavatsky's devotional classic, *The Voice of the Silence* (1889 Pasadena: Theosophical University Press, 1976). She claimed to have taken the "Stanzas" from *The Book of Golden Precepts*, compiled by Aryasanga for Tibetan monks. No extant texts have ever been found to correspond to Mme Blavatsky's "Stanzas." Professor Max Müller suggested that the "Stanzas" and the text of *The Voice of the Silence* were Mme Blavatsky's own brilliant forgeries; that is still the prevailing assumption. Regardless of their provenance, the "Stanzas" are marvelously poetic. As monumental, mythopoetic texts they certainly made an impression on various Russian Symbolist poets, notably Konstantin Bal'mont and Andrei Belyi. See the "Introductory" to *The Secret Doctrine*.

4. One of the major reasons that Theosophy and Anthroposophy are difficult to define and outline concisely is that both doctrines continually redefine basic concepts (such as Logos, Christ, soul, spirit, plane, and so forth) according to the immediate demands of the point under discussion. The understanding of the various terms also change with time, topic, exegete, and the point of the argument: Mrs. Besant and Rudolf Steiner, for example, frequently (though not always) mean very different things when they use the word *Logos*; their definitions are, in turn, different from either the traditional Christian or the Gnostic understanding of that important term. At the same time, enough points of coincidence lull the reader into a false sense of identity of concepts. The result is that it becomes impossible to get a real grip on what should be basic building-block ideas.

Furthermore, occultists tend to develop their arguments not by deduction or even induction, but by *analogy*. The reader, at the time of reading, momentarily senses the relationship of terms and intuitively or sympathetically perceives the parallel; afterward, understanding dissipates.

Finally, not only do the Theosophists constantly redefine their own terms, but they "translate" the statements of non-Theosophists into their own terminology, invariably muddling the translation. Their definitions of basic concepts are unfortunately so loose and subjective that just about any alien concept can be subsumed by them. Thus, for example, Anna Kamenskaia, discussing Fedor Dostoevskii (who was not much taken with oriental philosophy) blithely attributes to him the idea that mankind will achieve spiritual heights not through sorrow and suffering, but through the radiant flight of an exultant soul liberated from the chains of karma (!), although Dostoevskii would never have chosen to express himself in this way.

5. Sinnett, *Esoteric Buddhism*, viii.

6. Compare the One Unity with Vladimir Solov'ev's "Vse-Edinstvo," which stands at the beginning of his universe as the One Unity stands at the beginning of the universe in Valentinian Gnosticism.

7. Compare to the emanation of the Aeons into the Pleroma as described in the Syrian-Egyptian Gnosis of Valentinus.

8. If the positivists assumed that matter produced human thought (in the sense that the physical brain produced chemical and electric reactions that were called "thought"), the Theosophists, to the contrary, assumed that thought generated matter. The form of physical matter was, in their view, the creation of an acting consciousness. Mme Blavatsky expounded: "As God creates, so man can create. Given a certain intensity of will, and the shapes created by the mind become subjective. . . . Given a more intense and intelligent concentration of this will, and the form becomes concrete, visible, objective; the man has learned the secret of secrets; he is a MAGICIAN" (*Isis Unveiled*, vol. 1 [New York: J. W. Bouton 1877], 62).

Theosophy subscribed to the belief in the magical, creative power of thought and word, or *theurgy* [from the Greek, *theourgia*, divine rite; literally, "god-working," or even "working on (or like) the gods"]. Edouard Schuré called theurgy "the supreme art of the magus" (*The Great Initiates*, vol. 1 [1889; London: William Rider & Son, 1913], xxii). Mrs. Besant, in *Esoteric Christianity*, explained it as the ascent of the "intellectual and divine part" of man to the "gods" in order to learn "the truths of the intelligible world" (*Esoteric Christianity* [1901; Adyar: Theosophical Publishing House, 1966], 16). Theosophical definitions of theurgy were based primarily on popular concepts deriving from the French occult revival. The French occultist Paul Christian defined theurgy as the creation of "works similar to those of God by the progressive discovery of the secrets of universal life" (*The History and Practice of Magic* [1870; Secaucus, N.J.: Citadel, 1972], 246, 121). The most powerful theurgic act was the act of creation.

Theosophy accommodated theurgy because the syncretic Theosophical doctrine embraced not only theoretical occultism, but applied occultism (or magic) as well. Originally used as a synonym for sorcery, theurgy came to be associated by the Theosophists with the magic potency of the spoken word, whether spoken by the Creator or by an occultist-mage; both *create* by the magic power of the word/sound. Theurgy is, first and foremost, a direct means of contact with the superhuman or divine.

Clearly theurgy as a concept would appeal tremendously to the Symbolist poets, especially to Andrei Belyi and Viacheslav Ivanov, both of whom used the term frequently in this context (of the spermatic word, capable of creating alternative aesthetic universes). They used Vladimir Solov'ev (as well as Theosophy) to buttress their claim that the true and highest purpose of the poet is "theurgic service" (Viacheslav Ivanov, *Borozdy i mezhi* [Moscow: 1916], 115; the article that develops this thought, "Religioznoe delo Vladimira Solov'eva," was first delivered as a lecture in February 1911 and published shortly afterward in the journal *Put'*).

9. To summarize the precise sevenfold sequence in the "Outbreathing" of the Universe: (1) the unmanifested Logos *is*; (2) Universal Ideation (latent) be-

gins; (3) Universal Active Intelligence is formed; (4) Cosmic (Chaotic) Energy is generated; (5) Astral Ideation (the paradigm of terrestrial things) occurs; (6) Life Essence, or Energy, arises; and (7) the Earth (Matter) is formed.

In "The Stanzas of Dzyan," which forms the basis of her *Secret Doctrine*, Mme Blavatsky expands the seven principles into ten: (1) Parabrahma (the absolute Absolute); (2) the First Logos (Unmanifested Primal Cause); (3) the Second Logos (Spirit-Matter, potential differentiation); (4) the Third Logos (World Consciousness); (5) *Buddhi* (Wisdom); (6) *Manas* (Mind); (7) Causal Plane; (8) Mental Plane; (9) Astral Plane; and (10) Physical Plane. While breaking several of the steps into their component parts, Mme Blavatsky preserves the overall intention of the original sequence, movement from unconscious non-manifestation to conscious manifestation.

10. Mme Blavatsky, *The Secret Doctrine*, vol. 2 (London: The Theosophical Publishing Co., 1888), 81.

11. Mrs. Annie Besant, *The Ancient Wisdom* (1897; Adyar: The Theosophical Publishing House, 1977), 180.

12. Sinnett, *Esoteric Buddhism*, 33. Mme Blavatsky elaborates: "The world moves in cycles. The coming races will be but the reproductions of races long bygone; as we, perhaps, are the images of those who lived a hundred centuries ago" (*Isis Unveiled*, vol. 1, 51). On this point (as well as on others) Mme Blavatsky anticipates Friedrich Nietzsche's notion of Eternal Recurrence (*Also Sprach Zarathustra* was not published until 1883–1892). The Theosophists viewed Nietzsche as one of their own "prophets."

13. Mme Blavatsky, *The Secret Doctrine*, vol. 2, 69–70. Mme Blavatsky's use of "cosmic mathematics" in this passage is a good example of the way in which Theosophy unites science and metaphysics. The Buddhist calculation of time creates the illusion of "scientific fact"; actually it is scientific methodology applied to an unprovable premise without scientific basis.

14. Mme Blavatsky, *The Secret Doctrine*, vol. 1, 233.

15. Mme Blavatsky, *Isis Unveiled*, vol. 2, 112.

16. Mme Blavatsky, *The Secret Doctrine*, vol. 1, 192.

17. In Russian terminology the descent into matter is *niskhozhdenie* and ascent into spirit is *voskhozhdenie*; the very same terminology was used by Viacheslav Ivanov to describe the creative movement between the noumenal and phenomenal worlds.

18. Mme Blavatsky, *The Secret Doctrine*, vol. 1, 268.

19. Viacheslav Ivanov's concept of the mystery drama corresponds to this view. Compare also Joseph Campbell's *Hero with a Thousand Faces* (Princeton, N.J.: Princeton University Press, 1968).

20. Rudolf Steiner, *An Esoteric Cosmology* (Blauvelt, N.Y.: Spiritual Science Library, 1987), 123; lectures delivered in Paris May 25, to June 14, 1906.

21. Mme Blavatsky, *The Secret Doctrine*, vol. 1, 232; Mme Blavatsky poetically describes the Pilgrim-Soul's journey: "Starting upon the long journey immaculate; descending more and more into sinful matter, and having connected himself with every atom in manifested *Space*—the *Pilgrim*, having struggled through and suffered in every form of life and being, is only at the bottom of the valley of matter, and half through his cycle, when he has identified himself with

collective Humanity. This, *he has made in his own image*. In order to progress upwards and homewards, the 'God' has now to ascend the weary uphill path of the Golgotha of Life. It is the martyrdom of self-conscious existence. Like Visvakarman [a Vedic deity] he has to sacrifice *himself to himself* in order to redeem all creatures, to resurrect from the many into the *One Life*. Then he ascends to heaven indeed; where, plunged into the incomprehensible absolute Being and Bliss of Paranirvana, he reigns unconditionally, and whence he will re-descend again at the next 'coming'" (*The Secret Doctrine*, vol. 1, 268).

22. Sinnett, *Esoteric Buddhism*, 61–63.

23. Mrs. Besant, *The Ancient Wisdom*, 174.

24. Mme Blavatsky's Mahatmas are an exception: through massive spiritual effort, some human monads have reached the spiritual level that others will achieve only in the next round. These are the great adepts and teachers who help present humanity move forward.

25. Mrs. Besant, *The Ancient Wisdom*, 184.

26. Steiner, *An Esoteric Cosmology*, 58.

27. Ibid., 60, 63.

28. Ibid., 64.

29. C. W. Leadbeater, *The Astral Plane* (1895; Adyar: Theosophical Publishing 3 House, 1977), 21.

30. Theosophical aura colors and their relations to thoughts were extensively developed in Mrs. Annie Besant's and C. W. Leadbeater's book *Thought-Forms* (1901; Wheaton, Ill. Theosophical Publishing House, 1971). See also "Colors and Their Meaning," in Charles Leadbeater's *Man Visible and Invisible* (1902; Wheaton, Ill.: Theosophical Publishing House, 1925); and Rudolf Steiner's "Thought-Forms and the Human Aura," in his *Theosophy: An Introduction to the Supersensible Knowledge of the World and the Destination of Man* (1904, 1908; New York: Anthroposophic Press, 1971).

The Theosophists' color-feeling-thought-form paradigm attracted the attention of the Russian creative intelligentsia, producing some interesting results, such as Andrei Belyi's 1903 article "Sviashchennye tsveta" (in his *Arabeski* [Moscow: Skorpion, 1911], 115–29), and his sophisticated use of color imagery in his works, and Wasily Kandinsky's Theosophically permeated color theory as outlined in his essay *Über das Geistige in der Kunst* (Munich: 1912).

31. Edouard Schuré, *The Great Initiates*, trans. Fred Rothwell, vol. 1 (London: William Rider & Son, 1913), xxii.

32. Mme Blavatsky, *The Secret Doctrine*, vol. 1, 39.

33. This profoundly Gnostic paradigm is also the foundation of second-generation Symbolism's theory of Symbolism as a worldview. Vladislav Khodasevich explained how this noumenal-phenomenal dualism gripped his generation: "Everything seemed to have a double meaning, a second level; the contours of objects appeared to fluctuate. Reality, dispersing itself through consciousness, became transparent. We lived in a real world—and, at the same time, in its special, nebulous, and complex reflection, where everything was 'that, and yet not that.' Every object, every step, every gesture was as if conditionally reflected, projected into other planes on a nearby but intangible screen. Phenomena became visions. Every event acquired, beyond its obvious meaning, a second

meaning that needed to be deciphered. It was not always easy for us to decipher it, but we knew that this second meaning was actually the right one.

"Thus we lived in two worlds. But unable to discover the laws by which events occurred in this second world, seemingly more real than simply real to us,—we only languished in dark and troubled presentiments. We felt that everything that happened to us was an *omen*. But of what?" (Khodasevich, *Nekropol';* *Vospominaniia* [Paris: YMCA, 1976], 102–3).

34. Mme Blavatsky, *The Secret Doctrine,* vol. 2, 377.

35. Mme Blavatsky, *The Key to Theosophy,* 341.

36. Mrs. Besant, *The Ancient Wisdom,* 274.

37. Ibid., 235–36.

38. Ibid., 265.

39. C. G. Jung, *Alchemical Studies,* trans. R. F. C. Hull, vol. 13 of the *Collected Works* (Princeton, N.J.: Princeton University Press (Bollingen), 1968), 7.

40. Nikolai Berdiaev, "Tipy religioznoi mysli v Rossii," *Russkaia mysl'* 11(1916): 7 (2d pagination).

41. Ibid., 17.

42. See, for example, P. I. Mel'nikov-Pecherskii, *Belye golubi* and *Tainye sekty,* vol. 14 of his *Polnoe sobranie sochinenii* (Petersburg-Moscow: 1898), 203–353; also the numerous works of A. S. Prugavin, M. V. Muratov, and D. G. Konovalov. The literature on Russian mystical sectarianism is extensive.

43. Steiner's two programmatic works from the early period are *Theosophy: An Introduction to the Supersensible Knowledge of the World and the Destination of Man* (1904; 1908; and numerous subsequent eds.) and *An Outline of Occult Science* (1909; subsequent eds.). *Occult Science* outlines Steiner's complex cosmology in great detail.

44. Rudolf Steiner, *Christianity as Mystical Fact and the Mysteries of* Antiquity (1902; 2d rev. ed. 1910; Blauvelt, N.Y.: Steinerbooks, 1961), 43, 45.

45. "According to esoteric Christianity, it is correct to say that through his processes of initiation the Christian esotericist attains the purification and cleansing of his astral body; he makes his astral body into the Virgin Sophia and is illuminated from above—if you wish, you may call it overshadowed—by the 'Holy Spirit,' by the Cosmic, Universal Ego," elaborated Steiner (*The Gospel of St. John* [Spring Valley, N.Y.: The Anthroposophic Press, 1962], 179; lectures read in Hamburg May 18–31, 1908). He also identified the Mother of Jesus in the Gospel of St. John as the external historical personality of the Virgin Sophia. Explanations such as this, using familiar terminology (but frequently with real difference in meaning) allowed Russian Theosophists and Anthroposophists to point to the "parallels" between Steiner and Vladimir Solov'ev; in many cases (but not in all) these parallels are fallacious.

46. See Steiner's discussion of Mme Blavatsky's "enticement" into oriental forms in his lecture of October 23, 1911, printed in *Earthly and Cosmic Man* (Blauvelt, N.Y.: Spiritual Science Library, 1986), 23ff.

47. The eminent psychologist C. G. Jung eventually came to a similar conclusion about the psychic dangers of oriental thought for occidental man. Although Jung did not find Steiner or Anthroposophy congenial, Steiner actually anticipated many of Jung's concepts: the anima, the Christ as archetype of the

Self and symbol of ego-consciousness, initiation as individuation, and so forth. This is scarcely surprising since both scholars came from the same German academic tradition, with its particular emphasis on metaphysical idealism, philosophy of religion, and psychology. See: Gerhard Wehr, *C. G. Jung und Rudolf Steiner: Konfrontation und Synopse* (Frankfurt am Main: Klett-Cotta im Ullstein-Taschenbuch, 1982). Steiner would have been a fascinating subject for Jung; in many cases the two men were discussing the same psychic processes, but using different metaphors and vocabularies.

48. Steiner, *The Gospel of St. John*, 167.

49. Rudolf Steiner, *Rosicrucian Esotericism* (Spring Valley, N.Y.: The Anthroposophical Press, 1978), 121–22; lectures read in Budapest June 3–12, 1909.

50. Mrs. Besant, *Esoteric Christianity*, 42.

51. Steiner, *The Gospel of St. John*, 82.

52. Steiner, *An Esoteric Cosmology*, 118.

53. Steiner, *Christianity as Mystical Fact*, 66–67. Steiner seems never to have been concerned by his decided doctrinal divergence from traditional Christianity; he also attended and participated in various Christian services and liturgies, including the Orthodox (as, for example, during his lecture series in Helsinki during Orthodox Easter, 1913). On several separate occasions he pointed out the following: "Spiritual science does not want to usurp the place of Christianity; on the contrary it would like to be instrumental in making Christianity understood. Thus it becomes clear to us through spiritual science that the being whom we call Christ is to be recognized as the center of life on earth, that the whole Christian religion is the ultimate religion for the earth's whole future" (Steiner, "Anthroposophy and Christianity" [Spring Valley, N.Y.: The Anthroposophic Press, 1985], 17; lecture delivered at Norrköping, July 13, 1914).

54. Steiner, *The Gospel of St. John*, 56.

55. Ibid., 86. Steiner's Christ Impulse is a contemporary variant of the Gnostic "Call from Without." The Gnostic Christos is the "Caller of the Call," the call that awakens the spiritual man from the dream of this material world to the recognition of his spiritual nature. The Call *(Zov)* appears frequently in early Russian Symbolist literature.

56. Mme Blavatsky, *The Secret Doctrine*, vol. 1, 70–71.

57. Ibid., vol. 2, 237.

58. Eliphas Lévi, *The History of Magic* (1860), trans. A. E. Waite (1913; New York: Weiser, 1969), 159. Mme Blavatsky quotes this passage in *The Secret Doctrine*, vol. 2, 511.

59. Rudolf Steiner, *Secrets of the Threshold* (Hudson, N.Y.: The Anthroposophic Press, 1987), 33; lectures given in Munich August 24–31, 1913.

60. Ahriman is chief of the fallen angels, the tempter of mankind, and the principle of evil in Zoroastrianism; Lucifer, in Christian tradition, is one of the names of Satan, or the Devil. In Christian mythology Lucifer, cast out of heaven for hubris and arrogance, reigns in hell.

61. Steiner, *Secrets of the Threshold*, 19–20.

62. Rudolf Steiner, *Balance in the World and Man: Lucifer and Ahriman* (North Vancouver, Canada: Steiner Book Centre, 1977), 22; three lectures given in Dornach November 20–22, 1914.

63. Rudolf Steiner, *The Influences of Lucifer and Ahriman* (North Vancouver, Canada: Steiner Book Centre, 1954), 10; lectures from November 1919.

64. Steiner, *Balance in the World and Man*, 18.

65. Steiner, *The Gospel of St. John*, 191.

Chapter Six
The Russian Reception of Theosophical Thought

1. *Rebus* 13(1912): 3.

2. K. D. Kudriavtsev, *Chto takoe teosofiia i teosoficheskoe obshchestvo* (St. Petersburg: 1912; 2d rev. and exp. ed. 1914).

3. Ibid., 5–6.

4. Ibid., 20.

5. Ibid., 44–45.

6. Papus also belonged to the *Ordre Kabbalistique de la Rose-Croix*, an esoteric order spuriously connected with the Rosicrucian tradition. In late Renaissance Rosicrucian literature, from which many ideas were later appropriated by Freemasonry, there is a claim that Rosicrucian adepts went off to live in Tibet; the Theosophists claimed that this was a reference to their Mahatmas, whose Lodge was in the Himalayas. In this was a perceived continuity among Rosicrucianism, Masonry, and Theosophy. The leaders of the *Ordre* were Joséphin Péladan and the Marquis Stanislas de Guaita, one of the more prominent occultists associated with the French Occult Revival. See relevant entries in Kenneth Mackenzie's *The Royal Masonic Cyclopaedia* (1877).

7. Letter from Mme Blavatsky (to A. N. Aksakov), October 2, 1877; cited in Vs. Solov'ev's *Sovremennaia zhritsa Izidy* (St. Petersburg: Obshchestvennaia Pol'za, 1904), 287.

8. Kudriavtsev, *Chto takoe teosofiia*, 16.

9. V. P. Bykov, *Spiritizm pered sudom nauki, obshchestva i religii* (Moscow: Izdanie E. I. Bykovoi, 1914), 36.

10. Lev Kobylinskii-Ellis, *Vigilemus!* (Moscow: Musaget, 1914), 101.

11. "Novoe v teosoficheskom obshchestve," *Rebus* 14(1912): 4.

12. Kudriavtsev, *Chto takoe teosofiia*, 55–56.

13. Mme Blavatsky, *The Secret Doctrine*, vol. 1 (London: The Theosophical Publishing Co., 1888), xx.

14. Kudriavtsev, *Chto takoe teosofiia*, 25. Mme Blavatsky did not actually say the words as Kudriavtsev attributed them to her; the *Pall Mall Gazette* records only that "she dilated for nearly half an hour with much fervour and natural eloquence concerning the melancholy contrast between the professed creed of Christendom and the political actions of Christian nations, proclaiming herself on the side of the heathen whom they despise." She did add, rather arrogantly, that her Theosophical Society "aims, first, at the restoration of Buddhism to its original purity," and, second, "to restore Brahmanism to the purer ideal which finds expression in the Vedas." Only then did she plan to "combat a false materialism by the establishment of pure spiritual truth." The *Gazette*, a respectable miscellany of articles on politics, business, society, and the arts, concluded that Mme Blavatsky "is a woman who, regarded from the purely intellectual standpoint, deserves more attention than she has hitherto received," although it

found her Theosophy "inexpressibly bizarre and paradoxical" (*Pall Mall Gazette* [London], April 26, 1884, 3–4).

15. Mme Blavatsky, *The Key to Theosophy* (1889; Pasadena: Theosophical University Press, 1972), 61.

16. Nikolai Berdiaev, *Samopoznanie* (1949; Paris: YMCA, 1983), 207.

17. L. E. O., "Teosoficheskoe obshchestvo v Smolenske," *Rebus* 39(1907): 5.

18. V. I. Shtal'berg, "Khristianskaia i indo-buddiiskaia teosofiia," *Teosofskaia zhizn'* 2/3(1908): 116.

19. Ibid., *Teosofskaia zhizn'* 4/5(1908/1909): 197.

20. "Alba" [Anna Kamenskaia], "Protivorechit li teosofiia khristianstvu? (po A. Bezant)," *Voprosy teosofii*, vol. 1 (St. Petersburg: Gorodskaia tipografiia, 1907), 149.

21. Anna Kamenskaia, "Zadachi teosofii," *Rebus* 6/7(1907): 6.

22. Mrs. Annie Besant, *Esoteric Christianity* (1901; Adyar, Madras: Theosophical Publishing House, 1953), 90.

23. Numerous legends about Christ existed among Theosophists, many of them contradictory. Some examples: Christ was divine only during the years of mission, when he was animated by the Mahatma Illarion; Christ was a *chela* [disciple] who revealed the Word too soon; and so forth.

24. Archimandrite Varlaam, *Teosofiia pered sudom khristianstva* (Poltava: G. E. Markevich, 1912), 43–44.

25. Bykov, *Spiritizm pod sudom*, 35.

26. N. N., "Teosofskoe uchenie," *Khristianin* 4(1910): 775.

27. Mme Blavatsky, *The Key to Theosophy*, 325.

28. Rudolf Steiner, *The Gospel of St. John* (Spring Valley, N.Y.: The Anthroposophic Press, 1962), 159; lectures given in May 1908.

29. *Voprosy teosofii*, vol. 1; 159–68; materials based on Mrs. Annie Besant's *Esoteric Christianity* (1901; Adyar: Theosophical Publishing House, 1953), 159n.

30. Mrs. Besant's work was additionally influenced by the Theosophist G. R. S. Mead's translation of the Gnostic texts of the *Pistis Sophia*; in *Esoteric Christianity* she uses the Valentinian cosmogony as her starting point (the fall of Sophia from the Pleroma into matter, and so on).

31. Mrs. Besant, *Esoteric Christianity*, 126, 151.

32. Vladimir Solov'ev, "Dukhovnye osnovy zhizni," in his *Sobranie sochinenii*, 2d ed., vol. 3 (St. Petersburg: Prosveshchenie, 1911–1913), 402.

33. Timothy Ware, *The Orthodox Church* (Baltimore: Penguin, 1964), 236; Ware quotes from the Canon for Matins of Holy Thursday, Ode 4, Troparion 3.

34. Ibid., 237.

35. Mrs. Besant, *Esoteric Christianity*, 290.

36. Fr. Ioann Dmitrevskii, *Teosofiia—Religioznaia filosofiia nashego vremeni* (Khar'kov: Tip. Mirnyi trud, 1911), 78.

37. Nikolai Berdiaev, "Tipy religioznoi mysli v Rossii," *Russkaia mysl'* 11(1916): 5, 2d pagination). Berdiaev continued: "Theosophy does not wish to know this mystery of Christ, this miraculous liberation through grace from the yoke of the past, from the power of time, this abridgement of endless time into

one moment. Everything in Theosophy is based on a terrible and inevitable conformity [to the law of *karma*]; it applies even to the very depths of divine life. Karmic fate is just and appropriate, but it knows no forgiveness or mercy, it knows no love or freedom. Christianity is above all a religion of love and freedom, not of justice and conformity to [karmic] law." Berdiaev was particularly irritated by Theosophy's inability to accommodate the concepts of Redemption and Grace.

38. Dmitrevskii, *Teosofiia*, 59, 80. Father Dmitrevskii's opinion is echoed in N. N.'s article in *Khristianin*: "There is no reason to descend into the underground vaults of ancient pagan temples, there to root in the dust and garbage of the obsolete pagan cultures that destroyed the antique world" (5[1910], 111).

39. Kobylinskii-Ellis, *Vigilemus!*, 41.

40. Vs. Solov'ev, "Chto takoe 'doktrina teosoficheskogo obschestva,'" *Voprosy filosofii i psikhologiii* 18(1893), Book 3, 67–68, 2d pagination.

41. Mme Blavatsky, *The Key to Theosophy*, 362–63.

42. The doctrine of the Incarnation affirms that, as an act of the whole Godhead, Christ, the eternal Son of God, was born of a human mother and became simultaneously Man and God, thus excluding the partial, incomplete actualization implied by cyclical reincarnation; the doctrine also affirms the uniqueness of this historical event. As both Man and God, Christ was the bridge between the human and divine that would make possible the eventual redemption of fallen man and his reconciliation with God. The doctrine of the Atonement affirms man's reconciliation with the Godhead through Christ's Sacrifice of Himself for the sins of all men. The Atonement for sin is complete, obviating any need for repetition. The doctrine of resurrection in the body, which had a particular hold on the Orthodox mind at the end of the nineteenth century (see Nikolai Fedorov, *Filosofiia obshchego dela*, 1906, 1913), affirms the resurrection in the body of all departed souls at the time of the *Parousia*, or Second Coming. The promise of this resurrection is implicit, by analogy, in the resurrection of Christ. This resurrection is to eternal life, not to the endless recapitulations of imperfect mortal existences. All three doctrines, and especially the last, assume the uniqueness of historical manifestation and thus deny any form of reincarnation or metempsychosis.

43. Steiner, *The Gospel of St. John* (Spring Valley, N.Y.: The Anthroposophic Press, 1973), 121, 120; lectures given in Hamburg May 18–31, 1908.

44. Steiner, *An Esoteric Cosmology* (Blauvelt, N.Y.: Spiritual Science Library, 1987), 118; lectures read in Paris May 25 to June 14, 1906.

45. Mrs. Annie Besant, *The Ancient Wisdom* (1897; Adyar: Theosophical Publishing House, 1939), 289. Mrs. Besant may be suggesting that freedom requires a structure in which to operate, otherwise it is mere chaos. The logical conclusion of this approach is that greater freedom requires greater structure, and that final, true freedom is to be found only in complete necessity. However congenial this position might be to some Protestants (following St. Augustine, for example, or Martin Luther) and Marxists ("Freedom is the recognition of necessity"), it would have had limited appeal to most of her Russian Orthodox contemporaries.

46. See, for example, Berdiaev's discussion in chapter 13, "Tvorchestvo i mistika. Okkul'tizm i magiia," of *Smysl tvorchestva*, vol. 2 of his *Sobranie sochinenii* (1916; Paris: YMCA, 1985), 332–54.

47. Steiner, *An Esoteric Cosmology*, 119.

48. *Rebus* 37(1911): 6. "Freemasonry" was one of the most damning indictments in the entire lexicon of Russian Orthodox intellectual thought.

49. Mme Blavatsky's book *The Key to Theosophy* provides a convenient glossary of Theosophical terms; here: *chela*, disciple; *devachan*, the state between two earth lives; *Gupta Vidya*, the secret science; *kamaloka*, the semimaterial plane; paranirvana, beyond nirvana; see also glossary, this volume.

50. *Rebus* 18(1895): 181.

51. Rama-Krishna (1834–1896), Hindu philosopher and reformer; Yogi Ramacharaka (1862–1932; pseud. of American occultist William Walker Atkinson), prolific author of popular texts about Hatha-Yoga, Raja-Yoga, Jnana-Yoga, oriental philosophy, and so forth; Swami Vivekananda (1863–1902), a disciple of Rama-Krishna, popularized the philosophy of the Vedanta in Europe; Sri-Shankara-Acharya (c. 688–720 A.D.), Hindu metaphysician, most influential of all Hindu occultists, famous for his commentaries to the *Brahma Sutra, Upanishads, Bhagavad Gita*. See Bibliography of Theosophical and Related Works.

52. During the period of the formation of the Russian Theosophical Society (1907–1908), the International Society was under the leadership of Mrs. Besant, who had been born and raised in England during the time of the Raj; who had converted to Brahmanism; who resided in Adyar, Madras, where the Theosophical Headquarters were; and who was an active force in the movement for Indian independence.

Ironically, the neo-Buddhism of the Theosophists did not have the unqualified approval of the Hindus. The guru Mahatma Agamia Paramakhanza, head of the Indian Society of Representatives of Vedantic Philosophy, "considered it his duty, for the sake of Hindu youth, to protest against the distortion of ancient Hindu doctrines and against their appearance in the diluted and entirely distorted form in which Mrs. Besant and the Theosophists offered it both in India and in the West" ("Otzyvy Indusov o teosofakh," *Rebus* 28[1905]: 3). The guru did not understand why Mrs. Besant had decided to become an honorary Hindu, nor did he have a high opinion of the invisible Mahatmas.

53. Dmitrevskii, *Teosofiia*, 47, referring to Kamenskaia's article "Russkaia ideia," *Vestnik teosofii* 1(1910): 4–5; 9(1910): 69, 87.

54. Pisareva, review of Berdiaev's "Tipy" (*Russkaia mysl'* 11[1916]) in *Vestnik teosofii* 2(1917): 9–10.

55. "Taos," "Literaturnoe obozrenie," *Vestnik teosofii* 9(1915): 94; reference to Nikolai Shapir, "Natsional'nye tipy kul'tury," *Severnye zapiski* 3(1915).

56. *Vestnik teosofii* 9(1915): 95.

57. Kudriavtsev, *Chto takoe teosofiia*, 24; Kudriavtsev was referring to Mrs. Besant's socialist past. Kudriavtsev's conclusion was more succinctly formulated by Boris Vysheslavtsev: "Buddhism is *a religion without God*; Buddhism knows a certain higher mystical state, *nirvana*, but its mysticism is an atheistic mysticism. In India everything is religious and mystical—even atheism" ("Krishnamurti [zavershenie teosofii]," *Put'* [Paris] 14[December 1928], 95).

58. Vs. Solov'ev, *Sovremennaia zhritsa*, 293.

59. N. N., "Teosofskoe uchenie," *Khristianin* 4(1910): 795.

60. Mme Blavatsky, *The Secret Doctrine*, vol. 1, xx.

61. "S.," "30-tiletie Teosoficheskogo Obshchestva," *Rebus* 43/44(1905): 4.

62. F. Max Müller, "Esoteric Buddhism," in *The Nineteenth Century*, May 1893, 770–71. This well-known article was translated into German and published in *Spiritualistische Blätter* (4[1894]); excerpts were translated into Russian and appeared in *Rebus* as "Maks Miuller o noveishei teosofii i ee rasprostraniteliakh" (*Rebus* 21[1894]: 213).

63. Blavatsky, *Isis Unveiled*, vol. 2 (New York: J. W. Bouton, 1877), 143.

64. Müller, "Esoteric Buddhism," 783. Müller's position was that "if there is any religion entirely free from esoteric doctrines, it is Buddhism. There never was any such thing as mystery in Buddhism" (776). And Mme Blavatsky's esoteric Buddhism was "nothing very new, nothing very old, but simply a medley of well-known though generally misunderstood Brahmanic or Buddhistic doctrines" (775).

65. Kamenskaia, *Rebus* 7, 11(1907).

66. Berdiaev, "Tipy," 5.

67. Ibid., 16.

68. Ivan Il'in, "Filosofiia kak dukhovnoe delanie," *Russkaia mysl'* 3(1915): 125, 2d pagination.

69. Ibid., 126, 125.

70. Kobylinskii-Ellis, *Vigilemus!*, 102.

71. Ernst Haeckel (1834–1919) began with Darwinism, but soon developed a theory of the essential unity of the organic and inorganic. Haeckel's anti-idealistic, anti-agnostic, materialist position did not accept revealed religions, but posited a monistic religion of nature (see his *Riddle of the Universe* [1899]). His work was popular in its time.

72. Berdiaev, "Tipy," 15–16.

73. Kobylinskii-Ellis, *Vigilemus!*, 102.

74. See Leonid Sabaneev, *Skriabin* (Moscow: Skorpion, 1916); Boris Schloezer, *A. Skriabin: monografiia o lichnosti i tvorchestve* (Berlin: Grani, 1923).

75. See Mikhail Agursky, "Maksim Gorky and the Decline of Bolshevik Theomachy," in *Christianity and Russian Culture in Soviet Society* (Boulder: Westview Press, 1990), 81, 84ff. Agursky discusses in greater detail Gorkii's contacts with Theosophy.

76. See, for example, Kamenskaia's brochure, "Zadachi teosofii," also reprinted in *Rebus* 6–7(1907), which relies on Berdiaev and Solov'ev to lend credence to her position.

77. Vl. Solov'ev, "Retsenziia na knigu E. P. Blavatskoi: *The Key to Theosophy*," in his *Sobranie sochinenii*, vol. 6, 292.

78. Berdiaev, "Tipy," 1.

79. Lev Tolstoi, *Polnoe sobranie sochinenii*, vol. 49 (Moscow: Goslitizdat [iubileinoe izdanie], 1952), 84.

80. "Yesterday the Theosophists were here," Tolstoi laconically noted in his diary the next day. He did not seem particularly impressed, but then Tolstoi was not impressed by organizations, but by ideas (Lev Tolstoi, *Polnoe sobranie sochinenii*, vol. 56 [Moscow: Goslitizdat [iubileinoe izdanie], 1937], 138).

81. "Stenograficheskii otchet zasedaniia Rel.-Filos. Obshchestva v Spb. 24 noiabria 1909 g. po dokladu Alba 'Teosofiia i bogostroitel'stvo,'" *Vestnik teosofii* 2(1910): 62; the text of the entire lecture and discussion is given on pages 62 to 111.

82. *Vestnik teosofii* 2(1910): 86.

83. Ibid., 102.

84. Ironically, Theosophy would become, if not a church, at least a religion, by the end of 1925. At that time the Theosophical Council voted to accept Theosophy as the "One Universal Religion."

85. *Vestnik teosofii* 2(1910): 108.

86. Ibid., 106.

87. Ibid., 103.

88. Ibid., 98.

89. Woloschin, *Die grüne Schlange* (Frankfurt am Main: Fischer Verlag, 1968), 246.

90. Berdiaev even pointed out that the activities of Belyi, Metner, and the *Logos* and *Trudy i dni* writers were too "German." "Even A. Belyi was of a purely German persuasion, in spite of his Russian lack of organization and chaotic habits" (*Samopoznanie*, 188).

91. Berdiaev, "Tipy," 13.

92. Ibid., 11.

93. Ibid., 10.

94. Berdiaev's criticism here is not meticulously fair, as many of his criticism are, since Theosophy never claimed to be either mysticism or religion.

95. Regarding Belyi (whom he considered to possess "possibly the greatest creative gift in Russia"), Berdiaev wrote that "A. Belyi is very Russian, and his path is characteristic of the Russian soul. Steinerianism can scarcely be good for artistic creativity. Steiner's path can actually weaken creativity. Creativity assumes the overcoming of *karma* once and for all, it assumes a victory over it, and not an eternal, gradual overcoming of it. Creativity assumes the dualism of the world of spiritual freedom and the world of natural necessity. Insofar as A. Belyi receives creative impulses from Anthroposophy, he represents an exception to the rule" ("Tipy," 17).

96. "Dva pis'ma N. A. Berdiaeva Andreiu Belomu," published in *Mosty* 11(1965) by L. Murav'ev, with commentaries by Fedor Stepun, 359–68. (Republished in *Novyi zhurnal* 137[December 1979], 118–23.) Letter of June 8, 1912, 360–61. Berdiaev approved of Belyi's going to Rudolf Steiner, but suggested that Belyi ask Steiner "why there is no Saviour, and no Christ" in Steiner's system of salvation, and "why Steiner so completely denies the Dionysian element in life, why he does not wish to know the instinctive, passionate, and sub-conscious value" (119–20).

97. Berdiaev, *Samopoznanie*, 219–22.

98. Ibid., 219.
99. Berdiaev, "Tipy," 9.
100. Varlaam, *Teosofiia*, 25.
101. Kobylinskii-Ellis, *Vigilemus!*, vii.
102. Vs. Solov'ev, "Chto takoe 'doktrina,' " 68, 2d pagination.
103. Berdiaev, *Samopoznanie*, 219.
104. Dmitrii Stranden, *Teosofiia i ee kritiki* (St. Petersburg: Stasiulevich, 1913).
105. Ibid., 7.
106. *Vestnik teosofii* 4(1912): 83.
107. *Rebus* 11(1914): 6.
108. Stranden, *Teosofiia*, 6.

Chapter Seven
The Russian Theosophical Movement after 1917

1. *Izvestiia RTO* 2(1917): 41; after an initially rapturous reaction to events at home, Kamenskaia's subsequent letters referred only to events at Adyar, such as the "holiday of light" that commemorated the anniversary of Colonel Olcott's death. Today her letters sound remote, even insular, when read in the context of the first Russian revolution and what followed.
2. *Vestnik teosofii* 2(1917): 5–6.
3. E. Pisareva, "Na storozhevom postu," *Vestnik teosofii* 3/5(1917): 7; according to both Theosophy and Anthroposophy, the world was completing the cycle of the fifth, the Aryan, root-race, and beginning the sixth Earth root-race, which would be dominated by the Slavs.
4. Ibid., 9.
5. *Izvestiia RTO* 2(1917): 10; here are echoes of Theosophist P. D. Uspenskii's earlier "mystical socialism" and "creative labor." For a modern discussion of occultism and socialism as the strangest bedfellows of the nineteenth century, see Philippe Muray, *Le dix-neuvième siècle à travers les âges* (Paris: Denoël, 1984). Muray discusses the hybridization of occultism and socialism to produce a notion of modernity based on regimented humanity organized according to a principle of higher Harmony; P. D. Uspenskii said much the same thing.
6. A. Kamenskaia, "Moi vstrechi s A. Bezant," *Vestnik: Satyat Nasti Paro Dharmah* (Geneva) 3(May 1938): 5.
7. Ibid., 5–6.
8. The outbreak of the war had complicated life in the Anthroposophical community in Dornach; Steiner complained about the Anthroposophists' inability to overcome feelings of nationalism and chauvinism. Most of the Russians in Dornach had left for their homeland in the first weeks of the war, while it was still possible for them to travel through Germany. Andrei Belyi and his brother-in-law, Aleksandr Pozzo, left in 1916, taking a round-about path through France and Scandinavia. Trifon Trapeznikov left in January 1917 by the same route; Margarita Sabashnikova-Voloshina traveled by sealed train through Germany that summer.
9. Members and participants of *Vol'fila* included, inter alia, the famous poet

Aleksandr Blok, the critic Ivanov-Razumnik (R. V. Ivanov), the philosopher and journalist Aaron Shteinberg, the minor poet Konstantin Siunnerberg-Erberg, the philosopher and critic Aleksandr Meier, the painter Kuz'ma Petrov-Vodkin, Professor N. O. Losskii, Professor S. A. Askol'dov, the teacher L. V. Pumpian-skii, who later introduced the famous pianist Maria Iudina to Anthroposophy, the avant-garde artist Mikhail Matiushin, the writer Ol'ga Forsh, Margarita Sa-bashnikova-Voloshina, and others; most of them had had some contact with Theosophy or Anthroposophy.

10. The members of the Moscow Dukhovnaia Akademiia included critics and philosophers Gustav Shpett, M. P. Stoliarov, and Mikhail Gershenzon, as well as three major figures of the Russian religious renaissance, Nikolai Berdiaev, Boris Vysheslavtsev, and Fedor Stepun.

11. Russia's leading idealist philosophers (Nikolai Berdiaev, Fedor Stepun, Sergei Bulgakov, Boris Vysheslavtsev, and Semen Frank), along with many other academics and members of the intelligentsia, were deported from Russia by order of the Bolsheviks in the fall of 1922.

12. M. Zhemchuzhnikova, "Vospominaniia o Moskovskom Antroposofi-cheskom Obshchestve 1917–1923," 1975 ms. in private hands, fol. 50. The RAO did submit a registration request, which was denied by the authorities.

13. Belyi received permission to leave Russia because of his deteriorating health. His plan was to rejoin the Dornach community, but both his wife, Asya Turgeneva, and Dr. Steiner advised against it. Belyi felt rejected and furious at first, but eventually understood that his task in this life was to continue the work in Russia. Klavdiia Nikolaevna Vasil'eva was sent from Russia to bring him back, and in October 1923 Belyi returned to Moscow. He remained in the Soviet Union for the rest of his life. Despite some critics' claims to the contrary, Belyi never abandoned Anthroposophy but lived within its spiritual context for the rest of his life; see Boris Christa, "Andrey Bely's Connections with European Occultism," *Russian and Slavic Literature* (Selected Papers in the Humanities from the Banff 1974 International Conference), ed. Freeborn, Milner-Gulland, Ward (Ann Arbor: Slavica, 1976), 213–23.

14. Andrei Belyi, *Pochemu ia stal simvolistom* (Ann Arbor: Ardis, 1982), 117.

15. Many Russian occult texts would be offered to the West for purchase with gold-based currencies; the "Vsesoiuznoe mezhdunarodnoe auktsionnoe obshchestvo 'Mezhdunarodnaia Kniga'" prepared a catalog of such materials for sale to the West in the 1930s. Such books have always been available in the USSR to trusted customers in second-hand bookshops.

16. See Charlotte Douglas's article "Beyond Reason: Malevich, Matiushin, and Their Circles," in *The Spiritual in Art: Abstract Painting 1890–1985*, ed. Edward Weisberger, 185–200 [Exhibition Catalog, Los Angeles County Museum of Art] (New York: Abbeville, 1986), in which she explores in detail the manner in which the Cubo-Futurists united the Theosophical, neo-Buddhist idea that higher consciousness and supersensible sight can be achieved by organic evolution, with Uspenskii's theory of multiple dimensions.

17. Petr Demianovich Uspenskii, *Chetvertoe izmerenie* (St. Petersburg: Trud, 1910), 29.

18. Aleksandr Aseev, "Okkul'tnoe dvizhenie v Sovetskoi Rossii," *Okkul'tizm*

i ioga 3(1934), 90–91. As new organizations he names the "Bratstvo svetlogo goroda" and the "Severo-kavkazskie soedinennye shtaty." Kamenskaia also wrote about the "Knights of the Radiant City," defining them as a grass-roots "Gnostic-mystical movement"; "they use Russian folklore as material and speak in terms very dear to the Russian heart in the language of ancient heroic poems and of national legends and fairy-tales. The legend of Kitej, the Radiant City, is the basis of their symbolic teaching" ("Russia and Russian Theosophy," *The Theosophist* (Adyar), November 1931, 204).

The myth of Kitezh has always been a potent archetype in Russian culture and appears regularly in Russian art, music, and literature. According to legend, the city of Kitezh was originally located in the forests near Lake Svetloiar. God placed this holy city on the bottom of the lake to prevent it from being sacked by the Tatars. Those who are pure of heart can, on St. John's Eve, hear the bells of the churches of Kitezh and see their golden spires from Svetloiar's shore. Kitezh will rise from the waters and appear again when Russia is no longer "godless" and once more worthy to see it and its priceless treasures. Kitezh was an important symbol of the Russian sectarians, especially the Old Believers, the Flagellants, and the White Doves, who gathered at the shore of Lake Svetloiar every year on June 24.

The Kitezh myth particularly captured the imagination of the early twentieth century. In 1905 the Kitezh legend was associated with the hopes of the revolution (cf. Mstislav Dobuzhinskii's 1905 illustration, "Umirotvorenie," which shows the Moscow Kremlin rising from the waters, covered by a rainbow). After 1918 "godless Russia" was equated with the Bolshevik regime, and Kitezh became a symbol of spiritual opposition (as in the "Knights of the Radiant City").

19. Aseev, "Okkul'tnoe dvizhenie," 92. Aseev is quoting from an unspecified issue of *Vecherniaia Moskva* from the early 1930s.

20. Zhemchuzhnikova, fol. 52.

21. One of these was in Kuokkala; their leader, Vera Kholshevnikova, was invited to lecture on Theosophy at "Penaty," the studio-dacha of the famous painter, Ilya Repin. See *Vestnik* (Geneva) 4(September 1924): 10.

22. At the time of the Fiftieth Anniversary Congress, the Theosophical Society worldwide had 1,540 lodges and 41,492 officially registered members. This does not exhaust the number of actual Theosophists; many had broken with the Society or chose not to pay dues (*Vestnik* [Geneva] 4[April 1925]: 19).

23. The national sections were always the foundation of the Theosophical structure. Unlike the Anthroposophists, who were more cosmopolitan in outlook and seemed satisfied with their world center in Dornach and the general use of the German language, the Theosophists emphasized the distinctive national coloring of its sections. One is tempted to draw a parallel between the Anthroposophical and Theosophical societies, on the one hand, and the Western and Eastern churches, on the other: while the more rational Catholic church universally retained Latin as the ecclesiastical language and had its center in the Vatican with a single pope, the more mystical Eastern Orthodox church maintained seven (later more) patriarchs and used some form of the local vernacular as its ecclesiastical language.

24. *Vestnik* (Geneva) 1(April 1924): 1.

25. The Belgrade occult community had strong Theosophical interests. One of their number, Dr. Aleksandr Aseev, edited and published the journal *Okkul'tizm i ioga* (10 books, 1932–1938); he subsequently moved to South America and continued his occult activities there. Elena Pisareva made occasional contributions and Aseev planned an all-Blavatsky issue (which did not materialize), but closer relations with the Geneva Theosophists, who tended to remain aloof, never developed.

26. Elena Pisareva, "Rostki budushchego," *Vestnik* (Geneva) 1(April 1924): 6.

27. It is difficult to gauge the degree of the Theosophists' own belief in their mission and in their role in the future resurrection of Russia. Enthusiasts like Professor Nikolai Erassi, who must have realized that he would not see the New Russia in his lifetime (Erassi died in 1930), claimed that "the Great Russia of the Future is already built and lives on the higher planes in the world of true, eternal Reality" ("Krest russkoi emigratsii," *Vestnik* [Geneva] 6/8[June/August 1926]: 20).

28 E. Pisareva, "Rostki budushchego," *Vestnik* (Geneva) 1(April 19): 9. Metallurgy and alchemy have always been connected by the analogical imagination since both deal with transmutation; both processes aim to destroy impure elements with fire and release thereby a refined product, whether that be forged metal (the smith) or spiritual gold (the alchemist). Fire is associated with transfiguration, regeneration, and purification, while iron is associated with the astral world (as well as with Mars, the god of war). Thus in many primitive societies, the blacksmith is a magical, numinous figure. That this imagery complex (visually incorporated in the forging hammer and the forged sickle [scythe], and uniting war, death, and transmutation) was chosen by the Soviets as their "icon," must have seemed relevant and symbolic to the Theosophists.

29. A. Kamenskaia, "Na storozhevom postu," *Vestnik* (Geneva) 7(December 1924): 4.

30. A. Kamenskaia, "Mezhdunarodnaia missiia slavian," *Vestnik* (Geneva) 1(January 1925): 14.

31. A. Kamenskaia, "Missiia slavian," *Vestnik* (Geneva) 2(February 1925): 7.

32. Ibid., 9.

33. "Khronika teosoficheskogo dvizheniia," *Vestnik* (Geneva) 4(September 1924): 15.

34. E. Pisareva, "Pis'ma k chitatel'iam," *Vestnik* (Geneva) 3(March 1925): 9.

35. Theosophists unaffiliated with the RTOvR kept lines of communication open and shared many of the Society's optimistic visions. Dr. Aleksandr Aseev, editor of *Okkul'tizm i ioga*, wrote the following from Belgrade: "We know that the White Brotherhood [of the Mahatmas] has already more than once saved our homeland in difficult moments of its existence. The national soul knows several of them as saints and holy men of the Orthodox church, and today, during the difficult period of the Kali Yuga [the dark age, fourth age of the world, violent and bloody], during the days of the intensified struggle between darkness and light, *these* Brothers invisibly assist our homeland, and through the crucible of suffering and mourning will lead it to the Radiant City" ("Put' zarubezhnogo okkul'tizma," *Okkul'tizm i ioga* 2[1934], 5).

36. A. Kamenskaia, "Na storozhevom postu," *Vestnik* (Geneva) 6/8(June/ August 1928): 1. She referred to Berdiaev and Vysheslavtsev; the latter answered her obliquely in *Put'*: "Only a complete incomprehension of the fundamental differences between Christian and Hindu religious thought makes possible the strange fact that some Theosophists also consider themselves members of the church, whether Orthodox or Catholic. Hearing Krishnamurti speak just once, or reading just one of his works is sufficient to perceive once and for all the impossibility of the Theosophists' naive confusion of all altars, dogmas, faiths, and philosophies" (Boris Vysheslavtsev, "Krishnamurti [zavershenie teosofii]," *Put'* [Paris] 14[December 1928], 106).

37. A. Kamenskaia, "Na storozhevom postu," *Vestnik* (Geneva) 2(March 1938): 1.

38. Obituary notice, *Journal de Genève* 147(June 25, 1952): 5.

Afterword
Theosophy's Impact on Fin de siècle Russian Culture

1. C. G. Jung, *Civilization in Transition*, trans. R. F. C. Hull, vol. 10 of the *Collected Works* (Princeton, N.J.: Princeton University Press, 1970), 82.

2. Nicolas Berdiaev, *Freedom and the Spirit* (New York: Scribner's, 1935), 272.

3. James Webb, *The Occult Underground* (LaSalle, Ill.: Open Court, 1974), 1–2.

4. Sixten Ringbom, *The Sounding Cosmos. A Study of the Spiritualism of Kandinsky and the Genesis of Abstract Painting*, Acta Academiae Åboensis, Ser. A: Humaniora, vol. 38, nr 2 (Åbo [Turku], Finland: Åbo Akademi, 1970), 24. Discussing the source of Kandinsky's innovations in the area of abstraction, Ringbom points out, "It is one of the ironies of art history that the abstract idiom which its founders intended as a vehicle for communicating an essential content actually came to be regarded as a play with forms, that 'inhaltsloses Spiel mit den Formen' which Kandinsky dreaded. If expressed publicly in our own day, the claims made by the pioneers of abstract art would probably be dismissed as expressions of naiveté or affectation" (113).

5. Although Voloshin's Theosophical dimensions have as yet only been hinted at in the secondary literature, Aleksandr Skriabin's mystical theories of music and debt to Theosophical thought have been discussed both by Boris Schloezer and Leonid Sabaneev; Sixten Ringbom has meticulously outlined the influence of selected Theosophical ideas on Kandinsky's art in *The Sounding Cosmos*; see the general bibliography.

6. See V. V. Stasov, "Proiskhozhdenie russkikh bylin," *Vestnik Evropy* 1–4(1868).

7. *Tsvety Morii* (Berlin: Slovo, 1921) was recently published for the first time in the Soviet Union (Moscow: Sovremennik, 1988). Elena Roerich published two volumes of her translation of *The Secret Doctrine* in Riga shortly before the Second World War; the third volume was not printed (*Tainaia doktrina; sintez nauki, religii i filosofii*, trans. Elena Rerikh [Riga: Uguns, 1937]). The Russian Theosophical Movement has ironically been hampered for most of its history by

the lack of complete and accurate translations into Russian of the founder's two major texts, *Isis Unveiled* and *The Secret Doctrine*.

8. Reported by I. V. Mantsiarli, "Pis'mo iz Adiara," *Vestnik* (Geneva) 4(April 1925): 17–19; an author's copy of the painting is in the Museum of Oriental Art in Moscow.

9. Letter by Elena Roerich to an unspecified individual, dated December 17, 1936: "I must say that Kamenskaia is clearly an enemy of the Doctrine. We have information from many sources about her harmful, slanderous activities. Of course we were warned in advance about Mme Kamenskaia and thus know that she is hurting the Great Task. But we have more than a few friends among the Theosophists, and her calumnies have alienated those who know how to think independently" (cited in *Vest' E. P. Blavatskoi*, Leningrad: 1991, 81).

10. *Roerich Museum: A Decade of Activity 1921–1931* (New York: Roerich Museum Press, 1931), 11.

11. This enormous legacy consists of more than four hundred paintings, the ashes of N. K. and E. I. Roerich, their letters, documents, and manuscripts. See Irma Mamaladze and L.V. Shaposhnikova, "Nasledie Rerikha," in *Literaturnaia gazeta* 22(May 30, 1990): 8.

12. Aleksandra Unkovskaia, "Metoda tsveto-zvuko-chisel," *Vestnik teosofii* 1, 3(1909). Kandinsky refers to this work in various writings. As Unkovskaia's work was never published separately, Kandinsky could only have read it in *Vestnik teosofii* or received the manuscript from the author. Kandinsky and Unkovskaia were acquainted and shared friends in art, music, and Theosophical circles.

13. Mrs. Annie Besant and C. W. Leadbeater, *Thought-Forms* (London: Theosophical Publishing House, 1901; numerous subsequent eds. in all major languages).

14. Wasily Kandinsky, *Über das Geistige in der Kunst; insbesondere in der Malerei* (Munich: 1912; 7th ed. Bern: 1973); the essay was written over the course of 1910. It reflects many of the ideas in Mrs. Besant's and Leadbeater's *Thought-Forms*; it also mentions the works of Steiner and Mme Blavatsky. Kandinsky's work contains references to a number of artists and musicians who were interested in Theosophy (Mondrian, Skriabin, Sabaneev).

15. Andrei Belyi, "Material k biografii (intimnyi)," (Central Archives of Literature and Art (TsGALI), Moscow, MS# 53;2;3 (1923; covers 1880–1915), fol. 41a.

16. Aleksandr Blok, "O sovremennom sostoianii russkogo simvolizma," *Apollon* 8(1910): 22.

17. For a detailed discussion of this aspect of the novel, see Maria Carlson, "*The Silver Dove*," in *Andrey Bely: Spirit of Symbolism*, ed. John Malmstad (Ithaca, N.Y.: Cornell University Press, 1987), 60–96.

18. H. P. Blavatsky, *Isis Unveiled*, vol. 1 (New York: J. W. Bouton 1877), 62.

19. Mrs. Annie Besant, *The Ancient Wisdom* (1897; Adyar: Theosophical Publishing House, 1977), 63.

20. Ibid., 65.

21. Ibid., 67.

22. Mrs. Annie Besant, *Man and His Bodies* (1896; Adyar: Theosophical Publishing House, 1975), 39.

23. Andrei Belyi, *Peterburg* (Moscow: Nauka, 1981), 298.

24. Belyi, *Peterburg*, 214.

25. Belyi, *Peterburg*, 99.

26. Nikolai Berdiaev, "Astral'nyi roman (Razmyshleniia po povodu romana A. Belogo *Peterburg*)," *Birzhevye vedomosti* 15652(1916); also in his *Krizis iskusstva* (Moscow: 1918) and *Tipy religioznoi mysli v Rossii*, vol. 3 of his *Sobranie sochinenii* (Paris: YMCA Press, 1989), 430–40.

27. S. A. Levitskii, *Ocherki po istorii russkoi filosofskoi i obshchestvennoi mysli*, vol. 2 (Frankfurt am Main: Possev, 1981), 35.

28. Nataliia Turgeneva, "Otvet N. A. Berdiaevu po povodu Antroposofii," *Put'* (Paris), 25(December 1930): 93–104.

Glossary _____

Theosophical Vocabulary

THE THEOSOPHISTS drew much of their occult vocabulary from exotic Eastern religions and were often creative in their definitions; Mme Blavatsky's definitions are particularly opaque and changed as she developed her doctrine. Nor did all Theosophists agreed on a single meaning for their terminology. Theosophical definitions should, in many cases, not be identified entirely with the meanings of the terms in the original languages and religious contexts.

This glossary provides Theosophical definitions of some of the more commonly encountered terms, mostly taken from Sanskrit. The reader is additionally referred to the following works: H. P. Blavatsky's *Theosophical Glossary*, ed. G. R. S. Mead (1892 and subsequent editions); *The Key to Theosophy* (1889 and subsequent editions), which contains a glossary with highly questionable definitions and etymologies; Rudolf Steiner's *Foundations of Esotericism* (London: Rudolf Steiner Press, 1982; English translation of lectures read in 1905), which contains a brief "Glossary of Indian Theosophical Terms," as well as outlines of the Theosophical cosmology; and *The New Steinerbooks Dictionary of the Paranormal* (New York: Steinerbooks, 1980).

Akasha — Mme Blavatsky defines this elementary principle as "the astral light," "the universal Soul, the Matrix of the Universe, the 'Mysterium Magnum' from which all that exists is born by separation or *differentiation*. It is the cause of existence; it fills all the infinite Space; *is Space itself*" (*The Secret Doctrine*, vol. 2 [London: The Theosophical Publishing Co., 1888], 511–12). All feelings, thoughts, actions, and events in world history are impressed into this fine etheric matter that surrounds the world. Those individuals who have achieved supersensible sight can "read" the entire history of the world (as a *tableau vivant*) in the *Akashic Record* preserved in the world ether.

Astral — The astral world, sphere, or plane is the second of seven levels of being. It surrounds and interpenetrates the lowest plane, the physical, but is invisible to ordinary sight because astral matter is finer than gross, physical matter. The astral plane is inhabited by *elementals* and by the recently deceased, whose physical body has dropped away but whose astral matter has not yet disintegrated.

The astral body is the double of the physical body (the human being wears physical, astral, and mental bodies simultaneously while in earth incarnation); it is the doppelgänger of the psychologists. It is the instrument of passion, desire, feeling, and carries the human aura. The "spiritual scientist" is able to project his astral body out of his physical body and move about the astral plane at will (which he does at his own risk).

Atma, Atman — The Universal Spirit; the Spirit Self; pure consciousness. The highest, and most divine, of the seven principles of man. Written with a capital

"A," it is identifiable with *Brahman*; with a small "a," it refers to the individual Ego, the "higher self" of the human being.

Aura — A psychic essence that emanates from bodies, invisible to most humans. The aura radiates certain colors that reveal the spiritual, mental, and physical state of the individual emanating it. Thus, a predominantly black aura indicates hatred and malice; blood-red indicates sensuality, while crimson reveals love; dull brown-grey is selfishness, and yellow is intellectuality. Dark blue is religious feeling, while lilac blue indicates spiritual idealism. Green is one of the more difficult colors to interpret, indicating adaptability in both positive and negative aspects. (See Leadbeater, *Man Visible and Invisible*.)

Avatar — Incarnation of a divine being in a physical body.

Brahman — The Soul of the Universe, from which everything emanates and into which everything returns; Brahman cannot be created, destroyed, or even cognized; it is without beginning and without end; it is the Divine Essence.

Brahman is not to be confused with *Brahma*, the Creator, who exists for the duration of the *Manvantara* and then is annihilated.

Buddhi — The Spiritual Soul; the Universal Mind; the sixth principle of man.

Causal Body — The "incarnating entity" of man that follows him through his multiple reincarnations; a vehicle for the ego without gender distinction, it is composed of "higher mental matter." Not a "body" at all, according to Mme Blavatsky, the Causal Body is really a merging of *Buddhi*, the Spiritual Soul, and *Manas*, the Mind, the Higher Ego. The causal body is the permanent carrier of the personality.

Chela — A student of the occult, a follower of a guru or *mahatma*.

Devachan — The mental plane, also called Spirit Land, or Dwelling of the Gods. It corresponds roughly to Christian Heaven. After death, the impersonal ego, separated from the lower, material bodies, spends its time between incarnations in Devachan.

Devas — Spiritual, celestial beings, they live on planes higher than the physical. Mme Blavatsky attributes their "resplendence" as stemming from the root *div, to shine*.

Dharma — The laws of religion; the cosmic principles according to which all things exist; the divine and cosmic order of things.

Dhyan-Chohans — "The Lords of Light"; they correspond to Christian Archangels. Perfected human beings from previous planetary incarnations, they supervise the development of the cosmos.

Ego — Ego is the consciousness of the "I AM." Theosophy defines two egos in every being: a mortal, personal ego that characterizes a particular individual incarnation (called the "personality"), and the divine, impersonal ego that ties together the sequence of incarnations (called the "individuality").

Elementals — The astral plane is inhabited not by people, but by all the thoughts, feelings, fears, desires, wishes, and impulses that human beings feel or think on the physical plane. On the astral plane they take on visible, concrete forms and become a living force. "While they maintain a separate existence they are living entities, with bodies of elemental essence and thoughts as the ensouling lives, and they are then called artificial elementals, or thought-forms," Mrs. Besant explains (*The Ancient Wisdom* [1897; Adyar: The Theosophical Publishing House, 1977] 67). Thus thought and action are the same in the astral world, as thought on the physical plane is transformed into deed on the astral plane. Elementals may resemble human beings, or they may take abstract forms of their own.

Astral matter, or elemental essence, has considerable fluidity. Thus elementals continually change shape as human thought-impulses massage the elemental essence. Elementals are potentially dangerous, since many of them "incorporate" negative thoughts and feelings (rage, hatred, envy, avarice, malice).

Ether — The substance that pervades the entire universe; ether is a higher form of matter.

Gupta Vidya — Secret science, occult knowledge.

Individuality — See *Ego*.

Kali Yuga — The "Dark Age," the fourth and present Age of the world and the one most characterized by destruction and war; it began in 3102 B.C. The Kali Yuga lasts a total of 432,000 years.

Kama — The quality of being astral; associated with the substance of thoughts and desires; hence *Kama rupa*, astral body, and *Kamaloka*, the semimaterial plane, sometimes identified with the astral plane.

Karma — The cosmic law of cause and effect, or ethical causation; Mme Blavatsky called it the "Law of Retribution." Each individual's life in a particular incarnation depends on the balance of his or her positive and negative actions in previous incarnations. Karma becomes a form of cosmic justice that explains why bad things happen to people, seemingly without reason.

Linga sharira — The etheric body, or "life" body. Made of finer matter than the physical body, but of coarser matter than the astral body. While the astral body can leave the physical body and roam at will, the separation of etheric from physical body will cause death.

Mahatma — A combination of "Mahat," *great*, and "Atman," *spirit*; meaning a "great soul," a sage or guru. Mme Blavatsky used the word to refer to her invisible guides, adepts of the highest order, far ahead of mankind's development and already living in their spiritual bodies. Guiding the development of humanity from afar, they formed the Brotherhood of the White Lodge (the Great White Brotherhood).

Manas — Mind; the intellectual, mental principle; the Higher Ego, or individuality.

Manvantara — One Cosmic Day; it alternates equally with *Pralaya* (Cosmic Night). Together, Manvantara and Pralaya constitute 8,640,000,000 years; seven Days and seven Nights constitute a Great Age, or Maha Yuga.

Maya — The illusion and deception of the world of physical matter, symbolized by Maya, the Spider which weaves the web of world illusion in order to trap the ignorant. Only the noumenal world of the spirit, eternal and unchanging, is real; the phenomenal world of differentiation and change is demonic delusion.

Metempsychosis — The notion, central to Buddhism, Hinduism, and Theosophy, that the immortal soul may incarnate repeatedly, passing from one mortal body to another in succession; reincarnation.

Nirvana — The extinction of existence in the body, escape from matter, breaking away from the tyranny of the wheel of reincarnation; the achievement of the state of absolute consciousness and at the same time absorption into Spirit. There are three states of nirvanic being (from lowest to highest): nirvana, paranirvana, and mahaparanirvana.

Personality — See *Ego*.

Plane — A plane can refer to an extension of a state of consciousness or a state of matter (thus being simultaneously a metaphysical and physical concept). There are seven planes (from lowest to highest): physical, astral, mental, intuitional, spiritual, monadic, and divine (see chapter 6). The planes interpenetrate each other and exist simultaneously on different levels of being, for they are made of various kinds of matter (from gross to ultrarefined).

Pralaya — Period of dissolution, or rest, between manvantaric rounds.

Prana — The general Principle of Life.

Raja Yoga — In Theosophy, a moral and virtuous life is not enough to awaken the spiritual faculty. Theosophy advocates the physical and spiritual exercises of Raja Yoga, an advanced Yoga system that, through highly developed physical and spiritual meditation exercises, allows for the development of a high level of consciousness. While these exercises entail a certain amount of psychic risk, Theosophy points out that only the most strenuous efforts will lead to true spiritual revelation.

Rupa — Having form; a body; cf. *arupa*, without form.

Tat Twam asi — "That thou art" or "That art thou," a Vedic formulation that reveals that the individual Ego and Brahman-Atman are One, i.e., a pantheistic formulation of man's identity with the cosmic divinity.

Bibliography

Theosophical and Related Works Published in Russia between 1881 and 1918

The Russian Theosophical Society published popular Theosophical brochures in numerous editions between 1907 and 1918. Each brochure appeared in a run of 700 to 1200; some went through as many as ten editions. These included:

Alba [Anna Kamenskaia]. *Chto takoe teosofiia.*

No. 1. [Charles Leadbeater]. *Chelovek i ego vidimyi i nevidimyi sostav.* Translated by E[lena] P[isareva]. Translation of *Man, Visible and Invisible* (1902).

No. 2. E[lena] P[isareva]. *Zakon prichin i posledstvii (Karma).*

No. 3. E[lena] P[isareva]. *Perevoploshchenie.*

No. 4. Annie Besant and Charles Leadbeater. *Sila mysli i mysle-obrazy.* Translated by E[lena] P[isareva]. Translation of *Thought-Forms* (1902).

No. 5. A[nnie] Besant. *Zakony vysshei zhizni.*

No. 6. Ch[arles] Leadbeater. *Zhizn' posle smerti po ucheniiu teosofii.*

Monographs and Articles

Abedananda, Suomi. *Kak sdelat'sia iogom.* St. Petersburg: Novyi chelovek, 1913.

Adams, Marsham. *Skrizhali uchitelia, ili Egipetskoe uchenie o svete, rozhdennom ot Materi-Devy.* Translated by V. Pushkina. *Vestnik teosofii* 1–12(1916).

Alba. See Kamenskaia, Anna.

Anatolii. "Teosofiia i nauka." *Vestnik teosofii* 11(1913): 67–74.

Antoshevskii, I. K. *Orden Martinistov.* St. Petersburg: Izd. *Izidy*, Tip. "Pechatnyi Trud," 1912.

Arnold, Edwin. *Svet Azii.* Translated by Ivan Sabashnikov. St. Petersburg: 1893; 2d abridged ed. 1903. Translation of *Light of Asia*; or *The Great Renunciation (Mahabhinishkramana), Being the Life and Teaching of Gautama, Prince of India and Founder of Buddhism* (Boston: Roberts, 1861); more than a hundred subsequent editions and translations.

———. *Svet Azii.* Translated by A. M. Fedorov. Commentaries by the Orientologist Professor Sergei Ol'denburg. St. Petersburg: "Svetocha," 1906.

[Arnold, Edwin]. "Tseilon i Buddisty." Translated by A. S. Petrunkevich. *Russkaia Mysl'* 8 (1887): 36–51. Excerpted from Edwin Arnold's *India Revisited.*

Arnol'd, G. *Tainy indiiskikh fakirov.* Trans. from German. Saratov: Izd. Nauchno-Psikhologicheskogo Knigoizdatel'stva, 1912.

Asvagosha. *Zhizn' Buddy.* Translated by Konstantin Bal'mont. Moscow: Sabashnikovy, 1913.

[Atkinson, William Walker] Iogi Ramacharaka. *Karma-ioga.* St. Petersburg: Novyi chelovek, 1914.

[Atkinson, William Walker] Iogi Ramacharaka. *Khatkha-ioga. Uchenie iogov o fizicheskom zdorov'i s mnogochislennymi uprazhneniiami.* Translated by V. Sing. St. Petersburg: 1909; also St. Petersburg: Novyi chelovek, 1914.

———. *Nauka o dykhanii indiiskikh iogov.* St. Petersburg: Novyi chelovek, 1914.

———. *Osnovy mirosozertsaniia indiiskikh iogov.* St. Petersburg: Novyi chelovek, 1913, 1914.

———. *Put' dostizheniia indiiskikh iogov.* St. Petersburg: Novyi chelovek, 1913.

———. *Radzha-ioga. Uchenie iogov o psikhicheskom mire cheloveka.* St. Petersburg: Novyi chelovek, 1914; 2d ed. Petrograd: 1915.

———. *Religiia i tainye ucheniia vostoka.* St. Petersburg: Novyi chelovek, 1914.

———. *Zhnani-ioga.* St. Petersburg: Novyi chelovek, 1914.

Barabash, E. "Teosofiia i teosofy." *Rebus* 41(1884): 375–77; 42: 383–85; 43: 393–95.

Barker, Elsa. *Pis'ma zhivogo usopshego.* Translated by E. P[isareva]. *Vestnik teosofii* 2–12(1915); 1–3(1916).

Barth, Auguste. *Religii Indii.* Translated and edited by Prince S. Trubestkoi. Moscow: Kushnerev, 1897. Translation of *Les Religions de l'Inde* (1879).

Batiushkov, Pavel Nikolaevich. "Blizhaishie zadachi teosoficheskogo obshchestva." *Vestnik teosofii* 2(1915): 10–12.

———. "Chto daet nam teosofiia." *Vestnik teosofii* 5/6(1911): 57–59.

———. "Dukhovnaia al'khimiia." *Vestnik teosofii* 12(1909): 4–8.

———. "Ezoterizm religii." *Vestnik teosofii* 12(1911): 23–27.

———. "Karma." In *Al'manakh "Grif."* 143–48. Moscow: Grif, 1904.

———. "Karma-ioga." *Vestnik teosofii* 10(1909): 19–22.

———. "Mirovoe proiavlenie po teosofskomu mirosozertsaniiu." *Vestnik teosofii* 9(1909): 9–13.

———. "Mistika i poeziia zvuka." *Vestnik teosofii* 10(1910): 46–52.

———. "Osnovy teosofskogo sinteza." *Vestnik teosofii* 3(1908): 52–53.

———. "Perevoploshchenie." *Vestnik teosofii* 11(1913): 36–40.

———. "Put' dukhovnogo soznaniia." *Vestnik teosofii* 5/6(1913): 51–55.

———. "Sinteticheskoe mirosozertsanie i monadologicheskoe miroponimanie. *Vestnik teosofii* 5/6(1908): 62–66.

———. "Teosoficheskoe miroponimanie." *Vestnik teosofii* 12(1908): 1–5.

———. "Karma." *Voprosy teosofii* 1(1907): 85–90. Petersburg: Gorodskaia tipografiia.

Belotsvetov, Nikolai. *Religiia tvorcheskoi voli.* Chertyre lektsii, chitannye v Russkom Antroposoficheskom Obshchestve: 1. Nad istinoi i zabluzhdeniem (problema teorii znaniia); 2. O postoiannoi tsennosti (problema etiki); 3. Golos mirov (problema religii); 4. Vozvrashchenie Zaratustry (religioznaia estetika budushchei kul'tury). Petrograd: F. F. Tum, 1915.

Belyi, Andrei. *Rudol'f Shteiner i Gete v mirovozzrenii sovremennosti.* Moscow: Dukhovnoe znanie, 1917.

Berdiaev, Nikolai. "Gnoseologicheskie razmyshleniia ob okkul'tizme." *Trudy i dni,* Book 8 (1916), 49–69.

———. *Smysl tvorchestva; opyt opravdaniia cheloveka.* Moscow: 1915. 2d ed. Paris: YMCA, 1985.

———. "Tipy religioznoi mysli v Rossii. Teosofiia i antroposofiia." *Russkaia mysl'* 11(1916): 1–34, 2d pagination.

Besant, Annie. *Avtobiografiia.* Translated by Alba [Anna Kamenskaia] and V. P[ushkina]. St. Petersburg: Izdanie *Vestnika teosofii,* 1912. Translation of *My Autobiography* (1893).

———. "Bratstvo i voina." Translated by E. P[isareva]. *Vestnik teosofii* 10(1915): 8–20.

———. *Bratstvo religii; vseobshchie osnovaniia religii i nravstvennosti.* Translated by E. Pisareva. St. Petersburg: Izdanie *Vestnika teosofii,* 1912. First published in *Teosoficheskoe obozrenie* 1–2(October–November 1907). Subsequently serialized in *Vestnik teosofii* 1–8(1911). Reissue authorized in Geneva [printed in Tallinn] in 1927. Translation of *Brotherhood of Religions* (1897).

———. "Chelovecheskaia volia i sud'ba." *Vestnik teosofii* 11(1908): 1–5.

———. *Chetyre velikie religii.* Translated by E. Dandre. *Vestnik teosofii* 2–12(1917). Translation of *Four Great Religions: Hinduism, Zoroastrianism, Buddhism, Christianity* (1897).

———. *Chaianie novogo veka* [Teosofiia]. Petrograd: Pervaia gosudarstvennaia tipografiia sovetskikh rabochikh i krasnoarmeiskikh deputatov, 1918.

———. "Chto chelovek poseet, to i pozhnet." Translated by A. K[amenskaia]. Geneva: Izd. *Vestnika,* 1925. Translation of no. 3 of *The Great Truths* series. *Teosofskaia zhizn'* (3[1907]: 36–43) has an unspecified translation by A. Bornio of "Karma, ili chto poseesh', to i pozhnesh.'"

———. *Dkharma.* Translated by N. V. Pshenetskaia. St. Petersburg: Izd. *Vestnika teosofii,* 1910. Originally serialized in *Vestnik teosofii* 1–3(1910). Translation of *Dxarma* (1899).

———. "Dogmatizm i mistitsizm v religii." *Vestnik teosofii* 9(1909): 1–8.

———. *Drevniaia mudrost'.* Translated by E. Pisareva. St. Petersburg: Izd. *Vestnika teosofii,* 1910; 2d ed. 1913. Serialized in *Vestnik teosofii* 1–12(1908); 1–3, 5–8, 11–12(1909). Reprinted in Paris in 1925. Translation of *The Ancient Wisdom* (1897). Circulated widely in French: *La Sagesse antique; le Christianisme au point de vue théosophique; l'Idéal théosophique* (Paris, 1899); or *La Sagesse antique, exposé sommaire d'enseignement théosophique* (Paris, 1905).

———. *Dzhordano Bruno.* Translated by A. K[amenskaia]. *Vestnik teosofii* 1–2, 4(1914). "Dzhordano." Separate ed. Petrograd: Izd. *Vestnika teosofii,* 1914.

———. *Evoliutsiia zhizni i formy.* Translated by S. V. Tatarinova. Petrograd: Izd. *Vestnika teosofii,* 1918.

———. *Ezotericheskoe khristianstvo, ili malye misterii.* Translated by E. F. Pisareva. *Vestnik teosofii* 1(1918): 11–26; 2(1918): 16–38. This major Theosophical text was not yet completed when *Vestnik teosofii* ceased publication. The complete text was published only in 1930 in Geneva, through Anna Kamenskaia's efforts. Translation of *Esoteric Christianity, or the Lesser Mysteries* (1901).

———. "Intuitsiia s tochki zreniia teosofii i filosofii." Translated by E. P[isareva]. *Vestnik teosofii* 12(1913): 1–13.

———. "Ioga." Translated by D. Stranden. *Vestnik teosofii* 2(1909): 1–31.

Besant, Annie. "Iskanie Boga." Translated by Alba [Anna Kamenskaia]. In *Voprosy teosofii*, vol. 1, 131–34. St. Petersburg: Gorodskaia tipografiia, 1907.

———. "Khristos." Translated by P. N. Batiushkov. *Voprosy teosofii*, vol. 1, 159–68. St. Petersburg: Gorodskaia tipografiia, 1907.

———. *Kommentarii k Bkhagavad-Gite*. Translated by E. P[isareva]. Petrograd: Izd. *Vestnika teosofii*, 1915. Serialized in *Vestnik teosofii* 11(1914); 1–4(1915).

———. "Kratkii ocherk Teosoficheskogo dvizheniia." *Vestnik teosofii* 1(1908): 16–34.

———. "Mistitsizm." Translated by A. V. *Vestnik teosofii* 12(1910): 39–44.

———. "Neobkhodimost' perevoploshcheniia." Translated by Alba [Anna Kamenskaia]. In *Voprosy teosofii*, vol. 1, 67–84. St. Petersburg: Gorodskaia tipografiia, 1907.

———. "O Karme." *Vestnik teosofii* 1–8(1911).

———. "O nastroeniiakh." Translated by E. Pisareva. *Vestnik teosofii* 10(1909).

———. "O nekotorykh zatrudneniiakh vo vnutrennoi zhizni." Translated by E. I. In *Voprosy teosofii*, vol. 1, 181–96. St. Petersburg: Gorodskaia tipografiia, 1907.

———. "O znachenii teosoficheskogo obshchestva." Translated by A. Bornio. *Vestnik teosofii* 5/6(1909).

———. *Obshchedostupnye lektsii po teosofii*. Prague: 1927. Originally 1910 typed ms.

———. *Osnovy religii i etiki*. Translated by V. Pushkina. *Vestnik teosofii* 1, 3–4, 9–11(1912).

———. "Osviashchennaia zhizn'." Translated by V. Molokina. *Vestnik teosofii* 5/6(1912): 68–74.

———. "Preddver'e (Ochishchenie)." Translated by Alba [Anna Kamenskaia]. In *Voprosy teosofii*, vol. 1, 169–80. St. Petersburg: Gorodskaia tipografiia, 1907.

———. "Problema stradaniia." Translated by M. R[obinovich]. *Vestnik teosofii* 4(1911): 53–65.

———. "Problema zla i stradaniia." Translated by M. Robinovich. *Vestnik teosofii* 11(1910): 24–41.

———. "Protivorechit' li teosofiia khristianstvu? (po A. Bezant)." Paraphrased by Alba [Anna Kamenskaia]. In *Voprosy teosofii*, vol. 1, 149–58. St. Petersburg: Gorodskaia tipografiia, 1907.

———. "Psikhizm i dukhovnost'." *Vestnik teosofii* 7/8(1908): 44–57.

———. *Put' k posviashcheniiu i sovershenstvovaniia cheloveka*. Translated by V. Pushkina. St. Petersburg: Izd. *Vestnika teosofii*, 1914, 1918. First serialized in *Vestnik teosofii* 1–6(1913). Also Boston: Alba, 1963 [reproduction of typewritten ms.].

———. *Put' uchenichestva*. S predisloviem Alba [Anna Kamenskaia]. Translated by N. Nikol'skii. St. Petersburg: Izd. *Vestnika teosofii*, 1911.

———. "Religiia i muzyka." Translated by A. Unkovskaia. *Vestnik teosofii* 9(1911): 46–58.

———. "Religioznye problemy: dogmatizm ili mistitsizm." Translated by Alba [Anna Kamenskaia]. *Vestnik teosofii* 7/8(1914): 4–15.

———. "Sfinks teosofii." *Vestnik teosofii* 9(1908): 1–14.

———. *Sila mysli.* Translated by N. T. *Vestnik teosofii* 5–12(1911); 1–2, 4(1912). Originally adapted and paraphrased by P. N. Batiushkov in *Voprosy teosofii*, vol. 1, 197–210. St. Petersburg: Gorodskaia tipografiia, 1907; also Boston: Alba, 1967. Translation of *Thought Power* (1901).

———. "Smert' za grobom." Translated by A. Bornio. *Vestnik teosofii* 9(1909): 46–54.

———. *Stroenie kosmosa.* Translated by S. Tatarinova. St. Petersburg: Izd. *Vestnik teosofii,* 1914. Originally in *Vestnik teosofii* 1–6(1914).

———. "Sverkhfizicheskie issledovaniia." Translated by A. L['vov]. *Vestnik teosofii* 11(1914): 81–94; 12(1914): 117–38. Reprinted Boston: Alba, 1961.

———. *Teosofiia i novaia psikhologiia.* Translated by E. Pisareva. St. Petersburg: Izd. *Vestnika teosofii,* 1908; 2d. ed. Petrograd: 1915. Originally in *Voprosy teosofii,* vol. 1, 28–66. St. Petersburg: Gorodskaia tipografiia, 1907. Also serialized as supplement in *Vestnik teosofii:* 1–2, 4–6(1908).

———. "Tsarstvo mira." Translated by I. Mantsiarli. *Vestnik teosofii* 7/8(1909): 1–6. Translation of "The Place of Peace."

———. "Uchenie serdtsa." Translated by N. Dmitrieva. *Vestnik teosofii* 10(1914): 7–17.

———. *V preddverii khrama.* Translated by Alba [Anna Kamenskaia]. Kaluga: Tip. Gubernskoi zemskoi upravy, 1910; 2d ed. St. Petersburg: Izd. *Vestnika teosofii,* 1913; 3d ed. 1918. Translation of *In the Outer Court* (1895); transcripts of five lectures: "Purification," "Thought Control," "The Building of Character," "Spiritual Alchemy," and "On the Threshold." French translation: *Vers le temple* (Paris, 1899; 1906; subsequent eds.).

———. *Zagadki zhizni i kak teosofiia otvechaet na nikh.* Translated by E. Pisareva. *Vestnik teosofii* 3–11(1915). Separate ed. Kaluga: Lotos, 191?.

———. *Zakovy vysshei zhizni.* Translated by M. A. Ertel'. *Vestnik teosofii* 3–6(1909). Issued as a popular pamphlet published by the Russian Theosophical Society in numerous editions and large quantities. Editions appeared in Russia as late as 1918. Reprinted Boston: Alba, 1967.

———. "Zhivet li chelovek posle smerti?" [Speech read in London in April 1905.] *Rebus* 20(May 14, 1906): 4–6.

Bettany, George T. *Velikie religii Vostoka.* Translated by L. B. Khavkina and edited by Professor A. Krasnov. Moscow: P. Sytin, 1899. Translation of *The Great Indian Religions* (1892).

Bezhan, S. *Psikhologiia buddizma.* Khar'kov: Eparkhial'naia tipografiia, 1913.

Bibikova, A. "Karmicheskie iavleniia v svete vysshego izmereniia." *Vestnik teosofii* 5/6(1916): 67–78.

Bibliografiia okkul'tizma. Edited by I. K. Antoshevskii. St. Petersburg: Izd. *Izidy,* 1910; 2d rev. ed. 1911.

Bibliotheca Buddhica; sobranie buddiiskikh tekstov. Monograph series of the Academy of Sciences in St. Petersburg. 1897–. Twenty volumes were published before 1917.

Bkhagavad Gita. Translated from Sanskrit by M. E. *Voprosy teosofii,* vol. 1, 224–32. St. Petersburg: Gorodskaia tipografiia, 1907.

Bkhagavad Gita, ili Pesn' Gospodnia. Translated by Anna Kamenskaia and I. V. Mantsiarli. Kaluga: Izd. *Vestnika teosofii,* 1914. The translation was made three years before, in 1910 (see *Vestnik* 12[1913]: 54); it ran in *Vestnik teosofii* 11(1909), 1–12(1910). Translated freely from French.

Bkhagavat Gita; misticheskaia chast' Magabgaraty. Verse translation by A. P. Kaznacheeva. Vladimir: Tip. V. A. Parkova, 1909.

Blavatskaia, E. P. "Est' li dusha u zhivotnykh?" Translated by A. Bornio. *Voprosy teosofii,* vol. 2, 181–207. St. Petersburg: Gorodskaia tipografiia, 1910.

———. *Evoliutsiia simvolizma.* Excerpts from *The Secret Doctrine.* Addendum to *Vestnik teosofii* 1–2, 4–12(1913), 1, 3, 5/6, 11(1914).

———. *Golos bezmolviia.* Translated by E. Pisareva. Kaluga: Lotos, 1908. Also in *Voprosy teosofii.* Vol. 1. St. Petersburg: Gorodskaia tipografiia, 1907. 211–223. Translation of *The Voice of the Silence* (1889). French trans.: *La Voix du silence* (1899).

———. *Isis Unveiled.* New York: J. W. Bouton, 1877. Although this was Mme Blavatsky's first major Theosophical text, it was never published in Russia. Parts of it circulated in manuscript translation. Most Russian Theosophists read both *Isis Unveiled* and *The Secret Doctrine* in French. The work existed in French translation as early as 1884 (see Vs. Solov'ev, *Sovremennaia zhritsa Izidy,* 64).

———. "Izlecheniia iz *Golosa Bezmolviia; sem' vrat, dva puti.* Translated and with notes by E. Pisareva. In *Voprosy teosofii,* vol. 2, 167–73. St. Petersburg: Gorodskaia tipografiia, 1907.

———. *The Key to Theosophy.* London: Theosophical Publishing Co., 1889. Like many of her other major texts, Mme Blavatsky's *Key* also remained long untranslated into Russian; nevertheless, Vl. Solov'ev reviewed it in 1890 (see Solov'ev). A French translation was available: *La Clef de la théosophie* (Paris, 1895). A German translation, edited by Rudolf Steiner, was printed in Leipzig in 1907.

———. "Kitaiskie teni." *Novoe Vremia* 1493(1888).

———. "Nauka o zhizni (L. N. Tolstoi)." Translated by D. Stranden. *Vestnik teosofii* 12(1910): 6–16.

———. *Ob okkul'tnoi i sovremennoi nauke.* Excerpts from *The Secret Doctrine.* Published as an addendum to *Vestnik teosofii* 1–12(1915); 2–7/8, 10(1916); 3/5(1917).

———. "Okkul'tizm i magicheskoe iskusstvo." Translated by E. P[isareva]. *Vestnik teosofii* 1(1912): 3–14.

———. "Peshchera Ozerkov." *Rebus* 1–3(January 5,12,19, 1886).

———. "Pis'mo" [To the *Times* of London, October 9, 1884]. *Rebus* 41(October 14, 1884): 380.

———. "Pis'mo" [letter to the editor]. *Rebus* 37 (September 22, 1885): 335–36.

———. "Prakticheskii okkul'tizm." Translated by R. T. In *Voprosy teosofii,* vol. 2, 174–80. St. Petersburg: 1910.

———. "Prolog ["Proem" from *The Secret Doctrine*]." Translated by E. P[isareva]. In *Voprosy teosofii,* Vol. 2, 122–45. St. Petersburg: 1910.

———. "Sem' stans 'Knigi Dzian.'" Translated by P. Batiushkov. In *Voprosy teosofii*, vol. 2, 146–56. St. Petersburg: 1910. The "Seven Stanzas from the Book of Dzyan" is the text on which *The Secret Doctrine* is based.

———. "Sokrovennoe znanie i tainye iskusstva." Translated by R. T. *Vestnik teosofii* 5/6(1910): 1–13.

———. *Tainaia doktrina*; izvlechenie iz otdela "Evoliutsiia simvolizma." Edited by A. Kamenskaia and E. P[isareva]. Part 1. Petrograd: Izd. *Vestnika teosofii*, 1915. Originally published in *Vestnik teosofii* as an addendum (see *Evoliutsiia simvolizma*; see also *Ob okkul'tnoi i sovremennoi nauke*). Translation of excerpts from *The Secret Doctrine: The Synthesis of Science, Religion, and Philosophy* (1888). French editions include *La Doctrine secrète, synthèse de la science, de la religion et de la philosophie*. Translated by D. -A. Courmes (Paris, 1899; 2d ed., 1906); *La Doctrine secrète*. Publications théosophique françaises (Paris, 1901); there were dozens of French eds. by 1910.

———. "Vvedenie k *Tainoi doktrine*." Translated by Alba [Anna Kamenskaia]. In *Voprosy teosofii*, vol. 2, 93–121. St. Petersburg: Gorodskaia tipografiia, 1910.

[Blavatskaia, E. P.]. "Golos s togo sveta." *Tifliiskii Vestnik* April; May 17; September 13, 16, 23, 29, 1878. Signed "Golos."

———. "G-zha Blavatskaia." [Editorial mention in] *Rebus* 16(April 22, 1884): 155–56.

[Blavatskaia, E. P.] Radda-Bai. *Iz peshcher i debrei Indostana; pis'ma na rodinu.* Addendum to *Russkii vestnik* 1–8(1883). Originally published in *Moskovskie Vedomosti* from November 30, 1879, through January 1882.

———. *Iz peshcher i debrei Indostana; pis'ma na rodinu.* 2d series. *Russkii vestnik* 11(1885), 2–3; 8(1886).

———. *Iz peshcher i debrei Indostana. Zagadochnye plemena na "Golubykh Gorakh." Durbar v Lagore.* St. Petersburg: V. I. Gubinskii, 1893. 2d ed. St. Petersburg: Suvorin, 1912. The second edition was published with numerous illustrations in the text and without Zhelikhovskaia's panegyrics, under the name "Blavatskaia," not the pseudonym "Radda-Bai."

———. *Zagadochnye plemena. Tri mesiatsa na "Golubykh Gorakh" Madrasa. Russkii vestnik* 12(1884); 1–4(1885) (okonchanie).

———. "Zakoldovannaia zhizn'." *Rebus* 24–29(1891). Also in *Voprosy teosofii*, vol. 2, 208–43. Translated by E. P[isareva]. St. Petersburg: 1910. Russian version of a literary attempt by H. P. B. during her last illness, when she amused herself by writing fantastic stories, posthumously gathered in the volume *Nightmare Tales* (1892).

Boehme, Jacob. *Aurora, ili utrenniaia zaria.* Translated by Aleksei Petrovskii. Moscow: Musaget, 1914.

Bogushevskii, L. L. "Spinoza kak teosof." *Teosoficheskoe obozrenie* 1(1907): 26–32.

Boianus, N. K. "Chto takoe teosofiia." [brochure] 1907? Printed in *Spiritualist* 1(January 1908): 14–19, as "Universal'naia religiia."

———. Review of *Voprosy teosofii*, Vol. 1. *Spiritualist* 1(1908): 43–44.

Boulanger, Pavel Aleksandrovich. *Zhizn' i uchenie Siddarty Gotamy, prozvannogo Buddoi, t.e. 'Sovershenneishim.'* S prilozheniem izvlecheniia iz buddiiskikh pisanii. Edited by Lev Tolstoi. Moscow: Posrednik, 1911.

Boutroux, Emile. *Nauka i religiia v sovremennoi filosofii.* Translated and edited by N. M. Solov'ev. Moscow: Tvorcheskaia mysl', 1910.

———. *Nauka i religiia v sovremennoi filosofii.* Translated by V. Bazarov. St. Petersburg: Shipovnik, 1910.

Buddiiskie Sutty. Translated by N. Gerasimov. Moscow: 1900.

Buddiiskii katekhizis. St. Petersburg: Mitiurnikov, 1902.

Bulgakov, S. V. "Teosofy (sovremennye)." In his *Nastol'naia kniga dlia sviashchenno-tserkovno-sluzhitelei.* Otdel istoriko-statisticheskii, 205–6. Khar'kov: Tipografiia gubernskogo pravleniia, 1900.

Chatterji, Mohini. *Sokrovennaia religioznaia filosofiia Indii.* Translated and with forward by E. P[isareva]. Kaluga: Lotos, 1906; 2d ed. Kaluga: 1908; 4th ed. 1915.

[Chistiakov, P. A. (?) and Bobrov, S. D. (?)]. "Ne-posviashchennyi." "Chto takoe teosofiia. (Pis'mo vo redaktsiiu)." *Rebus* 44/45(December 5, 1904): 9–10.

Clery, Leon. "Chto takoe teosofiia?" *Rebus* 1–4(January 7–28, 1901). Translation of "Qu'est-ce que la théosophie," from *La Revue bleu,* February 10, 1900.

Collins, Mabel. *Idilliia belogo lotosa.* Translated by M. Rodon. *Teosoficheskoe obozrenie* 4–5, 7–12(1908).

———. *Idilliia belogo lotosa.* Translated by E. P[isareva]. *Vestnik teosofii* 1–12(1915).

———. *Istoriia goda.* Translated and with foreword by E. P[isareva]. Kaluga: Lotos, 1909.

———. *Kogda solntse dvizhetsia na sever.* Translated by Mariia Depp. Moscow: Dukhovnoe znanie, 1914.

———. *Svet na puti.* Translated by P. Batiushkov. In *Svobodnaia sovest',* vol. 1, 140–52. Moscow: Sytin, 1906.

———. *Svet na puti; Iz drevnego indusskogo pisaniia Kniga zolotykh pravil.* Translated by E. P[isareva]. Published with her *Uchenie o Karme.* Separate edition with commentaries. Moscow: Posrednik, 1905.

———. *Svet na puti i Karma* (Otryvok iz *Knigi zolotykh pravil.* [Translated by E. Pisareva.] Commentaries by M. K[amenskaia]. St. Petersburg: Novyi chelovek, 1914.

Denis, Leon. *Posle smerti; nauchnye i moral'nye vyvody filosofii.* Translated from French by V. K. 3d ed. St. Petersburg: Gubinskii, 1910.

Deussen, Paul. *Vedanta i Platon v svete kantovoi filosofii.* Translated by Mikhail Sizov. Moscow: Musaget, 1911.

Dmitrevskii, Fr. Ioann. *Teosofiia—Religioznaia filosofiia nashego vremeni.* Khar'kov: Tip. Mirnyi trud, 1911. Reviewed in *Vestnik teosofii* 4(1913): 80.

DuPrel, Karl. *Filosofiia mistiki, ili dvoistvennost' chelovecheskogo sushchestva.* Translated by M. S. Aksenov. St. Petersburg: Kushnerev, 1895.

———. *Monisticheskoe uchenie o dushe. Posobie k resheniiu zagadki o cheloveke.* Translated from German by M. Aksenov. Moscow: Kushnerev, 1908.

———. *Zagadochnost' chelovecheskogo sushchestva. Vvedenie v izuchenie okkul'tnykh nauk.* Translated from German by M. Aksenov. 2d ed. Moscow: Kushnerev, 1904.

Dzhinaradzhadaza. *Vo imia Ego.* St. Petersburg: Izd. *Vestnika teosofii,* 1914.

Dzhonston, V. V. "Novyi perevod Upanishad." *Voprosy filosofii i psikhologii* 51(1900): Book 1, 21–42, 2d pagination.

———. "Ocherk Bkhagavad-gity." *Voprosy filosofii i psikhologii* 47(1899): Book 2, 173–213; 48(1899): Book 3, 359–82.

———. "Otryvki iz Upanishad." *Voprosy filosofii i psikhologii* (31)1896: Book 1, 1–34.

"E. P. Blavatskaia i teosofisty." *Rebus* 28–29(1884).

Eckhart, Meister. *Izbrannye propovedi.* Translated from German by M. V. Sabashnikova. Moscow: Dukhovnoe znanie, 1912.

Ellis. See Kobylinskii, Lev.

Fechner, Gustav. *Knizhka o zhizne posle smerti* (cover title), *Zhizn' posle smerti.* Petrograd: Suvorin, 1915.

"Fenomeny okkul'tnyoi sily g-zhi Blavatskoi." *Rebus* 50(1884).

Fielding-Hall, Harold. *Vnutrennii svet.* Translated by N. Dmitrieva. 1913? Translation of *The Inward Light* (1908), about Buddhism in Burma. 2d ed. St. Petersburg: B. M. Vol'ff, 1913.

Gerasimov, N. *Filosofiia dushi.* Moscow: 1897.

———. *Filosofiia soznaniia bytiia bezkonechnogo.* Moscow: 1898.

———. *Nirvana i spasenie.* Moscow: Levenson, 1914.

de Gernet, Nina K. "The Rosy Cross in Russia." *Theosophical Review* (London) 38(1906): 489–501; 39(1907): 9–20, 138–44, 201–11, 304–6.

Gladkov, B. I. *Besedy o pereselenii dush i snosheniiakh s zagrobnym mirom (Buddizm i spiritizm).* St. Petersburg: Tip. "Obshchestvennaia pol'za, 1911.

Hartmann, Franz. "Chto takoe teosofiia?" *Teosoficheskoe obozrenie* 1(1907): 18–25.

———. "Ob opastnostiakh okkul'tizma." Translated by N. B[oianus]. *Vestnik teosofii* 9(1909): 38–41.

———. *Obshchenie s mirom dukhov.* Translated by D. Stranden. *Vestnik teosofii* 9–10(1910). Separate ed. 1910.

Hübbe-Schleiden, Wilhelm. "Teosoficheskoe dvizhenie i ego protivniki." *Teosoficheskoe obozrenie* 2(1907): 82–88.

Iasinskii, T. "Lektsiia g-zhi Kamenskoi v Rige." *Rebus* 13(April 28, 1913): 4–6.

Il'in, Ivan. "Filosofiia kak dukhovnoe delanie." *Russkaia mysl'* 3(1915): 112–28, 2d pagination.

Ivanov, Ivan. *Rasskazy o starine. Budda i buddizm. Kul'turno-istoricheskii ocherk.* Moscow: D. Tikhomirov, 1907.

Izvestiia Rossiiskogo Teosoficheskogo Obshchestva. Edited and published by Ts. L. Gel'mbol'dt. St. Petersburg: 1914–1917 (1914, nos. 1–3; 1915, nos. 1–4; 1916, nos. 1–4; 1917, nos. 1–2).

Jacolliot, Louis. *Spiritizm v Indii. Fakiry ocharovateli.* Moscow: S. Rumilov, 1883.

James, William. *Mnogoobrazie religioznogo opyta.* Translated by Malakhieva-Mirovich i M. V. Shik. Edited by S. V. Lur'e. Moscow: Izd. *Russkoi mysli,* 1910. Translation of *Varieties of Religious Experience* (1902).

Johnston, Charles. "Religiia drevnego Egipta." Translated by O. Annenkova. *Teosoficheskoe obozrenie* 4(January 1908): 226–34.

Johnston, Vera. See Dzhonston, Vera.

"Kaled." "Chto takoe Teosofiia? (K dokladu Kamenskoi)." Originally published in *Peterburgskie Vedomosti*; reprinted in *Vestnik teosofii* 3(1913): 82–83.

[Kamenskaia, Anna Alekseevna] Kamenski, Dr. Anna. "La Bhagavad-Gîtâ; son rôle dans le mouvement religieux de l'Inde et son unité." Dissertation. Geneva: 1926.

[Kamenskaia, Anna Alekseevna] Alba. *Chto takoe Teosofiia*. Popular pamphlet published by the Russian Theosophical Society in numerous editions and large quantities.

———. "G. S. Ol'kott. Biograficheskii ocherk." *Vestnik teosofii* 9(1910): 4–10.

———. "Missiia krasoty v svete Teosofii." *Vestnik teosofii* 1(1914): 27–33.

———. "Missiia E. P. Blavatskoi." *Voprosy teosofii* 2: 53–59. St. Petersburg: 1910.

———. "Teosofiia i bogostroitel'stvo." *Vestnik teosofii* 2(1910): 62–79. See also "Stenograficheskii otchet zasedaniia Rel.-Filos. Obshchestva v Spb. 24 noiabria 1909 goda po dokladu Alba "Teosofiia i Bogostroitel'stvo." *Vestnik teosofii* 2(1910): 79–111.

———. "Teosofiia i ee veianie v Rossii." *Vestnik teosofii* 1(1911): 1–11.

———. "Teosofiia v Rossii" (Speech from November 21, 1908, Russian Theosophical Society meeting). *Vestnik teosofii* 1(1909): 4–11.

———. *Teosofiia i bogostroitel'stvo*. St. Petersburg: Izd. *Vestnika teosofii*, 1910. Text of lecture delivered to St. Petersburg Religious-Philosophical Society on November 24, 1909.

———. *Voprosy vospitaniia v sviazi s zadachami dukhovnoi kul'tury*. St. Petersburg: Izd. *Vestnika teosofii*, 1912.

———. 'Zadachi dukhovnoi kul'tury." *Vestnik teosofii* 4(1911): 8–14.

———. *Zadachi teosofii*. (1907?) Reprinted in *Rebus* 6(February 6, 1907): 5–8; 7(February 11, 1907): 7–11.

Kamenskaia, A[nna Alekseevna]. "Istinnyi okkul'tizm." *Vestnik teosofii* 11/12(1916): 95–101.

———. "Nevidimyi mir i okkul'tizm." *Vestnik Teosofii* 1(1916): 65–76.

———. "Religioznaia filosofiia drevnei Indii. *Vestnik teosofii* 12(1915): 58–67.

Kamenskaia, Anna Alekseevna. *Madame Annie Besant et la campagne electorale*. 1913. A defence of Mrs. Besant from the attacks of Eugène Lévy, representative of the Anthroposophical Society in Paris. Lévy was the author of *Annie Besant et la crise théosophique* (Paris: G. Dussardier et P. Frank, 1913).

K[amenskaia], A[nna Alekseevna]. "Theosophy in Russia." *Theosophic Messenger* (American) X:6 (March 1909): 234–35.

———. "Teosofiia v Germanii v kontse XVIII i v nachale XIX veka (rech' Doktora Shteinera na Teosoficheskom kongresse v Parizhe v 1906)." In *Trudy pervogo vserossiiskogo s"ezda spiritualistov*, 248–55. Moscow: 1907.

Kamenskaia, M. "Istoricheskii ocherk buddizma." *Vestnik teosofii* 7–11(1913).

Kariagin, K. M. *Sakiia-muni (Budda); ego zhizn' i filosofskaia deiatel'nost'*. St. Petersburg: 1897.

———. *Budda*. Orenburg: Bakt, 1913.

"Karma" [Indian legend]. *Rebus* 33/34, 35, 36/37, 39(1907). Reprinted from *Priroda i liudi*.

Kellet, A. *Okkul'tizm, ego sushchnost', razvitie, i otnoshenie k khristianstvu. Teosofskaia zhizn'* 1(September 1907)–1(September 1908).

Knizhnik-Vetrov, I. S. Review of *Bkhagavad-Gita, ili Pesn' Gospodnia*. Translated from English and Sanskrit by A. Kamenskaia and I. Mantsiarli. St. Petersburg: 1914. Reviewed in *Russkaia mysl'* 2(1915): 8–9, 3d pagination.

———. Review of Rudolf Steiner's *Das Christentum als mystische Tatsache* (1910). *Russkaia mysl'* 9 (1912): 326–27.

[Kobylinskii, Lev] Ellis. *Vigilemus!* Traktat. Moscow: Musaget, 1914.

Koni, A. F. "Misticheskie sluchai v zhizni V. S. Solov'eva." *Rebus* 2(January 11, 1909): 6. Paraphrase of article from *Moskovskii ezhenedel'nik* 49(1908).

Konissi, D. P. "'Tao-te-king' of Lao Si." *Voprosy filosofii i psikhologii* 18(1893), Book 3, 27–45; 23(1894), Book 3, 363–79.

Kozhevnikov, Vladimir. *Buddizm v sravnenii s khristianstvom*. Petrograd: Merkulev, 1916.

Kozitskii-Fidler, A. "Spiritizm i teosofiia." *Rebus* 1(January 6, 1902): 10–12.

Kratkaia entsiklopediia tainykh nauk. St. Petersburg: 1903.

Krishnamurti, Jiddu. *U nog uchitelia*. 2d rev. ed. Kaluga: Lotos, 1912.

———. *Vospitanie kak vid sluzheniia*. St. Petersburg: Gorodskaia tipografiia, [1913].

Kudriavtsev, K. D. *Chto takoe teosofiia i teosoficheskoe obshchestvo*. St. Petersburg: Gorodskaia tipografiia, 1912; 2d rev. and exp. ed. 1914.

———. "Intelligentsiia i narod." *Vestnik teosofii* 1(1909): 69–73. Report of St. Petersburg Religious-Philosophical Society Meeting.

———. "Magnetizm i gipnotizm, ikh skhodstvo i razlichie." St. Petersburg: Izd. *Vestnika teosofii*, 1911. Originally in *Vestnik teosofii* 1(1911): 64–80.

———. *Tselitel'naia zhiznennaia sila*. St. Petersburg: Izd. *Vestnika teosofii*, 1913.

Kuz'min, E. *Tsel' i put'*. I. *Zakon chistoty*. St. Petersburg: Izd. *Vestnika teosofii*, 1911. First in a series of popularizing texts of Theosophy. Originally published in *Vestnik teosofii* 3–4(1911).

———. *Tsel' i put'*. II. *Zakon svobody*. St. Petersburg: Izd. *Vestnika teosofii*, 1913. First published in *Vestnik teosofii* 3(1913): 33–46.

Lavrova, P. M. "Otrechenie E. Shure ot Teosoficheskogo Ob-va." *Rebus* 14(May 25, 1914): 3.

Leadbeater, Charles. "Aromat Egipta." Translated by K. Trunevoi. *Vestnik teosofii* 3(1916): 29–38.

———. *Astral'nyi plan*. Translated from French by A. V. Troianovskii. St. Petersburg: V. L. Bogushevskii, [1908]. Addendum: Bibliography of occult works. Translation of *The Astral Plane* (1895; German trans. 1896; French trans. 1899).

———. *Belaia i chernaia magiia*. In *Izida* 3ff.(1912); separate ed. St. Petersburg: Izd. *Izidy*, 1913.

———. *Iasnovidenie*. Translated by M. Staniukovich. St. Petersburg: Izd. *Vestnika teosofii*, 1914. Staniukovich's translation was originally printed in *Vestnik teosofii* 11(1912); 1–11(1913). Translation of *Clairvoyance* (1899).

———. *Kratkii ocherk Teosofii*. Translated by E. P[isareva]. Kaluga: Lotos, 1911. Translation of *An Outline of Theosophy* (1902; French trans. 1903).

Leadbeater, Charles. "Melkie trevogi." Translated by Essel'. *Vestnik teosofii* 9(1910): 36–41.

———. "Mental'noe telo." Translated by E. Rodzevich. *Vestnik teosofii* 9(1916): 83–88.

———. *Mental'nyi plan.* Translated by A. V. Troianovskii. St. Petersburg: Izd. Naumova, Tip. Pechatnyi trud, 1912.

———. *Nevidimye pomoshchniki* i *Nevidimyi mir.* Translated by E. P[isareva]. Kaluga: Lotos, 1909. Translation of *Invisible Helpers* (1899; German trans. 1897; French trans. 1902).

———. *Nevidimyi mir.* Translated by M. S. *Vestnik teosofii* 3(1909).

———. "Poiavlenie novoi pod-rasy." Translated by I. Matveeva. *Vestnik teosofii* 6/9–10/11(1917).

———. "Posle smerti." Translated by E. P[isareva]. *Vestnik teosofii* 1(1916): 77–85.

———. "Predvidenie budushchego." Translated by A. I. *Vestnik teosofii* 2(1916): 67–70.

———. "Razvitie okkul'tnykh sil." Translated by V. Laletin. *Vestnik teosofii* 5/6(1914): 47–50.

———. "Sfery." Translated by V. Laletin. *Vestnik teosofii* 2(1915): 85–89.

———. *Sny; teosoficheskoe issledovanie.* Translated from German by A. V. Bornio. Moscow: Tip. A. I. Mamontova, 1909.

———. "Tsentry mysli." *Vestnik teosofii* 2(1918): 39–43.

———. "Tsentry sily." Translated by V. Laletin. *Vestnik teosofii* 2–3(1912).

———. "Usloviia posle smerti." Translated by E. Rodzevich. *Vestnik teosofii* 3(1916): 57–60.

———. "Vysshie izmereniia." Translated by E. P[isareva]. *Vestnik teosofii* 11/12(1916): 146–49.

———. *Zhizn' posle smerto po ucheniiu teosofii.* Translated by E. F. Pisareva. Kaluga: Lotos, 1914.

Lebedev, P. *Budda i buddizm.* 2d ed. Moscow: Sytin, 1911.

Leman, Boris. *Sen-Marten* [Saint-Martin]. Moscow: Dukhovnoe znanie, 1917.

Lesevich, V. V. "Buddiiskii nravstvennyi tip." *Severnyi vestnik* 5(1886): 41–77.

———. "Noveishie dvizheniia v Buddizme." *Russkaia mysl'* 8(1887): 1–17, 2d pagination.

Lévi, Eliphas [Constant, Alphonse Louis]. *Uchenie i ritual vysshei magii.* Vol. 1. *Uchenie.* Biblioteka okkul'tnykh nauk. Translated by A. Aleksandrov. St. Petersburg: Mil'shtein, 1910.

Lodge, Sir Oliver. "Bessmertie dushi." *Teosoficheskoe obozrenie* 3(1907): 115–24.

Lodyzhenskii, M. V. *Misticheskaia trilogiia:* I. *Sverkhsoznanie i puti k ego dosti-zheniiu; indusskaia radzha-ioga i khristianskoe podvizhnichestvo.* St. Petersburg: Tip. Sel'skogo vestnika, 1911; 2d ed. 1912; 3d ed. 1915. II. *Svet nezrimyi (iz oblasti vysshei mistiki).* St. Petersburg: Tip. Sel'skogo vestnika, 1912; 2d ed. 1915. III. *Temnaia sila.* Petrograd: Tip. "Ekaterininskaia," 1914.

———. *Vragi khristianstva.* Petrograd: 1916.

Lomakin, I. S. *Mudrost' iogov i khristianskie idealy Evropy.* Moscow: Dziubenko, 1914.

Lukinskii, A. "Teosofiia i khristianstvo." *Rossiia* 1412(June 17, 1910).

Mariupol'skii, N. [Pseud. of I. G. Aivazov). "Pravoslavnyi arkhimandrit-uchreditel' 'Teosofskogo Obshchestva.'" *Kolokol*; politicheskaia, tserkovno-narodnaia i literaturnaia gazeta, May 31, 1908, 4 (in letter to editor).

Mead, G. R. S. "Po povodu Eleny Petrovny Blavatskoi." Translated by E. P[isareva]. *Voprosy teosofii* 2:76–89. St. Petersburg: 1910. Originally in *Theosophical Review* (April 1904).

———. "Real'nost' mistiki." Translated by E. P[isareva]. *Vestnik teosofii* 12(1912): 1–8.

Ménard, Louis. *Germes Trismegist*: Translated by A. K[amenskaia]. *Vestnik teosofii* 7–11(1911); 1(1912). Translation of *Hermès Trismégiste; traduction complète précédée d'une étude sur l'origine des livres hermétiques* [par Ménard]. Paris: 1866, 1867.

Metner, Emilii Karlovich. *Razmyshleniia o Gete.* [Razbor vzgliadov R. Shteinera v sviazi s voprosami krititsizma, simvolizma, i okkul'tizma.] Moscow: Musaget, 1914.

"Miatushchaiasia dusha. K sovremennomu teosoficheskomu dvizheniiu." *Moskovskie vedomosti* 114(May 20, 1910); 115(May 21, 1910).

Mintslova, Anna Rudol'fovna. "O teosoficheskom kongresse. Pis'mo iz Londona. *Iskusstvo* 5/7(1905): 152.

Morsier, Eduard. "Evoliutsiia okkul'tizma." Translated by O. Famintsyna. *Vestnik teosofii* 7/8(1913): 75–85.

Müller, Max Friedrich. *Shest' sistem indeiskoi filosofii.* Translated by N. Nikolaev. Moscow: 1901.

"N. N." "Teosofskoe uchenie (kratkii kriticheskii razbor ego)." *Khristianin* 4(1910): 767–98; 5(1910): 72–111.

"N. S." "Karma." *Rebus* 6(February 11, 1901): 59–60.

Nikolaev, Iurii. *V poiskakh za bozhestvom. Ocherki iz istorii gnostitsizma.* St. Petersburg: Suvorin, 1913.

Nirvana; Buddiiskoe skazanie. Translated by P. Bulanzhe. Moscow: Kushnerev, 1901.

Nirvana; iz oblasti buddiiskoi psikhologii. St. Petersburg: 1909.

Novoselov, Mikhail Aleksandrovich. *Zabytyi put' opytnogo bogopoznaniia v sviazi s voprosom o kharaktere pravoslavnoi missii.* Religiozno-filosofskaia biblioteka. Vol. 1. V.-Volochek: 1903.

"Obshchestvo Teosofov." *Rebus* 22(June 3, 1884): 208.

[Olcott, Colonel Henry S.]. "Katekhizis Buddizma." Translated by A. S. Petrunkevich. *Russkaia mysl'* 8(1887): 18–35, 2d pagination.

Olcott, Colonel Henry S. "Teosofiia, kak nauchnoe obosnovanie religii." Translated by Alba [Anna Kamenskaia]. *Vestnik teosofii* 10(1912): 17–28.

Oldenburg, Hermann. *Budda; ego zhizn, uchenie, i obshchina.* Translated by P. Nikolaev. 3d ed. Moscow: 1989.

Ol'denburg, Sergei Fedorovich. *Buddiiskie legendy i buddizm.* St. Petersburg: 1894, 1896, and subsequent eds.

———. *Buddiiskii sbornik "Girlianda Dzhatak" i zametki o zhatakakh.* St. Petersburg: Akademiia Nauk, 1892.

Osnovy Upanishad. Sbornik vyderzhek, aforizmov, tekstov iz Upanishad, sviashchennykh indusskikh knig. Translated by V. Sing. St. Petersburg: 1909.

"Otzyvy indusov o teosofakh." *Rebus* 28(July 17, 1905): 2–3.

Papus [Encausse, Gerard]. *Chelovek i vselennaia.* Moscow: Spiral', 1909.

————. *Pervonachal'nye svedeniia po okkul'tizmu.* Translated by A. V. Troianovskii. St. Petersburg: 1904; 3d ed. St. Petersburg: Trud, 1911.

————. *Prakticheskaia magiia.* Translated by A. V. Troianovskii. St. Petersburg: Luch, 1913.

Parker, John. *Sila vnutri nas.* St. Petersburg: Tainy zhizni, n.d.

Pascal, Théophile. "Bratstvo." *Vestnik teosofii* 1(1909): 12–24.

————. *Drevniaia mudrost' na protiazhenii vekov.* Translated by A. Gralevskaia. St. Petersburg: Izd. *Vestnika teosofii,* 1911. Originally in *Vestnik teosofii* 2–11(1910).

Pavlinova, N. "Orficheskie misterii." *Vestnik teosofii* 7/8(1913): 34–44.

Petrovo-Solovovo, Mikhail, Graf Perovskii. Review of Edmund Garrett's *Isis Very Much Unveiled; The Story of the Great Mahatma Hoax.* London: Westminster Gazette, 1894. *Rebus* 18(April 30, 1895): 181–83.

P[isareva], E[lena Fedorovna]. *Chelovek i ego vidimyi i nevidimyi sostav.* Popular pamphlet published by the Russian Theosophical Society in numerous editions and large quantities; based on C. W. Leadbeater's *Man Visible and Invisible* (1902).

————. "Elena Petrovna Blavatskaia." In *Voprosy teosofii,* vol. 2, 7–52. St. Petersburg: 1910. 2d ed. Geneva: 1937. Reprinted Boston: "Alba," 1966.

————. *Sila mysli i mysle-obrazy.* Popular pamphlet based on Annie Besant's and Charles Leadbeater's work *Thought-Forms* and published by the Russian theosophical Society in numerous editions and large quantities.

————. *Zakon prichin i posledstvii (Karma).* Popular pamphlet published by the Russian Theosophical Society in numerous editions and large quantities.

Pisareva, Elena Fedorovna. "Missiia E. P. Blavatskoi." *Vestnik teosofii* 1(1913): 15–28.

————. "O razvitii psikhicheskikh sil cheloveka." *Vestnik teosofii* 4(1914): 26–49.

————. *Perevoploshchenie.* Popular pamphlet published by the Russian Theosophical Society in numerous editions and large quantities.

————. "Tsennost' teosoficheskikh uchenii dlia chelovecheskoi zhizni." *Vestnik teosofii* 4(1916): 14–26.

[Pisareva, Elena Fedorovna]. *O skrytom smysle zhizni. Pis'ma teosofa k russkim chitateliam.* Kaluga: Lotos, 1913. 2d ed. Geneva: Izd. *Vestnika,* 1931.

P[isareva], E[lena Fedorovna], trans. *Svet na puti i Karma.* See Collins, Mabel. *Light on the Path.*

P[isareva], E[lena Fedorovna], and Alba [Anna Kamenskaia], comps. "O simvolizme po A. Bezant." In *Voprosy teosofii,* vol. 1, 135–48. St. Petersburg: Gorodskaia tipografiia, 1907.

Pisareva, Elena Fedorovna, and Anna Alekseevna Kamenskaia. *Zadachi Soiuza vospitaniia svobodnogo cheloveka.* Petrograd: 1918.

Pistis Sophia; gnosticheskii pamiatnik. Translated by A. Vinogradov. Moscow: Dukhovnoe znanie, ?. This book was advertised, but may never have appeared because of the events of 1917–1918; Lenin Library could find no indication of its publication, although publication had been announced.

Probably a translation of G. R. S. Mead's *Pistis Sophia; A Gnostic Gospel* (1896). Fragments of these Gnostic texts were accessible in circulating manuscript.

Pogosskaia, Aleksandra Loginovna. *Idealy truda kak osnova shchastlivoi zhizni.* Kaluga: Lotos, 1914.

Poiasnitel'nyi slovar' k teosoficheskoi literature. Moscow: Kushnerev, 1912.

du Prel: see DuPrel.

Pratimoksha-sutra; buddiiskii sluzhebnik. Translated by I. Minaev. *Zapiski Akademii Nauk* 16(1869), Addendum I.

Pushkina, V. N. *Skoro Spasitel' pridet.* Petrograd: Izd. Ordena Zvezdy na Vostoke, 1918.

————. *Uznaem li my ego?* Petrograd: Izd. Ordena Zvezdy na Vostoke, 1918.

Put' k istine. Izrecheniia buddiiskoi nravstvennoi mudrosti. Translated, with introduction by Gerasimov. Moscow: 1898.

Radda-Bai. See Blavatskaia, E. P.

Ramacharaka, Iogi. See Atkinson, William Walker.

Ramakrishna [Paramahamsa]. *Izbrannye pritchi Rama-Krishny.* Paraphrased by V. Altukhov i I. Sanin. *Rebus* 1(January 2, 1905): 6–7; 7(February 13, 1905): 8; 18/19(May 15, 1905): 10.

————. *Prozvestie Ramakrishny, s predisloviem i vvedeniem Suomi Abedanandy.* St. Petersburg: Gorodskaia tipografiia 1914. Translation of *The Sayings of Sri Ramakrishna,* comp. Swâmi Abhedânanda. New York: Vedânta Society, 1903.

Rebus. Ezhenedel'nyi zhurnal. From 51(1905): *Nezavisimyi organ russkikh spiritualistov;* from 1905: *Populiarno-nauchnyi zhurnal po voprosam spiritualizma, psikhizma i mediumizma;* from 1909: *Zhurnal psikhizma, mediumizma, i spiritualizma.* St. Petersburg: 1881–1903; edited and published by V. I. Pribytkov. Moscow: 1904–1917; edited and published by P. A. Chistiakov. V. I. Pribytkov edited the journal from no. 1 to no. 1125 (Dec. 21, 1903), when he retired because of ill health; P. A. Chistiakov assumed editorship in Moscow from no. 1126. 52 nos. annually until 1903; thereafter from 30–52 nos. annually. Jubilee No. 9/1000 (March 4, 1901).

Rees-Davies, Professor T. V. *Ocherk zhizni i ucheniia Gautamy Buddy.* Translated from the eighteenth English ed. by M. Giunsburg. 2d ed. St. Petersburg: Gubinskii, 1906.

Richet, Charles. *Opyt obshchei psikhologii.* Translated from French by N. Fedorov. St. Petersburg: 1895; 2d ed. St. Petersburg: 1903.

————. *Somnambulizm, demonizm i iady intellekta.* St. Petersburg: 1885.

Rozenbakh, Dr. Pavel Iakovlevich. *Sovremennyi mistitsizm.* St. Petersburg: Rikker, 1891. See especially "Teosoficheskii kul't," 32–38.

Ryshkovskii, N. I. *Individualizm i bessmertie.* Smolensk: Izd. "*Teosofskaia zhizn',*" 1910.

"S." "30-tiletie Teosoficheskogo Obshchestva." *Rebus* 43/44(1905): 4.

Sabashnikova, M. V. *Sviatoi Serafim.* Moscow: Dukhovnoe znanie, 1913.

Saint-Yves d'Alveydre, Joseph. "Gimn Luny" (poetic cycle). Rendered by A. V. Troianovskii. *Teosoficheskoe obozrenie* 4 (January 1908): 277–83.

————. *Kliuchi vostoka. Tainy rozhdeniia. Pol i liubov'. Tainy smerti. Soglasno ukazaniiam Vostochnoi Kabbaly.* Translated by M. A. Radynskii; edited by A. V. Troianovskii. St. Petersburg: Izd. *Izidy*, 1912.

Saint-Yves d'Alveydre, Joseph. *Missiia Indii v Evrope. Missiia Evropy v Azii.* Petrograd: Novyi chelovek, 1915.

Sbornik pamiati A. P. Filosofovoi; stat'i i materialy. 2 vols. Petrograd: M. O. Wol'f, 1915.

Schuré, Edouard. "Dionis i Persefona." Translated by E. P[isareva]. In *Voprosy teosofii*, vol. 1, 255–58. St. Petersburg: Gorodskaia tipografiia, 1908.

———. *Ocherki iz istorii religii. "Rama." Teosoficheskoe obozrenie* 4–6, 8/9(1908).

———. *Poety zar' i sumerek.* Translated by M. Staniukovich. *Vestnik teosofii* 1–2(1912).

———. *Velikie posviashchennye.* Translated by E. Pisareva. St. Petersburg: Izd. N. V. Pisareva, Gorodskaia tipografiia, 1910; 2d ed. Kaluga: Lotos, 1913. First appeared in *Vestnik teosofii* 2–12(1908); 3–8, 10–12(1909). Translation of his major work, *Les grands initiés* (Paris: Perrin, 1889); more than a hundred French editions alone; translated into all major languages.

———. *Zhritsa*: Antichnaia biblioteka (series). Translated by K. Zhikhareva. Moscow: Sfinks, 1911.

Scott-Elliot, W. *Istoriia Atlantidy.* Translated by N. Dmitrieva. *Vestnik teosofii* 9–12(1916).

Shcherbatskoi, Fedor Ippolitovich. *Teoriia poznaniia i logika po ucheniiu buddistov.* 3 vols. St. Petersburg: Gerol'd, 1903–1909.

Shtal'berg, V. I. *Bor'ba dukha s materieiu.* Smolensk: Izd. *"Teosofskaia zhizn',"* n.d. Orig. published in the journal *Teosofskaia zhizn'* 1(September 1907)–12((August 1908); 1(September 1908)–2/3(October/November 1908).

———. *Khristianskaia i indo-buddiiskaia teosofiia.* Smolensk: Izd. *"Teosofskaia zhizn',"* n.d.

Sinnett, Alfred Percy. *Okkul'tnyi mir.* Translated by A. *Vestnik teosofii* 12(1912): 9–11. Translation of *The Occult World* (1881).

[Sizov, Mikhail] Sedlov, M. *Tsezar' Lombroso i spiritizm. Istoricheskii i kriticheskii ocherk.* Moscow: Musaget, 1913.

Soiuz vospitaniia svobodnogo cheloveka. *Otchet deiatel'nosti za 1917/18 (pervyi) god.* Petrograd: 1918.

———. *Vekhi. Pervoe i vtoroe semiletiia rebenka.* Papers of the Pedagogical Circle of the Russian Theosophical Society, 1910–1915. Edited by M. F. Gardenina. Petrograd: 1918.

Solov'ev, Vladimir Sergeevich. "Blavatskaia, Elena Petrovna." In S. A. Vengerov, *Kritiko-biograficheskii slovar'*, vol. 2, 315–19. St. Petersburg: Semenovskaia tipografiia, 1892. Also in Solov'ev *Sobranie sochinenii*, ed. E. L. Radlov and S. M. Solov'ev, vol. 6, 2d ed., 394–98. (Title: "Zametka o E. P. Blavatskoi.")

———. "Retsenziia na knigu E. P. Blavatskoi *The Key to Theosophy.*" *Russkoe obozrenie* 8(1890). Also in *Sobranie sochinenii*, ed. by E. L. Radlov and S. M. Solov'ev, vol. 6, 2d ed., 287–92. St. Petersburg: Prosveshchenie, 1912.

———. "V. Solov'ev o teosofii." *Rebus* 1(January 11, 1915): 2–3. Reprint of

Solov'ev's review of *The Key to Theosophy*; his "Zametka o E. P. Blavatskoi" was begun in *Rebus* 4(January 25, 1915): 1–2, but never completed.

Solov'ev, Vsevolod Sergeevich. "Chto takoe 'doktrina teosoficheskogo obshchestva'." *Voprosy filosofii i psikhologii* 18(1893), Book 3, 41–68, 2d pagination.

———. "Interesnyi fenomen." Letter from Paris, June 10/22. Published in *Rebus*, 26(July 1, 1884): 243.

———. *Sovremennaia zhritsa Izidy. Russkii vestnik* 2–5, 9–12(1892), [*not* 1–6 as is usually given in bibliographies]. Separate ed. St. Petersburg: Obshchestvennaia Pol'za, 1893; numerous subsequent eds. English translation: *A Modern Priestess of Isis.* Translated by W. Leaf (member of the Society for Psychical Research). London: Longmans, Green & Co., 1895.

———. *Velikii Rozenkreitser. Okku'tyni roman.* St. Petersburg: 1890.

———. *Volkhvy. Okkul'tnyi roman.* St. Petersburg: 1889.

Sredi Rozenkreitserov. Prikliucheniia odnogo issledovatelia okkul'tizma. Rebus 40/41(November 21, 1904): 8–10; 46/48 (December 12, 1904): 13–15; 51/52 (December 26, 1904): 12–13; 1(January 2, 1905): 8–10; 2(January 9, 1905): 6–7; 3(January 16, 1905): 7–8; 4(January 23, 1905): 7–8; 5(January 30, 1905): 7–9; 6(February 6, 1905): 8–10; 8(February 20, 1905): 8; 10(March 6, 1905): 8–9; 11(March 13, 1905): 10–11; 13(March 27, 1905): 10–12; 14(April 3, 1905): 8–10; 15(April 10, 1905): 7–8; 16(April 17, 1905): 7–8; 17(May 8, 1905): 7–8.

Sri-Sankara-Acharya. *Atma-Bodkha, ili samopoznanie.* Khar'kov: Tip. Radomyshel'skogo, 1912.

———. *Tattva-Bodkha, ili poznanie bytiia.* Translated by N. A. Sheierman. Khar'kov: Tip. Radomyshel'skogo, 1913.

———. *Viveka Chudamani, ili sokrovishcha premudrosti.* Translated by N. A. Sheierman. Khar'kov: tip. Radomyshel'skogo, 1912.

Steiner, Rudolf. Brochure series published by "Dukhovnoe Znanie":

    I. *Teosofiia i sotsial'nyi vopros* (1917).

    II. *Filosofiia i teosofiia* (1917).

    III. *Sushchnost' iskusstva* (1917). Authorized trans. of stenograph of lecture read October 23, 1909.

    IV. *Otche nash* (1917). Authorized trans. by E. P. Mashkovtseva.

    V. *Rozhdestvo.* Razmyshlenie iz zhizni-mudrosti (Vitaesophia) (1918). Based on Christmas lecture, December 13, 1907. Authorized trans.

    VI. *Posviashchenie i misterii* (1918).

———. *Akasha-Khronika* (Istoriia proiskhozhdeniia mira i cheloveka). Translated by A. Bornio. Moscow: Moscovskaia tipografiia, 1912. Reviewed in *Vestnik teosofii* 9(1913). Translation of *Aus der Akasha-Chronik* (1904).

———. *Dukhovedenie; vvedenie v sverkhchuvstvennoe poznanie mira i naznachenie cheloveka.* Dornach: 1927.

———. *Evoliutsiia mira i cheloveka.* Lectures read in Paris in 1906. Paraphrased and edited by E. Pisareva. *Vestnik teosofii* 1–9(1911).

———. "*Faust* Gete (tolkovanie)." Translated by A. M[intslova]. In *Voprosy teosofii*, vol. 1, 233–54. St. Petersburg: Gorodskaia tipografiia, 1908.

Steiner, Rudolf. *Filosofiia svobody* was announced in 1918 by Dukhovnoe znanie, but was never published.

———. "Gekkel', mirovye zagadki, i Teosofiia." *Vestnik teosofii* 11(1908): 56–74.

———. *Istina i nauka*. Prolog k *Filosofii svobody*. Moscow: Dukhovnoe znanie, 1913. Authorized trans. by B. Grigorov. Translation of *Die Philosophie der Freiheit* (1894).

———. *Iz letopisi mira*. Authorized trans. of *Aus der Akasha-Chronik* (which appeared serially in *Luzifer-Gnosis* in 1904). Moscow: Dukhovnoe znanie, 1914.

———. *Kak dostich' poznaniia vysshikh (sverkhchuvstvennykh) mirov*. [1911?]. Translation of *Wie erlangt man Erkenntnisse der höheren Welten?* (1904).

———. *Kak dostigaetsia poznanie vysshikh mirov*. Translated by A. V. Bornio. *Teosofskaia zhizn'* 1(September 1907); 3–7(November 1907–March 1908); 12(August 1908); 1–12(September 1908–August 1909). Separate ed. Smolensk: Izd. "*Teosofskaia zhizn'*," n.d. Translation of *Wie erlangt man Erkenntnisse der höheren Welten?* (1904).

———. *Kak dostignut' poznaniia vysshikh mirov*. Translated by V. Laletin. Serialized in *Vestnik teosofii* 1–12(1908); 1–11(1909). Translation of *Wie erlangt man Erkenntnisse der höheren Welten?* (1904).

———. *Kak dostignut' poznaniia vysshikh mirov*. Authorized trans. Moscow: Dukhovnoe znanie, 1918. Contains Steiner's intro. to his rev. 5th ed. (1914). Translation of *Wie erlangt man Erkenntnisse der höheren Welten?* (1904).

———. *Khristianstvo kak misticheskii fakt i misterii drevnosti*. Translated by [Ol'ga Nikolaevna Annenkova]. 2d ed. Moscow: Dukhovnoe znanie, 1917. The 1st Russian ed. appeared under the title *Misterii drevnosti i khristianstvo* (see). Translation of *Das Christentum als mystische Tatsache und die Mysterien des Altertums* (1902; 2d ed. 1910).

———. "Kul'tura piatoi rasy." In *Voprosy teosofii*, vol. 1, 91–108. St. Petersburg: Gorodskaia tipografiia, 1908. Text of lecture read in Berlin in November 1906, prepared by Elena Pisareva.

———. *Misterii drevnosti i khristianstvo*. Moscow: Dukhovnoe znanie, 1913. Authorized trans. of 2d German ed., 1910 (*Das Christentum als mystische Tatsache*. 2d rev. and enl. ed. Leipzig: 1910). The 2d Russian ed. appeared under the title *Khristianstvo kak misticheskii fakt i misterii drevnosti* (see). Before this work appeared in Russian, it was known in the French translation of Edouard Schuré: *Le Mystère chrétien et les mystères antiques* (1908).

———. *Mistika na zare dukhovnoi zhizni novogo vremeni i ee otnosheniia k sovremennym mirovozzreniiam*. Moscow: Dukhovnoe znanie, 1917.

———. *Mistiki*. Translated by E. P[isareva]. *Vestnik teosofii* 3–10 (1910).

———. "O chelovecheskoi aure." Translated by E. P[isareva]. *Vestnik teosofii* 10–12(1911).

———. *Ocherki tainovedeniia*. Authorized trans. of 6th ed. Moscow: Dukhovnoe znanie, 1916.

———. *Ocherki teorii poznaniia getevskogo mirovozzreniia* was announced by Dukhovnoe znanie in 1918, but never published.

———. *Porog dukhovnogo mira*. Moscow: Dukhovnoe znanie, 1917.

————. *Put' k posviashcheniiu i kak dostignut' poznaniia vysshikh mirov.* Translated from German. Kaluga: Lotos, 1911.

————. *Put' k samopoznaniiu cheloveka. V vos'mi meditatsiiakh.* Authorized trans. Moscow: Dukhovnoe znanie, 1913.

————. *Sokrovennye znaniia.* Moscow: Dukhovnoe znanie, ?. Listed as in preparation in 1913, but could not verify. Translation of *Geheimwissenschaft im Umriss* (1909).

————. "Teosofiia i Graf L. N. Tolstoi." *Vestnik teosofii* 7/8(1908): 58–64.

————. *Teosofiia i nauka.* Translated by O. A[nnenkova]. *Vestnik teosofii* 1(1910): 21–28.

————. "Teosofiia i sotsial'nyi vopros." Translated by E. P[isareva]. *Vestnik teosofii* 3(1912): 7–14; 4(1912): 23–33.

————. *Theosofiia.* Translated by by A[nna] M[intslova]. St. Petersburg: Stasiulevich, 1910. Translation of *Theosophie; Einführung in Übersinnliche Welterkenntnis und Menschenbestimmung,* 2d German ed. (1908; orig. 1904).

Stranden, Dmitrii. *Germetizm. Ego proiskhozhdenie i osnovnye ucheniia. (Sokrovennaia filosofiia Egiptian).* St. Petersburg: A. Voronets, 1914. Reprinted Beograd: 1937.

————. *Teosofiia i ee kritiki. Otvet ottsu I. Dmitrevskomu, arkhim. Varlaamu i K. D. Kudriavtsevu.* St. Petersburg: Stasiulevich, 1913.

————. "Teosofiia i filosofiia." *Vestnik teosofii* 5/6(1912): 41–59.

S[trande]n, D[mitrii]. *Zabytaia storona khristianstva. Taina Khrista.* St. Petersburg: Kirshbaum, 1912.

Sutta-Nipata; buddiiskaia kanonicheskaia kniga. Translated by N. I. Gerasimov. Moscow: 1899.

Suvorin, A. A. [Aleksei Poroshin]. *Novyi chelovek.* St. Petersburg: Novyi chelovek, 1913.

Teosoficheskoe obozrenie. Ezhemesiachnyi zhurnal, posviashchennyi teosofii i teosoficheskomu dvizheniiu v Rossii i za-granitsei; with 1907, No. 3: *Put' k vsemirnomu bratstvu. Zhurnal, posviashchennyi bratstvu chelovechestva, teosofii, i izucheniiu etiki, filosofii, nauk i iskusstv.* Edited and published by V. L. Bogushevskii. St. Petersburg: 1907–1908 (1907, no. 1 [October]–no. 3 [December]; 1908, no. 4 [January]–no. 12 [September]). 918 pp. Superceded by *Mir,* a general journal with no occult content.

"Teosofiia i spiritizm." *Rebus* 7(February 16, 1886).

Teosofskaia zhizn'. Posviashcheno teosofskomu dvizheniiu i izucheniiu filosofii, nauk i religii. Organ Smolenskogo Teosofskogo Obshchestva. From 1909, no. 6/7: "Khristianskogo" instead of "Smolenskogo." Edited and published by V. I. Shtal'berg. Smolensk: 1907–1909 (1907, no. 1 [September]–no. 4 [December]; 1908, no. 5 [January]–no. 12 [August], no. 1 [September]–no. 2/3 [October/November]; 1908/1909, no. 4/5 [December/January]; 1909, no. 6/7 [February/March]–no. 12 [August]). Superceded by *Zhizn' dukha.*

Timofeevskii, P. I. *Ot smerti k bessmertiiu.* 1914.

————. *Voprosy vechnye i teosofiia.* St. Petersburg: Izd. *Vestnika teosofii,* 1914. Reprinted from *Vestnik teosofii* 5/6(1913): 11–33. Lecture read January 17, 1913, in the Russian Theosophical Society.

Tits, L. "Rol' Teosoficheskogo Obshchestva v perezhivaemuiu epokhu." *Vestnik teosofii* 12(1914): 31–39.

Tsiolkovskii, Konstantin. *Nirvana*. Kaluga: Lotos, 1914.

Tukholka, Sofiia Ivanovna. *Okkul'tizm i magiia*. 2d ed. St. Petersburg: Suvorin, 1907; 4th ed. 1917.

Turaev, B. *Bog Tot*. Leipzig: 1989. A study of Hermes Trismegistus.

Unkovskaia, Aleksandra Vasil'evna. "Metoda tsveto-zvuko-chisel." *Vestnik teosofii* 1, 3(1909).

———. "Pis'ma o muzyke." *Vestnik teosofii* 9–12(1912); 7, 10, 12(1913); 5/ 6(1914).

Uspenskii, Petr Demianovich. *Chetvertoe izmerenie. Opyt issledovaniia oblasti neizmerimogo*. St. Petersburg: Trud, 1910. *Chetvertoe izmerenie. Obzor glavneishikh teorii i popytok issledovaniia oblasti neizmerimogo*. 2d rev. ed. St. Petersburg: Trud, [1913] 1914. Originally published in *Vestnik teosofii*: 7–12(1909). Book ed. has additional chapter on the Theosophical worldview.

———. *Iskaniia novoi zhizni. Chto takoe ioga*. St. Petersburg: Gerol'd, 1913. 2d ed. Petrograd: Novyi chelovek (Suvorin), 1915.

———. *Kinemodrama (Ne dlia kinematografa); okkul'tnaia povest'*. Petrograd: Brianchaninov, 1917.

———. "Mir kazhushchii i mir real'nyi." *Biulleteni literatury i zhizni* (Moscow), 7/8(1915/1916): 335–49. Three chapters from *Tertium Organum*.

———. *Razgovory s diavolom. Okkul'tnye rasskazy*. Petrograd: Brianchaninov, 1916.

———. *Simvoly Taro. Filosofiia okkul'tizma v risunkakh i chislakh (Ocherk iz knigi Mudrosti bogov)*. St. Petersburg: Gorodskaia tipografiia, 1912. Originally in *Vestnik teosofii* 3(1912): 40–84. English trans. by A. L. Pogossky: *The Symbolism of the Tarot: Philosophy of Occultism in Pictures and Numbers* (with pen drawings of the twenty-two Tarot cards). St. Petersburg: Trud, 1913.

———. *Tertium Organum. Kliuch k zagadkam mira*. St. Petersburg: Trud, 1911. 2d. rev. and exp. ed. Petrograd: N. I. Taberio (Trud), 1914; 3d ed. 1916.

———. *Vnutrennii krug*. St. Petersburg: Trud, [1912] 1913.

Varlaam, Arkhimandrit. *Teosofiia pered sudom khristianstva*. Poltava: G. E. Markevich, 1912.

Vasil'ev, Vasilii Pavlovich. *Buddizm; ego dogmaty, istoriia i literatura*. Parts 1 and 3 (no others published). St. Petersburg: 1857, 1869.

———. *Religii vostoka: Konfutsianstvo, Buddizm, i Daosizm*. St. Petersburg: 1873.

Vedy. Vosem' gimnov Rig-Vedy. Translated by A. Krushevskii. Kazan': 1879.

Vengerova, Zinaida. "Blavatskaia, Elena Petrovna." In *Kritiko-biograficheskii slovar'*, ed. S. A. Vengerov, vol. 3, 301–15. St. Petersburg: Semenovskaia tipografiia, 1892.

Vestnik teosofii. Religiozno-filosofsko-nauchnyi zhurnal. Edited and published by Anna Kamenskaia; from 1912, published by Kamenskaia and Ts. L. Gel'mbol'dt. Seven hundred copies published in 1911. St. Petersburg: 1908–

1918 (1908–1916, nos. 1–12; 1917, Nos. 1–2, 3/5, 6/9, 10/12; 1918, Nos. 1–2). Publication ceased in 1918.

Vivekananda, Suomi. *Bkhakti-ioga*. Translated by Ia. K. Popov. St. Petersburg: Tip. A. Leont'eva, 1914.

———. *Dzhnana-ioga*. Translation of 2d ed. by Ia. K. Popov. St. Petersburg: Leont'ev, 1914.

———. *Filosofiia ioga. Lektsii o Radzha-Ioge, chitannye v Niu-Iorke zimoiu 1895-1896 g. Suomi Vivekananda o Radzha-Ioga ili podchinenii vnutrennei prirody*. Translated by Ia. K. Popov. Sosnitsa: 1906; 2d ed. Sosnitsa: Tip. Uezdnogo zemstva, 1911.

———. *Karma Ioga*. Translated by Ia. K. Popov. St. Petersburg: Leont'ev, 1914.

Voloshin, Maks. "Anni Bezant i 'russkaia shkola.'" (Pis'mo iz Parizha.) *Rus'* 186(August 12, 1905): 3.

Voprosy teosofii. Sbornik statei. Vol. 1. St. Petersburg: Gorodskaia tipografiia, 1907, 1908. Reviewed by N. Boianus in *Spiritualist* 1(1908): 43–44.

Voprosy teosofii. Sbornik statei. V pamiati Eleny Petrovny Blavatskoi. Vol. 2. St. Petersburg: Gorodskaia tipografiia, 1910. The second volume of *Voprosy teosofii* was reissued in 1911 as *Elena Petrovna Blavatskaia, ee biografiia, otzyvy o nei uchenikov, i obraztsy ee sochinenii, vyshedshikh v Anglii*.

Vvedenskii, A. I. "Buddiiskaia nirvana." *Russkii vestnik* 7(1901): 133–47; 8(1901): 421–34.

———. "Buddiiskii 'put' k spaseniiu.'" *Russkii vestnik* 11(1911): 123–35; 12(1911): 543–60.

Ward, Edith. "Teosofiia i nauka." Translated by D. S[tranden]. In *Voprosy teosofii*, vol. 1, 109–30. St. Petersburg: Gorodskaia tipografiia, 1908.

Wood, Michael. *Iz letopisi chelovecheskoi dushi*. Translated by E. P[isareva]. Kaluga: Lotos, 1913.

———. "Mat' vsekh skazanii." Translated by E. P[isareva]. *Vestnik teosofii* 2(1913): 41–50.

Woodhouse, E. A. *Mir v ozhidanii*. Petrograd: Izd. Ordena Zvezdy Vostoka, 1917.

[Zhelikhovskaia, Vera Petrovna]. *E. P. Blavatskaia i sovremennyi zhrets istiny* (*otvet gospozhy Igrek g. Vsev. Solov'evu*). St. Petersburg: 1893. Zhelikhovskaia published her response to Vs. Solov'ev's negative article as a separate brochure at her own expense because *Russkii vestnik* refused it.

Zhelikhovskaia, Vera Petrovna. "E. P. Blavatskaia i teosofisty." *Odesskii vestnik* 123(June 5, 1884): 1–3. Reprinted in *Rebus* 28(July 15, 1884): 263–65, 29(July 22, 1884): 274–75.

———. "Elena Petrovna Blavatskaia (biograficheskii ocherk)." *Russkoe obozrenie* 11(1891): 242–94; 12(1891): 567–621.

———. *Neob"iasnimoe ili neob"iasnennoe iz lichnykh i semeinykh vospominanii*. St. Petersburg: Izd. *Rebusa*, 1885. Materials originally published in *Rebus* 43–48(October 28–December 2, 1884) as "Pravda o E. P. Blavatskoi" and in 4(January 27,1885), as "Neob"iasnimoe i neob"iasnennoe."

———. "Pis'ma iz-za granitsy." Series written for *Novorossiiskii telegraf* (Odessa newspaper) in May and June 1884.

Zhelikhovskaia, Vera Petrovna. "V oblasti okkul'tizma i magnetizma." *Odesskii vestnik* 166(July 26, 1884): 1–3; 172(August 2, 1884): 1–3; 181(August 14, 1884): 1–2; 184(August 18, 1884): 1–2. Abridged in *Rebus* as "Fenomeny okkul'ticheskoi sily g-zhy Blavatskoi," 50(December 16, 1884): 465–67.

[Zhelikhovskaia, Vera Petrovna] I. Ia. "Pravda o E. P. Blavatskoi." *Rebus* 40(October 16, 1883), 41, 43–44; 46–48(October 23–December 11, 1883).

Zhelikhovskaia, Vera Vladimirovna. "Iasnovidenie i psikhometriia." *Novosti* [newspaper] 348–50(1890). First published in *Rebus* 3(January 19, 1886).

Zhizn' dukha. Spiritualisticheskii religiozno-filosofskii zhurnal. On cover: *Teosofiia. Okkul'tizm. Religiia. Nauki.* Supercedes *Teosofskaia zhizn'.* Edited and published by V. I. Shtal'berg. Smolensk: 1910 (1910, no. 1 [January]–no. 11/12 [November–December]).

Selected Bibliography

This bibliography does not pretend to be complete. It lists only secondary sources that I found particularly helpful in reaching an understanding of the topic under discussion.

Agni Yoga series. [Vols. 1–2] *Leaves of Morya's Garden* ("The Call" and "Illumination"), by N. K. Roerich 1923; 1924–26 [1952–53]; [Vol. 3] *Community* 1926 [1951]; [Vol. 4] *Agni Yoga* 1929 [1954]; [Vol. 5] *Infinity*, pt. 1, 1930 [1956]; [Vol. 6] *Infinity*, pt. 2, 1930 [1957]; [Vol. 7] *Hierarchy* 1931 [1944]; [Vol. 8] *Heart* 1932 [1934]; [Vol. 9] *Fiery World*, pt. 1, 1933; [Vols. 10–11] *Fiery World*, pts. 3 and 4, 1934–35 [1946–48]; [Vol. 12] *Aum* 1936 [1959]; [Vol. 13] *Brotherhood* 1937 [1962]. New York: Agni Yoga Society.

Ahern, Geoffrey. *Sun at Midnight; The Rudolf Steiner Movement and the Western Esoteric Tradition*. Wellingborough, G.B.: Aquarian, 1984.

Allen, Paul M. *Vladimir Soloviev, Russian Mystic*. Blauvelt, N.Y.: 1978.

Andrej Belyj und Rudolf Steiner; Briefe und Dokumente. Beiträge zur Rudolf Steiner Gesamtausgabe, Nr. 89/90. Edited by Walter Kugler and Victor B. Fedjuschin. Dornach: 1985.

Aseev, Aleksandr. "Okkul'tnoe dvizhenie v Sovetskoi Rossii." *Okkul'tizm i ioga*. Book 3 (1934): 90–98.

Barborka, Geoffrey A. *H. P. Blavatsky, Tibet and Tulku*. Adyar, Madras: Theosophical Publishing House, 1974.

Belyi, Andrei. "Die Anthroposophie und Russland," *Die Drei* (Stuttgart) 4–5(1923). Separate English ed.: *Anthroposophy and Russia*. Translated by Linda Maloney. Spring Valley, N.Y.: St. George, 1983.

———. "Antroposofiia i Doktor Gans Lezegang." *Beseda* (Berlin) 2(1923): 378–92.

———. "Iz vospominanii." *Beseda* (Berlin) 2(1923): 83–127.

———. *Mezhdu dvukh revoliutsii*. Leningrad: Isdatel'stvo pisatelei, 1934.

———. "Nachalo veka." 1928–30. Unpublished ms. Manuscript Division, Saltykov-Shchedrin Library, Leningrad. Fond 60; item 13; 128 fols.

———. "Material k biografii (intimnyi)." 1923. Unpublished ms. Central State Archive for Literature and Art, Moscow. Fond 53, k. 2; item 3; 164 fols.

———. *Vospominaniia o Bloke*. Monograph publ. in *Epopeia*, vols. 1–4. Moscow and Berlin: 1922–1923. Reprinted as *Vospominaniia ob A. A. Bloke*. Munich: Fink Verlag, 1969.

———. *Vospominaniia o Shteinere*. Edited and annotated by Frédéric Kozlic. Paris: La Presse Libre, 1982.

Berberova, Nina N. *Liudi i lozhi; russkie masony xx stoletiia*. New York: Russica, 1986.

Berdiaev, Nikolai. "Dva pis'ma N. A. Berdiaeva Andreiu Belomu." Published by L. Murav'ev, with afterword by F. Stepun. *Mosty* 11(1965): 358–68.

Berdiaev, Nikolai. *Filosofiia svobodnogo dukha.* 2 vols. Paris: 1927. See esp. section on Theosophy. Translation: *Freedom and the Spirit.* New York: Scribner's, 1935.

———. *Samopoznanie.* 2d rev. ed. Paris: YMCA, 1983. See especially chaps. 6–8 for an account of the Russian occult revival of the Silver Age.

———. *Symsl tvorchestva.* Moscow: 1915. 2d ed. Paris: YMCA, 1985. See especially chap. 13: "Tvorchestvo i mistika. Okkul'tizm i magiia" (332–54).

———. "Spor ob Antroposofii (Otvet N. Turgenevoi)." *Put'* (Paris), 25(December 1930): 105–14.

Berry, Thomas. *Spiritualism in Tsarist Society and Literature.* Baltimore: Edgar Allan Poe Society, 1985.

Bland, Rosamund. *Extracts from Nine Letters Written . . . at the Beginning of P. D. Ouspensky's London Work in 1921.* Cape Town: Stourton, 1952.

Blavatsky, H. P. *H. P. B. Speaks.* 2 vols. Adyar, Madras: Theosophical Publishing House, 1951.

Bowlt, John. "Esoteric Culture and Russian Society." In *The Spiritual in Art: Abstract Painting 1890–1985,* ed. Edward Weisberger, 165–84 [Exhibition Catalog, Los Angeles County Museum of Art]. New York: Abbeville, 1986.

Bragdon, Claude. *Merely Players.* New York: Knopf, 1905, 1928. Freeport, N.Y.: Books for Libraries Press, 1972.

Britten, E. H. *Nineteenth Century Miracles; or Spirits and Their Work in Every Country of the Earth.* New York: Lovell, 1884.

Bugaeva, Klavdiia Nikolaevna. *Vospominaniia o Belom.* Edited and annotated by John Malmstad. Berkeley: Berkeley Slavic Specialties, 1981.

Bulgakov, Sergei. *The Orthodox Church.* Rev. trans. New York: St. Vladimir's, 1988.

Butkovsky-Hewitt, Anna. *Gurdjieff in St. Petersburg and Paris.* London: Routledge and Kegan Paul, 1978.

Campbell, Bruce F. *Ancient Wisdom Revived. A History of the Theosophical Movement.* Berkeley: University of California Press, 1980.

Carlson, Maria. "Ivanov-Belyj-Minclova: The Mystical Triangle." In *Cultura e Memoria. Atti del terzo Simposio Internazionale dedicato a Vjaceslav Ivanov.* I. Testi in italiano, francese, inglese, ed. Fausto Malcovati, 63–79. Firenze: 1988.

Christa, Boris. "Andrey Bely's Connections with European Occultism." In *Russian and Slavic Literature,* ed. Freeborn, Milner-Gulland, and Ward, 213–23. Selected papers in the humanities from the Banff 1974 International Conference. Ann Arbor: Slavica, 1976.

Christian, Paul. *The History and Practice of Magic.* Translated by James Kirkup and Julian Shaw. Secaucus, N.J.: Citadel, [1972]. Translation of *Histoire de la magie du monde surnaturel et de la fatalité à travers les temps et les peuples.* Paris: 1870.

Conan Doyle, Arthur. *History of Spiritualism.* 2 vols. London: 1924.

[Constant, Alphonse Louis] Lévi, Eliphas. *The History of Magic.* 1860. Translated by A. E. Waite. London: 1913. Reprinted New York: Weiser, 1969.

Cooper, Martin. "Scriabin's Mystical Beliefs." *Music and Letters* 16(1935): 110–15.

Decter, Jacqueline. *Nicholas Roerich; The Life and Art of a Russian Master*. Rochester, Vt.: Park Street Press, 1989.

Douglas, Charlotte. "Beyond Reason: Malevich, Matiushin, and Their Circles." In *The Spiritual in Art: Abstract Painting 1890-1985*, ed. Edward Weisberger, 185–200 [Exhibition Catalog, Los Angeles County Museum of Art]. New York: Abbeville, 1986.

The Theosophical Movement 1875–1950. Rev. ed. Los Angeles: Cunningham Press, 1951.

Eliade, Mircea. *The Sacred and the Profane*. Translated by W. R. Trask. New York: Harcourt, Brace, and World, 1959.

Ellis [Kobylinskii, Lev]. *Russkie simvolisty*. Moscow: Musaget, 1910.

[Encausse, Gerrard] Papus. *Les Doctrines théosophiques*; les sept principes de l'homme au point de vue scientifique. Paris: Conférence de la Société théosofique "Hermes," 1889.

Encyclopedia of Occultism and Parapsychology. Edited by Leslie A. Shepard. 2 vols. New York: Avon/Gale, 1978.

Fedjuschin, Victor B. *Russlands Sehnsucht nach Spiritualität*. Theosophie, Anthroposophie, Rudolf Steiner und die Russen; eine geistige Wanderschaft. Schaffhausen, Switzerland: Novalis Verlag, 1988.

Florovskii, Georgii. *Puti russkogo bogosloviia*. 2d ed. Paris: YMCA, 1981. Originally Paris: 1937.

Fodor, Nandor. *An Encyclopedia of Psychic Science*. 1934. Reprinted Secaucus, N.J.: Citadel Press, 1966.

A Further Record Chiefly of Extracts from Meetings Held by P. D. Ouspensky Between 1928 and 1945. Cape Town: Stourton Press, 1952.

Garrett, Edmund. *Isis Very Much Unveiled; The Story of the Great Mahatma Hoax*. London: Westminster Gazette, 1894.

Gertsyk, Evgeniia. *Vospominaniia*. Paris: YMCA, 1973.

Gol'denberg, V. *Antroposofskoe dvizhenie i ego prorok*. Vseobshchaia biblioteka, 45/46. Berlin: Russkoe universal'noe izdatel'stvo, 1923.

Gomes, Michael. *The Dawning of the Theosophical Movement*. Wheaton, Ill.: Theosophical Publishing House, 1987.

Grigorenko, A. Iu. *Raznolikaia magiia*. Moscow: Sovetskaia Rossiia, 1987.

Hanson, Virginia, ed. *H. P. Blavatsky and The Secret Doctrine; Commentaries on her Contribution to World Thought*. Wheaton, Ill.: Theosophical Publishing House, 1971.

Hemleben, Johannes. *Rudolf Steiner; A Documentary Biography*. East Grinstead, Sussex: Henry Goulden, 1975.

Howell, B. P., ed. *The Theosophical Society. The First Fifty Years*. London: Theosophical Publishing House, 1925.

Huxley, Aldous. *The Perennial Philosophy*. New York and London: Harpers, 1945.

Inge, William. *Christian Mysticism*. London: 1899; London: Methuen, 1948.

James, William. *The Varieties of Religious Experience*. 1902. Reprinted New York: Penguin, 1982.

Theosophical Society. *The Golden Book of the Theosophical Society 1875–1925*. Edited by C. Jinarajadasa. London: Theosophical Publishing House, 1925.

Jonas, Hans. *The Gnostic Religion. The Message of the Alien God and the Beginnings of Christianity.* 2d rev. ed. Boston: Beacon, 1963.

Jullian, Philippe. *Dreamers of Decadence; Symbolist Painters of the 1890s.* Translated by Robert Baldick. New York: Praeger, 1971.

Jung, Carl Gustav. *Aion: Researches into the Phenomenology of the Self.* Translated by R. F. C. Hull. Vol. 9, pt. 2 of the *Collected Works.* Princeton, N.J.: Princeton University Press, 1959.

———. *Archetypes of the Collective Unconscious.* Translated by R. F. C. Hull. 2d ed. Vol. 9, pt. 1 of the *Collected Works.* Princeton, N.J.: Princeton University Press: 1970.

Kamensky, Dr. Anna. "Russia and Russian Theosophy." *The Theosophist* (Adyar) (November 1931), 203–10.

Kandinsky, Wasily. *Über das Geistige in der Kunst, insbesondere in der Malerei.* Munich: R. Piper, 1912.

Kasinec, Edward, and Boris Kerdimun. "Occult Literature in Russia." In *The Spiritual in Art: Abstract Painting 1890-1985,* ed. Edward Weisberger, 361–66 [Exhibition Catalog, Los Angeles County Museum of Art]. New York: Abbeville, 1986.

Knight, Richard Payne. *Symbolical Language of Ancient Art and Mythology; An Inquiry.* 1818; New York: J. W. Bouton, 1876.

Kozlik, Frédéric C. *L'influence de l'anthroposophie sur l'oeuvre d'Andréi Biélyi.* 3 vols. Frankfurt am Main: Fischer Verlag, 1981.

Landau, Rom. *God is my Adventure.* [London]: Nicholson and Watson, 1935. New York: Knopf, 1936. See especially chap. 8, "War Against Sleep: P. D. Ouspensky."

Leisegang, Dr. Hans. "Antroposofiia." *Beseda* (Berlin) 1(1923): 237–63.

Lossky, Vladimir. *The Mystical Theology of the Eastern Church.* Cambridge: Clark, 1957.

Mackenzie, Kenneth. *The Royal Masonic Cyclopedia.* 1877. Reprinted Wellingborough, G.B.: Aquarian Press, 1987.

McIntosh, Christopher. *Eliphas Lévi and the French Occult Revival.* New York: Weiser, 1972.

McNeile, E. R. *From Theosophy to Christian Faith.* London: Longmans, Green, 1919.

Macoy, Robert. *General History, Cyclopedia and Dictionary of Freemasonry.* New York: Masonic Publishing Company, 1870.

Meade, Marion. *Madame Blavatsky. The Woman Behind the Myth.* New York: Putnam's, 1980.

Mil'don, V. I. "Blavatskaia, Elena Petrovna." In *Russkie pisateli 1800–1917; biograficheskii slovar',* vol. 1, 272–73. Moscow: Sovetskaia entsiklopediia, 1989.

Muray, Philippe. *Le dix-neuvième siècle à travers les âges.* Paris: Denoël, 1984.

Nemanov, I. N., M. A. Rozhnova, and V. E. Rozhnov. *Kogda dukhi pokazyvaiut kogti.* Moscow: Politizdat, 1969. See especially pages 143–68 on Blavatsky and Theosophy.

Neumann, Erich. *The Origins and History of Consciousness.* Translated by R. F. C. Hull. Princeton, N.J.: Princeton University Press, 1954.

Nicoll, Maurice. *Psychological Commentaries on the Teaching of G. I. Gurdjieff and P. D. Ouspensky.* 5 vols. London: V. Stuart, 1952–1956.

Nott, C. S. *Journey Through This World.* The Second Journal of a Pupil. Including an Account of Meetings with G. I. Gurdjieff, A. R. Orage, and P. D. Ouspensky. New York: Weiser, 1978.

Okkul'tizm i Ioga. Journal edited by Aleksandr Aseev. Belgrade: 1934–1936; Sofia: 1937-1939.

Olcott, Henry Steel. *Old Diary Leaves.* New York: G. P. Putnam's, 1895.

Pereselenie dush. Problema bezsmertiia v okkul'tizme i khristianstve. Paris: YMCA, [1935]. Articles by Nikolai Berdiaev, Sergei Bulgakov, Boris Vysheslavtsev, Vladimir Zenkovskii, Georgii Florovskii, and Semen Frank.

"Peterburgskie satanisty." *Golos Moskvy* 34(1913). Reprinted in *Rebus* 9(February 24, 1913): 4–5.

Pierrot, Jean. *The Decadent Imagination 1880–1900.* Translated by Derek Coltman. Chicago: University of Chicago Press, 1981.

Praz, Mario. *The Romantic Agony.* 2d ed. London: Oxford, 1970.

Ransom, Josephine. *Short History of the Theosophical Society.* Adyar: Theosophical Publishing House, 1938.

Reyner, J. H. *Ouspensky: The Unsung Genius.* London: George Allen and Unwin, 1981.

Ringbom, Sixten. "Art in the 'Epoch of the Great Spiritual': Occult Elements in the Early Theory of Abstract Painting." *Journal of the Warburg and Courtauld Institutes* 24(1966): 386–418.

———. *The Sounding Cosmos. A Study of the Spiritualism of Kandinsky and the Genesis of Abstract Painting.* Åbo [Turku], Finland: Åbo Akademi, 1970. *Acta Academiae Åboensis,* ser. A: Humaniora. Vol. 38, nr 2.

Roerich, Elena. *Letters 1929–1938.* New York: Agni Yoga Society, 1954. Originally published in Russian by the Latvian Roerich Society in Riga in 1939.

Ryan, C. J. *H. P. Blavatsky and the Theosophical Movement.* Pasadena: Theosophical University Press, 1937.

Rozhnov, V. E. *Proroki i chudotvortsy.* Moscow: Politicheskaia literatura, 1977.

[Sabaneev] Sabaneef, Leonid. "Religious and Mystical Trends of Russia at the Turn of the Century." *Russian Review* 24:4(October 1965): 354–68.

Sabaneev, Leonid. *Skriabin.* Moscow: Skorpion, 1916.

Schloezer, Boris Fedorovich. *A. Skriabin: monografiia o lichnosti i tvorchestve.* Berlin: Grani, 1923. English translation, *Scriabin: Artist and Mystic.* Translated by Nicholas Slonimsky. Berkeley: University of California Press, 1987.

Scholem, Gershom. *On the Kabbalah and Its Symbolism.* New York: Schocken, 1969.

Seligmann, Kurt. *Magic, Supernaturalism and Religion.* New York: Pantheon, 1948.

Sinnett, Alfred Percy. *The Early Days of Theosophy in Europe.* London: Theosophical Publishing House, 1922.

———. *Incidents in the Life of Mme Blavatsky.* London: George Redway, 1886.

Solov'ev, S. M. *Zhizn' i tvorcheskaia evoliutsiia Vladimira Solov'eva.* Brussels: Foyer Oriental Chrétien, 1977.

Spence, Lewis. *An Encyclopaedia of Occultism.* 1920. Reprinted Secaucus, N.J.: Citadel Press, 1977.

Steiner, Rudolf. *An Autobiography.* Blauvelt, N.Y.: Rudolf Steiner Publications, 1977.

————. *The Essential Steiner.* Edited by Robert A. McDermott. San Francisco: Harper and Row, 1984.

Steiner, Rudolf, and Marie Steiner-von Sivers. *Correspondence and Documents 1901–1925.* London: Rudolf Steiner Press, 1988.

Taylor, Merrily E. *Remembering Pyotr Demianovich Ouspensky.* New Haven: Yale University Press, 1978.

The Theosophical Movement 1875–1925; A History and a Survey. New York: E. P. Dutton, [1925].

Trubetskoi, E. N. *Mirosozertsanie Vl. S. Solov'eva.* 2 vols. Moscow: Izdanie avtora, 1913.

Tumins, V. A. "Enlightenment and Mysticism in Eighteenth-Century Russia." *Studies on Voltaire and the Eighteenth Century.* 58(1967): 1671–88.

Turgeneva, Asya. "Andrei Belyi i Rudol'f Steiner." *Mosty* 13–14(1967–1968): 236–51.

[Turgeneva] Turgenieff, Asya. *Errinerungen an Rudolf Steiner.* Stuttgart: Freies Geistesleben, 1973.

Turgeneva, N. "Otvet N. A. Berdiaevu po povodu Antroposofii." *Put'* (Paris), 25(December 1930): 93–104.

Underhill, Evelyn. *Mysticism. A Study in the Nature and Development of Man's Spiritual Consciousness.* 1910. New York: New American Library, 1955.

Vestnik. Satyat Nasti Paro Dharmah. Geneva [printed in Bruxelles, Geneva, Tallinn]: 1924–1939. Edited by Anna Kamenskaia, Tsetsiliia Gel'mbol'dt, and Elena Solovskaia.

Vysheslavtsev, Boris. "Krishnamurti (zavershenie teosofii)." *Put'* (Paris) 14(December 1928): 91–107.

Wachsmuth, Guenther. *The Life and Work of Rudolf Steiner.* 2d ed. Blauvelt, N.Y.: Spiritual Science Library, 1989.

Wachtmeister, Countess Constance. *Reminiscences of H. P. Blavatsky and The Secret Doctrine.* London: Theosophical Publishing Society, 1893. Reprinted Wheaton, Ill.: Theosophical Publishing House, 1976.

Waite, Arthur Edward. *A New Encyclopedia of Freemasonry.* New York: Weathervane, 1970. Reprint of 1937 edition, published in one volume, of original 1911 edition, published in two volumes.

————. *Lamps of Western Mysticism.* 1923. Blauvelt, N.Y.: Rudolf Steiner Publications, 1973.

Ware, Timothy. *The Orthodox Church.* Baltimore: Penguin, 1964.

Webb, James. *The Occult Underground.* LaSalle, Ill.: Open Court, 1974.

Weber, Eugen. *France, Fin de Siècle.* Cambridge, Mass.: Harvard University Press, 1986.

Weisberger, Edward, ed. *The Spiritual in Art: Abstract Painting 1890–1985* [Exhibition Catalog, Los Angeles County Museum of Art]. New York: Abbeville, 1986.

Wiesberger, Hella. *Aus dem Leben Marie Steiner-von Sivers; Biographische Beiträge und eine Bibliographie.* Dornach: Der Rudolf Steiner-Nachlassverwaltung, 1956.

Wiesberger, Hella, and Walter Kugler, eds. *Im Mittelpunkt der Mensch. Ein Einführung in die ausgewählten Werke Rudolf Steiners.* Frankfurt am Main: Fischer, 1985.

Woloschin [Sabashnikova-Voloshina], Margarita. *Die grüne Schlange. Lebenserinnerungen einer Malerin.* 1965. Frankfurt am Main: Fischer, 1982.

Zirkoff, Boris de. *How The Secret Doctrine of H. P. Blavatsky Was Written.* Adyar: Theosophical Publishing House, 1977.

Index